Data Acquisition and Process Control with the M68HC11 Microcontroller

Data Acquisition and Process Control with the M68HC11 Microcontroller

Frederick F. Driscoll
Robert F. Coughlin
Robert S. Villanucci
Wentworth Institute of Technology

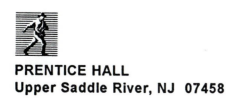

PRENTICE HALL
Upper Saddle River, NJ 07458

Library of Congress Cataloging in Publication Data
Driscoll, Frederick F.
    Data acquisition and process control with the M68HC11
microcontroller/Frederick F. Driscoll, Robert F. Coughlin, Robert
S. Villanucci.
        p. cm.
    Includes index.
    ISBN 0-02-330555-X
    1. Process control-Data processing.   2. Digital control systems-
Design and Construction.   3. Microprocessors.   I. Coughlin, Robert
F. II. Villanucci, Robert S., 1944   III. Title.
TS156.8.D75   1994   93-2671
629.8'95416   CIP

Editor: David Garza
Production Supervisor: Bookworks
Production Manager: Aliza Greenblatt
Cover Designer: Cathleen Norz
Illustrations: Academy Art Works, Inc.

This book was set in 10/12 Palatino by The Clarinda Co.

 © 1994 by Prentice-Hall, Inc.
A Simon & Schuster Company
Englewood Cliffs, New Jersey 07632

Printed in the United States of America
10 9 8 7 6 5 4

ISBN 0-02-330555-X

Prentice-Hall International (UK) Limited, *London*
Prentice-Hall of Australia Pty. Limited, *Sydney*
Prentice-Hall Canada Inc., *Toronto*
Prentice-Hall Hispanoamericana, S.A., *Mexico*
Prentice-Hall of India Private Limited, *New Delhi*
Prentice-Hall of Japan, Inc., *Tokyo*
Simon & Schuster Asia Pte. Ltd., *Singapore*
Editora Prentice-Hall do Brasil, Ltda., *Rio de Janeiro*

Preface

Modern instrumentation and control system are low-cost, versatile, and flexible because of the availability of a device called the microcontroller (μC). This device is a single high-density integrated circuit that contains a complete central processing unit (CPU) plus on-chip peripheral capabilities. For example, Motorola's M68HC11 family of microcontrollers contain a central processing unit, three kinds of memory (ROM, RAM, and EEPROM), A/D converter, both synchronous and asynchronous serial interfaces, an on-board clock and pulse accumulator subsystem, plus a variety of input and output ports.

The development of a microcontroller-based product requires the coordination of many skills. Measuring a process variable such as temperature and converting this measurement into a form acceptable to the A/D converter input of a microcontroller requires knowledge of sensors, transducers and analog circuitry. Interfacing output commands from the microcontroller to heaters, motors, or relays, for example, requires knowledge of digital technology and semiconductor power control devices like transistors, MOSFETs, SCRs, and triacs. Most important however is knowing how to program the microcontroller for a system solution.

This text shows how these many diverse skills can be organized effectively by employing an engineering design procedure with practical application examples. It is broadly divided into three sections, beginning with an Introduction and the first four chapters, which are devoted totally to the M68HC11 microcontroller and an Evaluation Board (EVB) system. Chapters 5 and 6 are hybrid chapters detailing software consideration and hardware design procedures to both acquire input data and provide output control with the microcontroller. The third section, Chapters 7 through 10, presents four practical data acquisition and control problems with complete hardware and software designs given and each problem completely explained.

An overview of the design process is presented in the Introduction. Since a programmer needs a way to turn on and communicate with a microcontroller in order to develop the application software, Chapter 4 shows how this can be accomplished using an Evaluation Board system.

Chapter 1 covers the pin designations of the M68HC11 microcontroller and the function of a port replacement unit (PRU) on the Evaluation Board system. Chapter 2 describes the programmer's model and addressing modes for the microcontroller. Chapter 3 presents the M68HC11's instruction set. Both of these chapters are necessary to understand how to use the M68HC11 Evaluation Board introduced in Chapter 4.

Chapter 5, the first hybrid chapter, shows how to interface analog signals to the M68HC11 and describes all of the analog interfacing circuits that will be used in the application chapters. An analog interface design procedure is given here to illustrate how it is done. Basic output interfacing hardware and software control commands are given in Chapter 6, the second hybrid chapter.

Design applications of microcontroller systems are presented in the remaining chapters. Chapter 7 shows the design procedure for a temperature measuring system with a computer terminal or printer display. It also is used to present the complete design procedure introduced in Chapter 5 for the analog interface. This design procedure can be generalized to handle *any* linear analog design problem involving conversion of a physical quantity to an electrical quantity. The software routines input the temperature data every 30 seconds, perform a binary BCD conversion, and output the information to the pc terminal used as a monitor.

In this first applications chapter you are introduced to a modular approach to software development. Software subroutines, written in Chapters 1 through 6, are combined in this and the remaining applications chapters to produce complete programs. This building block approach to programming aids in understanding and reducing lengthy programs to manageable tasks by reusing previously developed subroutines.

Chapter 8 shows how a microcontroller is used in a weight measuring system. Operation of a load cell is explained, equations are derived for the transducer and required signal conditioning circuits to show how easy it is to design the analog interface with the design procedure. Software application includes lookup tables, scaling, decimal multiplication, and output routines.

Pressure measurement is shown in Chapter 9, which also gives a tutorial on semiconductor pressure sensors. The design procedure is used again to complete the analog interface. This application requires the software to display updated information and warning notices to a supervisor.

Chapter 10 shows how programming techniques can linearize the output of a nonlinear transducer. The thermocouple is a nonlinear temperature-to-voltage converter and chosen for this nonlinear example. First, thermocouple basics are discussed along with how to apply cold junction compensation. Approximate linear transducer equations are derived for the thermocouple to introduce the linearization technique. Then the transducer's piecewise-linearization equations are derived to design the analog interface, and finally, the equations are derived for use by the programmer who identifies which piecewise-linear equation should be used, performs look-up information for slope and offset terms, then a decimal addition and multiplication routine is required to solve the equation before outputting the temperature.

TARGET AUDIENCE

The material in this textbook can be understood by a student who has had *some* background in basic microprocessor terminology and programming concepts. Also helpful, but not necessarily mandatory, would be an exposure to analog circuits using operational amplifiers. All of these topics are covered in most associate level programs.

It has been the authors' intent to develop a text that would be useful to people who will be designing real systems using the M68HC11 as an embedded microcontroller. Of course this text can be used as a first course in microcontrollers at either the associate or bachelor's level, and can be taught to both electrical and non-electrical majors. Expected audiences would include students studying design and applications in such courses as *Engineering Design, Senior Design, Instrumentation for Process Control, Electromechanical Control Systems, Measurement and Control Systems,* as well as manufacturing and mechanical engineering technology programs that use embedded controllers as part of their curricula.

We would like to especially thank Jean Driscoll for her skillful preparation and editing of the original manuscript. A special thank you goes to our students, who saw the need for such a text and encouraged us to write it. A final thanks goes to Mr. Joseph Diecidue, for his generous help with the many and varied problems of software utilization.

F.F.D.
R.F.C.
R.S.V.

Contents

CHAPTER 9   MEASURING PRESSURE WITH SEMICONDUCTOR SENSORS   295

CHAPTER 10   THERMOCOUPLE HIGH-TEMPERATURE MEASUREMENT WITH SOFTWARE LINEARIZATION   321

Introduction

THE MICROCONTROLLER

This text uses a microcontroller as the basic building block for data acquisition and control applications. Before proceeding to microcontroller technology, we need to describe briefly how a *microcontroller* differs from the more familiar terms *microcomputer* and *microprocessor*. Let's begin with the microcomputer.

When someone says microcomputer or *personal computer* (PC), we usually think of a desktop stand-alone computer system that performs a variety of applications such as word processing, spreadsheet analysis, record keeping, inventory control, and so on. IBM, Apple, Compaq, or other manufacturers' products may come to mind. When purchasing one of these products, you obtain hardware and enough software to operate the system as soon as it is turned on.

A microcomputer's hardware comprises its physical components: keyboard, monitor, chassis (the actual computer enclosure), printer, mouse, connecting cables, etc. The software that comes with your purchase is stored on floppy disks and includes an operating system and usually one or two application packages. If you open the chassis, you can identify other hardware components: power supply, hard disk (if any), floppy disk(s), main computer board, possibly input/output boards, and expansion sockets. One of the integrated circuits on the main pc board is the computer's electronic brain, know as its central processing unit (CPU) or more often referred to as the *microprocessor*. Thus, the microprocessor is the central processing unit of a *microcomputer*.

Once, CPUs required several large-size printed circuit boards to contain all their logic circuitry. With today's IC manufacturing techniques of very large-scale integration (VLSI), hundreds of thousands of transistors can be fabricated on a silicon substrate and housed in a single package. VLSI fabrication permitted the rapid advances in microprocessor technology. The microprocessor, like any CPU, contains counters, registers, buffers, latches, clock circuitry, arithmetic logic unit(s), timing and control circuitry to name only some of the circuitry in today's microprocessors.

Other components on the main computer board are memory, and input/output (I/O) chips. Memory chips store data and instructions used by the microprocessor during program execution. Most memory chips are RAM (Random-Access Memory) which store information *temporarily* and can be written to and read from by the microprocessor. If power to the system is lost, the information in these chips is lost, hence the word temporarily. There are one or two other memory chips on the main computer board, that do not lose their information when power is turned off. These chips are *read-only memory* (ROM). The programs stored in these chips are "burned-in" and then used by the microprocessor to get the system "up and running" each time the system is turned on. In addition to the system's main memory, there is storage space on the hard and floppy disks. The microprocessor transfers data to and from these mass storage devices through I/O chips. Other I/O chips allow the microprocessor to communicate to other peripheral equipment: keyboard, monitor, printer, and so on.

The system that we are describing here is for general purpose computing applications. However, the first applications using the microprocessor were not for general purpose work, but rather were designed for embedded control applications. When engineers saw the microprocessor's flexibility, they began using it to design new products and modify present ones to add more features at a lower cost. Their designs incorporated pc boards with a microprocessor, memory (RAM and ROM), and I/O chips similar in structure but with a lot less capacity than today's microcomputers. Semiconductor manufacturers working with product designers were able to fabricate in a single integrated circuit the most commonly needed features for an embedded controller IC; hence the birth of the *microcontroller*. The microcontroller that you will study in this text contains a CPU, memory (RAM and ROM), serial and parallel I/O lines, analog-to-digital converter (ADC), and a timer unit. Remember that the microcontroller is optimized for data acquisition and control applications, while today's microprocessors are designed to support high-level languages for general purpose applications. Let's learn what is necessary to develop a microcontroller-based product to solve application problems.

A review of the current trade literature suggests that products solving measurement and control problems use at least one microcontroller IC. All indications are that this trend will continue and that the sales of microcontroller chips will increase. While there are many secondary reasons for this trend toward new microcontroller-based products, the overwhelming attractions are lower product cost and superior performance. Since microcontroller-based products are rapidly becoming commonplace, we need to learn how to design products using this device. Although this task may seem formidable, such an engineering problem can be solved by a *systematic design procedure*.

I.1

DESIGN PROCEDURE

Most data acquisition and control problems begin with the measurement of physical quantities by an appropriate sensor. The sensor's analog output is then signal-conditioned for acceptance by the microcontroller. Within the microcontroller, the analog signal is converted to a digital value. Under software control, the microcontroller can compare the digital value against a preset value, make logical decisions based on this comparison, perform scaling or other mathematical operations, and perform control functions. The tasks performed by the microcontroller are limited only by the ingenuity of the programmer. Output interface devices such as opto-isolators, SCRs, or triacs allow the microcontroller to control peripherals such as LED indicators, motors, fans, heaters, and printers.

Thus, the design procedure required to implement a microcontroller-based engineering solution is as follows:

1. Select a sensor to measure the physical quantity.
2. Design signal conditioning circuitry (SCC) to interface the sensor's output with the microcontroller's on-board analog-to-digital converter.
3. Write the program necessary to acquire data, solve the engineering problem, and provide output control.
4. Design interfacing circuitry between the microcontroller's digital output control lines and peripheral devices.

I.2

PROBLEM SOLVING

The steps above clearly demonstrate the need to merge knowledge of analog technology, programming, and digital circuitry. This text addresses these issues by providing a single volume reference covering all areas of interest.

The following descriptions are some of the types of practical problems that could be solved with a microcontroller.

- A *biologist* must monitor and record the temperature of a specimen slide to ensure that it is not adversely affected by the microscope's illumination.
- A *mechanical engineer* needs to measure intake manifold pressure of a gasoline engine as a monitor of performance.
- A *civil engineer* must monitor and control the curing temperature of concrete to guarantee proper hydration (bonding process).
- A *naturalist* wishes to weigh birds in the wild and requires a weight system camouflaged as a rock.

- A *research physicist* must measure and control the magnetic field strength of electromagnetics for alignment of a particle accelerator system.
- A *farmer* must monitor and control the relative humidity of a grain silo to prevent an explosion.

The solution to all of these problems can use a microcontroller along with input and output circuitry. The application chapters 7 through 10 of this text show how to design other typical microcontroller applications.

I.3

MICROCONTROLLER DEVELOPMENT PLATFORM

The complete hardware for any of the microcontroller-based applications above appears deceptively simple. As shown in Figure I.1, the finished product consists of a sensor, a few support components, and a microcontroller IC with a "burned-in" dedicated software program. However, the finished product is ready for market only after a considerable amount of design effort followed by extensive testing of both hardware and software.

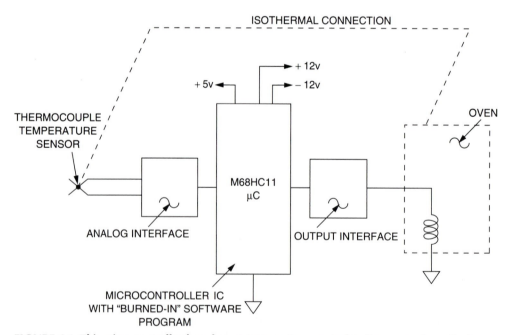

FIGURE I.1 This microcontroller-based oven temperature control unit appears deceptively simple. However, a considerable amount of development time followed by extensive testing is needed to bring an application design to a finished product.

The design cycle of a microcontroller-based product begins with a *microcontroller development platform* (MDP). This MDP should have as much flexibility and as many features as possible. MDPs are printed circuit boards that contain, in addition to a microcontroller, a set of monitor programs stored in ROM chips, I/O connections, and interfacing capacity to a dumb (or smart) terminal. These development systems are usually available from manufacturers of the microcontroller chips and sometimes from third-party vendors. One source of such products is Motorola, which sells two low-cost MDPs for its M68HC11 microcontroller. One is known as the EVBU, Universal Evaluation Board, and a larger version, the M68HC11 Evaluation Board—known as the EVB—is shown in Figure I.2.

For this text, the authors have chosen the M68HC11 EVB-based development platform. This system is the topic of Chapter 4 but some of the on-board features are introduced now.

- Monitor/debugger program called BUFFALO, which stands for *Bit User Fast Friendly Aid to Logical Operations*. BUFFALO is contained in an EPROM external to the microcontroller
- One-line assembler/disassembler
- Ability to evaluate microcontroller unit (MCU) circuitry
- *Port replacement unit* (PRU) for MCU I/O expansion
- Computer downloading capability
- Terminal I/O port circuitry, RS-232-C compatible
- Host I/O port, RS-232-C compatible
- 60-pin I/O connector

I.4

SOFTWARE DEVELOPMENT

Software development, a key component in any microcontroller product, begins either on this platform or on a personal computer. Thus, there are two ways to enter instructions or entire programs into the EVB's RAM. The first method is under control of the BUFFALO's monitor programs. The second is to use a cross-assembler on a PC and then download the assembled code (developed program) to the EVB's RAM. We will use both methods in this text. Even when you download a program from a PC, you may still use the BUFFALO's monitor to check and modify your software. Caution: If you modify the working program using the on-board assembler/disassembler after the original program has been downloaded to the EVB, you now have *two* program versions, one in EVB RAM and one in a file on the PC. It is prudent to ensure that both versions are identical before turning off power. Once power is lost to the EVB, programs and data stored in RAM are gone forever.

The M68HC11 EVB has been designed so that the MCU operates in its *expanded*

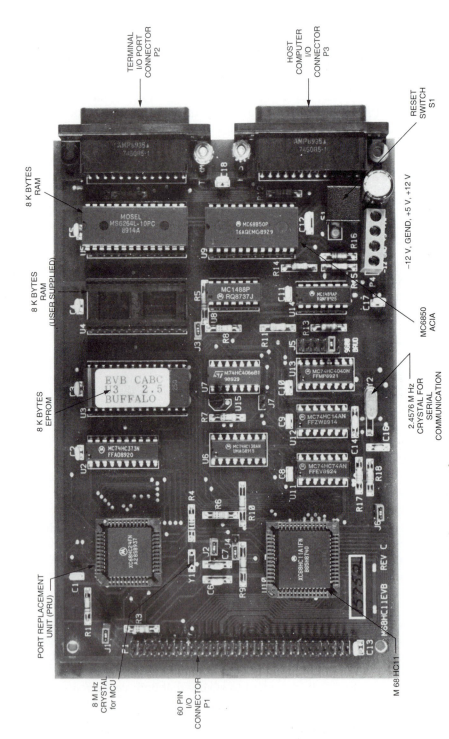

FIGURE 1.2 M68HC11 Evaluation Board (EVB)

6

mode. This means the version of the M68HC11 IC chosen for the EVB allows it to be interfaced with external EPROMS, RAM, and a port replacement unit (PRU), thereby providing a development platform that emulates the single-chip mode of operation found in the finished product.

I.5

MICROCONTROLLER DEVELOPMENT SYSTEM

Figure I.3 shows the block diagram of a *complete development system* (CDS). Note: It contains at its core the M68HC11 development platform (EVB hardware, PC, and software). To complete the development system, we must provide a transducer and signal conditioning circuitry to measure physical quantities and output circuitry to solve control problems.

The EVB's 60-pin I/O connector P1 allows easy access to the MCU's analog-to-digital converter (ADC) from the outside world. Port P1 can also be used to input

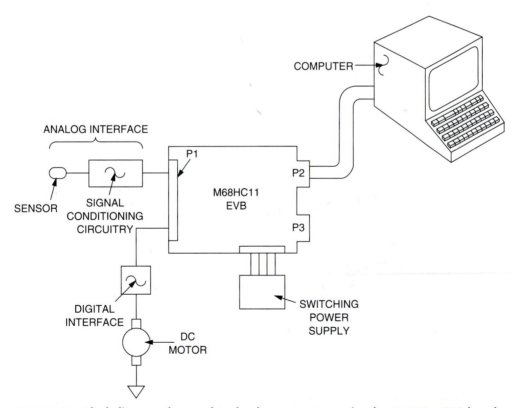

FIGURE I.3 Block diagram of a complete development system using the M68HC11 EVB board

and output digital data. Figure I.4 shows the pin assignment for P1. The functions of these pins are studied in Chapter 1. Figure I.5 shows the pin assignments for P2 and P3. It is through this I/O connector that a dumb terminal or PC can communicate with the EVB over a serial RS-232 line.

I.6

INPUT: ANALOG INTERFACE

The analog technology necessary to develop a complete microcontroller-based product requires the design of input circuitry to acquire data and output signals to fit the MCU's ADC. Figure I.6 shows the block diagram of a typical analog interface that can be described by an *analog interface equation* (AIE). The design of such a system begins by first selecting the transducer to sense the physical quantity to be measured. The transducer converts the physical quantity into an electrical parameter such as voltage, current, or resistance, and it is characterized by a transducer equation.

Unfortunately, transducers rarely, if ever, output the exact electrical parameter, or value, suitable for direct input into the microcontroller's analog-to-digital converter. Therefore, Figure I.6 shows that a signal conditioning circuitry (SCC) must be designed. This circuit is the interface between the transducer's output and the input to the microcontroller. The typical SCC includes both *span* and *offset* adjustments or trims so that its output signal interfaces to the full input span of the microcontroller's A/D converter. This allows for maximum measurement resolution. Design of signal conditioning circuitry is made easy by writing an SCC design equation. The applications in Chapters 7 through 10 illustrate how to write analog interface, transducer, and design equations and how to implement the mathematical design with hardware. This systematic design procedure greatly simplifies the analog input design portion of a microcontroller-based product.

I.7

OUTPUT: DIGITAL INTERFACE

Figure I.7 illustrates how a microcontroller's digital output line is interfaced to the outside world. Usually, the low-power TTL level (+5V) of an output line must be buffered to perform such functions as (a) activating LED indicators, (b) turning on or off dc motors, or (c) controlling ac load currents to oven heaters. A commonly used output interface device is the opto-isolator. As its name indicates, this device provides electrical isolation between the microcontroller and the load. The output circuitry of an opto-isolator can be a transistor, SCR, triac, or logic circuit. Thus, opto-isolators are used to drive a variety of loads. The principles of output devices are covered in Chapter 6.

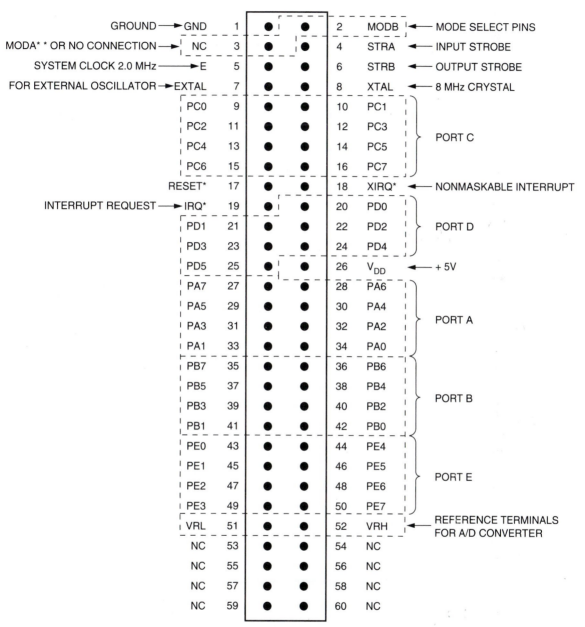

* ACTIVE LOW STATE
* * MAY BE AVAILABLE ON SOME SYSTEMS

FIGURE I.4 I/O connector P₁ on the EVB

9

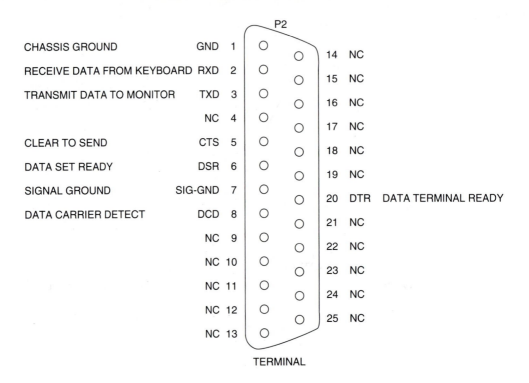

CHASSIS GROUND	GND	1			14	NC
RECEIVE DATA FROM KEYBOARD	RXD	2			15	NC
TRANSMIT DATA TO MONITOR	TXD	3			16	NC
	NC	4			17	NC
CLEAR TO SEND	CTS	5			18	NC
DATA SET READY	DSR	6			19	NC
SIGNAL GROUND	SIG-GND	7			20	DTR DATA TERMINAL READY
DATA CARRIER DETECT	DCD	8			21	NC
	NC	9			22	NC
	NC	10			23	NC
	NC	11			24	NC
	NC	12			25	NC
	NC	13				

TERMINAL

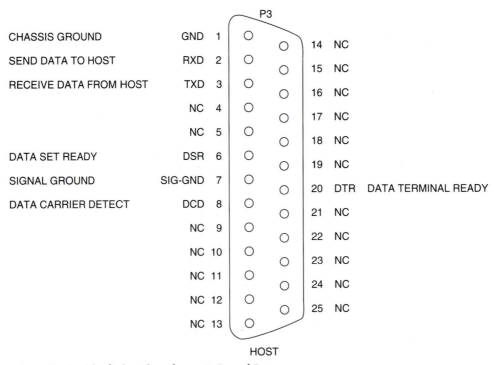

CHASSIS GROUND	GND	1			14	NC
SEND DATA TO HOST	RXD	2			15	NC
RECEIVE DATA FROM HOST	TXD	3			16	NC
	NC	4			17	NC
	NC	5			18	NC
DATA SET READY	DSR	6			19	NC
SIGNAL GROUND	SIG-GND	7			20	DTR DATA TERMINAL READY
DATA CARRIER DETECT	DCD	8			21	NC
	NC	9			22	NC
	NC	10			23	NC
	NC	11			24	NC
	NC	12			25	NC
	NC	13				

HOST

FIGURE 1.5 Pin designations for ports P_2 and P_3

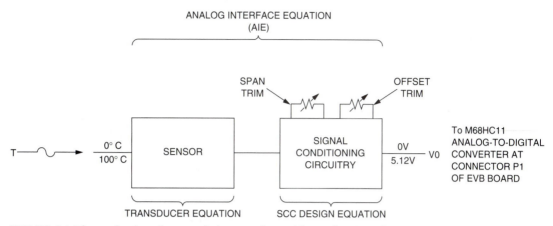

FIGURE I.6 The analog interface needed to acquire and input data into the M68HC11 microcontroller can be described by a block diagram.

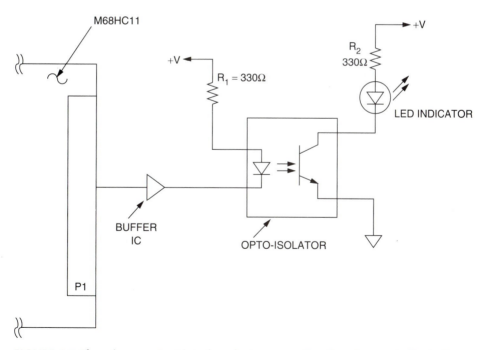

FIGURE I.7 The primary output interface device connecting the microcontroller to the outside world is the opto isolator. Opto-isolators eliminate ground problems and are available with outputs such as a transistor (shown), SCR, and triac, to name a few.

I.8

CONCLUSION

Before designing an entire system, we will study the microcontroller, and EVB, and input and output interface circuitry separately. In Chapters 1–3, you will study the M68HC11 microcontroller, by first looking at it externally, to learn the functions of its pins, and then internally beginning with a programmer's model, addressing modes, and instruction set. Chapter 4 introduces some of the EVB features. Chapter 5 describes the basic principles of signal conditioning circuits and how to use the microcontroller's analog-to-digital converter. Chapter 6 covers the microcontroller's timer unit and how to test logic states on its I/O pins as well as covering output control devices. The applications chapters (7 to 10) show how to design four microcontroller-based systems.

CHAPTER 1

M68HC11 Microcontroller

1.0

INTRODUCTION

As previously discussed, the design of a microcontroller-based product is usually done using a microcontroller development system so that your ideas in hardware and software may be tested and any modifications incorporated into the design before it is finished. After your application software is tested and debugged, it can be "burned into" a microcontroller's ROM for the finished product. Remember that the final design or product usually does not contain the development system, even a small one like the EVB. Such systems are needed only in the design stages. Before beginning a design, we need to understand the microcontroller's hardware and software, thereby gaining insight to its power and flexibility. This chapter discusses the hardware, primarily the function of its pins, while Chapters 2 and 3 examine the software.

The M68HC11 has two modes of operation: single-chip and expanded. The single-chip mode is normally used in the final product and in particular for high-volume dedicated applications. The expanded mode uses some of the microcontroller's I/O pins for address and data lines. A port replacement unit (PRU) restores these I/O functions and is transparent to the software. Section 1.4 introduces this device. To understand how the CPU communicates with memory (ROM, RAM) and I/O, section 1.5 covers the topic called memory map. This chapter begins with a list of microcontrollers that are part of the M68HC11 family.

1.1

M68HC11 FAMILY

The M68HC11 product is a family of 8-bit microcontrollers available from Motorola. They are software compatible, but some of their hardware features, such as the size of ROM and/or RAM, differ. This product line allows the end user to choose the best microcontroller for the application. All of these microcontrollers are fabricated using high-density complementary metal-oxide semiconductor (HCMOS) technology. The basic microcontroller is the MC68HC11A8. Table 1.1 lists the different versions available at this time and the unique advantages of each (new products are always emerging).

TABLE 1.1   M68HC11 Family Members (Courtesy of Motorola, Inc.)

Part Number	EPROM	ROM	EEPROM	RAM	CONFIG[2]	Comments
*MC68HC11A8	—		512	256	$0F	Family built around this device
MC68HC11A1	—	—	512	256	$0D	'A8 with ROM disabled
MC68HC11A0	—	—	—	256	$0C	'A8 with ROM and EEPROM disabled
MC68HC811A8	—	—	8K+512	256	$0F	EEPROM emulator for 'A8
MC68HC11E9	—	12K	512	512	$0F	Four input capture/bigger RAM 12K ROM
MC68HC11E1	—	—	512	512	$0D	'E9 with ROM disabled
MC68HC11E0	—	—	—	512	$0C	'E9 with ROM and EEPROM disabled
MC68HC811E2	—	—	2K[1]	256	$FF[3]	No ROM part for expanded systems
MC68HC711E9	12K	—	512	512	$0F	One-time programmable version of 'E9
MC68HC11D3	—	4K	—	192	N/A	Low-cost 40-pin version
MC68HC711E9	4K	—	—	192	N/A	One-time programmable version of 'D3

TABLE 1.1   M68HC11 Family Members (Courtesy of Motorola, Inc.) (continued)

Part Number	EPROM	ROM	EEPROM	RAM	CONFIG[2]	Comments
MC68HC11F1	—	—	512[1]	1K	$FF[3]	High-performance nonmultiplexed 68-Pin
MC68HC11K4	—	24K	640	768	$FF	>1 Meg memory space, PWM, CS, 84-Pin
MC68HC711K4	24K	—	640	768	$FF	One-time programmable version of 'K4
MC68HC11L6	—	16K	512	512	$0F	Like 'E9 with more ROM and more I/O, 64/68
MC68HC711L6	16K	—	512	512	$0F	One-time programmable version of 'L4

*Basic microcontroller
NOTES:
1. The EEPROM is relocatable to the top of any 4K memory page. Relocation is done with the upper four bits of the CONFIG register.
2. CONFIG register values in this table reflect the value programmed prior to shipment from Motorola (Internal MCU register).
3. At the time of this printing, a change was being considered that would make this value $0F.

The alphanumeric code for this family of microcontrollers is shown in Figure 1.1. Note: When a feature applies to all family members, the general coding sequence of M68HC11 is used. However, when a specific part is used or ordered, such as the A8 version, then the coding sequence is MC68HC11A8. The EVB system used in this text has been shipped with the MC68HC11A1 microcontroller. Table 1.1 shows that the A1 version is the same as the A8 but with its internal ROM disabled. On the EVB, the monitor programs are stored in an external EPROM chip because the microcontroller is operated in the expanded mode. Since the A8 version is the basic device, the following sections describe its pin functions.

1.2

MC68HC11A8 MICROCONTROLLER

The MC68HC11A8 version has 8k bytes of read-only memory (ROM), 512 bytes of electrically erasable read-only memory, and 256 bytes of random-access memory (RAM). Therefore, after the microcontroller-based system has been designed

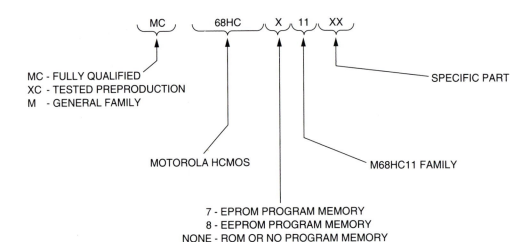

FIGURE 1.1 Part numbering for Motorola's microcontroller family (Courtesy of Motorola, Inc.)

and tested using a development platform, the finalized software for the application can be "burned into" the ROM. The advantage of using a microcontroller in a dedicated control application is not only having on-chip ROM and RAM, but also having access to many peripheral functions. Such functions include an analog-to-digital converter, asynchronous and synchronous serial communication ports, timer unit, pulse accumulator, as well as general purpose I/O ports.

Figure 1.2 is an internal block diagram of the MC68HC11A8 microcontroller IC. The dashed box in the lower right-hand corner shows a parallel I/O subsystem. When the MCU is operated in an expanded mode, the functions of the I/O subsystem are lost and a multiplexed address bus is available. It is the lower eight lines (0–7) that are multiplexed to carry either address or data; hence, the notation A (for address) and D (for data). The parallel I/O functions are regained if an MC68HC24 device, known as a port replacement unit (PRU), is used (see section 1.4). To the software developer, there is no difference between these two hardware configurations. The advantage of using the microcontroller in the expanded mode is that external EPROM and RAM can be interfaced to the MCU for the design stages of software development and still allow the user to know how the single-chip version will work. The microcontroller on the EVB is configured for the expanded mode. The BUFFALO monitor programs are contained in an 8K EPROM and there is 8K of RAM for user programs. A socket is provided for another 8K of RAM (MCM6164) if so desired by the user. The EVB system also contains the MC68HC24 (the port replacement unit).

The EVBU, universal evaluation board system, is not configured in the expanded mode. The BUFFALO monitor programs are "burned into" the microcontroller's on-chip ROM and the user is limited to the on-chip RAM of 256 bytes.

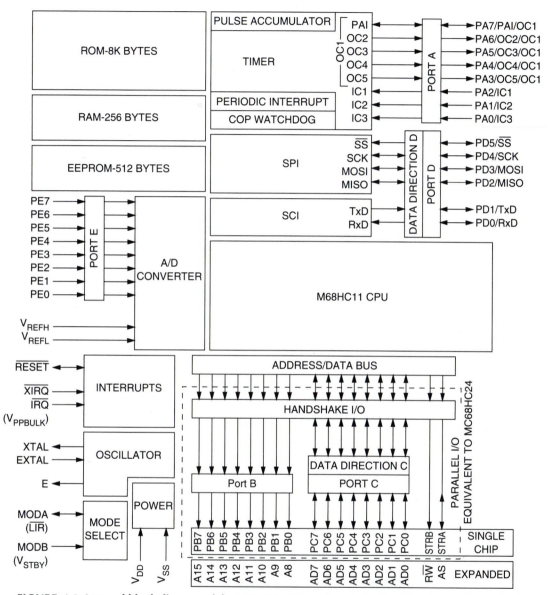

FIGURE 1.2 Internal block diagram of the MC68HC11A8 microcontroller (Courtesy of Motorola, Inc.)

1.3

PACKAGE STYLE AND PIN ASSIGNMENTS

This section introduces the package syles, name of each pin or group of pins, and a brief description of the pin(s) function. The MC68HC11A8 is available in a 52-pin quad package for use with a plastic leaded chip carrier (PLCC) or a 48-pin dual-in-line package (DIP). Both package styles are shown in Figure 1.3. The difference is only in the number of available analog-to-digital input pins. The 52-pin package has eight inputs, while the 48-pin package has only four. In this text, all pin assignments are for the 52-pin quad package. (Note: In Figure 1.3 the pin assignments are not the same for each package.)

The MC68HC11A1 MCU used on the EVB is housed in the 52-pin package and has the same pin assignments as the MC68HC11A8. The difference is that the on-chip EEPROM of the A1 version is disabled by a bit contained in a nonvolatile register within the MCU. This register is known as the configuration (CONFIG) register.

1.3.1 Power Supply Pins (V_{DD} and V_{SS})

The MCU is a +5 volt device for most applications. Pins 26 and 1 are the +5V and ground pins, respectively. However, optional supplies may be added for battery backup for the on-chip RAM or for the analog-to-digital reference voltages. Power supply bypass capacitors should be used as close to the MCU pins as possible. If the MCU is being used in the expanded mode, a 1μF in parallel with a 0.01μF disc capacitor (with good high-frequency characteristics) should be used. For single-chip applications, a single 0.1μF disc may be sufficient.

To power-up the EVB system, the authors have used a switching power supply because it was available, but a linear supply could also be used. The EVB requirements are +5V @ 0.5A, +12V @ 0.1A, and −12V @ 0.1A. The ±12V are required for the serial communication lines.

1.3.2 Mode Select Pins (MODA/$\overline{\text{LIR}}$ and MODB/V_{STBY})

The mode select pins 2 and 3 are used by the MCU to select the operating mode during a reset condition. Table 1.2 summarizes the logic state of the mode pins for single-chip and expanded mode operation. Other binary states on these pins select either a special bootstrap or test operating mode. The MCU on the EVB is wired for the expanded operating mode (pins 2 and 3 are connected to V_{DD} through 10kΩ pull-up resistors). After reset, the MCU no longer requires input logic states on pins 2 and 3 to keep the device in the selected operating mode. These pins may now be used for their alternate function.

The alternate function of the MODA pin 3 is as an output signal indicating a load instruction resister ($\overline{\text{LIR}}$) operation has taken place within the MCU. On each

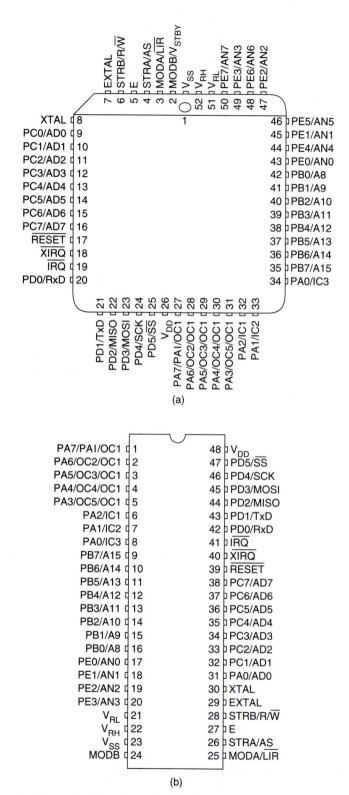

FIGURE 1.3 Pin assignments for the MC68HC11A8 (a) 52-pin PLCC, and (b) 48-pin DIP (Courtesy of Motorola, Inc.)

TABLE 1.2   Logic States for Single-chip and Expanded Operating Modes

Select Inputs		
MODB	MODA	Operating Mode
1	0	Single-chip
1	1	Expanded

new instruction, pin 3 outputs a low during the first MCU clock signal (E clock, which is covered in section 1.3.4). This signal can be used for software debugging purposes. In single-chip applications, this pin is usually wired to V_{SS}. The reason is that debugging is usually not done in the finalized product, which contains a single-chip MCU. Pin 3's internal circuit is an open-drain output so no damage is done when it is connected to V_{SS}.

The alternate function of the MODB pin 2 is to provide standby power (V_{STBY}) to the on-chip RAM when V_{DD} is not present. Another way to maintain the RAM contents is to use the STOP instruction (see section 3.14) with V_{DD} still applied. This is a preferred method because it does not require a separate supply. In the STOP mode, the MCU draws only microamperes of current.

1.3.3 Crystal Oscillator Pins (EXTAL, XTAL)

Oscillator pins 7 and 8 are used to connect a crystal network shown in Figure 1.4. Within the M68HC11, the oscillator circuitry consists of a two-input NAND gate. One input is connected to the MCU's STOP mode circuitry, which disables the

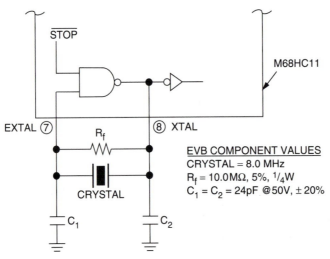

FIGURE 1.4 Typical connections to an M68HC11 (Courtesy of Motorola, Inc.)

oscillator to halt all system clocks and place the microcontroller in a standby mode to draw minimum supply power. The other input to the NAND gate is connected to the EXTAL pin 7. The output of the NAND gate is connected to the XTAL pin 8.

If the MCU's clock signals are being generated by a CMOS compatible clock source and not by a crystal, then the clock input is applied to the EXTAL pin. The XTAL pin is either left unterminated or connected through a 10kΩ–100kΩ pull-down resistor to ground.

1.3.4 E Clock Signal

As long as the oscillator is operating, the E clock is running at ¼ the crystal frequency (remember the STOP mode stops all MCU clock signals). For the EVB system, the E clock is 2.0 MHz and the time for one clock cycle is 0.5μs. The E clock is the basic clock signal for all MCU internal and external operations. In a single-chip system, the E clock pin 5 is not used and left unterminated.

In the expanded mode of operation, such as on the EVB, the E clock pin is connected to external ROM, RAM, and I/O chips in order to synchronize data transfers between these devices and the CPU. It is possible to connect an oscilloscope to the E clock pin to observe the clock signal. However, an oscilloscope's probe connected to EXTAL (pin 7) will modify and may even disable the oscillator circuitry.

1.3.5 Reset Signal

The $\overline{\text{RESET}}$ line connected to pin 17 is used for a bidirectional control signal. As an input, a low active signal initializes the MCU to a known state. As an output, it is used to signal external circuitry that the MCU has had an internal failure.

1.3.6 Interrupt Pins ($\overline{\text{IRQ}}$, $\overline{\text{XIRQ}}$)

The M68HC11 has two input interrupt request pins: $\overline{\text{IRQ}}$ pin 19 and $\overline{\text{XIRQ}}$ pin 18. The $\overline{\text{IRQ}}$ pin is known as the maskable interrupt request pin. This means that an interrupt signal may or may not be recognized, and this ability is under the programmer's control. The interrupt mask bit (I bit) in the CPU's condition code register (this topic is covered in Chapter 2) may be set or cleared under programmer's control. If the I bit is set, the CPU does not recognize interrupt signals; otherwise, interrupt signals are recognized. The XIRQ bit provides a means of having nonmaskable interrupts after reset. During reset, the X bit in the microcontroller's condition code register (see Chapter 2) is set and any interrupts on pin 18 are masked. This enables the programmer to write software to initialize the system without having the microcontroller receive an interrupt on the $\overline{\text{XIRQ}}$ pin. After the software initialization procedure is completed, the X bit can be cleared by a TAP instruction (see Chapter 2) but cannot be set by an instruction; hence the $\overline{\text{XIRQ}}$ pin now becomes nonmaskable.

In addition to $\overline{\text{IRQ}}$ and $\overline{\text{XIRQ}}$, the MC68HC11A8 has five other pins capable of generating an interrupt request. These pins are part of the MCU's on-chip peripherals. Examples are the timer unit and handshake I/O lines. These pins are PA0/IC3 (pin 34), PA1/IC2 (pin 33), PA2/IC1 (pin 32), PA7/PA1/OC1 (pin 27), and STRA/AS (pin 4). In some applications, there are advantages in using these pins, but before comparing any advantages or disadvantages you need to know more about how to program and use the on-chip peripherals. This topic is covered in Chapter 6.

1.3.7 Port A/Timer Pins

The port A/timer pins 27–34 can be used either as I/O lines for general purpose applications or lines for specific timer applications. In either case, the eight pins are configured as three input-only pins, four output-only pins, and one pin that can be programmed as either an input or output. As general purpose lines, the pins are referred to as port pins PA0–PA7. PA0–PA2 are the three input pins, PA3–PA6 are the four output pins, and PA7 may be programmed either as an input or as an output.

For timer applications, the three input pins 32–34 are referred to as input-capture pins (IC1–IC3). The four output pins 28–31 are referred to as output-compare pins (OC2–OC5). The MCU's circuitry allows the output-compare one (OC1) to control any combination of PA7–PA3 pins; hence the reason for the notation in Figures 1.2 and 1.3.

Pin 27 (PA7/PAI/OC1) is also used as the MCU's pulse-accumulator input pin, which can be used as an event counter or for gated time accumulations. The functions of these pins are discussed in more detail in Chapter 6.

1.3.8 Port B, Port C, STRA, and STRB Pins

As shown in Figure 1.3, these 18 pins (pins 35–42, 9–16, 4 and 6) have different functions depending on the operating mode of the MCU. In the single-chip mode, port B is an 8-bit output-only port for general purpose applications. Port C lines can be configured either as input or output lines. Note: some port C lines can be programmed as output lines and the other lines stay as inputs. The primary function of STRA and STRB, in the single-chip mode, is for strobe and handshake functions with peripheral circuitry.

In the expanded mode, these 18 pins are used as a multiplexed address/data bus, a read/write (R/$\overline{\text{W}}$) line, and an address strobe (AS) line. The 16 address lines allow the CPU to access 64K (2^{16} = 64K) bytes of memory and I/O space. Time multiplexing is used on the low-order address (AD0–AD7) pins to provide either an 8-bit address or data. When the AS line (pin 4) is high, an address is outputted by the CPU and is used by external circuitry as an enable signal. When the AS line goes low, the address information should be latched into an external device—such as an octal D-latch.

The R/$\overline{\text{W}}$ line is used to control the direction of data. The CPU reads data when the line is high and writes data when the line is low. Chapter 6 will show how to use port B and C for its I/O capability.

1.3.9 Port D

The six port D pins can be configured either as general purpose bidirectional I/O lines or as serial communication lines. Some I/O lines can be programmed as output lines and the remaining ones as inputs. This I/O capability is similar to port C, but there are only six lines associated with port D. In addition to general I/O capability, these lines can be used for both asynchronous and synchronous communication.

For asynchronous communication, PD0/RxD pin 20 is used to receive serial data and PD1/TxD pin 21 is used to transmit serial data. As shown in Figure 1.2, these two pins are associated with an internal MCU block labeled SCI, which is the MCU's asynchronous serial communications interface circuitry. It performs the functions of a general purpose UART (universal asynchronous receiver/transmitter).

The other four lines of port D can also be configured for serial communication. These lines are associated with the SPI (serial peripheral interface) block as shown in Figure 1.2. They may be used for synchronous communication or to transfer data to peripheral equipment such as a liquid crystal display or to receive data from a serial analog-to-digital (A/D) converter. The MCU can be used in a multiple-master processor system by using these lines. When the MCU is the master, the input line is pin 22 (MISO) and the output line is pin 23 (MOSI). As a slave, pin 22 is output and pin 23 is input.

The SCK pin 24 is the clock line. It is used as an output clock signal to synchronize data transfer when the MCU is configured as a master. When the MCU is being used as a slave unit, pin 24 may be used for input clock signals. In some applications, slave units do not require a clock signal and the SCK signal is ignored.

The $\overline{\text{SS}}$ pin 25 is the slave select input pin. It is used to enable the SPI unit for data transfer. A master unit normally keeps the SS pin high (its inactive state).

1.3.10 Port E, V$_{RL}$, and V$_{RH}$

Port E may be programmed for 8-bit general purpose input only pins or as 8 input channels to the MCU's analog-to-digital converter. All of the applications in this text require A/D conversion, so this port is discussed in detail in Chapter 5. Chapter 5 also discusses the analog reference pins, V$_{RL}$ and V$_{RH}$, and how they should be used in an application.

1.4

PORT REPLACEMENT UNIT

You have learned that the M68HC11 microcomputer can be operated either in the single-chip or expanded mode. Your final product will most likely use the single-chip microcomputer, but you may wish to design using the expanded mode so that additional RAM and ROM may be added. When an M68HC11 is operated in the expanded mode, ports B and C as well as strobe lines A and B (STRA, STRB) are lost because these lines are used for address and data lines, read/write (R/$\overline{W}$) line, and address strobe (AS). The MC68HC24 is a peripheral device referred to as a port replacement unit (PRU). It replaces ports B, C, STRA, and STRB and is transparent to the software. The other peripheral lines on the microcontroller are not affected. Figure I.2 shows the location of the PRU on the EVB. The M68HC11 microcontroller is wired in the expanded mode with external RAM (8K on board and 8K optional), 8K of EPROM, and a PRU.

PRU devices are available in dual-in-line packages, both plastic and ceramic, and quad packages in a plastic leadless chip carrier. The quad package is used on the EVB and the pin assignments are shown in Figure 1.5. The pins for low numbered address lines are multiplexed with the data bus (AD0 through AD7). Address lines A_{12} through A_{15} are nonmultiplexed. The PRU does not use address lines A_9 through A_{11}.

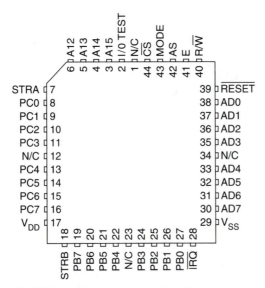

FIGURE 1.5 Pin assignments for the
MC68HC24 port replacement unit (Courtesy of
Motorola, Inc.)

Since this unit is software transparent to the user, the operation of the port and strobe lines are the same as those on the MCU and described in section 1.3.8. Technical data, pin descriptions, and internal register descriptions are given in Appendix B.

In general, a PRU device can be configured for any page boundary. On the EVB, the PRU's internal registers along with the microcontroller's other internal registers associated with I/O operations are at locations $1000 through $103F. To understand how external devices are connected to the CPU, we must describe a scheme called memory mapped.

1.5

MEMORY MAP

In the Introduction, we described how the CPU is the electronic brain of a computer and, in particular, the CPU of a microcomputer is called a microprocessor. As shown in Figure 1.2, one part of the microcontroller is labeled CPU. Like any CPU, it is this section that decodes instructions, performs the arithmetic and logic operations, has latches, buffers, registers, and control circuitry. Thus, this section is the electronic brain of the microcontroller. Note: the CPU section of a micro-controller is *not* referred to as a microprocessor but just as the CPU.

All registers outside of the CPU section are associated with I/O operations or the timer unit. These registers, whether they are part of the microcontroller or the PRU, are addressable by the CPU. This means that these registers are located by their address and are "viewed" by the CPU the same as any memory location; therefore, no special instructions are required to read or write data to these registers. This technique of having I/O registers as easily addressable as memory locations is known as *memory mapped I/O*. This scheme places memory (RAM and ROM) and registers associated with I/O operations within the 64K address range of the CPU. Figure 1.6 is the memory map for the EVB system. Address space $1000 through $103F are the locations reserved for microcontroller's I/O registers. An expanded view of this section of the memory map is shown in Figure 1.7. Many of these registers will be used in Chapters 5–10 and Figure 1.7 will be used as a reference.

INTERNAL RAM (MCU RESERVED)	$0000
	$00FF
NOT USED	$0100
	$0FFF
PRU + REG. DECODE	$1000
	$17FF
NOT USED	$1800
	$3FFF
FLIP-FLOP DECODE	$4000
	$5FFF
OPTIONAL 8K RAM	$6000
	$7FFF
NOT USED	$8000
	$97FF
TERMINAL ACIA	$9800
	$9FFF
NOT USED	$A000
	$B5FF
EEPROM	$B600
	$B7FF
NOT USED	$B800
	$BFFF
USER RAM	$C000
	$DFFF
MONITOR EPROM	$E000
	$FFFF

FIGURE 1.6 EVB memory map diagram

Address	Bit 7	6	5	4	3	2	1	Bit 0	Register
$1000	Bit 7							Bit 0	PORTA
$1001									Reserved
$1002	STAF	STAI	CWOM	HNDS	OIN	PLS	EGA	INVB	PIOC
$1003	Bit 7							Bit 0	PORTC
$1004	Bit 7							Bit 0	PORTB
$1005	Bit 7							Bit 0	PORTCL
$1006									Reserved
$1007	Bit 7							Bit 0	DDRC
$1008			Bit 5					Bit 0	PORTD
$1009			Bit 5					Bit 0	DDRD
$100A	Bit 7							Bit 0	PORTE
$100B	FOC1	FOC2	FOC3	FOC4	FOC5				CFORC
$100C	OC1M7	OC1M6	OC1M5	OC1M4	OC1M3				OC1M
$100D	OC1D7	OC1D6	OC1D5	OC1D4	OC1D3				OC1D
$100E	Bit 15							Bit 8	TCNT
$100F	Bit 7							Bit 0	
$1010	Bit 15							Bit 8	TIC1
$1011	Bit 7							Bit 0	
$1012	Bit 15							Bit 8	TIC2
$1013	Bit 7							Bit 0	
$1014	Bit 15							Bit 8	TIC3
$1015	Bit 7							Bit 0	
$1016	Bit 15							Bit 8	TOC1
$1017	Bit 7							Bit 0	
$1018	Bit 15							Bit 8	TOC2
$1019	Bit 7							Bit 0	
$101A	Bit 15							Bit 8	TOC3
$101B	Bit 7							Bit 0	
$101C	Bit 15							Bit 8	TOC4
$101D	Bit 7							Bit 0	
$101E	Bit 15							Bit 8	TOC5
$101F	Bit 7							Bit 0	

Address	Bit 7	6	5	4	3	2	1	Bit 0	Register
$1020	OM2	OL2	OM3	OL3	OM4	OL4	OM5	OL5	TCTL1
$1021			EDG1B	EDG1A	EDG2B	EDG2A	EDG3B	EDG3A	TCTL2
$1022	OC1I	OC2I	OC3I	OC4I	OC5I	IC1I	IC2I	IC3I	TMSK1
$1023	OC1F	OC2F	OC3F	OC4F	OC5F	IC1F	IC2F	IC3F	TFLG1
$1024	TOI	RTII	PAOVI	PAII			PR1	PR0	TMSK2
$1025	TOF	RTIF	PAOVF	PAIF					TFLG2
$1026	DDRA7	PAEN	PAMOD	PEDGE			RTR1	RTR0	PACTL
$1027	Bit 7							Bit 0	PACNT
$1028	SPIE	SPE	DWOM	MSTR	CPOL	CPHA	SPR1	SPR0	SPCR
$1029	SPIF	WCOL		MODF					SPSR
$102A	Bit 7							Bit 0	SPDR
$102B	TCLR		SCP1	SCP0	RCKB	SCR2	SCR1	SCR0	BAUD
$102C	R8	T8		M	WAKE				SCCR1
$102D	TIE	TCIE	RIE	ILIE	TE	RE	RWU	SBK	SCCR2
$102E	TDRE	TC	RDRF	IDLE	OR	NF	FE		SCSR
$102F	Bit 7							Bit 0	SCDR
$1030	CCF		SCAN	MULT	CD	CC	CB	CA	ADCTL
$1031	Bit 7							Bit 0	ADR1
$1032	Bit 7							Bit 0	ADR2
$1033	Bit 7							Bit 0	ADR3
$1034	Bit 7							Bit 0	ADR4
$1035									Reserved
$1036									Reserved
$1037									Reserved
$1038									Reserved
$1039	ADPU	CSEL	IRQE	DLY	CME		CR1	CR0	OPTION
$103A	Bit 7							Bit 0	COPRST
$103B	ODD	EVEN		BYTE	ROW	ERASE	EELAT	EEPGM	PPROG
$103C	RBOOT	SMOD	MDA	IRV	PSEL3	PSEL2	PSEL1	PSEL0	HPRIO
$103D	RAM3	RAM2	RAM1	RAM0	REG3	REG2	REG1	REG0	INIT
$103E	TILOP		OCCR	CBYP	DISR	FCM	FCOP		TEST1
$103F					NOSEC	NOCOP	ROMON	EEON	CONFIG

FIGURE 1.7 MCU's I/O registers and bit assignments. Note: On the EVB some of these registers are inside the PRU because the microcontroller is operated in the expanded mode.

27

PROBLEMS

1. If the M68HC11 is operated in the expanded mode, the I/O subsystem is _____ (lost, maintained).
2. The microcontroller on the EVB board is configured for the expanded mode. _____ (True, False)
3. How much RAM is available on the EVB board? _____
   How much ROM? _____
4. Which microcontroller package configuration has 8 ADC pins? _____
5. Distinguish between the MC68HC11A1 and the MC68HC11A8. _____
   _____
   _____
6. What is the recommended power supply bypass configuration for the M68HC11 MCU?
7. Explain the two functions of the (a) MODA and (b) MODB pins.
8. Which pins are used to wire an external master clock to the MC68HC11 MCU?
9. Compute one clock cycle if an E clock is operated at (a) 4MHz, (b) 2MHz, and (c) 1MHz.
10. To initialize the M68HC11 MCU, the $\overline{\text{RESET}}$ line (pin 17) must be an active _____.
11. Contrast the differences between the $\overline{\text{IXQ}}$ and $\overline{\text{XIRQ}}$ interrupt pins.
12. Which MCU pin is used as the pulse-accumulator input?
13. What are the primary uses for STRA and STRB in the single-chip mode?
14. Explain the main function of the Read/Write line.
15. Which two pins on the M68HC11 MCU are used to transmit and receive asynchronous serial data?
16. Which pin is used to enable the serial peripheral interface (SPI) of the MCU?

CHAPTER 2

M68HC11 Programmer's Model and Addressing Modes

2.0

INTRODUCTION

This chapter and Chapter 3 introduce a programmer's CPU model, addressing modes, and the instruction set for the M68HC11 microcontroller. This chapter concentrates on the first two topics, while Chapter 3 focuses on the instructions and short programs to illustrate how the instructions are combined to form assembly language programs.

A model aids the programmer to visualize how data is transferred between registers when an instruction is executed. This chapter concentrates primarily on the CPU registers. Other chapters introduce registers located in the different parts of the microcontroller.

In order to give the programmer the most flexibility, manufacturers design into their instruction set a number of different operational codes (op codes) and addressing modes. The op code "tells" the CPU what to do; the addressing mode "tells" the CPU how to obtain the data. Hence, the addressing modes are different ways that the CPU addresses data or instruction words. Addressing modes provide the programmer with various ways of handling data to speed up the processing operation and/or reduce the number of instructions required to write the program. The M68HC11 microcontroller uses the same addressing modes as the MC6800 microprocessor but has two index registers, while the MC6800 has only one.

Similar to other Motorola products, the M68HC11 uses a memory mapped I/O scheme. This technique allows all registers within I/O devices and memory locations to be treated identically, thus simplifying the programming.

The M68HC11 can execute all MC6800 instructions plus more than 90 new instructions. For the MC6800, there are less than 256 instructions and the entire instruction set is easily encoded into 8 bits (the width of the data bus). However, there are more than 256 instructions for the M68HC11, and since the data bus is still 8 bits wide, this requires that some of the new instructions be specified by a 2-byte op code. The first byte, called a *prebyte,* is followed by a second byte to designate the entire instruction. Although the topic of prebyte is mentioned in this chapter, it will be encountered more often in Chapter 3. The M68HC11 instruction set is covered in Chapter 3. However, a few instructions will be introduced in this chapter where needed to clarify the use of a particular addressing mode.

2.1

PROGRAMMER'S MODEL

A programmer's model for the M68HC11 CPU is shown in Figure 2.1. It includes seven registers available to the user: accumulator A, accumulator B, two index registers (X and Y), stack pointer (SP), program counter (PC), and condition code register (CCR). Similar to the MC6800 microprocessor, this microcontroller is an 8-bit device because its data bus is 8 bits wide. However, there are several instructions that permit 16-bit operations. These instructions use accumulators A and B as a single 16-bit register known as accumulator D. Since accumulator D comprises accumulators A and B together, it is not counted as a separate register. The function of each of the CPU registers is discussed in the following sections.

2.2

ACCUMULATORS (A AND B)

Like the MC6800 CPU, accumulators A and B in the M68HC11 are general purpose 8-bit registers. They are used to store data from or send data to either memory or an I/O device and to hold the results of arithmetic operations. Although most operations use accumulator A or B interchangeably, there are some instructions that only use accumulator A or in which the result is always stored in accumulator A. Some examples are: (1) if you want to perform decimal arithmetic, then you must use accumulator A; (2) the contents of the condition code register

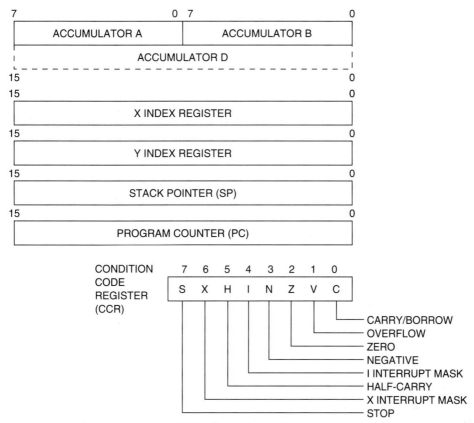

FIGURE 2.1   Programmer's model for the M68HC11 CPU

can only be transferred to accumulator A or from accumulator A to the condition code register; (3) the add, subtract, and compare instructions (whose mnemonics are ABA, SBA, and CBA) use data in accumulators A and B but the result is always put into accumulator A. For example, the Boolean expression for the instruction ABA is $A + B \rightarrow A$, which states that the contents of accumulator A is added to the contents of accumulator B and the result is put into accumulator A.

Figure 2.2 may help to visualize what happens within the CPU when the ABA instruction is executed. Note: The original contents of accumulator A are lost because the result is now stored in that register. However, the contents of accumulator B are not changed because it is not the location of the answer. In this example, accumulators A and B are known as *source* registers and accumulator A is also the *destination* register. The conclusion is data that comes from a source register (or memory location) is never lost, but the original data at a destination register (or memory location) is always lost because it is overwritten by the new data going into it.

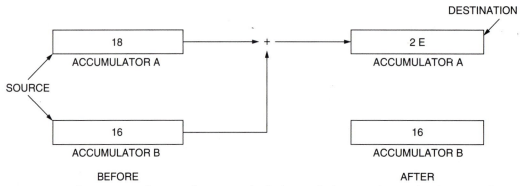

FIGURE 2.2 The contents of accumulators A and B before and after ABA instruction is executed. Data is in hexadecimal.

2.3

ACCUMULATOR D

Unlike the MC6800, the M68HC11 CPU contains instructions that treat the combination of accumulator A and B as a single 16-bit double accumulator called accumulator D or the D register. Accumulator D is used for 16-bit add, subtract, multiply, and divide operations as well as exchanging data with an index register. As you will see in Chapter 3, a 16-bit accumulator saves programming steps when binary values greater than 8 bits are being manipulated. By using the exchange instruction (XGDX or XGDY), accumulator D allows the contents of an index register to be manipulated easily and then returned to the index register. There are more powerful instructions associated with accumulator D than with either index register. This feature is very helpful when memory pointers have to be modified.

Note: The D register is not a separate register. It is accumulator A and accumulator B used together for a particular operation. Accumulator A is the upper byte, while accumulator B is the lower byte. As shown in Chapter 4, when we use the EVB system and obtain a display of the CPU registers, there isn't a separate D register. You use the contents of both accumulators A and B to perform a 16-bit operation and you need accumulators A and B to store a 16-bit result.

2.4

CONDITION CODE REGISTER (CCR)

The CCR as shown in Figure 2.1 is an 8-bit register that contains five status bits, two interrupt masking bits, and a stop disable bit. The five status bits, also called status flags or flag bits, are: carry/borrow (C), overflow (V), zero (Z), negative (N), and half-carry (H). The two interrupt bits are the I and X bits. The S bit is the stop bit. The logic states of the C, V, Z, and N bits are used by the CPU's branch instructions to make decisions. Appendix A summarizes the function of every instruction and how it affects each flag bit. Let's now introduce the function of each bit in the CCR and explain some of the conditions that cause the bit to be set or cleared.

2.4.1 Carry Flag (C Flag)

The C bit indicates a carry from an addition operation or a borrow from a subtraction operation. For an addition operation, the C flag is set to a logic 1 if there is a carry out of the most significant bit of the result; otherwise, C = 0. For 8-bit addition, the carry is from bit position 7 as shown in Figures 2.3(a) and (b). For 16-bit addition, the carry is from bit position 15 as shown in Figure 2.3(c).

As with other CPUs, the M68HC11 is capable of handling 2's complement

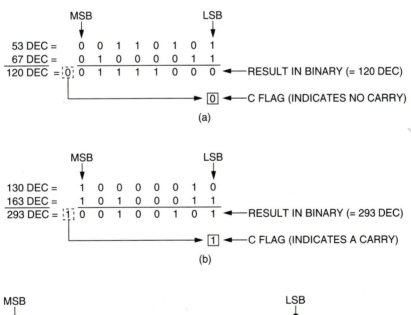

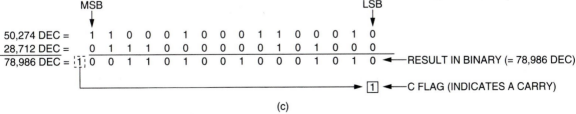

FIGURE 2.3 For addition, the C flag indicates a carry out of the MSB (most significant bit). LSB represents least significant bit.

MSB (SIGN BIT)   LSB   MSB (SIGN BIT)   LSB

```
  + 3 = 0   0   0   0   0   0   1   1      − 3 = 1   1   1   1   1   1   0   1
 + 26 = 0   0   0   1   1   0   1   0     − 26 = 1   1   1   0   0   1   1   0
 + 40 = 0   0   1   0   1   0   0   0     − 40 = 1   1   0   1   1   0   0   0
+ 102 = 0   1   1   0   0   1   1   0    − 102 = 1   0   0   1   1   0   1   0
```

(a)

2'S COMPLEMENT NUMBER	STATUS OF MSB	STATUS OF N FLAG
POSITIVE NUMBER	0	0
NEGATIVE NUMBER	1	1

(b)

FIGURE 2.4 (a) Example of positive and negative numbers expressed in two's complement form. (b) Summary of the N flag status.

numbers. In 2's complement form, the most significant bit (MSB) is the sign bit. Positive numbers have the MSB as a logic 0 and remaining bits are in straight binary. Negative numbers, however, have the MSB as a logic 1 and the remaining bits are the 2's complement of the number. Figure 2.4 shows examples of positive and negative values expressed in 2's complement form.

The range of 2's complement numbers for an 8-bit register is from −128 to +127 decimal, and for a 16-bit register it is from −32,768 to +32,767 decimal. Section 2.4.2 shows how the CPU determines if a result is within or outside of this range.

The M68HC11 stores all negative numbers in 2's complement form, and subtraction is performed using 2's complement arithmetic. Negative results are stored in 2's complement form. Figure 2.5 gives examples of the subtraction operation using 2's complement arithmetic and how the C flag is set to a logic 1 (if there is a borrow from the most significant bit) or how it is cleared to a logic 0. Note: After the subtraction operation, the carry out of the MSB is internally complemented before being stored in the C flag.

2.4.2 Overflow Flag (V Flag)

Many programs and some CPU operations require 2's complement arithmetic. The previous section introduced 2's complement numbers and showed that the range held by an 8 bit register is from −128 to +127 decimal, and for a 16-bit register it is from −32,768 to + 32,767 decimal. The CPU sets the V flag to a logic 1 when a number is outside of this range. This is known as a 2's complement overflow. The CPU clears the V flag to a logic 0 when a number is within the range for the register that is being used.

The input to the V flag can be generated from a two-input exclusive OR gate

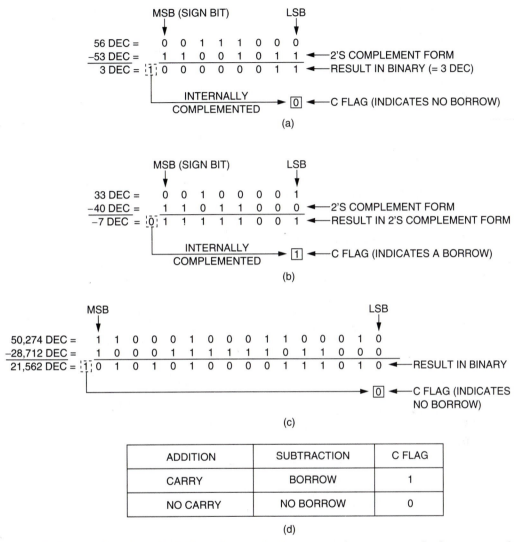

FIGURE 2.5 For subtraction, the C flag indicates whether or not a borrow occured. (d) Summary of C flag bit status.

inside the CPU, as shown in Figure 2.6. One input comes from the carry out of the most significant bit (MSB). The other input comes from a carry generated from bit 6 to bit 7 for 8-bit operations, and from bit 14 to bit 15 for 16-bit operations. Figure 2.6 show three examples when the V flag is set or cleared for operations on 8-bit numbers. Since the V flag is set in examples (a) and (b), the answers are outside of the range for an 8-bit register and therefore incorrect. Consequently, if you are doing 2's complement arithmetic, the program must include instructions to check the status of the V flag and decide what to do next.

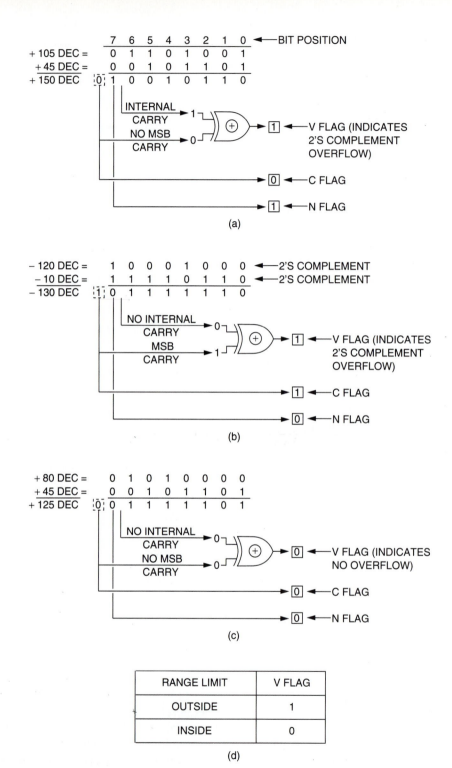

FIGURE 2.6 A 2's complement overflow occurs in examples (a) and (b), but not (c). Therefore, only the answer for part (c) is correct. (d) Summary of V flag bit status.

2.4.3 Zero Flag (Z Flag)

The Z bit is set to a logic 1 when the result is zero; otherwise Z = 0. Figure 2.7 illustrates two subtraction examples. One shows the conditions for the Z bit to be set to a logic 1, and the other for the Z bit to be cleared to a logic 0. Although arithmetic operations always affect the logic state of the Z flag, most of the M68HC11 instructions also affect it. For example, if a value of zero is moved into any accumulator, the Z flag will be set. Remember that if the result of any operation is zero, Z = 1; otherwise, Z = 0.

2.4.4 Negative Flag (N Flag)

The N bit indicates the state of the MSB of a result. If the MSB is a logic 1, then the N flag is a logic 1; otherwise, it is a logic 0. The N bit is used in 2's complement arithmetic to indicate the sign of a number. A result is positive when the

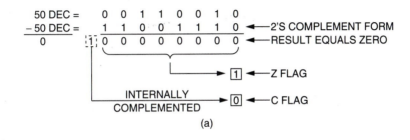

(a)

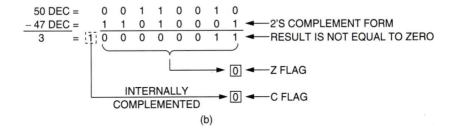

(b)

RESULTS OF OPERATION	STATUS OF Z FLAG
= 0	1
≠ 0	0

(c)

FIGURE 2.7 The Z flag is set to a logic 1 if the result equals zero as in (a). If the result is not equal to zero, the Z flag is cleared to a logic 0 as in (b). (c) Summary of Z flag bit status.

MSB is zero and thus N is zero. A result is negative when the MSB is a logic 1 and thus N is 1. Remember from Figure 2.6 for 2's complement arithmetic that the V flag must equal 0 for the answer to be within the range. Refer to example (c) in Figure 2.6: since there is no overflow (V flag = 0), the N flag indicates the correct sign of the result.

Another use for the N flag is to check the most significant bit of the status register of an I/O device. This bit is used by many I/O devices to indicate whether or not the device has requested an interrupt.

2.4.5 Half-Carry Flag (H Flag)

The half-carry flag is used only for BCD (binary coded decimal) arithmetic operations, while the other four status bits can be used for branching based on the results of a previous operation. The H flag is updated only by three add instructions—the ABA, ADD, and ADC—which are discussed fully in Chapter 3. The H flag indicates a carry from bit 3 to bit 4 during an 8-bit BCD addition operation. If decimal addition is being performed, then the status of the H flag along with the C flag and the temporary binary result are used by the DAA (decimal adjust accumulator A) instruction to correct the temporary binary result to the final decimal answer. In a program, the DAA instruction follows one of the add instructions previously mentioned whenever a decimal result is needed. Figure 2.8 shows the different combinations that can exist between the H flag, C flag, and temporary result, and also the value that must be added to the temporary result to produce the final decimal answer.

STATUS OF FLAG BITS		TEMPORARY BINARY RESULT		ADJUSTMENT VALUE TO BE ADDED BY THE DAA INSTRUCTION	
C	H	UPPER 4 BITS	LOWER 4 BITS		
0	0	0 – 9	0 – 9	0	0
0	0	0 – 8	A – F	0	6
0	0	A – F	0 – 9	6	0
0	0	9 – F	A – F	6	6
0	1	0 – 9	0 – 3	0	6
0	1	A – F	0 – 3	6	6
1	0	0 – 2	0 – 9	6	0
1	0	0 – 2	A – F	6	6
1	1	0 – 3	0 – 3	6	6

FIGURE 2.8 In decimal addition, an adjustment value is added to the temporary binary result to yield the final result.

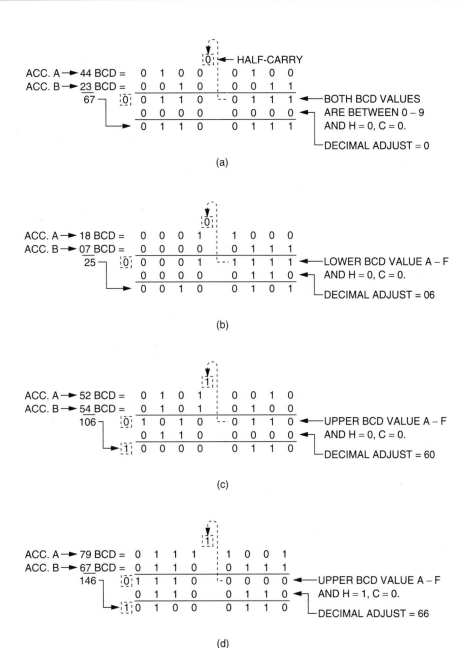

FIGURE 2.9 The CPU uses the logic states of the C and H flags along with upper and lower BCD values to determine if 00, 06, 60, or 66 should be added for the decimal adjust. Decimal adjust can be used in conjuction with ABA, ADD, ADC instructions.

Figure 2.9 shows examples of how the CPU uses the adjustment value to accomplish decimal addition. Note: Before the addition begins, the numbers that are being added must be BCD values (values 0 to 9) and not hexadecimal values (values 0 to F).

2.4.6 I Interrupt Mask Flag (I Flag)

The I bit is the interrupt request ($\overline{\text{IRQ}}$) bit. It disables all maskable interrupts. When the I bit is set (logic 1), the CPU will not recognize interrupts and will continue normal execution of the program until the I bit is cleared (to a logic 0). When a reset condition occurs, the I bit is set and can only be cleared by a software instruction. If the I bit is cleared and an interrupt occurs, the CPU registers are placed on the stack before the interrupt vector is fetched. Section 2.9 covers interrupt operation in more detail.

2.4.7 X Interrupt Mask Flag (X Flag)

The X bit is used to enable or disable interrupt signals that occur on the $\overline{\text{XIRQ}}$ pin. Interrupts on this pin are recognized by the CPU when the X bit is a logic 0 and are not recognized by the CPU when the X bit is a logic 1. The operation of the $\overline{\text{XIRQ}}$ pin was covered in Section 1.3.6.

2.4.8 Stop Flag (S Flag)

The S bit is the stop bit. It is used to allow or disallow the stop instruction. If the stop bit is set to a logic 1 and the STOP instruction is executed by the CPU, it will be treated like a no operation (NOP) instruction and the CPU executes the next instruction. If the S bit is cleared to a logic 0 and the STOP instruction is executed, all system clocks halt, and the system is placed in a power standby condition. All CPU registers remain unchanged and I/O pins remain unaffected. Recovery from a stop condition is either by a reset or an interrupt request ($\overline{\text{IRQ}}$ or $\overline{\text{XIRQ}}$). To assure proper recovery for all versions of the M68HC11, a NOP instruction should precede the STOP instruction.

2.5

INDEX REGISTERS (X AND Y)

As shown in Figure 2.1, the M68HC11 has two 16-bit registers, X and Y, used for the indexed addressing mode. This topic is covered in Section 2.8.6. When the index addressing mode is used, the contents of a 16-bit index register is added to an 8-bit offset which is part of the instruction. This sum forms the effective address that is used by the CPU to fetch the data. Figure 2.10 shows how the CPU calculates an effective address using an index register. The LDAA mnemonic

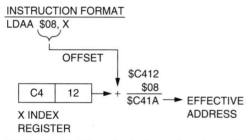

FIGURE 2.10 When the index register is used, its contents (such as $C412) are added to the contents of the instruction's offset (such as $08). The $ symbol indicates a hexadecimal value.

used in Figure 2.10 stands for load accumulator A. This means that the data at the effective address will be moved to accumulator A.

2.6

STACK POINTER (SP)

The stack is an area of RAM used for temporary storage of data and/or return addresses when the CPU is executing a subroutine call or an interrupt service routine. The stack pointer is a 16-bit register within the CPU that points to the next free location on the stack. Each time a byte is put onto the stack, the stack pointer is automatically decremented (reduced by one), and each time a byte of

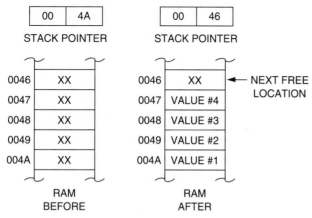

FIGURE 2.11 The stack pointer keeps track of the next free memory location where data can be stored. The symbol pair XX represents any hexadecimal pair.

data is retrieved from the stack the stack pointer is automatically incremented (increased by one). Normally, the stack pointer is initialized by one of the first instructions in an application program. Thus, the programmer does not have to be concerned about the stack other than its size; that is, does it contain sufficient memory space to hold the temporary data and addresses for your application? Figure 2.11 shows the contents of the stack pointer before and after 4 bytes of data are put onto the stack.

2.7

PROGRAM COUNTER (PC)

The program counter is also a 16-bit register within the CPU. It holds the address of the next instruction to be executed. When the CPU executes a subroutine call or an interrupt routine, the contents of the program counter are automatically saved or "pushed" onto the stack. Figure 2.12 shows the order in which the program counter is saved on the stack. The last instruction of a subroutine is a return from subroutine (RTS) instruction. This instruction "pulls" the stored contents from the stack and returns it to the program counter.

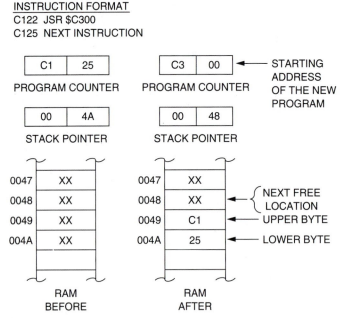

FIGURE 2.12 The stack is used to save the contents of the "old" program counter. The value $C300 is used only as an example of a new starting location for the subroutine program (Note: JSR stands for jump to subroutine).

We now discuss the M68HC11's addressing modes to gain insight on the flexibility of the microcontroller's instruction set.

2.8

ADDRESSING MODES

M68HC11 CPU has the same six addressing modes as the MC6800. They are: immediate, extended, direct, inherent, relative, and indexed. Except for the immediate and inherent modes, each of the other addressing modes generates a double byte effective address. The effective address is the address where the data is located. The CPU puts this address onto the address bus during the beginning portion of the instruction. The following subsections provide a description of each addressing mode with examples.

2.8.1 Immediate (IMM)

In this addressing mode, data follows the op code and is put immediately into the register specified by the instruction. Thus, the data is part of the instruction. Instructions that use the immediate addressing mode are 2, 3, and 4 bytes in length. The first byte (or the second byte for those instructions that require a prebyte) is the op code. The remaining byte(s) of the instruction are data. Note: The immediate value is limited to either 1 or 2 bytes depending on the size of the register used in the instruction. The immediate addressing mode is always specified by the character # and is also used by the assembler (more on this topic in Chapter 4) to detect this type of addressing mode. Other symbols that may precede the data and be recognized by an M68HC11 assembler are as follows:

Prefix	Type of Data
none	decimal
$	hexadecimal
@	octal
%	binary
'	single ASCII character

Note: these symbols are for the cross assembler loaded on a personal computer. The BUFFALO assembler recognizes all values as hexadecimal numbers.

As previously mentioned, the LOAD instruction permits data to be moved into one of the CPU's registers. For example, LDAA means to move data into accumulator A. Figure 2.13 shows five examples of what data will be loaded into accumulator A using the immediate addressing mode.

	INSTRUCTION	COMMENTS
(a)	LDAA #10	DECIMAL VALUE 10 ——————▶ ACC. A
(b)	LDAA # $1C	HEXADECIMAL VALUE 1C ——▶ ACC. A
(c)	LDAA # @03	OCTAL VALUE 3 ——————————▶ ACC. A
(d)	LDAA # %11101100	BINARY VALUE 11101100 ——▶ ACC. A
(e)	LDAA # ´C´	ASCII C ——————————————————▶ ACC. A

FIGURE 2.13 Five examples of how data is moved into a register using the immediate addressing mode. An assembler always interprets the # symbol to mean the immediate addressing mode.

2.8.2 Extended (EXT)

In this addressing mode, the effective address (where data is located) is part of the instruction; it is the 2 bytes following the op code. Most of the instructions that use the extended addressing mode are 3 bytes in length. The first byte is the op code. The second is the high address byte, and the third byte is the low address byte. Figure 2.14 shows how this instruction is used with a LOAD instruction. Those instructions that require a prebyte have a total of four bytes in the instruction. The first byte is the prebyte, the second byte is the op code, and the third and fourth bytes are the effective address. Figure 2.15 illustrates how 3-byte and 4-byte instructions are stored in memory.

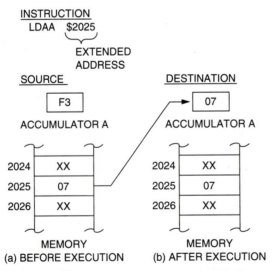

FIGURE 2.14 Contents of accumulator A and location $2025 before and after execution of LDAA $2025. The value 20 is the high (or upper) address byte and the value 25 is the low address byte.

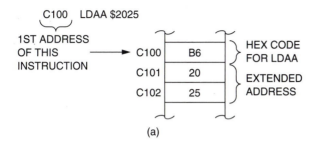

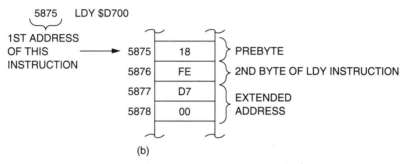

FIGURE 2.15 (a) The instruction in part (a) requires 3 bytes of memory to be stored. (b) The LDY instruction uses a prebyte, thus the extended addressing mode with this instruction requires a total of 4 bytes of memeory to be stored. Prebyte hex codes are either 18, 1A, or CD.

2.8.3 Direct (DIR)

In the direct addressing mode, the least significant byte of the effective address appears in the instruction. The high order byte is "understood" by the CPU to be $00. Therefore, it is not included as part of the instruction. The use of the direct addressing mode limits the addressing range from $0000 to $00FF. Note: This range of 256 bytes is on page zero and this addressing mode is also referred to as zero page or direct page.

Most of the instructions that use this addressing mode are two bytes in length: the first byte is the op code and the second byte is the least significant (or lower) byte of the effective address. Instructions that use a prebyte are 3 bytes in length: 2 bytes, one for the prebyte and one for the op code, and the third byte is the least significant byte of the effective address.

Direct addressing mode allows the programmer to use instructions that take one less byte of program memory space than the equivalent instruction using the extended addressing mode. This also reduces by one cycle the CPU's execution time. Such a feature might be desirable to locate RAM for temporary data storage or I/O devices on page zero so that they can be accessed quickly. Figure 2.16 shows how the CPU executes a LOAD instruction using the direct addressing mode.

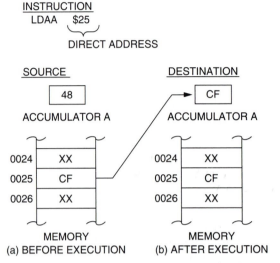

FIGURE 2.16 **In the direct addressing mode, the
high order byte of the address is $00.**

2.8.4 Inherent (INH)

In the inherent addressing mode, the instruction contains everything the CPU needs to execute the instruction. Therefore, no additional information or data is needed from memory. Usually, these instructions are 1 or 2 bytes in length, such as choosing whether we want to increment or decrement a register or add accumulator A to accumulator B. Refer back to Figure 2.2, which shows that the contents of accumulator A can be added to the contents of accumulator B and their sum automatically stored into accumulator A by using one instruction—the ABA instruction. This instruction uses the inherent addressing mode because when the CPU executes this instruction, it knows which registers the data is coming from and which register the data will be going to. The SBA instruction whose Boolean expression is A − B → A also uses the inherent addressing mode and is shown in Figure 2.17.

2.8.5 Relative (REL)

The relative addressing mode is used only for branch instructions. Except for the branching versions of the bit manipulation instructions, branch instructions require 2 bytes of code: the first byte is the op code and the second byte is the relative offset. These offset values are in 2's complement form. This permits branching forward and backward with a decimal range of −128 to +127 bytes. If the branch condition is true, the offset value is added to the contents of the program counter to form the new effective branch address. Before the addition, the program counter contains the address of the instruction immediately following the

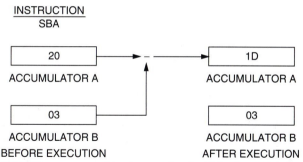

FIGURE 2.17 **Everything is contained within the CPU when it executes an inherent addressing mode instruction. The Boolean expression for SBA is A − B → A. Accumulator values are in hexadecimal.**

branch instruction. If the branch is not taken, the CPU executes the instruction following the branch instruction.

The BCC (Branch on Carry Clear) instruction used in Figure 2.18 means that the CPU checks the logic state of the C flag, and if it is a logic 0 then the offset is added to the contents of the program counter. Hence, the branch is taken. Figure 2.18 shows what values are added by the CPU to calculate the effective address when a branch is taken. Note: The branch instruction is a 2 byte instruction—the first byte is the op code and the second byte is the offset.

2.8.6 Indexed (INDX, INDY)

As previously mentioned, the M68HC11 has two index registers, X and Y. The indexed addressing mode uses the contents of either the X or Y register and adds it

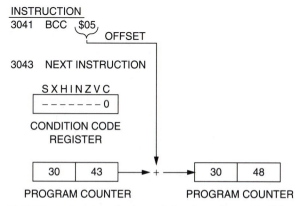

FIGURE 2.18 **When the branch is taken, the CPU adds the instruction's offset to the contents of the program counter to obtain the new address.**

to an offset contained in the instruction to calculate the effective address. As will be shown in Chapter 3, there are a number of instructions that can be used to modify the contents of the X or Y register. Therefore, the effective address can be considered a variable which depends on the current contents of the index register. Unlike the offset used in the relative addressing mode, this offset is treated by the CPU as an 8-bit unsigned value. Note: Since the offset is part of the instruction, the programmer should consider it as a fixed value and not a variable that the assembler may change.

Figure 2.19 shows how the CPU calculates the effective address using the X index register. However, the Y register could have been used just as easily.

2.9

INTERRUPTS

The microcontroller's CPU executes instructions sequentially. However, many applications require it to execute another program(s) in response to requests from peripheral devices. These requests are called interrupts and they may occur at any time. Depending on the type of interrupt and the logic state of the I bit in the condition code register, the CPU may suspend its normal operation and service the interrrupt. If an interrupt service routine is executed, the CPU usually re-

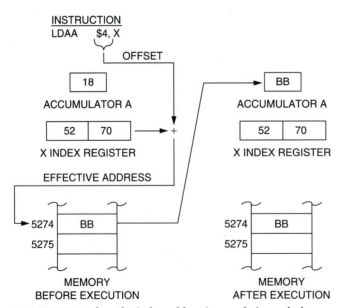

FIGURE 2.19 **When the index addressing mode is used, the effective address is calculated by adding the instruction's offset and the contents of the index register.**

turns to the original program and resumes execution as if no interrupt occurred. This requires the CPU's registers to be saved when the CPU services an interrupt and returned unaltered when the routine is finished. When an interrupt is acknowledged, the CPU's hardware saves the registers' contents on the stack. An interrupt service routine ends with a RTI instruction. This instruction automatically returns the CPU registers. Appendix C shows the flowcharts associated with the M68HC11 interrupts. The topic of interrupts is covered in more detail in Chapter 4.

PROBLEMS

1. How many of the MC6800 instructions can the MC68HC11 microcontroller execute?
2. List the seven CPU registers in a M68HC11 microcontroller.
3. Write the Boolean expression for the nmemonics (a) SBA and (b) CBA.
4. Accumulator A is the _____ (upper/lower) byte and accumulator B is the _____ (upper/lower) byte of accumulator D.
5. List the five status bits within the condition code register.
6. Perform the following 8-bit additions and indicate the carry bit status.
   (a) $46_{hex} + 50_{hex}$ (b) $A3_{hex} + 57_{hex}$
7. In 2's complement form, the sign bit for negative numbers is a logic 1 and the remaining bits are in straight binary. (True/False)
8. Write the following decimal numbers in 2's complement form:
   (a) +18   (b) −55   (c) −1   (d) +101
9. The range of 2's complement numbers for 8-bit wide registers is _____. What flag in the CCR indicates to the CPU if data is within or outside of this range?
10. Perform the following 2's complement subtraction and indicate the C flag status. The following values are in hexadecimal form.
    (a) 48−15   (b) 74−5A   (c) 24−3C
11. Execution of an SBA instruction sets the C flag and clears the V flag. What can be told from this CCR information?
12. Why must your program include checking the V status bit when doing 2's complement arithmetic?
13. Only arithmetic operations affect the status of the Z flag. (True/False)
14. Explain the function of the N flag in 2's complement arithmetic.
15. What are the three instructions that will update the H flag and what type of arithmetic operations do they represent?
16. Explain how the CPU determines the offset needed in an index addressing mode.
17. The stack pointer (SP) is a _____ bit wide register that points to the _____ location in memory.

18. When the program counter (PC) is loaded onto the stack, the lower byte is entered first followed by the upper byte. (True/False)
19. Name the six addressing modes used in the MC68HC11.
20. The immediate addressing mode is recognized by BUFFALO with what symbol?
21. Write an extended addressing mode instruction to load the contents of accumulator A with data from location 14_{dec}.
22. How many address locations are allotted for the direct addressing mode and where do these addresses reside in memory?
23. Write a direct addressing mode instruction to load the contents of accumulator A with the data found in location 64_{dec}.
24. Explain the inherent addressing mode for the CBA instruction. Show a diagram similar to Figure 2.17.
25. The relative addressing mode is limited to what range?

CHAPTER 3

M68HC11 Instruction Set

3.0

INTRODUCTION

This chapter introduces the M68HC11 instructions. The M68HC11 can execute all the MC6800 and MC6801 instructions plus more than 90 additional instructions. Similar to the MC6800/1, the data bus of the M68HC11 is 8 bits wide. For the MC6800/1, there are less than 256 instructions and the entire instruction set is easily encoded into 8 bits. However, there are more than 256 instructions for the M68HC11 and since the data bus is still 8 bits wide, this requires some of the new instructions to be specified by a 2-byte op code. The first byte is called a prebyte and it is followed by a second byte to designate the entire instruction.

Similar to other Motorola products, the M68HC11 uses a memory mapped I/O scheme. This technique allows all peripheral I/O and memory locations to be treated identically, thus simplifying the programming.

Unlike the MC6800, the M68HC11 CPU contains a second 16-bit index (Y) register, bit manipulation instructions, a multiply instruction, and two divide instructions. There are also several instructions that allow the CPU to perform 16-bit arithmetic operations. In addition to introducing the M68HC11 instructions, this chapter also illustrates how many of the instructions operate and how they can be used to write programs.

3.1

M68HC11 INSTRUCTION SET

The following sections organize the instructions into different functional groups and show examples of how some of these instructions operate. The function groups are:

1. Data Movement
2. Arithmetic
3. Multiply and Divide
4. Logical Operation
5. Data Testing and Bit Manipulation
6. Shift and Rotate
7. Condition Code Register (CCR)
8. Branch
9. Jump
10. Subroutine Calls and Return
11. Stack Pointer and Index Register
12. Interrupt Handling
13. Miscellaneous

Some instructions appear in more than one functional group to best show their different uses. For example, transfer the condition code register to accumulator A (TPA) appears in both the data movement group and the CCR group. Another example is the bit test accumulator A (BITA) with memory; it appears in both the logical operations and the data test and manipulation groups. The authors have used the same functional groups as those given by the manufacturer so that the user may easily cross-reference material in the M68HC11 reference manual available from Motorola. An alphabetical summary of all the instructions is given in Appendix A of this text for quick reference. Appendix A also gives, for each instruction, the Boolean expression, hexadecimal machine code, the number of bytes, the number of clock cycles for each instruction, and how the flag bits are affected by an instruction. Hence, it is a quick and easy reference to use for future programming.

3.2

LOAD, STORE, TRANSFER, AND EXCHANGE DATA MOVEMENT INSTRUCTIONS

There are four sub-groups of data movement instructions:. load, store, transfer, and exchange . All microcontroller programs include one or more of these instructions. Load instructions move data either from memory or an I/O device to an internal CPU register. Store instructions move data from an internal CPU register to memory or an I/O device. Transfer instructions move data from one internal CPU register to another. Exchange instructions swap data between two CPU registers. If data is moved to and from the stack area of memory, the instructions are known as *push* and *pull* instructions, respectively. A special case of load and store instructions is the clear instruction. Table 3.1 summarizes the data movement instructions for the M68HC11 including the clear instructions. An X in Table 3.1 or any of the following tables indicates the addressing modes used with a particular op code.

As an example of what happens when the CPU executes a load accumulator A (LDAA) instruction, review Figures 2.13 to 2.15. Figures 2.14 and 2.15 show a typical instruction, the contents of memory, and the contents of the accumulator before and after execution of the instruction. Note: The contents of the source location does not change, only the contents of the destination location changes. This is true of all load, store, and transfer instructions.

When the push and pull instructions are executed, the address does not have to be specified as part of the instruction because the CPU uses the address contained in the stack pointer registers as the effective address. Examples of how

■■■■ **TABLE 3.1   Load, Store, Transfer, and Exchange Instructions**

Function	Mnemonic	IMM	DIR	EXT	INDX	INDY	INH
Clear Memory Byte	CLR			X	X	X	
Clear Accumulator A	CLRA						X
Clear Accumulator B	CLRB						X
Load Accumulator A	LDAA	X	X	X	X	X	
Load Accumulator B	LDAB	X	X	X	X	X	
Load Double Accumulator D	LDD	X	X	X	X	X	
Pull A from Stack	PULA						X
Pull B from Stack	PULB						X
Push A onto Stack	PSHA						X
Push B onto Stack	PSHB						X
Store Accumulator A	STAA		X	X	X	X	
Store Accumulator B	STAB		X	X	X	X	
Store Double Accumulator D	STD		X	X	X	X	
Transfer A to B	TAB						X
Transfer A to CCR	TAP						X
Transfer B to A	TBA						X
Transfer CCR to A	TPA						X
Exchange D with X	XGDX						X
Exchange D with Y	XGDY						X

(Courtesy of Motorola, Inc.)

the stack and stack pointer are used were shown in Figures 2.11 and 2.12. Figure 3.1 and 3.2 show how the load and store accumulator D instructions operate, respectively. Remember from Chapter 2 the upper byte of accumulator D is accumulator A and the lower byte of accumulator D is accumulator B.

Example 3.1:

Write the programming steps necessary to save the contents of accumulators A, B, and the condition code register on the stack. Assume the stack begins at location $004A. (This address would have previously been loaded into the stack pointer.)

Solution:

A method of accomplishing this task is:

PSHB   Save contents of accumulator B.
PSHA   Save contents of accumulator A.
TPA   Transfer CCR to A.
PSHA   Save contents of CCR.

After each push instruction is executed, the stack pointer is automatically decremented. Figure 3.3 shows typical contents of the internal registers and the stack

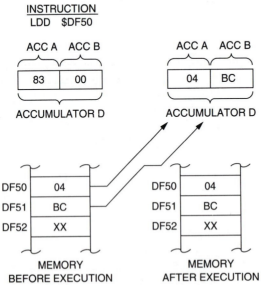

FIGURE 3.1 The load accumulator D instruction copies the contents of two consecutive memory locations into accumulators A and B. In this example, the extended adressing mode is used.

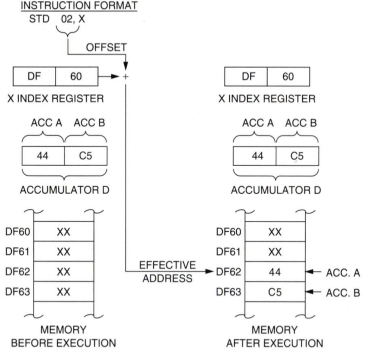

FIGURE 3.2 The store accumulator D instruction copies accumulator A into the effective address and accumulator B into the effective address plus one.

area of memory before and after the programming steps are executed. These programming steps as well as saving the contents of the X and Y registers are often the first instructions of a subroutine. The instructions to save the X and Y registers are given in section 3.12. At the end of a subroutine but before a return from subroutine instruction (RTS) is executed, pull instructions are used so that the original contents are restored, as will be shown in Example 3.2. Thus, the push and pull instructions are a quick way of temporarily saving and restoring data without using the load and store instructions. Load and store instructions affect the N, Z, and V flag bits (see Appendix A). Push and pull instructions do not affect the flag bits.

Example 3.2:

Consider that the stack pointer contains $0047. Show and explain how the following programming steps are used:

PULA
TAP
PULA
PULB

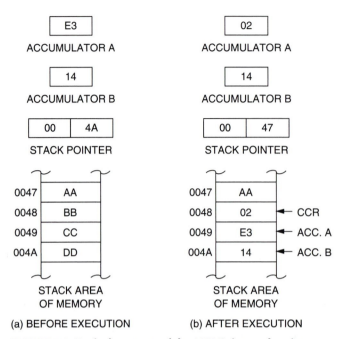

FIGURE 3.3 Typical contents of the MCU's internal registers and memory stack before and after the programming steps in Example 3.1.

Solution:

The push instructions shown below are usually the first programming steps of a subroutine and have been explained in Example 3.1. The stack pointer has automatically been decremented from $004A to $0047 as shown in Figure 3.3.

$$\left.\begin{array}{l} \text{PSHB} \\ \text{PSHA} \\ \text{TPA} \\ \text{PSHA} \end{array}\right\} \text{ from Example 3.1}$$

Main body of the subroutine

PULA	Bring back CCR to accumulator A.
TAP	Restore CCR.
PULA	Restore contents of accumulator A.
PULB	Restore contents of accumulator B.
RTS	Return from subroutine (see section 3. 11).

Thus, the pull instructions are used to restore the original contents to the CPU. The format shown in this example is used in most subroutine programs. After the last pull instruction (PULB) is executed, the stack pointer once again contains $004A. Note: When a pull instruction is executed, the stack pointer is first incremented and then the data is retrieved from the stack.

3.3

ARITHMETIC INSTRUCTIONS

3.3.1 Introduction

This group of instructions includes add, subtract, compare, increment (add 1), decrement (subtract 1), 2's complement, test, and a decimal adjust. See Table 3.2 for the entire list of arithmetic operations and the addressing modes supported by each instruction. Both 8- and 16-bit arithmetic operations are possible and can be extended for multiple byte or multiple word operations. For this group of instructions, the CPU is capable of performing both signed (2's complement) and unsigned (straight binary) operations. Also, the CPU is capable of performing decimal arithmetic by using the decimal adjust accumulator A (DAA) instruction. Refer to Figure 2.8 to see the adjustment value that the CPU adds to the temporary binary result to obtain the answer.

3.3.2 Add Operations

Since the addition operation is a vital part of any microcontroller application, let's first study how this instruction can be used.

Example 3.3:

Write a program that adds two (8-bit) values stored at memory locations $C100 and $C101. Store the result at location $C725. Use accumulator A for the addition.

Solution:

```
LDAA     $C100     Load the first value into accumulator A.
ADDA     $C101     Add value #1 to value #2.
STAA     $C725     Store the sum.
```

This program does not include the carry flag in the addition . If the carry flag was set as a result of the addition, then additional programming steps such as the following are required.

```
LDAA     #00       Load accumulator A with 0s.
ADCA     #00       Add accumulator A + 00 + C flag → A.
STAA     $C724
```

Now the status of the carry flag has been stored.

■■■■■ **TABLE 3.2   Arithmetic Operations**

Function	Mnemonic	IMM	DIR	EXT	INDX	INDY	INH
Add Accumulators	ABA						X
Add Accumulator B to X	ABX						X
Add Accumulator B to Y	ABY						X
Add with Carry to A	ADCA	X	X	X	X	X	
Add with Carry to B	ADCB	X	X	X	X	X	
Add Memory to A	ADDA	X	X	X	X	X	
Add Memory to B	ADDB	X	X	X	X	X	
Add Memory to D (16-Bit)	ADDD	X	X	X	X	X	
Compare A to B	CBA						X
Compare A to Memory	CMPA	X	X	X	X	X	
Compare B to Memory	CMPB	X	X	X	X	X	
Compare D to Memory (16-Bit)	CPD	X	X	X	X	X	
Decimal Adjust A (for BCD)	DAA						X
Decrement Memory Byte	DEC			X	X	X	
Decrement Accumulator A	DECA						X
Decrement Accumulator B	DECB						X
Increment Memory Byte	INC			X	X	X	
Increment Accumulator A	INCA						X
Increment Accumulator B	INCB						X
Two's Complement Memory Byte	NEG			X	X	X	
Two's Complement Accumulator A	NEGA						X
Two's Complement Accumulator B	NEGB						X
Subtract B from A	SBA						X
Subtract with Carry from A	SBCA	X	X	X	X	X	
Subtract with Carry from B	SBCB	X	X	X	X	X	
Subtract Memory from A	SUBA	X	X	X	X	X	
Subtract Memory from B	SUBB	X	X	X	X	X	
Subtract Memory from D (16-Bit)	SUBD	X	X	X	X	X	
Test for Zero or Minus	TST			X	X	X	
Test for Zero or Minus A	TSTA						X
Test for Zero or Minus B	TSTB						X

(Courtesy of Motorola, Inc.)

The M68HC11 is capable of adding two 16-bit values together using the ADDD instruction. Sixteen-bit addition is also referred to as double precision addition. This instruction does not include the carry flag in the addition, but the result may affect the logic state of the carry flag.

Example 3.4:

What programming steps are necessary to add with double precision the contents of $C100 and $C101 to the contents of $C200 and $C201. Store the result in locations $C300 and $C301.

Solution:

LDD	$C100	Data from $C100 and $C101 are moved to accumulators A and B, respectively.
ADDD	$C200	16-bit addition is accomplished.
STD	$C300	Result is stored. A → $C300, B → $C301.

When more than 8 bits are added, it is called multiprecision. Hence, double precision addition is a form of multiprecision addition; however, multiprecision is more general. The addition of 24 or 32 bits are examples of multiprecision problems. The D register can only be used for 16-bit application, so if your application requires more than 16-bit addition, you need to write a multiprecision addition program. Many such programs use a register to keep a count of how many additions have to be done. Using this method requires the use of other MCU instructions. Therefore, a multiprecision addition program will be covered in section 3.15.

The M68HC11 is also capable of adding decimal numbers and producing a decimal result. This requires the values to be added to be in a decimal format and the CPU to execute the DAA (decimal adjustment) instruction immediately after the add instruction. When the CPU executes the DAA instruction, it checks the logic state of the half-carry (H) and carry (C) flags as well as the upper and lower 4 bits of the binary addition to determine the correct adjustment to make. Figure 2.8 summarized the different conditions that can occur and the value that the CPU will add for the correct decimal result. The programmer does not have to worry about which correction value from Figure 2.8 must be used, but need only include the DAA instruction following the add instruction. Decimal addition is also referred to as BCD (binary coded decimal) addition because only binary values 0000 to 1001 are valid numbers.

Example 3.5:

Write the programming steps necessary to add decimal numbers stored at location $D400 to $D410. Store the sum at location $D500.

Solution:

The programming steps are similar to those of Example 3.3.

LDAA	$D400	Load the first value in accumulator A.
ADDA	$D410	Add the two values.
DAA		Decimal adjust.
STAA	$D500	Store the sum.

Since the DAA instruction applies only with accumulator A, accumulator D cannot be used for double precision decimal addition.

Example 3.6:

Modify Example 3.4 to show how double precision decimal addition can be accomplished. One 16-bit value is stored at locations $C100 and $C101. The other value is stored at locations $C200 and $C201. Store the results in locations $C300 and $C301. Locations $C100 and $C200 contain the most significant bytes.

Solution:

LDAA	$C101	Load least significant byte into accumulator A.
ADDA	$C201	Add second least significant byte.
DAA		Decimal adjust result.
STAA	$C301	Store result.
LDAA	$C100	Load most significant byte into accumulator A.
ADCA	$C200	Add second most significant byte and carry flag.
DAA		Decimal adjust result.
STAA	$C300	Store result.

3.3.3 Subtract Operations

The following examples show that binary subtraction can be done as easily as addition.

Example 3.7:

Subtract the contents of memory location $D120 from $D100 and store the result at location $D800. Use accumulator A for the subtraction.

Solution:

LDAA	$D100	Load accumulator A with data from $D100.
SUBA	$D120	Subtract data at $D120 from accumulator A.
STAA	$D800	Store result.

Example 3.8:

Subtract the contents of memory locations $D120 and $D121 from the contents in memory locations $D100 and $D101. Store the result in $D800 and $D801. (a) Use accumulator D, and (b) use only accumulator A. The most significant bytes are at the lowest numbered addresses.

Solution:

(a)	LDD	$D100	Load accumulator D with the data from $D100 and $D101.
	SUBD	$D120	16-bit subtraction is performed.
	STD	$D800	Store the result. A → $D800, B → $D801.
b)	LDAA	$D101	Load least significant byte.
	SUBA	$D121	Subtract data at $D121 from accumulator A.
	STAA	$D801	Store first result.
	LDAA	$D100	Load most significant byte.
	SBCA	$D120	Perform Acc. A–data at $D120–C flag.
	STAA	$D800	Store second result.

Remember from Chapter 2, that the carry flag for subtraction is referred to as the borrow flag. Refer to Figure 2.5 and to Example 3.10 to understand how this bit is set and cleared for subtraction.

3.3.4 Compare Operations

The compare instructions are extremely useful when you want to compare incoming data against a known set point. Compare instructions perform a subtraction to update the bits of the condition code register, but this instruction does not alter any data. Figure 3.4 shows the difference between a subtract (SBA) and a compare (CBA) instruction. Both instructions use the contents of accumulators A and B, but for a compare instruction the original contents in accumulator A is not lost, only the flag bits are updated.

Example 3.9:

What programming steps are needed to compare the data at address $1031 (which is one of the MCU's A/D result registers) with a set point value of $50? Use accumulator A.

Solution:

LDAA	#$50	Load the set point into accumulator A.
CMPA	$1031	Compare A to memory (A - M).

Example 3.10:

If the data at address $1031 in Example 3.9 is $45 and the contents of the condition code register is $EF, which flag bits if any will be set? Use Appendix A as a reference.

Solution:

The compare instruction, like the subtract instruction, uses 2's complement arithmetic.

Therefore, the N, Z, V, and C flag bits are cleared.

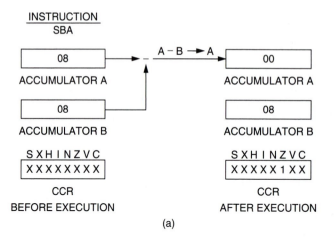

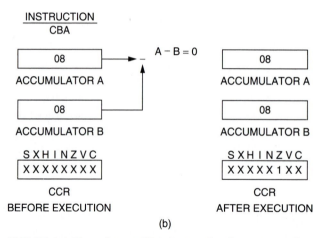

FIGURE 3.4 The subtract (SBA) instruction in (a) stores the result in accumulator A and updates the condition code register (CCR). The compare (CBA) instruction in (b) only updates the CCR.

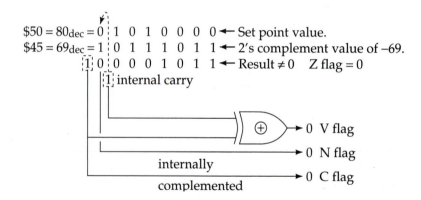

3.3.5 Test Operations

The test instructions (TST, TSTA, TSTB) allow the CPU to test for zero or minus. This instruction subtracts $00 either from the contents of a memory location, accumulator A, or accumulator B and then sets or clears the N and Z flags. This subtraction is accomplished without modifying the contents of an accumulator or memory location.

Example 3.11:

Port C of the MCU has been programmed as an input port and the data on these lines is in 2's complement form. If a test instruction is used, what condition code bits are set if the data is (a) positive value; (b) negative value; (c) zero.

Solution:

From Figure 1.7, we find the address of Port C is $1003. Then the instruction is TST $1003.

(a) Positive value　　$N = 0$　　$Z = 0$
(b) Negative value　　$N = 1$　　$Z = 0$
(c) Zero value　　　　$N = 0$　　$Z = 1$

A branch instruction usually follows a test instruction. Branch instructions are studied in section 3.9.

3.4

MULTIPLY AND DIVIDE INSTRUCTIONS

Although multiply and divide are arithmetic operations, they are grouped separately by the manufacturer. The M68HCll has one multiply and two divide instructions. The multiply instruction multiplies two unsigned 8-bit values and produces a 16-bit unsigned product. As shown in Table 3.3, the 8-bit values must reside in accumulators A and B and the result is placed in accumulator D. Using this instruction a multiple precision multiply can be performed without having to use a multiply algorithm.

TABLE 3.3　Multiply and Divide Instructions

Function	Mnemoic	INH
Multiply (A × B → D)	MUL	X
Fractional Divide (D ÷ X → X; r → D)	FDIV	X
Integer Divide (D ÷ X → X; r → D)	IDIV	X

(Courtesy of Motorola, Inc.)

Example 3.12:

What programming steps are necessary to multiply the data at location $D500 with the data at location $D510 and store the result at location $D520 and $D521?

Solution:

LDAA	$D500	Load value #1.
LDAB	$D510	Load value #2.
MUL		A × B → D (result is held in accumulator D).
STD	$D520	Store result.

Note that the values must be held in accumulators A and B before the multiplication instruction is executed. The upper byte of accumulator D (which is accumulator A) is stored at location $D520, and the lower byte of accumulator D (which is accumulator B) is stored at location $D521. In a later example, you will learn how to perform decimal multiplication because it will be useful for later applications.

Only the carry flag is affected by the multiply instruction. It is set only if bit 7 of the result is a logic 1; otherwise C = 0. This allows the programmer to use the instruction sequence of

    MUL
    ADCA #00

to round off the most significant byte of the result.

The divide operations use the D and X registers. The D register contains the dividend (numerator), the X register contains the divisor (demonimator), the resultant (quotient) is placed in the X register, and the remainder in the D register as shown in Table 3.3.

The CPU performs either an integer divide using the IDIV instruction or a fractional divide using the FDIV instruction. The fractional divide is used when the denominator is larger than the numerator. The result is a binary weighted fraction between 0 and 0.999998 that is stored in the X register and a 16-bit remainder is stored in the D register. In some applications, the FDIV instruction is used to further resolve the remainder from either the IDIV or FDIV operation. Figure 3.5 shows an example of the multiply instruction and Figure 3.6 shows examples of both types of divide instructions.

3.5

LOGICAL OPERATION INSTRUCTIONS

Table 3.4 lists the M68HC11's logical operations and the addressing modes supported by each instruction. This group of instructions perform the Boolean operations of AND, Inclusive OR, Exclusive OR, and 1's complement. The bit test

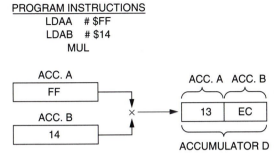

PROGRAM INSTRUCTIONS
LDAA   # $FF
LDAB   # $14
MUL

FIGURE 3.5 The result of a MUL instruction is placed in accumulator D. A STD instruction would store the 16 bits into two consecutive memory locations.

instructions (BITA) or (BITB) perform the AND operation to update the condition code bits; however, the data does not change. These bit test instructions are also given in the bit manipulation functional group, which is presented in section 3.6.

The AND instruction is often used to perform a mask operation. A mask operation occurs when we want to receive only certain bits and force the other bits in the byte to a known logic state. Figure 3.7 shows how the mask operation using the ANDA instruction converts the ASCII character 34_{hex} to its BCD equivalent.

Example 3.13:

What is the result of each of the following instructions if the contents of $D330 is $2F and the contents of accumulator A is $1C?

TABLE 3.4   Logical Operation Instructions

Function	Mnemonic	IMM	DIR	EXT	INDX	INDY	INH
AND A with Memory	ANDA	X	X	X	X	X	
AND B with Memory	ANDB	X	X	X	X	X	
Bit(s) Test A with Memory	BITA	X	X	X	X	X	
Bit(s) Test B with Memory	BITB	X	X	X	X	X	
One's Complement Memory Byte	COM			X	X	X	
One's Complement A	COMA						X
One's Complement B	COMB						X
OR A with Memory (Exclusive)	EORA	X	X	X	X	X	
OR B with Memory (Exclusive)	EORB	X	X	X	X	X	
OR A with Memory (Inclusive)	ORAA	X	X	X	X	X	
OR B with Memory (Inclusive)	ORAB	X	X	X	X	X	

(Courtesy of Motorola, Inc.)

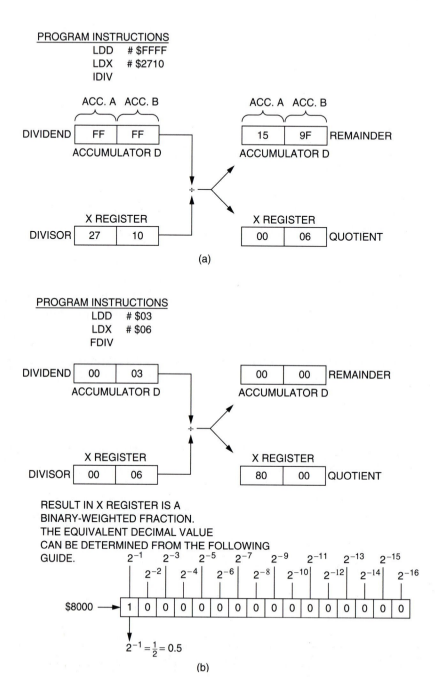

FIGURE 3.6 An example of integer divide in (a) and a fractional divide in (b).

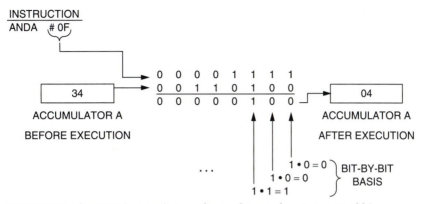

FIGURE 3.7 The AND instruction can be used to mask out unwanted bits.

(a) ANDA $D330
(b) EORA $D330
(c) ORAA $D330

Solution:

As shown in Figure 3.7, the logical operations are performed on a bit-by-bit basis.

(a) AND operation
        $D330   0 0 1 0 1 1 1 1 ← $2F
        Acc. A   0 0 0 1 1 1 0 0 ← $1C
        Result   0 0 0 0 1 1 0 0
(b) Exclusive OR operation
        $D330   0 0 1 0 1 1 1 1 ← $2F
        Acc. A   0 0 0 1 1 1 0 0 ← $1C
        Result   0 0 1 1 0 0 1 1
(c) Inclusive OR operation
        $D330   0 0 1 0 1 1 1 1 ← $2F
        Acc. A   0 0 0 1 1 1 0 0 ← $1C
        Result   0 0 1 1 1 1 1 1

3.6

DATA TESTING AND BIT MANIPULATION INSTRUCTIONS

This group of instructions is used to test or alter the contents of a register or memory location. The test may be from a single bit to 8-bits. Table 3.5 lists the instructions that belong to this functional group. As mentioned in the previous section, the BITA or BITB instructions perform an AND operation and update the N and Z

TABLE 3.5 Data Testing and Bit Manipulation Instructions

Function	Mnemonic	IMM	DIR	EXT	INDX	INDY
Bit(s) Test A with Memory	BITA	X	X	X	X	X
Bit(s) Test B with Memory	BITB	X	X	X	X	X
Clear Bit(s) in Memory	BCLR		X		X	X
Set Bit(s) in Memory	BSET		X		X	X
Branch if Bit(s) Clear	BRCLR		X		X	X
Branch if Bit(s) Set	BRSET		X		X	X

(Courtesy of Motorola, Inc.)

flags (V flag is always cleared) of the condition code register without altering either operand. Since only the N and Z are updated, the bit test instructions are a quick way of checking the sign of a number or testing for zero. The programmer must be careful of which branch instructions (see section 3.9) follow a bit test because some branch instructions also check the carry flag.

The clear bit or bits in memory (BCLR) and the set bit or bits in memory (BSET) instructions are a read/modify/write type of instruction. That is, the contents of the memory location are read, modified, and written back to the same address. A note of caution when using these instructions with I/O devices: The location read from is not always the same as the location written to. An example would be the MC6850 ACIA device, which transmits and receives serial data. Its control and status registers have the same address. It is the logic state of the read/write line that "tells" the ACIA whether the control register is being written to or the status register is being read from. Therefore, when the microprocessor reads the contents of the I/O location, data is read from the status register but writes it back to the I/O's control register. In all likelihood this will alter the format of how data will be transmitted and how the I/O device will try to interpret received serial data.

The instruction format for the BCLR and BSET instruction is

```
BCLR dd, mm
BSET dd, mm
```

where dd is a memory location on page zero ($00dd) and mm is the mask byte. When using these instructions, the bits to be cleared or set must be specified by logic 1s in the mask byte. All other bits at the memory location are unaffected. The following examples illustrate this principle.

Example 3.14:

What programming step is required to clear bit number 3 at memory location $0020?

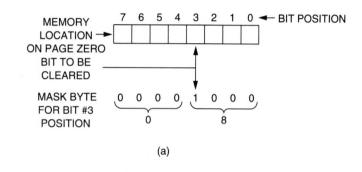

(a)

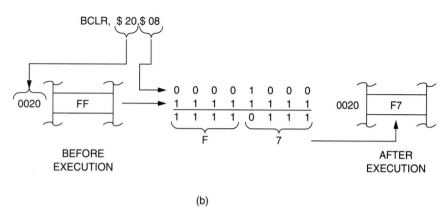

(b)

FIGURE 3.8 (a) Determine the mask byte, and (b) the contents location $0020 before and after the BCLR instruction is executed.

Solution:

Since location $0020 can be addressed using the direct addressing mode, the bit clear (BCLR) instruction can be used. Figure 3.8 shows how this can be done. It is assumed the data at $0020 is $FF before the instruction is executed.

Example 3.15:

Write the programming step necessary to clear or set the bit positions for each of the following conditions.

(a) Clear bit 0 of memory location $0020.
(b) Set bit 7 of memory location $0010.
(c) Set bits 3 and 4 of memory location $0030.

Solution:

Use the bit position placements of Figure 3.8 as a guide.

(a) The mask for bit position number 0 is $01, then the instruction is BCLR $20, $01.

(b) The mask for bit position number 7 is $80, then the instruction is BSET $10, $80.

(c) The mask for bit positions 3 and 4 is $18 and the instruction is BSET $30, $18.

3.7

SHIFT AND ROTATE INSTRUCTIONS

Table 3.6 lists the shift and rotate instructions for the M68HC11 CPU. All of these instructions involve the carry bit. Therefore, after a shift operation or rotate instruction is executed, the carry flag can be tested to determine the logic state of

TABLE 3.6   Shift and Rotate Instructions

Function	Mnemonic	IMM	DIR	EXT	INDX	INDY	INH
Arithmetic Shift Left Memory	ASL			X	X	X	
Arithmetic Shift Left A	ASLA						X
Arithmetic Shift Left B	ASLB						X
Arithmetic Shift Left Double	ASLD						X
Arithmetic Shift Right Memory	ASR			X	X	X	
Arithmetic Shift Right A	ASRA						X
Arithmetic Shift Right B	ASRB						X
(Logical Shift Left Memory)	(LSL)			X	X	X	
(Logical Shift Left A)	(LSLA)						X
(Logical Shift Left B)	(LSLB)						X
(Logical Shift Left Double)	(LSLD)						X
Logical Shift Right Memory	LSR			X	X	X	
Logical Shift Right A	LSRA						X
Logical Shift Right B	LSRB						X
Logical Shift Right D	LSRD						X
Rotate Left Memory	ROL			X	X	X	
Rotate Left A	ROLA						X
Rotate Left B	ROLB						X
Rotate Right Memory	ROR			X	X	X	
Rotate Right A	RORA						X
Rotate Right B	RORB						X

(Courtesy of Motorola, Inc.)

the least significant bit or the most significant bit of the register, depending on the direction of the shift or rotate instruction.

Arithmetic shift right instruction (ASR) retains the original value of the most significant bit. This function is desirable when performing 2's complement arithmetic. Figure 3.9 illustrates a programmer's model for each of the instructions. There is no difference between a logical shift left operation and an arithmetic shift left operation. Assembler language programs recognize them as equivalent. Both instructions are included in the instruction set because they make some programs easier to read.

If the carry bit is set or cleared before a rotate instruction, the programmer can control what logic state will be moved into the register. The carry bit is also used when the contents of two memory locations are shifted, as shown in the following example.

Example 3.16:

Write the instruction sequence necessary to shift the 16-bit number at locations $D300 and $D301 one bit to the left. Assume $D300 is the upper byte.

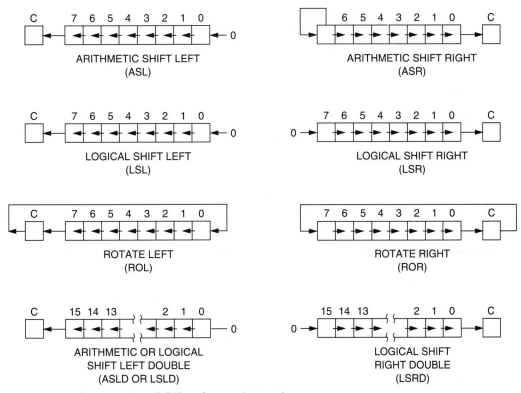

FIGURE 3.9 The operation of shift and rotate instructions.

Solution:

There are two methods of solving this problem:

(a) One method is to use the extended addressing mode.

     LSL $D301   Shift left one bit, MSB → C bit.
     ROL $D300   Rotate left one bit, C bit → LSB.

(b) Another method is to use accumulator D.

     LDD $D300   Load the 16-bit value.
     LSLD   Shift left one bit.
     STD $D300   Store result.

In both solutions, the most significant bit of the upper byte was shifted into the carry flag and was not saved. If you needed to save it, a rotate into another register or memory location could be used.

For some applications, it is necessary to move the upper four bits of a byte to the lower four bits of the same byte. Another application may require exchanging the upper and lower four bits of the same byte. (Note: Four bits are referred to as a nibble.)

Example 3.17:

Write the instructions necessary to move the upper nibble of accumulator B to the lower nibble. The upper nibble is to contain all logic 0s at the end of the instruction sequence.

Solution:

Use the LSR instruction to move the data to the right and shift in logic 0s. Figure 3.10 gives the instructions and illustrates the principle. Data 0101 has been lost.

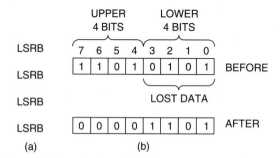

FIGURE 3.10 (a) Four LSRB instuctions move the upper nibble to the lower nibble as shown in (b).

Example 3.18:

Assume your application requires the upper and lower nibbles of memory locations $D360 to be exchanged. How can this be accomplished?

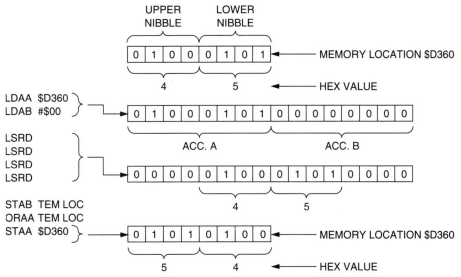

FIGURE 3.11 A method of exchanging the upper and lower nibbles of a memory location. TEMLOC represents a temporary memory location.

Solution:

A rotate of just location $D360 does not work because the logic state of the C bit will appear in the data. One method is to use accumulator D. The instructions and sequence of steps are shown in Figure 3.11.

3.8

CONDITION CODE REGISTER INSTRUCTIONS

Table 3.7 lists the instructions that allow a programmer to directly change 3 bits in the condition code register. They are the carry (C), interrupt (I), and overflow (V) bits. When the I bit is set, the CPU will not service any more interrupts that occur on the $\overline{\text{IRQ}}$ pin. However, the programmer needs the ability to clear this bit because many applications require the CPU to recognize and service another interrupt while in the middle of an interrupt subroutine; hence the need for the CLI instruction. Likewise, the user may wish to prevent the CPU from recognizing other interrupt request signals; hence the SEI instruction. In another application, the user may need to set or clear the C or V flag to be used by an instruction that follows.

The TPA instruction copies the 8 bits of the condition code register to accumulator A. The TAP is the reverse operation; it copies the 8 bits of accumulator A to the condition code register. These instructions are often used at the beginning

TABLE 3.7   Condition Code Register Instructions

Function	Mnemonic	INH
Clear Carry Bit	CLC	X
Clear Interrupt Mask Bit	CLI	X
Clear Overflow Bit	CLV	X
Set Carry Bit	SEC	X
Set Interrupt Mask Bit	SEI	X
Set Overflow Bit	SEV	X
Transfer A to CCR	TAP	X
Transfer CCR to A	TPA	X

(Courtesy of Motorola, Inc.)

and ending portions of a subroutine to save and retrieve the contents of the CCR on the stack. Examples 3.1 and 3.2 illustrated how these instructions are incorporated into a subroutine.

3.9

BRANCH INSTRUCTIONS

These instructions allow the CPU to make decisions based on the logic state of a condition code bit or bits. Table 3.8 lists the branch instructions. For every branch condition there is a branch for the opposite condition. For example, branch if carry clear (BCC); the opposite condition is branch if carry set (BCS). Remember from section 2.8.5 that branch instructions are 2-byte instructions. The first byte is the op code and the second byte is the offset in 2's complement form. If the branch is taken, the offset value is added to the contents of the program counter which contains the address of the instruction following the branch instruction. See Figure 2.18 as a review example. Since the offset value is only 8 bits and it is in 2's complement form, the range of a branch is from −128 to +127. In applications in which this range is not enough, the program must be rewritten. One method is shown in Figure 3.12 using a jump instruction.

Table 3.8 lists all the conditional branch instructions. Those branch instructions that have relative addressing modes (except BRN) can be divided into three categories: (1) tests of a single condition code bit, (2) tests for unsigned binary numbers, and (3) tests for signed binary numbers.

3.9.1 Single Condition Code Branches

The list on page 76 of eight branches is taken from Table 3.8 and shows that only a single flag bit is tested. If the condition is true, the branch is taken; if the condition is false, the CPU executes the instruction following the branch instruction.

███████ TABLE 3.8   Branch Instructions

Function	Mnemonic	REL	DIR	INDX	INDY	Comments
Branch if Carry Clear	BCC	X				C = 0?
Branch if Carry Set	BCS	X				C = 1?
Branch if Equal Zero	BEQ	X				Z = 1?
Branch if Greater Than or Equal	BGE	X				Signed ≥
Branch if Greater Than	BGT	X				Signed >
Branch if Higher	BHI	X				Unsigned >
Branch if Higher or Same (same as BCC)	BHS	X				Unsigned ≥
Branch if Less Than or Equal	BLE	X				Signed ≤
Branch if Lower (same as BCS)	BLO	X				Unsigned <
Branch if Lower or Same	BLS	X				Unsigned ≤
Branch if Less Than	BLT	X				Signed <
Branch if Minus	BMI	X				N = 1?
Branch if Not Equal	BNE	X				Z = 0?
Branch if Plus	BPL	X				N = 0?
Branch if Bit(s) Clear in Memory Byte	BRCLR		X	X	X	Bit Manipulation
Branch Never	BRN	X				3-cycle NOP
Branch if Bit(s) Set in Memory Byte	BRSET		X	X	X	Bit Manipulation
Branch if Overflow Clear	BVC	X				V = 0?
Branch if Overflow Set	BVS	X				V = 1?

(Courtesy of Motorola, Inc.)

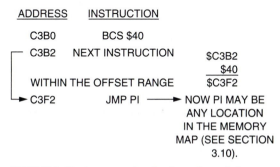

ADDRESS   INSTRUCTION

C3B0   BCS $40

C3B2   NEXT INSTRUCTION $C3B2
                                      $40
        WITHIN THE OFFSET RANGE $C3F2

C3F2   JMP PI ———→ NOW PI MAY BE
                            ANY LOCATION
                            IN THE MEMORY
                            MAP (SEE SECTION
                            3.10).

FIGURE 3.12 An example of using a branch jump instruction together to branch outside of the offset range. Note: If you use BUFFALO's one-line assembler to enter code, the assembler calculates the offset. For this example, you would enter BCS C3F2. For forward branches, you may have to enter a guess for the address and then correct it later.

This is the method of creating a loop in a program.

Instruction	Mnemonic	Flag Bit Tested
Branch if Carry Clear	BCC	C = 0
Branch if Carry Set	BCS	C = 1
Branch if Equal to Zero	BEQ	Z = 1
Branch if Not Equal to Zero	BNE	Z = 0
Branch if Minus	BMI	N = 1
Branch if Plus	BPL	N = 0
Branch if Overflow Clear	BVC	V = 0
Branch if Overflow Set	BVS	V = 1

We will use branch instructions often in the application chapters. A branch instruction may be used to create a loop so that the CPU executes the same set instructions for a specified count value. The following examples use a loop to create a timing delay in a program.

Example 3.19:

Refer to the flowchart of Figure 3.13 and write a time delay program.

Solution:

```
        LDAB  #$Count   Load accumulator B with count value (1µs).
DELAY:  DECB            Decrement accumulator B (1µs).
        BNE   DELAY     If Acc. B ≠ 0, branch to DELAY (1.5µs).
```

The times in parentheses in Example 3.19 are for the MCU operating from a 2MHz clock. The overall time delay can be calculated by

$$\underbrace{\text{LDAB}}\ \underbrace{\text{DECB}}\ \underbrace{\text{BNE}}$$
$$\text{Time Delay} = 1\mu s + (1\mu s + 1.5\mu s) \times \text{count} \qquad (3.1)$$

In most applications, you know how much time delay is needed; therefore, the count value must be determined to write the program. Rearranging Eq. (3.1) yields a general form of

$$\text{Count} = \frac{\text{Time delay} - \text{LDAB time}}{\text{DECB time} + \text{RNE time}} \qquad (3.2a)$$

If the MCU's clock frequency is 2MHz, then Eq. (3.2a) may be written as

$$\text{Count}_{\text{dec}} = \frac{\text{Time delay} - 1\mu s}{2.5\mu s} \qquad (3.2b)$$

Note that the count value obtained from Eq. (3.2b) is a decimal number. You will have to convert it to hexadecimal if you are using BUFFALO's one line assembler and entering instructions.

Example 3-20:

The MCU's A/D converter requires 64 µs to acquire, convert, and store the

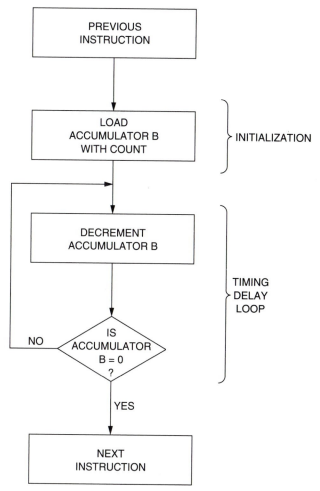

FIGURE 3.13 A flowchart for a time delay program.

data for four input samples. What count value should be used in Example 3.19 to generate a time delay of 64 μs?

Solution:

Begin by using Eq. (3.2b).

$$\text{Count} = \frac{64\mu s - 1\mu s}{2.5\mu s} = 25.2_{\text{dec}} \cong 26_{\text{dec}} = 1A_{\text{hex}}$$

To avoid errors in an A/D conversion you must provide sufficient time. Therefore, choose the next whole decimal number before converting to hex. Although the MCU has a timer unit that can be used to generate time delays, the three instructions of Example 3.19 and Eq. (3.2b) provide an easy method to generate approximate time delays.

3.9.2 Unsigned Binary Number Branches

Some applications use unsigned binary and others use signed binary numbers. An unsigned binary number is always a positive number. For an 8-bit CPU, the range of unsigned numbers is from 00000000 (0_{dec}) to 11111111 (255_{dec}). The most significant bit is not a sign bit. Unsigned binary numbers are also referred to as absolute values. The following list groups those branch instructions for testing flag bits when an application treats data as unsigned binary numbers.

Instruction	Mnemonic	Symbol	Flag Bits
Branch if Higher	BHI	>	C + Z = 0
Branch if Higher or Same (same as BCC)	BHS	≥	C = 0
Branch if Lower (same as BCS)	BLO	<	C = 1
Branch if Lower or Same	BLS	≤	C + Z = 1

The + symbol represents the inclusive OR operation

The terms higher and lower are used for unsigned binary numbers. The terms greater than or less than are used for signed binary numbers.

The above branch instructions usually follow CBA, CMP (A, B, or D), CP (X or Y), SBA, SUB (A, B, or D) instructions. If the contents of the CPU register makes the condition true, the branch is taken. Otherwise, there is no branch and the instruction following the branch instruction is executed. For the CBA and SBA instructions, consider accumulator B to be the primary CPU register.

Example 3.21:

Set a reference value at 25_{dec}. If this reference value is higher or the same as the input data, then the branch is to be taken; otherwise the instruction following the branch is to be executed. What is the instruction sequence to accomplish this task? Assume the input data is being stored at location $D380.

Solution:

The value $25_{dec} = 19_{hex}$, then

```
LDAA    #$19      Load the reference value.
CMPA    $D380     Compare data to reference.
BHS     P1        If reference ≥ data, branch to P1.
Next instruction
```

Note: if the contents of accumulator A (reference value in this example) is higher or the same as the data at location $D380, the branch is taken.

3.9.3 Signed Binary Number Branches

In Chapter 2, you were introduced to 2's complement numbers, which are a type of signed binary numbers. The range of signed numbers in 2's complement for 8 bits is from 10000000 (-128_{dec}) to 01111111 ($+127_{dec}$). In Example 3.21 if the input data was 11100101 (229_{dec}), it is certainly higher than 25 (00011001). If, however, our application is using 2's complement numbers, then 11100101 = -27. The reference value, 25, is greater than the input data value of -27. The following list groups those branch instructions that are used with signed binary numbers and which flag bits are tested for each instruction.

Instruction	Mnemonic	Symbol	Flag Bits
Branch if Greater Than	BGT	>	$Z \cdot (N \oplus V) = 0$
Branch if Greater Than or Equal	BGE	$\geq$	$N \oplus V = 0$
Branch if Less Than	BLT	<	$N \oplus V = 1$
Branch if Less Than or Equal	BLE	$\leq$	$Z + (N \oplus V) = 1$

Similar to the unsigned branch instructions, these instructions usually follow either CBA, CMP (A, B, or D), CP (X or Y), SBA, SUB (A, B, or D) instructions. If the contents of a CPU register makes the condition true, then the branch is taken. Otherwise, the branch is not taken and the instruction following the branch instruction is taken. Accumulator B is considered the primary CPU register for the CBA and SBA instructions.

Example 3.22:

If the instruction BHS in Example 3.21 is changed to BGE, will the branch be taken if the input data stored at location $D380 is (a) 25_{hex}, (b) 04_{hex}, (c) 90_{hex}?

Solution:

From the solution of Example 3.19, accumulator A is loaded with 19_{hex}. The branch will be taken if the contents of accumulator A is greater than or equal to the input data.

(a) $19_{hex} < 25_{hex}$ ∴ branch will not be taken.
(b) $19_{hex} > 04_{hex}$ ∴ branch will be taken.
(c) $90_{hex} = 10010000_{bin} = -112_{dec}$
   and $19_{hex} = 25_{dec}$
   Since $25_{dec} > -112_{dec}$, the branch will be taken.

3.10

JUMP AND BRANCH ALWAYS INSTRUCTIONS

The jump (JMP) and branch always (BRA) instructions are often referred to as unconditional instructions. This means that no flag bits are tested even for the branch instruction. When the CPU executes one of these instructions, a jump (or branch) to a new memory location always occurs.

TABLE 3.9   Unconditional Jump Instructions

Function	Mnemonic	DIR	EXT	INDX	INDY	INH	REL
Jump	JMP	X	X	X	X		
Branch Always	BRA						X

(Courtesy of Motorola, Inc.)

The differences between these instructions are the number of bytes of program memory and the range that can be obtained. The branch instruction requires only 2 bytes of program memory (op code and offset), but the range is limited from −128 to +127. The range of the jump instruction is 64K, the entire memory map, but it usually requires 3 bytes of program memory (op code plus 2 bytes of address). An example of using the jump instruction is given in Figure 3.12.

Table 3.9 summarizes the addressing modes of these instructions. The direct addressing mode has the same hex value as the extended addressing mode. Therefore, in Appendix A, the direct mode is not listed.

3.11

SUBROUTINE CALLS AND RETURN INSTRUCTIONS

The M68HC11 has three instructions in this functional group: a branch to, a jump to, and a return from subroutine instruction. When either the branch or jump to subroutine instruction is executed, the CPU automatically pushes onto the stack the return address. When the RTS instruction is executed, the CPU pulls from the stack the return address and returns to the main program. As shown in Table 3.10, the branch instruction uses the relative addressing mode only. This means that the second byte of the instruction is an offset and like other branch instructions, the offset is in 2's complement form and the range for the instruction is from −128 to +127. Whenever a subroutine is beyond this limited range, the JSR instruction should be used. The advantage of the branch instruction is that it requires fewer bytes of program memory. The disadvantage is with its limited range. Figure 3.14 shows these three instructions along with the contents of the stack after these instructions are executed.

TABLE 3.10   Subroutine Calls and Return Instructions

Function	Mnemonic	REL	DIR	EXT	INDX	INDY	INH
Branch to Subroutine	BSR	X					
Jump to Subroutine	JSR		X	X	X	X	
Return from Subroutine	RTS						X

(Courtesy of Motorola, Inc.)

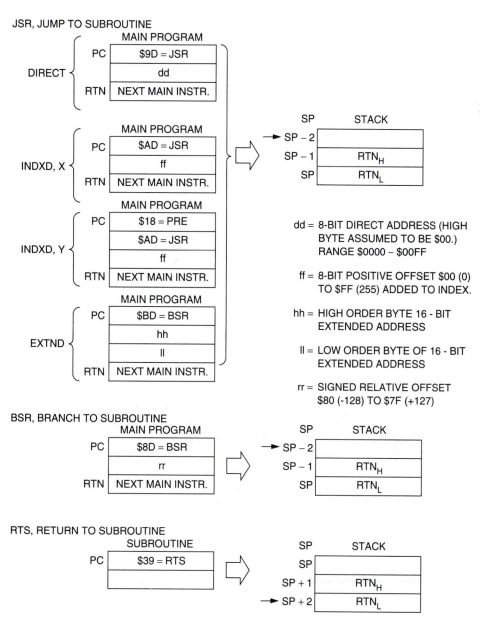

FIGURE 3.14 The JSR and BSR instructions store the return address on the stack. The RTS instruction pulls off the stack the return adress. RTN$_H$ is the most significant byte and RTN$_L$ is the least significant byte. (Courtesy of Motorola, Inc.)

3.12

STACK POINTER AND INDEX REGISTER INSTRUCTIONS

Table 3.11 lists the instructions in this functional group. The exchange D with X (XGDX) and exchange D with Y (XGDY) allow the CPU to transfer the contents of an index register to accumulator D. This allows the programmer to use the more powerful 16-bit arithmetic capabilities. The original contents of the D register are temporarily stored in the index register and can be returned to the D register by having the CPU execute another exchange instruction.

TABLE 3.11 Stack and Index Register Instructions

Function	Mnemonic	IMM	DIR	EXT	INDX	INDY	INH
Add Accumulator B to X	ABX						X
Add Accumulator B to Y	ABY						X
Compare X to Memory (16-Bit)	CPX	X	X	X	X	X	
Compare Y to Memory (16-Bit)	CPY	X	X	X	X	X	
Decrement Stack Pointer	DES						X
Decrement Index Register X	DEX						X
Decrement Index Register Y	DEY						X
Increment Stack Pointer	INS						X
Increment Index Register X	INX						X
Increment Index Register Y	INY						X
Load Index Register X	LDX	X	X	X	X	X	
Load Index Register Y	LDY	X	X	X	X	X	
Load Stack Pointer	LDS	X	X	X	X	X	
Pull X from Stack	PULX						X
Pull Y from Stack	PULY						X
Push X onto Stack	PSHX						X
Push Y onto Stack	PSHY						X
Store Index Register X	STX		X	X	X	X	
Store Index Register Y	STY		X	X	X	X	
Store Stack Pointer	STS		X	X	X	X	
Transfer SP to X	TSX						X
Transfer SP to Y	TSY						X
Transfer X to SP	TXS						X
Transfer Y to SP	TYS						X
Exchange D with X	XGDX						X
Exchange D with Y	XGDY						X

(Courtesy of Motorola, Inc.)

Jump or branch to subroutine instructions do not automatically save the contents of the CPU registers on the stack. Examples 3.1 and 3.2 showed how accumulators A, B, and the condition code register could be saved and retrieved from the stack. To save the X and Y registers on the stack in Example 3.1, include PSHX and PHSY. Since the X and Y registers are 16 bits, the data is saved as 2 bytes (low byte then high byte). The PULY and PULX instructions retrieve the data.

3.13

INTERRUPT HANDLING INSTRUCTIONS

There are three instructions in this functional group, as shown in Table 3.12. The CPU can be programmed to wait for an external interrupt to occur. It is placed in this wait state after it executes a WAI instruction. This allows the MCU to be in a standby mode to conserve power until an interrupt occurs.

The software interrupt instruction (SWI) is similar to the JSR instruction except the contents of all the working registers are stored on the stack. Remember for the JSR instruction, only the return address (contents of the program counter are stored) is stored. For the EVB system, the SWI instruction may be used to end a program and the contents of the CPU registers will be displayed. The RTI instruction restores the CPU registers. Figure 3.15 shows the order on the stack of the CPU registers.

TABLE 3.12   Interrupt Handling Instructions

Function	Mnemonic	INH
Return from Interrupt	RTI	X
Software Interrupt	SWI	X
Wait for Interrupt	WAI	X

(Courtesy of Motorola, Inc.)

3.14

MISCELLANEOUS INSTRUCTIONS

Three instructions that have not been grouped thus far are the no operation, stop, and test instructions. See Table 3.13. The no operation (NOP) instruction does not alter the contents of any of the CPU registers and it does not change the logic state of any of the CCR bits. It does, however, add a two-clock cycle time delay.

The STOP instruction causes the oscillator and all clock signals to stop, thereby reducing the power consumption of the MCU. In order for this instruction to be executed, the S bit (bit 7) in the CCR must be a logic 0. If the S bit is a logic 1, the

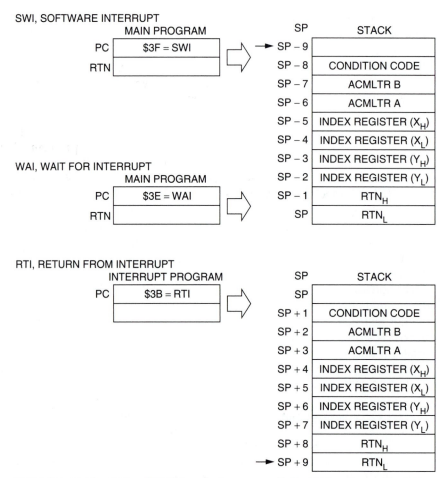

FIGURE 3.15 The SWI and WAI instructions store all the CPU registers. The RTI instructions pull the contents of the CPU registers off the stack. (Courtesy of Motorola, Inc.)

TABLE 3.13   Miscellaneous Instructions

Function	Mnemonic	INH
No Operation (2-cycle delay)	NOP	X
Stop Clocks	STOP	X
Test	TEST	X

(Courtesy of Motorola, Inc.)

STOP instruction is treated by the CPU as a NOP and the next instruction in the program is executed.

The TEST instruction is used by the manufacturer during factory testing and is treated as an illegal instruction when used during normal operation.

In the previous sections, you were introduced to the M68HC11 instruction set and some short programs to illustrate how a particular instruction or instructions are used. The next three sections show examples of longer programs using a number of instructions. These programs will be used in later chapters as part of the software solution to a particular problem. Similar to hardware design, there is no unique approach to writing a program. Although some of the programs could have been written with fewer instructions, it is not the authors' intention to optimize every program but rather to show a straight-forward approach to a problem. We may want to combine or modify some of these programs as part of the total solution for a particular solution in later chapters.

3.15

MULTIPRECISION ADDITION

A multiprecision addition program is needed when more than 8 bits are added. The double precision addition given in Example 3.6 is a form of multiprecision addition. The term multi is most often used where more than 16 bits are added. Figure 3.16 gives an example of 24-bit multiprecision addition and identifies the arithmetic terms of augend, addend, and sum.

Example 3.23 shows how a 24-bit multiprecision addition can be done. This program could be changed to any number of bytes (up to 255) by changing the count value loaded into accumulator B. The X and Y index registers are used as pointers to the memory buffers. In this program, the augend values are lost as the same locations are also being used by the sum.

Example 3.23:

Write a 24-bit multiprecision subroutine that adds the data beginning at location $D200 to data in memory beginning at location $D300. Store the result in memory beginning at location $D200. Use accumulator A for the addition and accumulator B for the count value. It is not necessary to include instructions to save the CPU registers on the stack.

```
MPADD:      LDX      #$D200      Initialize X index register.
            LDY      #$D300      Initialize Y index register.
            LDAB     #$03        Load count value (3 bytes
                                   = 24 bits).
            CLC                  Clear carry flag.
```

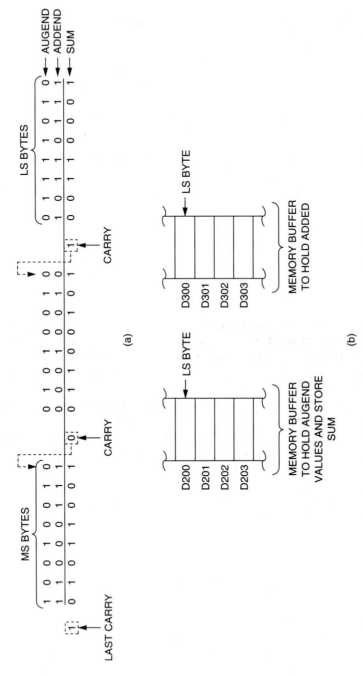

FIGURE 3.16 (a) An example of a 24-bit addition. Memory buffers are used to hold the augend, addend, and sum, as shown in (b).

```
MULTADD:    LDAA    00,X        Load augend value.
            ADCA    00,Y        Add with carry.
            STAA    00,X        Store result.
            INX                 Increment X pointer.
            INY                 Increment Y pointer.
            DECB                Decrement count value.
            BNE     MULTADD     If count ≠ 0 , branch to
                                    MULTADD.
            LDAA    #$00    ⎫
            ADCA    #$00    ⎬   Save last carry status.
            STAA    00,X    ⎭
            RTS                 Return from subroutine
```

3.16

BINARY-TO-BCD CONVERSION

Many control and monitor applications require an output displaying a decimal number indicating temperature, price, weight, voltage, etc. Since the CPU's operations are in binary, a binary-to-binary coded decimal (BCD) conversion routine is needed. The BCD value is converted to ASCII and transmitted to a peripheral device, usually a monitor or printer. This section shows how a 16-bit number can be converted to a 5-digit BCD number. Examples in Chapter 4 show how to use programs in the EVB monitor EPROM to convert a BCD value to ASCII and transmit the result to peripheral equipment. Both of these routines are used in later chapters to output and display decimal results. The following conversion routine is based on a program in Motorola's M68HC11 Reference Manual.

The greatest 16-bit number is $FFFF_{hex} = 65,535_{dec}$. Thus, a 16-bit number is capable of producing a 5-digit BCD value.

We know from arithmetic that a decimal number can be divided into its whole parts. For example,

$$
\begin{array}{r}
65,535 \longrightarrow 6 \times 10,000 = 60,000 \\
5 \times \quad 1000 = \quad 5,000 \\
5 \times \quad\ 100 = \quad\ 500 \\
3 \times \quad\ \ 10 = \quad\ \ 30 \\
5 \times \quad\ \ \ 1 = \quad\ \ \ 5 \\
\overline{\quad\quad 65,535}
\end{array}
$$

multiplier   weight   whole number

Our conversion is based on the reverse process because we know the whole number to be converted and we know the weights and must determine the multiplier. Therefore, the following routine divides the number to be converted by 10,000 (2710_{hex}) and then the remainders in order by 1,000 ($3E8_{hex}$), 100 (64_{hex}), 10 (A_{hex}), and 1. The following mathematical steps illustrate how this conversion routine works. All values are in hexadecimal.

	Quotient	Remainder
$\dfrac{FFFF}{2710} = 6$	+	159F
$\dfrac{159F}{3E8} = 5$	+	217
$\dfrac{217}{64} = 5$	+	23
$\dfrac{23}{A} = 3$	+	5
$\dfrac{5}{1} = 5$	+	0

From Figure 3.6a, we know that the dividend and divisor must be stored into accumulator D and X registers respectively. After each division, the quotient is in the X register and the remainder is in accumulator D.

Although the quotients in the X register are 16 bits, the actual result is in the lowest nibble. This will be saved in one byte of a memory buffer for easy conversion to ASCII or other operations at a later time. Two more pieces of information are needed: where is the data to be converted stored and where will the BCD values be saved? Let's choose locations $D100 and $D101 for the 16-bit number to be converted and a 5-byte memory buffer beginning at $DB00 to store the results. See Figure 3.17. With this background, we are ready to write a 16-bit binary-to-BCD conversion routine called BINBCD.

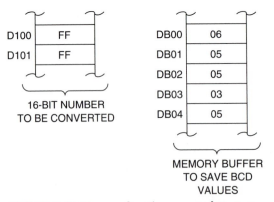

FIGURE 3.17 Memory location are used to store the original binary data and the converted BCD values.

Example 3.24:

Write a binary-to-BCD conversion subroutine. Use Figure 3.17 as guide for determining the location of the binary number and saved BCD values. This subroutine does not have to save the CPU registers on the stack. Therefore, it does not include push and pull instructions.

Solution:

BINBCD:	LDD	$D100	Load 16-bit number to be converted.
	LDX	#$2710	Load divisor 10,000 (2710_{hex}).
	IDIV		Integer divide.
	XGDX		Save remainder in X register.
	STAB	$DB00	Store quotient in memory buffer.
	XGDX		Return remainder back to D.
	LDX	#$3E8	Load divisor 1,000 ($3E8_{hex}$).
	IDIV		Integer divide.
	XGDX		Save remainder in X register.
	STAB	$DB01	Store quotient in memory buffer.
	XGDX		Return remainder back to D.
	LDX	#$64	Load divisor 100 (64_{hex}).
	IDIV		Integer divide.
	XGDX		Save remainder in X register.
	STAB	$DB02	Store quotient in memory buffer.
	XGDX		Return remainder back to D.
	LDX	#$A	Load divisor 10 (A_{hex}).
	IDIV		Integer divide.
	XGDX		Save remainder in X register.
	STAB	$DB03	Store quotient in memory buffer.
	XGDX		Return remainder back to D.
	STAB	$DB04	Store quotient in memory buffer.
	RTS		Return from subroutine.

3.17

DECIMAL MULTIPLICATION

In Section 3.4, we learned how the MUL instruction works and learned that it only multiplies two 8-bit unsigned binary values. However, applications such as point-of-sale terminals need input and output data as decimal numbers. It is possible to have a routine to convert the input data to binary, process the data in binary, then convert the results from binary to decimal, and output the results. Another technique is to keep the input data and intermediate results in decimal form, then the results are ready to output quickly after the last processing step. The all-decimal technique requires more memory because each number is stored as a BCD value and the main program requires more instructions, but long decimal-to-binary and binary-to-decimal routines are not required.

Before we write a program, let's study the steps involved. Consider the decimal numbers 7 and 9 are multiplied using the MUL instruction. The product is

Decimal Form			Binary Form	
Multiplicand	$\longrightarrow$	7	0111	
Multiplier	$\longrightarrow$	9	1001	
Product	$\longrightarrow$	63	$0011\overline{1111} = 63_{dec}$	
			3 F_{hex}	

This example shows the MUL instruction produces a binary result which must be converted to BCD. This conversion can be done by a single IDIV instruction. The conversion of $3F_{hex}$ is done by

	Quotient		Remainder
$\dfrac{3F}{A}$ =	6	+	$3 = 63$

Example 3.25:

> Write the instructions that multiply 7 times 9 and store the decimal product in a memory buffer. Store the units value at $DB51 and the tens value at $DB50.

Solution:

LDAA	#$07	Load multiplicand.
LDAB	#$09	Load multiplier.
MUL		Multiply A × B → D.
LDX	#$0A	Load divisor ($0A_{hex} = 10_{dec}$).
IDIV		D/X → X; r → D.
STAB	$DB51	Store units value.
XGDX		Move X register to D.
STAB	$DB50	Store tens value.

The result has been stored as its units and tens component so that the data can easily be processed at a later time such as converted to ASCII and sent to a peripheral device or be used as a partial product for the next multiplication. The previous example had one decimal number for the multiplicand and multiplier. Except for the conversion from binary to decimal, the following example shows the steps are the same as decimal multiplication using a paper and pencil.

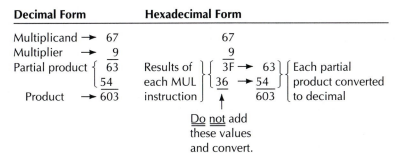

The following program retrieves the multiplicand values from a memory buffer ($D300 and $D301). The multiplier is a constant value, 9. The X and Y index registers are used as pointers to the multiplicand buffer and partial product buffers respectively. The multiplicand and results are all stored as unpacked BCD numbers; that is, one BCD number per byte, and in our example this is stored in the lower nibble. Location $D500 is used for temporary storage of the X register and $D506 is used as a counter register (count equals number of multiplicand values). Figure 3.18 helps us to visualize the buffers and temporary storage locations. Figure 3.19 shows a general flow chart of the program. Additional features have been built into this program because it will be a major building block for a longer program in Chapters 8 and 10.

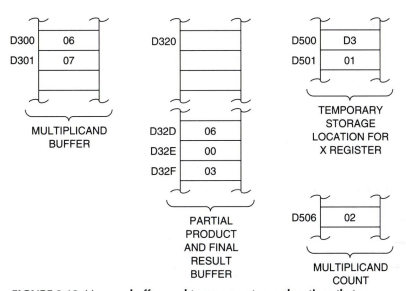

FIGURE 3.18 Memory buffers and temporary storage locations that are used for the MULx9 program. Data and results are stored as unpacked BCD values.

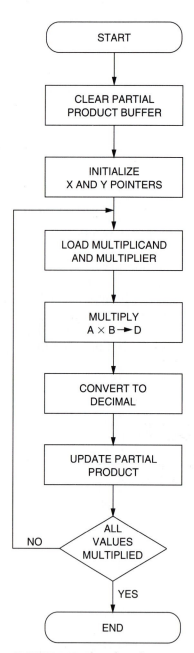

**FIGURE 3.19 Flowchart for a
decimal multiplication routine.**

```
MULx9:    LDY      #$D320  ┐
          LDAB     #$10    │
          CLRA             │  Clear partial product buffer
L1:       STAA     00,Y    ├  of 16 bytes in length
          INY              │  beginning at $D320.
          DECB             │
          BNE      L1      ┘

          LDX      #$D301     Initialize X register.
          STX      $D500      Store X temporarily.
          LDY      #$D32F     Initialize Y register.
          LDAA     #$02    ┐  Initialize multiplicand
          STAA     $D506   ┘  counter.

L2:       LDAA     00,X       Load a multiplicand value.
          LDAB     #$09       Load multiplier = 9_dec.
          MUL                 Multiply A × B → D.
          LDX      #$0A       Load divisor $0A = 10_dec.
          IDIV                Convert binary product to decimal
          TBA                 Transfer B → A.
          JSR      PARTPD     Jump to partial product subroutine

          XGDX                Move quotient to D register.
          TBA                 Transfer B → A.
          DEY                 Decrement Y register.
          JSR      PARTPD     Jump to partial product subroutine.

          LDX      $D500      Retrieve X pointer.
          DEX                 Decrement multiplicand pointer.
          DEC      $D506      Decrement multiplicand counter.
          BNE      L2         If count ≠ 0, branch to L2.
          SWI                 Software interrupt program will
                              stop.
```

This subroutine adds the partial products and stores the result in the partial product memory buffer. At the end of the program, the result is stored in this buffer, as shown in Figure 3.18.

```
PARTPD:   PSHY                Save Y register.
          CLC                 Clear C flag.
P1:       ADCA     $00,Y      Add partial product + A + C flag.
          DAA                 Decimal adjust.
          CMPA     #$10       Compare A with 10_hex.
          BLT      P2         If A < 10_hex, branch to P2.
          ANDA     #$0F       Mask out upper nibble.
          STAA     00,Y       Store result.
          CLRA                Clear accumulator A.
          SEC                 Set C flag.
          DEY                 Decrement Y pointer.
```

```
            BRA      P1             Branch to update partial product.

     P2:    STAA     00,Y           Store result.
            PULY                    Retrieve Y register.
            RTS                     Return from subroutine.
```

This program can be easily modified to have more than two multiplicand values (actually up to 15 for the same size result buffer) by changing the X pointer and multiplicand count. Constants other than 9 can be used by changing the LDAB #$09 instruction. A modification of this program will be used in Chapters 8 and 10.

PROBLEMS

1. Name at least 5 of the 13 function groups used to organize the M68HC11 instruction set.
2. What are the four subgroups of the data movement instructions?
3. Explain the difference between a load and store instruction.
4. Explain the difference between a transfer and exchange instruction.
5. Explain the difference between the push and pull instructions.
6. How does the CPU determine the effective address when executing a push instruction?
7. Assume the stack pointer is at location $0030. Write the programming steps necessary to save the contents of accumulators A, B on the stack.
8. Which of the following instructions affect the N, Z, and V flags: load, push, pull, and store?
9. Assume the stack pointer is at location $0040. Write the programming steps necessary to restore the original contents of the CPU from the stack.
10. The M68HC11 microcontroller is capable of performing signed operations in straight binary. (True/False)
11. Write a program to add two (8-bit) values stored in memory locations $A000 and $B000 and store results in accumulator B.
12. Which of the following additions are multiprecision and which are double precision?
   (a) 24-bit addition
   (b) 16-bit addition
   (c) 32-bit addition
13. Explain each of the following programming steps.
   LDAA $A100
   ADDA $A101
   DAA
   STAA $A102

14. Write a program to subtract the contents of location $A100 from $A101 and store the results in location $A102.
15. The original contents in accumulator A are lost when the compare instruction (CBA) is executed. (True/False)
16. What flag is affected by the MUL instruction and how is this flag set to a logic 1?
17. Write a program to multiply the data in location $A200 with the data present in accumulator A and store the results in memory location $A050.
18. When is the IDIV instruction used in preference to the FDIV instruction?
19. Determine the contents of accumulator B after the following instruction is executed: ANDB #$F0. Assume 15_{hex} resided in accumulator B before the logical AND operation is executed.
20. Write the single line code to (a) clear bit 5 of memory location $00A1, (b) clear bit 6 at location $00AA ,and (c) set bit 2 at $00FE.
21. Write code to shift the lower nibble of accumulator A to the upper nibble. The lower nibble of accumulator A is to contain all logic 1s after execution.
22. Write the code to exchange the upper two bits of memory location $D100 with the lower two bits of the same location.
23. What is the difference between an arithmetic shift right operation and the logical shift right operation?
24. Explain the following instructions.
    (a) CLI   (b) SEI
25. What is the reverse operation to the TAP instruction?
26. What is the range of an 8-bit branch instruction?
27. List 4 branch instructions that test a single flag bit.
28. For the delay loop of Figure 3.13, determine the count number (hex) required to set a delay of (a) 100 µs, (b) 540 µs, (c) 32 µs. Assume MCU's clock is 2MHz.
29. Write the program instructions for a 128 µs delay loop.
30. Which addressing mode is not supported by the JMP instruction?
31. What is the range of unsigned numbers?
32. Accumulator A is loaded with a reference value of $A2. Write code to check input data stored in $C100 against reference, and branch if data is equal to or less than reference; otherwise the instruction following the branch is to be executed.
33. Explain one disadvantage of the BSR instruction.
34. How many clock cycles does the NOP instruction use?
35. What must occur in the CCR for the STOP instruction to be ignored?
36. Explain the XGDY and XGDX instructions and their advantages.
37. Is TEST an illegal instruction for the M68HC11?
38. Write a 32-bit multiprecision addition subroutine. Use Example 3.23 as a guide.

CHAPTER 4

EVB Commands, Utility Subroutines, and M68HC11 Assembler Software

4.0

INTRODUCTION

As discussed in the Introduction, in order to quickly and easily use the M68HC11 microcontroller, Motorola designed a low-cost evaluation board (EVB) as shown in Figure I.2. Some of the EVB features are: (1) MC68HC11A8 MCU; (2) 8K of EPROM containing a monitor and debugging programs; (3) 8K of RAM expandable to 16K; (4) MC68HC24 port replacement unit (PRU) to replace the I/O lines lost because the MCU is used in its expanded mode; (5) serial and I/O ports; and (6) downloading capability from a host computer. Thus the EVB system contains both the hardware and software capabilities to design, build, and test your application ideas. The monitor program contained in the EVB's onboard EPROM is called BUFFA-LO, which stands for *Bit User Fast Friendly Aid to Logical Operation*. This monitor program contains 19 programs called commands that allow the user to write programs using assembly language; check the contents of memory, I/O, and the CPU registers; receive programs and data from a host computer, and so on. The assembly language programs that you write using BUFFALO do not permit labels to be used. However, the assembler that comes with the purchase of an EVB system and loaded onto a PC does allow labels, along with many other features, some of which you will study in sections 4.18 through 4.20 and use again in later chapters to write programs. After a program is written and assembled, it may be downloaded into the RAM on the EVB and executed. Hence, the purchase of an EVB system is a versatile product that allows you to get up and going quickly, either at the chip level, using BUFFALO commands and machine language, or at the assembly level and downloading your program. This chapter shows how to use: (1) most of the BUFFALO commands (sections 4.3 to 4.15), (2) utility subroutines that are also contained within the EPROM chip (section 4.16), (3) interrupt vectors (section 4.17), (4) assembler directives (sections 4.18 to 4.20), and (5) a general procedure of how to download an assembled language program to the EVB (section 4.22).

4.1

POWER REQUIREMENTS FOR THE EVB

Remember from Chapter 1 that the EVB system requires an external power supply, whose specifications are: +5Vdc at 0.5A, +12Vdc at 0.1A, −12Vdc at 0.1A. This supply does not come with the purchase of an EVB system. The authors have used a switching power supply with no problems.

4.2

INITIAL SETUP

To write and test programs, you may use either the BUFFALO monitor program to debug and assemble user code or use the software assembler that comes on a 5¼ inch floppy disk with an EVB and may be used on a PC. If you are using only BUFFALO, then you need only a dumb, asynchronous terminal with an RS-232 port. Another method is to use a communication program similar to KERMIT or PROCOMM and a serial port on the PC. In either case, the connection from the PC is through port 2 on the EVB, as shown in Figure I.3.

After power is applied, press the reset button, switch S1, on the EVB (see Figure I.2 for its location). Displayed on the screen will be Bit User Fast Friendly Aid to Logical Operation. Now press the ENTER or CARRIAGE RETURN <CR> key and the BUFFALO prompt (>) appears on the next line. It may be necessary to press the reset key more than once or hold it down for a few seconds to obtain the prompt.

4.3

MONITOR COMMANDS

Table 4.1 is an alphabetical listing of the BUFFALO commands stored in the EVB's EPROM chip. These commands are programs supplied to you by the manufacturer so that you can load, execute, and debug your application program. A standard input routine controls the EVB while the user types a command. The command is executed only after the command line has been terminated by pressing the ENTER or CARRIAGE RETURN key. Although the manufacturer's literature describes these commands in alphabetical order, the authors have chosen to cover most of the commands as a first-time user may need them or use them to learn how the MCU operates.

TABLE 4.1   An Alphabetical Listing of the BUFFALO Commands

Command	Description
ASM [⟨address⟩]	Assembler/disassembler
BF ⟨address1⟩ ⟨address2⟩ ⟨data⟩	Block fill memory with data
BR [–] [⟨address⟩]. . .	Breakpoint set
BULK	Bulk erase EEPROM
BULKALL	Bulk erase EEPROM + CONFIG register
CALL [⟨address⟩]	Execute subroutine
G [⟨address⟩]	Execute program
HELP	Display monitor commands
LOAD ⟨host download command⟩	Download (S-records) via host port
LOAD ⟨T⟩	Download (S-records) via terminal port
MD [⟨address1⟩ [⟨address2⟩]]	Dump memory to terminal
MM [⟨address⟩]	Memory modify
MOVE ⟨address1⟩ ⟨address2⟩ [⟨destination⟩]	Move memory to new location
P	Proceed/continue from breakpoint
RM [p,y,x,a,b,c,s]	Register modify
T [⟨n⟩]	Trace $1–$FF instructions
TM	Enter transparent mode
VERIFY ⟨host download command⟩	Compare memory to download data via host port
VERIFY ⟨T⟩	Compare memory to download data via terminal port

(Courtesy of Motorola, Inc.)

4.4

HELP COMMAND

The HELP command may be used as a quick reference to the EVB commands. It displays the information in a form similar to Table 4.1. Therefore, if Table 4.1 is not available use the HELP command to quickly check the function of the other commands.

4.5

REGISTER MODIFY COMMAND

The RM command is used to display and/or modify the CPU's seven internal registers, which are the program counter (P); the Y index register (Y); the X index register (X); A accumulator (A); B accumulator (B); condition code register (C); and stack pointer register (S). After the BUFFALO prompt, type RM and press the ENTER key. The contents of the CPU's internal registers will be displayed in the format shown in Figure 4.1(a). Note: Typical CPU values shown in Figure 4.1(a) are not what you may see on your screen. Also note that the P register appears again on the second line, indicating that the P register may be changed at this time. To enter a new value, type an address in hex (new value is underlined) and then the ENTER key; the program counter will be loaded with the new address. Also shown in Figure 4.1(a), $C200 is entered (the underlined values are those entered by the user). Now if you type RM again and press the ENTER key, you will see that $C200 has been loaded into the program counter and the other registers remain unchanged. See Figure 4.1(b). Note: When using a BUFFALO command, all values are treated as a hexadecimal number; therefore, you do not precede these values with the $ symbol.

To change the contents of a particular register, such as accumulator A, type RM A. Now when the ENTER key is pressed, you will see the contents of the CPU's registers displayed and on the second line the contents of accumulator A displayed again. This indicates that the A register can be modified at this time. Try entering FF. To see if the example has worked, type RM <ENTER>, and you will see the value FF has been loaded into accumulator A. See Figures 4.1(c) and (d).

To change the contents of more than one register at a time, you may type RM <ENTER>. Once again the program counter is displayed on the second line, ready to be modified. If you choose not to modify the program counter, just hit the space bar <SP> and the Y register's contents will be displayed. The Y register may be modified at this time. Pressing the space bar again displays the contents of the X register. Each time the space bar is pressed, the contents of the next register will be displayed. If you press only the space bar, the value remains unchanged. If you enter a new value and then press the space bar, the register will

```
>RM  <ENTER>
P-D500 Y-6018 X-45A2 A-37 B-22 C-E0 S-004A
P-D500 C200  <ENTER>
```
                        (a)


```
>RM  <ENTER>
P-C200 Y-6018 X-45A2 A-37 B-22 C-E0 S-004A
P-C200
```
                        (b)


```
>RM A  <ENTER>
P-C200 Y-6018 X-45A2 A-37 B-22 C-E0 S-004A
A-37 FF  <ENTER>
```
                        (c)


```
>RM  <ENTER>
P-C200 Y-6018 X-45A2 A-FF B-22 C-E0 S-004A
P-C200
```
                        (d)


```
>RM  <ENTER>
P-C200 Y-6018 X-45A2 A-FF B-22 C-E0 S-004A
P-C200  <SPACE BAR>
Y-6018  D750  <SPACE BAR>
X-45A2  D3A4  <SPACE BAR>
A-FF     <SPACE BAR>
B-22     80  <SPACE BAR>
C-E0     <SPACE BAR>
S-004A  <SPACE BAR>
>
```
                        (e)


```
>RM  <ENTER>
P-C200 Y-D750 X-D3A4 A-FF B-80 C-E0 S-004A
P-C200
```
                        (f)

**FIGURE 4.1 The RM command is used to
display and modify the CPU registers.**

be modified. Pressing the space bar after the stack pointer register is displayed or modified brings you back to the BUFFALO prompt. See Figures 4.1(e) and (f) as an example. Having a command that allows you to display the CPU registers is a valuable software debugging tool because it allows you to put a known value into a register before the CPU executes an instruction(s). The next command allows you to display the contents of a memory location.

MEMORY DISPLAY

The MD command allows you to display a block of memory beginning at one address and continuing to the second address. The MD command format is

```
MD <address 1> <address 2>
```

where <address 1> is the starting address and <address 2> is the ending address. In many applications, you would specify both addresses. However, three default conditions have been designed into this command. They are: (1) if address 2 is not entered, 9 lines, with 16 bytes per line, are displayed beginning at address 1; (2) if no addresses are specified, 9 lines with 16 bytes per line are displayed beginning at the last memory stored in the program counter; (3) if address 1 is greater than or equal to address 2, the display begins at address 1 and displays one line of 16 bytes. Figure 4.2 shows common examples of how to use the MD command. Note: A displayed line is always 16 bytes in length, a partial line is never displayed.

>MD EC00 <ENTER>

```
EC00  20 45 78 65 63 75 74  65 20 75 73 65 72 20 63 6F   Execute user co
EC10  64 65 2E 0D 4C 4F 41  44 2C 20 56 45 52 49 46 59   de. LOAD, VERIFY
EC20  20 5B 54 5D 20 3C 68  6F 73 74 20 64 6F 77 6E 6C   [T] <host downl
EC30  6F 61 64 20 63 6F 6D  6D 61 6E 64 3E 20 20 4C 6F   oad COMMAND> LO
EC40  61 64 20 6F 72 20 76  65 72 69 66 79 20 53 2D 72   ad or verify S-r
EC50  65 63 6F 72 64 73 2E  0D 4D 44 20 5B 3C 61 64 64   ecords. MD [<ADD
EC60  72 31 3E 20 5B 3C 61  64 64 72 32 3E 5D 5D 20 20   r1> [<addr2>]]
EC70  4D 65 6D 6F 72 79 20  64 75 6D 70 2E 0D 4D 4D 20   Memory dump. MM
EC80  5B 3C 61 64 64 72 3E  5D 20 20 4D 65 6D 6F 72 79   [<ADDR>] Memory
>
```

ASCII
READOUT

(a)

>MD E400 E41F <ENTER>

```
E400  05 A7 02 39 A6 01 84  01 27 04 A6 03 84 7F 39 7D    9       9
E410  00 A9 27 10 8D 0E 81  0D 26 04 86 0A 20 06 81 0A    '       &
>
```

NONPRINTABLE
ASCII CHARACTERS
APPEAR AS BLANK
SPACES

(b)

>MD F300 F300 <ENTER>

```
F300  20 72 61 6E 67 65 04  CE 00 00 DF AE BD E2 F1 81    range
>
```

(c)

FIGURE 4.2 Examples of using the MD display. The default condition (only one address specified) displays 9 lines and 16 bytes per line as shown in (a).

4.7

BLOCK FILL COMMAND

The BF command allows you to copy a byte into one RAM location or into an entire block of RAM. The command format is

```
BF <address 1> <address 2> <data>
```

where address 1 is the starting address, address 2 is the ending address. All values are hexadecimal.

Example 4.1:

Show how a block of memory from location $C100 to $C12F may be cleared with all logic 0s. This is a block of 48 bytes.

Solution:

After the BUFFALO prompt, type

```
> BF C100 C12F 00 <ENTER>
```

Each byte of memory from $C100 through $C12F now contains the data 00. To check the result, use the MD command.

```
> MD C100 <ENTER>
```

If you try to fill an invalid address, such as loading data into ROM, an invalid message will be displayed. The form of this invalid message is "rom xxxx" where xxxx is the invalid address.

Example 4.2:

What happens when you type

```
> BF E000 E020 FF <ENTER>
```

Solution:

The message rom E000 is displayed on the terminal because in the EVB system the ROM's address range is from $E000 to $FFFF. Refer back to the memory map diagram of Figure 1.6 as a guide.

4.8

MOVE COMMAND

The MOVE command allows you to copy a block of memory (RAM or ROM) to a new memory location. The command format is

```
MOVE <address 1> <address 2> [<destination>]
```

where <address 1> is the starting address of the data that is being moved; <address 2> is the ending address of the data that is being moved; and [<destination>] is the starting address of the destination. The bracket symbols [ ] indicate an optional condition. If a destination address is not specified, the data is moved up one memory location from its present location. This is the default condition for MOVE command.

When the MOVE command is being executed, there are no messages displayed on the screen. After it is completed, the BUFFALO prompt reappears.

This command is useful when programming the MCU's EEPROM. You create the program in RAM using the assembler, debug it, and then use the MOVE command to copy it into the EEPROM.

Example 4.3:

Use BUFFALO commands and show the steps involved to move the first 32 bytes of the monitor ROM to RAM beginning at address $D100. Then verify that data has been moved.

Solution:

The range for 32 bytes (decimal) is 0–1F. Therefore, the address space for the first 32 bytes in ROM are from $E000 to $E01F. This information is moved by

```
> MOVE E000 E01F D100 <ENTER>
```

Now use the memory display command twice to verify that the data has been transferred from ROM to RAM.

```
>MD E000 E01F <ENTER>
E000 CE 10 0A 1F 00 01 03 7E B6 00 86 93 B7 10 39 86
E010 00 B7 10 24 8E 00 68 BD E3 40 CE 00 4A DF A7 86
>MD D100 D11F <ENTER>
D100 CE 10 0A 1F 00 01 03 7E B6 00 86 93 B7 10 39 86
D110 00 B7 10 24 8E 00 68 BD E3 40 CE 00 4A DF A7 86
```

4.9

MEMORY MODIFY COMMAND

The MM command allows you to examine and/or modify the contents of a RAM location. This command is different than the memory display (MD) command. The MM command only allows you to examine one RAM location at a time; however, it does allow you to modify the contents of the location, which the MD command does not. The format of the MM command is

$$MM \ <address>$$

where <address> is the location whose contents are to be examined and/or modified.

4.9.1 Examining a Location(s)

Suppose you want to examine the contents of location $D400. Then

```
>MM D400 <ENTER>    Examines location $D400.
 D400 5F            Contents are displayed (typical value).
```

To examine the next location(s) press the space bar (SP). For example

```
>MM D400 <ENTER>  Examine memory beginning at $D400.
 D400 5F <SP> 4A <SP> 73 <SP> 84 <SP> C6 Typical values are shown.
```

4.9.2 Modifying a Location(s)

To change the contents of a location enter the new data immediately after the old data is displayed. If you also want to examine the location with the new data press the (/) key after the data has been entered. Let's change the data at memory $D400 to $AB and examine it.

```
>MM D400 <ENTER>
 D400 5F AB/  AB is the new data and $D400 is examined.
 D400 AB
```

Example 4.4:

Show how you could enter the ASCII hex values for the word volts starting at location $D400.

Solution:

From the ASCII matrix in Appendix D, we obtain the hex value for each letter:

```
                         v    o    l    t    s   Lowercase letter
                        76   6F   6C   74   73   ASCII value
```

Now use the MM command

```
>MM D400 <ENTER>
D400 XX 76 <SP> XX 6F<SP> XX 6C<SP> XX 74<SP> XX 73<SP> <ENTER>
```

The XX characters indicate old data. To check if the new data has been entered, use either the MM command or the MD command.

The MM command may also be used to change the data at a location and then back up one space. For example,

```
>MM D405 <ENTER>
D405 38 2E ^     Examine, change data $38 to $2E, and then back up.
D404 73          Typical data at location $D404.
```

4.9.3 Calculating an Offset

The MM command can be used to compute an offset that exists between two memory locations. The range is +127 ($7F) to −128 ($80). Consider that you want the offset between $D405 and $D321.

```
>MM D405 <ENTER>
D405 XX D321 E4  E4 is the offset value.
```

4.10

ASSEMBLER/DISASSEMBLER COMMAND

The ASM command allows the user to enter M68HC11 assembly language commands one at a time into user RAM on the EVB. The format for this command is

```
ASM <address>
```

where <address> is the starting address. After you press <ENTER>, the address is displayed and any present instruction at that address is disassembled and shown. Then the BUFFALO prompt appears on the next line. At this time, a new instruction may be entered. It will be assembled and displayed when you press the <ENTER> key. Then the next available location will be displayed and the instruction at that address is displayed. Figure 4.3 shows how the 8-bit addition program of Example 3.5 would be entered using the ASM command and starting at location $C200. The JMP instruction is not part of Example 3.5 but returns the CPU back to BUFFALO if the program is run (see section 4.11). To exit the BUFFALO assembler, hold down the CONTROL key and type A, <CTRL> A.

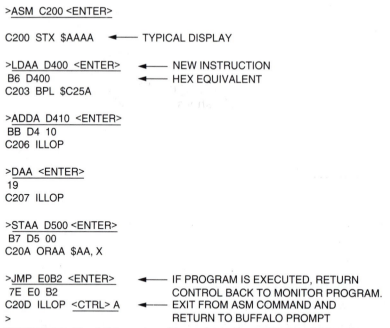

>ASM C200 <ENTER>

C200 STX $AAAA   ◄——— TYPICAL DISPLAY

>LDAA D400 <ENTER>   ◄——— NEW INSTRUCTION
B6 D400   ◄——— HEX EQUIVALENT
C203 BPL $C25A

>ADDA D410 <ENTER>
BB D4 10
C206 ILLOP

>DAA <ENTER>
19
C207 ILLOP

>STAA D500 <ENTER>
B7 D5 00
C20A ORAA $AA, X

>JMP E0B2 <ENTER>   ◄——— IF PROGRAM IS EXECUTED, RETURN
7E E0 B2   CONTROL BACK TO MONITOR PROGRAM.
C20D ILLOP <CTRL> A ◄——— EXIT FROM ASM COMMAND AND
>   RETURN TO BUFFALO PROMPT

FIGURE 4.3 The ASM command is used to enter M68HC11 instructions one at a time. The disassembled instructions that are read out are typical. ILLOP stands for illegal op code; the binary pattern was not able to be disassembled into a valid M68HC11 op code. After a new instruction is entered, its hex code is displayed immediately. Note the BUFFALO's disassembler does insert the $ symbol.

To check and see that your assembled program has been stored in RAM, use the ASM command again starting at the beginning address. Each time the ENTER key is pressed the next line of code will be displayed. Note: The MD command does not disassemble your program; it only shows line(s) of hex values.

4.11

GO COMMAND

The G command allows you to execute your program. This command's format is

```
G [<address>]
```

where the address is the starting location of your program. To execute the program given in Figure 4.3, type G C200 <ENTER>. Note: the program returns the CPU operation back to the BUFFALO prompt because of the JMP E0B2 instruction.

If the starting address is not specified, execution starts at the current contents of the program counter. In either case, program execution continues unless a breakpoint is encountered (see section 4.13), the EVB reset switch is pressed, another type of interrupt occurs, or a return to the BUFFALO prompt is encountered.

If you execute the program given in Figure 4.3, first use the MM command to preload known decimal values at locations $D400 and $D410.

4.12
▬

TRACE COMMAND

The T command allows the user to execute the program on an instruction-by-instruction basis and to have the CPU's internal registers displayed after each instruction. After each instruction is executed and the CPU registers are displayed, you must press the <ENTER> key to execute the next instruction. This command gives the user a valuable debugging tool by being able to check the CPU's registers after each instruction. Before using this command, you first must enter the starting address into the program counter (P register) by using the RM command. As an example, enter the starting address given in Figure 4.3 and then after the prompt type T <ENTER>. Single step through the program to understand what the contents of the CPU registers are at each step. If you do the example of Figure 4.3, stop when you get to the JMP E0B2 instruction; it is not necessary to single step through instructions in monitor ROM.

Another way to use the T command is by executing several instructions at a time. This procedure is initiated by entering a count value after T. The format is

```
T [<n>]
```

where n is the number of instructions that will be executed before the program stops. However, the contents of the CPU registers will be displayed after each instruction. Remember if no count value is specified, the default condition is 1 (single instruction execution). Another command that is useful in troubleshooting programs is the breakpoint set command given next.

4.13
▬

BREAKPOINT SET COMMAND

The BR command allows you to set a breakpoint which halts the program at the instruction immediately preceding the location of the breakpoint. A maximum of four (4) breakpoints may be set at any one time. Table 4.2 lists the breakpoint commands and their descriptions. A breakpoint is accomplished by a software

■■■■■ **TABLE 4.2   Listing of the Breakpoint Set Commands**

Command Formats	Description
BR	Display all current breakpoints.
BR <address>	Set breakpoint.
BR <addr1> <addr2>...	Set several breakpoints.
BR −	Remove all breakpoints.
BR −<addr1> <addr2>	Remove <addr1> and add <addr2>.
BR − <addr1><addr2>	Clear all entries, then add <addr1>, add <addr2>.
BR <addr1> −<addr2>	Add <addr1>, then remove <addr2>.

(Courtesy of Motorola, Inc.)

interrupt (SWI) instruction being automatically inserted at the breakpoint address. A breakpoint can only be used with instructions stored in RAM, and a breakpoint can not be inserted at an SWI instruction.

Example 4.5:

Show the breakpoint command needed to accomplish the following: (a) Set a breakpoint at address location $C100; (b) Set four breakpoints at the following locations—$C100, $C110, $C120, and $C130; (c) Display all breakpoints.

Solution:

From Table 4.2

```
(a) >BR C100 <ENTER>
      C100 0000 0000 0000  The breakpoint is set at location $C100.
(b) >BR C100 C110 C120 C130 <ENTER>
      C100 C110 C120 C130  A breakpoint is set at each one of
                               these addresses.
(c) >BR <ENTER>  This command displays all current breakpoints.
      C100 C110 C120 C130
```

If a fifth breakpoint is entered, only the first four breakpoints will be accepted. For example

```
>BR C100 C110 C120 C130 C140 <ENTER>
Full                   Breakpoint buffer full message.
C100 C110 C120 C130  Breakpoint at C140 is not accepted.
>                      (BUFFALO prompt)
```

Example 4.6:

Show how (a) the breakpoint at location C120 is removed and the other breakpoints remain set; (b) all breakpoints are removed.

Solution:

(a) >BR -C120 <ENTER>
    C100 C110 C130 0000   Breakpoint at $C120 has been
                            removed.
(b) >BR - <ENTER>
    0000 0000 0000 0000   All breakpoints have been removed.

4.14

PROCEED/CONTINUE COMMAND

The P command is used to proceed or continue program execution after a breakpoint has been encountered. Thus, the user does not have to remove the breakpoints to continue the program. Note that the breakpoints remain in place until removed by a BR – command. To use the Proceed/Continue command, type P <ENTER> and program execution continues.

4.15

CALL COMMAND

The call command allows you to execute a subroutine program. The format of this command is

                    CALL [<address>]

where <address> is the starting address of the subroutine. If the address is not specified at the call command, execution starts at the current contents of the program counter. Consider the binary-to-BCD (BINBCD) subroutine of Example 3.24. If the starting address of the subroutine is $C8FB, it can be executed by typing:

                  > CALL C8FB <ENTER>

Since the program has been designed to convert 2 binary bytes of data at $D100 and $D101, then values should be loaded into these locations prior to using the CALL command. To do this, use the MM command. The results of the conversion are stored in a memory buffer of 5 bytes beginning at location $DB00. The MD command can be used to check the results. This command and subroutine are tested in this manner in Chapter 8.

Although there are six other BUFFALO commands, only the LOAD T command will be covered (see section 4.21). The remaining five are usually not used by first-time users. There are other programs in monitor EPROM chip that EVB users will find helpful. They are utility subroutines.

4.16

UTILITY SUBROUTINES

In addition to the BUFFALO commands, there are 17 utility subroutines stored in the EPROM chip and available to the user. These subroutines are summarized in Table 4.3. To use one of these subroutines, you only have to include a jump to subroutine instruction. The instruction format is

```
JSR xxxx
```

where xxxx is the starting address of the subroutine as given in Table 4.3. Remember that if you are using the ASM command to enter instructions, do not include the $ symbol. If you are using the cross-assembler on a PC (section 4.21), include the $ symbol before the address (JSR $XXXX).

These utility programs have been written as subroutines. Therefore, they end with an RTS (return from subroutine) instruction and program execution returns to the instruction following the JSR instruction.

In the application Chapters 7 through 10, we will use the input and some of the output routines. The following examples illustrate how they can be used.

Example 4.7:

Consider the following message has been stored in a memory buffer starting at location $DB50.

```
Microcontroller applications using the M68HC11 ($04)
```

Show how you can output this message to a monitor.

Solution:

Use the OUTSTRG (output string) utility subroutine.

```
LDX #$DB50   Initialize X index register.
JSR $FFC7 Jump to OUTSTRG routine.
```

In this example the OUTSTRG routine outputs an ASCII string beginning at location $DB50 and continues until 04 (the ASCII character for end of transmission, EOT) is reached. The MM (memory modify) command could be used to enter the ASCII hexadecimal value for each alphanumeric character. However, an easier method is to use an assembler director command and download the message to the EVB. This easier method will be studied in section 4.20.6 and used in Chapters 7 through 10. Remember, do not include the $ symbol if the ASM command is used to enter instructions.

■■■ **TABLE 4.3   Summary of Utility Subroutines**

Address	Label	Description
FFA0	UPCASE	If the ASCII character in accumulator A is lowercase, convert it to uppercase.
FFA3	WCHEK	If the ASCII character in accumulator A is whitespace (space, comma, tab), set the Z flag.
FFA6	DCHEK	If the ASCII character in accumulator A is a delimiter (carriage return or whitespace), set the Z flag.
FFA9	INIT	Initialize I/O device.
FFAC	INPUT	Read from I/O device.
FFAF	OUTPUT	Write to I/O device.
FFB2	OUTLHLF	Convert left nibble (bits 7–4) of accumulator A to ASCII and then output result to terminal port (P2).
FFB5	OUTRHLF	Convert right nibble (bits 3–0) of accumulator A to ASCII and then output result to terminal port 2.
FFB8	OUTA	Output the ASCII character stored in accumulator A.
FFBB	OUT1BYT	Convert the binary byte at the address held by the X index register to two ASCII characters and output the result. The X index register is incremented, thus pointing to the next byte.
FFBE	OUT1BSP	Convert the binary byte at the address held by the X index register to two ASCII characters and output the result followed by a space. The X index register is incremented, thus pointing to the next byte.
FFC1	OUT2BSP	Covert two consecutive bytes starting at address in the X index register to four ASCII characters and output the result followed by a space. The X index registered is update and points to the next byte.
FFC4	OUTCRLF	Output a carriage return followed by a line feed. Both characters are in ASCII format.
FFC7	OUTSTRG	Output a string of ASCII characters until an end of transmission ($04). The X index register is used as a pointer to the character string.
FFCA	OUTSTRG0	This subroutine is the same as OUTSTRG except a leading carriage return and line feed are not included.
FFCD	INCHAR	Input an ASCII character to accumulator A and echos back the character. This routine is in an endless loop until a character is actually received.
FFD0	VECINIT	This routine is used during initialization to preset the indirect vector area in RAM. This routine or a similar routine should be included in a user program which is invoked by the jump to $B600 routine of BUFFALO.

(Courtesy of Motorola, Inc.)

Example 4.8:

Show how three BCD values which represent a voltage value of 2.34 V may be sent to a monitor. The data is stored as unpacked BCD values in a memory buffer as:

```
Memory
location   Contents
DB01       02
DB02       03
DB03       04
```

Solution:

In this application a decimal point must be inserted as well as a space and uppercase letter V. Since the BCD values are stored in the right half of each byte, the utility subroutine OUTRHLF will be used. This routine converts the 4 bits (nibble) to ASCII and outputs the result.

```
LDAA    $DB01    Load first significant value.
JSR     $FFB5    Convert right nibble to ASCII and output.
LDAA    #$2E     Load decimal point as ASCII character.
JSR     $FFB8    Output accumulator A.
LDAA    $DB02    Load second significant value.
JSR     $FFB5    Convert right nibble to ASCII and output.
LDAA    $DB03    Load third significant value.
JSR     $FFB5    Convert right nibble to ASCII and output.
LDAA    #$20     Load ASCII space character.
JSR     $FFB8    Output accumulator A.
LDAA    #$56     Load ASCII uppercase V.
JSR     $FFB8    Output accumulator A.
```

These three BCD values could be the result of the binary-to-BCD conversion subroutine studied in Example 3.24.

Note: The utility subroutines do not convert a binary number to BCD. If the result is already a BCD value, then a utility subroutine may be used to convert the BCD value to ASCII and output the result.

Example 4.9:

Write a program that monitors the keyboard waiting for an input character which is either 1, 2, 3, or 4. If it is one of these characters, have the program branch to a software interrupt to display the CPU registers. If the input character is other than 1, 2, 3, or 4, the program returns to the beginning, searching for one of these four numbers.

Solution:

Use the INCHAR utility subroutine to monitor the keyboard. This routine is in an endless loop searching for any key to be pressed, and when it is received it is stored in accumulator A and is also echoed back to the monitor. Data comes from a keyboard as an ASCII character. From Appendix D the ASCII representation for 1, 2, 3, and 4 is 31, 32, 33, and 34 respectively.

```
INPUT: JSR   $FFCD  Endless loop until a character is received.
       CMPA  #$31   Has number 1 been pressed.
       BEQ   P1     If yes, branch to P1.
       CMPA  #$32   Has number 2 been pressed.
       BEQ   P1     If yes, branch to P1.
       CMPA  #$33   Has number 3 been pressed.
       BEQ   P1     If yes, branch to P1.
       CMPA  #$34   Has number 4 been pressed.
       BEQ   P1     If yes, branch to P1.
       BNE   INPUT  Another key has been pressed, branch back
                    to INPUT.
P1:    SWI          Display CPU register.
```

This program is the basis for part of the input routine used in Chapter 8 to identify a part number being entered from a keyboard. Labels (INPUT and P1) have been used to easily identify program locations. If you enter this program using the ASM command, absolute addresses must be used. Sections 4.18 through 4.20 introduce the topic of assemblers which permit labels.

4.17

■■■

INTERRUPT VECTORS

Chapter 2 introduced the concept of interrupts and that the CPU can be interrupted by signals external or internal to the MCU. External interrupt signals are received on the $\overline{\text{IRQ}}$ and $\overline{\text{XIRQ}}$ pins. Internal interrupts can be generated from the serial interface unit, pulse accumulator, timer unit, a software interrupt instruction, an illegal op code, computer operating properly (COP) watchdog unit, and a clock monitor. A priority flow chart of the order in which the CPU responds is given in Appendix C.

Each interrupt is associated with a vector address that has been designed into the CPU's hardware and is given in Appendix C. On the EVB system, the contents of a vector address points to the beginning of a 3-byte location in RAM for each interrupt source. These RAM locations are used to contain a jump instruction and an absolute address where the user's interrupt service routine begins. The EVB system has been designed to allow users to write and execute their own interrupt service subroutines. Table 4.4 summarizes the interrupt vector jump table in RAM. Figure 4.4 shows what happens when an interrupt such as a signal from the MCU's timer unit for a real time interrupt (RTI) occurs and is recognized by the CPU. The sequence of steps are: (1) $FFF0 is automatically

■■■■ **TABLE 4.4   Interrupt Vector Jump Table**

Interrupt Vector	Ram Address on EVB
Serial Communications Interface (SCI)	$00C4-$00C6
Serial Peripheral Interface (SPI)	$00C7-$00C9
Pulse Accumulator Input Edge	$00CA-$00CC
Pulse Accumulator Overflow	$00CD-$00CF
Timer Overflow	$00D0-$00D2
Timer Output Compare 5	$00D3-$00D5
Timer Output Compare 4	$00D6-$00D8
Timer Output Compare 3	$00D9-$00DB
Timer Output Compare 2	$00DC-$00DE
Timer Output Compare 1	$00DF-$00E1
Timer Input Capture 3	$00E2-$00E4
Timer Input Capture 2	$00E5-$00E7
Timer Input Capture 1	$00E8-$00EA
Real Time Interrupt	$00EB-$00ED
IRQ	$00EE-$00F0
XIRQ	$00F1-$00F3
Software Interrupt (SWI)	$00F4-$00F6
Illegal Op Code	$00F7-$00F9
Computer Operating Properly (COP)	$00FA-$00FC
Clock Monitor	$00FD-$00FF

(Courtesy of Motorola, Inc.)

loaded into the CPU's program counter and the contents at that address is retrieved; (2) The program counter is incremented by one to $FFF1 and the next byte is retrieved. For the EVB system, this data is $00 and $EB for the RTI vector; (3) This data is loaded into the CPU's program counter and is used as an address into the interrupt vector jump table stored in RAM; (4) The CPU retrieves and executes the instruction starting at $00EB. The first byte in the

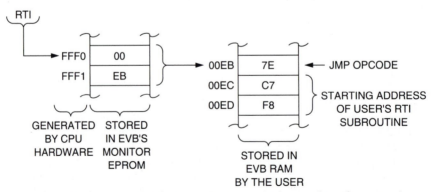

FIGURE 4.4 Users may write their own interrupt service routine. The vector jump table in RAM allows the user to write different routines, each having its own starting address.

vector jump table must always be a JMP (jump) instruction whose op code is $7E; (5) The starting address of the user's interrupt service routine which is stored in the following two bytes is retrieved. The example of Figure 4.4 has address $C7F8 as the starting address of a user's interrupt service routine. If you are working with the EVB, you usually do not need to know the hardware vector address, such as $FFF0/$FFF1, only the RAM address, and this information is given in Table 4.4.

Example 4.10:

Write the programming steps necessary to have the RTI service routine as shown in Figure 4.4 begin at $C7F8.

Solution:

The instruction JMP $C7F8 must be stored at locations $00EB–$00ED as shown in Figure 4.4.

```
LDAA   #$7E     Load op code for JMP instruction.
STAA   $00EB    Store op code.
LDD    #$C7F8   Load starting address of interrupt routine.
STD    $00EC    Store address.
```

During initialization, BUFFALO checks the first byte of each interrupt vector in the jump table. If the op code $7E is not found, BUFFALO inserts a jump to a routine in the EPROM called STOPIT. Thus there are no uninitialized interrupt vectors to cause problems. You may replace any of the JMP STOPIT instructions as was done in Example 4.10. A reset generated by switch S1 on the EVB (see Figure I.2) does not change the user's jump instructions. Therefore, they do not have to be re-initialized after every reset.

4.18

ASSEMBLER

An assembler is a program that translates source code into object code (machine language). A cross-assembler refers to a translating program that is executed on one computer and produces machine language for another CPU. Cross-assemblers for the M68HC11 are available for IBM or compatible computers or for the Macintosh. The authors used the IBM cross-assembler that came with the EVB system to develop the application programs for this text. They were written using an IBM-compatible computer, edited, assembled, and then the object code was downloaded into the EVB RAM (as will be studied in section 4.21).

Cross-assemblers are useful tools for writing, editing, adding comments, and using labels instead of absolute addresses. These are just some of the advantages of using assemblers. Another advantage of using a cross-assembler on a micro-computer system for writing an application program is that it can be saved as a file on disk for future use. Remember that when power is removed from the EVB, instructions and data in RAM are lost.

4.19

ASSEMBLER LINE STATEMENT FORMAT

A definite format must be followed when writing each line of the source code file. Each line is divided into four fields. They are: label field, op-code (operation code) field, operand field, and comment field. Figure 4.5 gives the four fields for the timing loop delay program of Example 3.19 to illustrate the information that may be contained in each field.

4.19.1 Label Field

The first field of a source line is the label field. All labels begin in column 1 and end with a space or colon. The assembler interrupts the colon or first space as the beginning of the operation field. Therefore, a colon or space can *not* be used as a part of the label. Many source code lines do not require a label, and for those lines the label field is left blank. This assembler allows labels of one to fifteen characters; however, most labels are not more than six characters long. Characters may be upper- or lowercase letters, numbers 0–9, period (.), dollar sign ($), or underscore (_). Upper- and lowercase letters are distinct (case sensitive). A number cannot be the first character, although a number can be used as part of the label. For example, TDREG1 is a valid label but 1TDREG is not.

4.19.2 Operation Field

The operation is the next field after the label field. If the label field is not being used, you must leave at least one space from the left margin. In most applications, the computer's tab key is used so that each field begins on the same column number. This produces the neatest display to read and study. The operation field contains an instruction mnemonic (i.e., LDAA, STAB, DECB, etc.); an

LABEL FIELD	OPERATION FIELD	OPERAND FIELD	COMMENT FIELD
	LDAB	#26	LOAD ACCUMULATOR B WITH COUNT = 26 $_{DEC}$
DELAY:	DECB		DECREMENT ACCUMULATOR B
	BNE	DELAY	IF ACC. B ≠ 0, BRANCH BACK TO DELAY

FIGURE 4.5 Assembler line statements are divided into four fields.

assembler directive (as will be covered in section 4.20); or a macro call (refer to Motorola's M6800 Family Assembler Reference Manual).

4.19.3 Operand Field

The operand field follows the operation field. At least one space must separate these fields. Usually, the tab key is used, inserting one or more spaces and aligning the operand field. This field contains instruction operands or arguments for assembler directives or macro calls. The operand field may contain numbers to be used as data or addresses. There are four symbols to identify the type of number:

No symbol	Decimal number
$	Hexadecimal number
@	Octal number
%	Binary number

Note that if no symbol is used, the assembler interprets the digits as a decimal number. If you are using the HC11 cross-assembler to write your programs and an address or data is to be interpreted as a hexadecimal number, be sure to include the $ symbol. This is different than using the BUFFALO commands on the EVB, where all values are interpreted as hexadecimal numbers.

4.19.4 Comment Field

The fourth and last field of a source line is a comment field. This field is optional. If it is included it must be separated from the operand field by at least one space. If there is no operand, then the separation of one space must be from the operation field. Once again the tab key is usually used for alignment of the comment field.

Comment fields may consist of any ASCII printable character. Comments are used for documentation for you and other users of your programs.

Refer to one of the application chapters such as Chapter 7, section 7.8, or Chapter 8, section 8.6 to see how these fields are used in longer programs.

4.19.5 Additional Comments

The previous subsection discussed how comments may be inserted as part of a line statement. Programmers often wish to insert additional comments within a long program. This is done by inserting an asterisk (*) as the first printable character in the line. The assembler interprets the entire line as a comment. Therefore, do not precede any instruction or assembler directive with an asterisk because it will not be recognized. Sections 7.8 and 8.6 show additional comments being used. Remember all comments are for reference purposes only. They are not assembled as part of the object code that is downloaded to the microcontroller.

4.20

ASSEMBLER DIRECTIVES

Assembler directives are instructions to the cross-assembler to perform a particular task(s). These instructions are not converted to machine language like M68HC11 instructions, but rather they are instructions to call a program or programs that perform a task.

There are 42 assembler directives listed in Motorola's reference manual and some of these have one or more options. Motorola also groups their directives in eight categories according to functions. It is not possible in the scope of this book to cover all of the directives, but we do want to use a few of them. Those that are encountered most often are:

Mnemonic	Description
NAM	Assign a program name
ORG	Set location counter
END	End of source
EQU	Equate symbol to a value
FCB	Form constant byte
FCC	Form character string constant
RMB	Reserve memory byte

A brief description of these directives is given below. A more complete description is given in Motorola's Portable Cross-Assembler Reference Manual. In the following statements, < > indicates a variable and [   ] indicates the field is optional.

4.20.1 NAM Directive

This directive assigns a name to the program and is usually the first statement of the program. Its use is optional, however. If used the format for this directive is

```
        NAM <program name> [<comment>]
```

where the <program name> can be of any length but only the first eight printable characters are used as the name. All characters after the eighth character are considered as part of the comment field.

4.20.2 ORG Directive

The ORG (or origin) sets the starting address for data or instructions to the value given in the operand field. The format for this directive is

```
        ORG <expression> [<comments>]
```

where <expression> is the address where you want data or instructions to be put into RAM when the object code is downloaded. As an example

```
ORG $C700 This is the starting address for the instructions in
          the application program of Chapter 7.
```

Note: The starting address must be given as a hexadecimal number. Check how the ORG directives are used in the application programs of Chapters 7 through 10. Remember the comment field is optional.

4.20.3 END Directive

This directive indicates the end of the source program and must be included. The format is

```
END [<expression>] [<comment>]
```

where <expression> specifies the starting address of the program that is given in the ORG directive. As an example

```
END $C700    Close the source program of Chapter 7.
```

If you refer to the application program of Chapter 7, you will note that the last statement is END with the operand and comment field left blank. If you wish to include a comment field, include an operand expression.

4.20.4 EQU Directive

This directive assigns the value given in the operand field to the label. The format is

```
<label> EQU <expression> [< comment>]
```

As an example

```
ADCTL EQU $1030  Location of the MCU's A/D control register.
```

Whenever the label ADCTL is encountered, the assembler assigns it to the memory address of $1030. Equate statements are usually included at the beginning of source programs. Refer to Chapters 7 through 10 for examples.

4.20.5 FCB Directive

Unlike most other directives, *form constant byte* (FCB) can have more than one value (expression) in the operand field. Each value must be separated by a comma. The format is

```
[<label>] FCB <expression>, [<expression>, ...] [<comment>]
```

where [<label>] is set to the address of the first byte expression and if other <expressions> exist they will be loaded into consecutive bytes. As an example

```
DIGITS FCB 0, 1, 2, 3  Fill a 4-byte memory buffer labeled
                       DIGITS with 0, 1, 2, and 3.
```

The location of the memory buffer may be established by an ORG directive. The application program of Chapter 7 uses several FCB statements. The reader may wish to refer to it to see how it was set up.

4.20.6 FCC Directive

This directive stores an ASCII character string in consecutive bytes. Although this directive has two formats, the format that we will use is

```
[<label>]  FCC  '<ASCII string>'  [<comment>]
```

where [<label>] is set to the first address in the string and the string is enclosed within identical deliminators (separators). The deliminators most often used are the apostrophe mark ('). This directive is very useful to include messages that you want displayed when your application program is executed. For an example of how this directive is set up, refer to the application programs of Chapters 7, 8, or 10.

4.20.7 RMB Directive

The RMB directive reserves a single byte or a block of memory. The format is

```
[<label>] RMB <expression> [<comment>]
```

An example of reserving several bytes is:

```
MRCNT  RMB  1  Reserve  1  byte
TREG1  RMB  2  Reserve  2  bytes
TEBUFF RMB  12 Reserve  12 bytes
```

In this example, 15 bytes will be reserved in consecutive order in memory. For additional examples, refer to Chapters 7 and 10. In both of these chapters, an ORG directive is used to select that portion of memory the authors wanted to reserve for temporary data.

4.21

SOURCE AND ASSEMBLER FILES

4.21.1 Creating the Source File

As previously mentioned, the authors used an IBM-compatible computer for all their development work. They set up a separate directory (HC11) and subdirectory (WORK) on the C drive for most of the examples and all the application program files for this text. One of the first files stored in this directory was an editor program so that source code could be created as easily as possible. Since an editor contains word processing functions such as insertion, deletion, alignment, etc., an application program containing CPU instructions and assembler directives as well as comments for documentation may be developed quickly. The editor program was invoked by typing EDIT after the DOS prompt. The authors created all their source programs with the extension SOR. The format for creating the source code was:

```
C:\HC11\WORK>EDIT (file name).SOR <ENTER>
```

The file name given for most of the applications was the chapter number. For example, the application program for Chapter 7 was created as CH7.SOR. This was done so that the authors could refer to the chapter number to retrieve a file. You may choose another method for saving your source programs. After the source code is complete, it is saved as a file. Figure 4.6 is the source program for Example 4.9. Although assembler directive NAM is used at the beginning of the program, the program was created and saved as a file named CH4.SOR.

Saving a source program does not invoke the cross-assembler. You may check this by using the DOS command DIR (directory) for a listing of the files in your working directory. (For the authors this would be HC11\WORK.) For the source program of Figure 4.6, you will see only CH4.SOR. At this time, you do not know if the program contains any errors whether they be wrong machine instructions, typos, wrong or missing assembler directives, missing labels, etc. It is necessary to run the cross-assembler to find this out. Note: A program that is error free after cross-assembling does not guarantee that the program will run when it is downloaded for the microcontroller's CPU to execute. A wrong placement of a label could cause the program to be assembled error free but not to execute the way you expect. As an example, if the label DELAY in Figure 4.5 preceded the LDAB instruction, the CPU would be in an infinite loop. This is not what the programmer intended.

4.21.2 Invoking the Assembler

After the source file is saved you want to invoke the assembler. The format for this is:

```
         NAM            KEYBOARD ENTRY
* * * * * * * * * * * * * * * * * * * * * * * * * * * * * * * * * * * * * * * * * * * * *
*   THIS ROUTINE IS IN AN ENDLESS LOOP WAITING FOR KEY 1, 2, 3, OR 4 TO          *
*   BE PRESSED. IF ONE OF THESE KEYS IS PRESSED THE PROGRAM EXECUTION            *
*   BRANCHES TO P1 AND THE CPU REGISTERS ARE DISPLAYED. THIS PROGRAM WILL        *
*   BE STORED IN RAM BEGINNING AT LOCATION $C400.                                *
* * * * * * * * * * * * * * * * * * * * * * * * * * * * * * * * * * * * * * * * * * * * *
*                  UTILIITY SUBROUTINE EQUATE

INCHAR EQU     $FFCD   STARTING ADDRESS OF UTILITY SUBROUTINE (SEE TABLE 4-3).

        ORG     $C400   STARTING ADDRESS.

INPUT:  JSR     INCHAR  ENDLESS LOOP UNTIL A CHARACTER IS RECEIVED.
        CMPA    #$31    HAS NUMBER 1 BEEN PRESSED.
        BEQ     P1      IF YES, BRANCH TO P1.
        CMPA    #$32    HAS NUMBER 2 BEEN PRESSED.
        BEQ     P1      IF YES, BRANCH TO P1.
        CMPA    #$33    HAS NUMBER 3 BEEN PRESSED.
        BEQ     P1      IF YES, BRANCH TO P1.
        CMPA    #$34    HAS NUMBER 4 BEEN PRESSED.
        BEQ     P1      IF YES, BRANCH TO P1.
        BNE     INPUT   ANOTHER KEY HAS BEEN PRESSED, BRANCH BACK TO INPUT.
P1:     SWI             SOFTWARE INTERRUPT INSTRUCTION.

        END     $C400   ENDING ASSEMBLER DIRECTIVE.
```
FIGURE 4.6 The source code for Example 4.10.

```
                         ASM (file name)
```

This is typed after the DOS prompt. For example, for the author's development, C:\HC11\WORK> ASM (file name). Note: Do not include any extension and the abbreviation ASM does not represent the BUFFALO command but rather a command that invokes the assembler. If there are no assembling errors, two additional files—LST (listing) file and an OUT (output) file—are created and stored on the disk. If an assembling error(s) is found, a line number and type of error is displayed. You should record all errors and using the editor return to the source file so it may be corrected. Then invoke the assembler again. Repeat the process until the assembled code is error free, after which you may want to use the DOS command DIR to see what files have been created and saved in the directory. If this is done for the source program of Figure 4.6, a DIR display shows three files: CH4.SOR, CH4.LST, and CH4.OUT.

If the assembler detects an error(s), a LST file is created but not an OUT file. This may be checked by using the DIR command to see what files exist whenever an assembling error occurs.

Figure 4.7 is a printout of the listing file for the source file given in Figure 4.6. The assembler listing format is

```
     Line#    Address    Object code    Source line statement
```

```
LINE   S  PC    OPCO OPERANDS  S  LABEL    MNEMO  OPERANDS  COMMENT
                                           NAM    KEYBOARD  ENTRY
00001                             *  * * * * * * * * * * * * * * * * * * * * * * * * * * * * * * * * * * * *
00002                             *  THIS ROUTINE IS IN AN ENDLESS LOOP WAITING FOR KEY 1, 2, 3, OR 4 TO    *
00003                             *  BE PRESSED. IF ONE OF THESE KEYS IS PRESSED THE PROGRAM EXECUTION      *
00004                             *  BRANCHES TO P1 AND THE CPU REGISTERS ARE DISPLAYED. THIS PROGRAM WILL  *
00005                             *  BE STORED IN RAM BEGINNING AT LOCATION $C400.                          *
00006                             *  * * * * * * * * * * * * * * * * * * * * * * * * * * * * * * * * * * * *
00007
00008                             *
00009                             *                           UTILITY SUBROUTINE EQUATE
00010
00011  P  0000  FFCD           A  INCHAR   EQU    $FFCD     STARTING ADDRESS OF UTILITY SUBROUTINE (SEE TABLE 4-3).
00012
00013  A  C400                 A           ORG    $C400     STARTING ADDRESS.
00014
00015  A  C400  BD   FFCD      A  INPUT:   JSR    INCHAR    ENDLESS LOOP UNTIL A CHARACTER IS RECEIVED.
00016  A  C403  81   31        A           CMPA   #$31      HAS NUMBER 1 BEEN PRESSED.
00017  A  C405  27   0E   C415 A           BEQ    P1        IF YES, BRANCH TO P1.
00018  A  C407  81   32        A           CMPA   #$32      HAS NUMBER 2 BEEN PRESSED.
00019  A  C409  27   0A   C415 A           BEQ    P1        IF YES, BRANCH TO P1.
00020  A  C40B  81   33        A           CMPA   #$33      HAS NUMBER 3 BEEN PRESSED.
00021  A  C40D  27   06   C415 A           BEQ    P1        IF YES, BRANCH TO P1.
00022  A  C40F  81   34        A           CMPA   #$34      HAS NUMBER 4 BEEN PRESSED.
00023  A  C411  27   02   C415 A           BEQ    P1        IF YES, BRANCH TO P1.
00024  A  C413  26   EB   C400 A           BNE    INPUT     ANOTHER KEY HAS BEEN PRESSED, BRANCH BACK TO INPUT.
00025  A  C415  3F             P1:         SWI              SOFTWARE INTERRUPT INSTRUCTION.
00026
00027  A                                   END    $C400     ENDING ASSEMBLER DIRECTIVE.


TOTAL NUMBER OF ERRORS: 0
TOTAL NUMBER OF WARNINGS: 0
TOTAL NUMBER OF LINES: 27

NUMBER OF BYTES IN SECTION ASCT: 22

NUMBER OF BYTES IN PROGRAM: 22
           CROSS REFERENCE TABLE
NAME    ATTRB  S  VALUE  P:LINE  LINE1....N

INCHAR  EQU    A  FFCD   2:11    15
INPUT   A  C400  2:15    24
P1      A  C415  2:25    17      19    21    23
```

FIGURE 4.7 The LST (listing) file for the source program of Figure 4.6.

123

The line number is for reference purposes only. It is a 4-digit decimal number. The address field displays the instruction's op code address as a hexadecimal number. For multibyte instructions, the op code is always the first byte. The object code field is the hexadecimal value of the instruction (op code and operand). The source line statement is the same as the source program.

At the end of the listing file is a cross-reference of all labels used in the program. It is the listing file that is most helpful when trying to analyze an application program because the address, instructions, comments, and cross-references are all available. Refer to sections 7.8 and 8.6 for additional examples of LST files. To obtain a display of a LST file, use the following format:

```
TYPE (file name).LST
```

after the DOS prompt. When obtaining a printout of a LST file use a wide format printer for best results.

The output (OUT) file is the file that is used to create the S-record (see section 4.21.3). It is a binary file which if displayed to the screen produces unrecognizable characters.

4.21.3 S-Record

Motorola uses character strings called S-records to encode programs and data for serial transmission between computers. Each string begins with the uppercase letter S and is divided into five fields as shown in Figure 4.8. Although there are ten possible types of S-records (S0–S9) for Motorola's microprocessor family, only three (S0, S1, and S9) are used with the EVB. An S-record encodes the object code into a printable ASCII format. This permits you to display and study it to understand how instructions and data are downloaded into the EVB. The last byte of each S-record is a checksum. This value is used for error checking to ensure that the information has been transmitted error free.

After the LST and OUT files have been stored, the S-records can be created. The format is:

```
UBS (file name)
```

This is typed after the DOS prompt. UBS is a utility builder program that creates the S-records. Note: File extensions are not used. For the example given in Figure

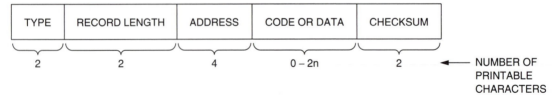

FIGURE 4.8 S-records are divided into five fields, although some S-records do not require all five fields.

S00A00006368342E4F5554D0
S119C400BDFFCD8131270E8132270A813327068134270226EB3FBF
S9030000FC

FIGURE 4.9 The S-record file for the source program of Figure 4.6.

4.6, the S-records are created by typing UBS CH4. Figure 4.9 is a printout of the S-records for this example. It is the S-record file that is downloaded into the EVB's RAM (see section 4.22).

Type of S-Record

An S0-record is always the first character string and is referred to as the header record. The address field may be all zeros in an S0 record. S1 records contain the instructions and data to be operated on by the microcontroller. The S9 record is the termination string. The address field may also be all zeros and there is no code/data field. The last byte of all S-records is a checksum. How it is determined will be shown later in this section.

Contents of S-Record Files

Let's examine the contents of the fields of each line in Figure 4.9.

```
S0        Indicates the record is a header record.
0A        The number of bytes (in hex) to follow in this string.
0000      Address field is all zeros.
63        \
68         |
34         |   ASCII representation for
2E         |   ch4.OUT
4F         |
55         |
54        /
D0        Checksum (see last part of this section).
S1        Indicates the record contains code/data.
19        Hexadecimal 19 (25 decimal). There are 25 bytes of binary
          data to follow.
C400      Starting address where the data is stored. (See ORG
          directive in Figures 4.6 and 4.7.)
BD FFCD   Machine code for first instruction, JSR INCHAR.
81 31     Machine code for CMPA #$31.
  .       ⎫Machine code for the
  .       ⎬other instructions
  .       ⎭in the program.
3F        Machine code for SWI.
BF        Checksum (see last part of this section).
S9        Indicates a termination record.
03        There are 3 bytes to follow.
0000      Address field is all zeros.
FC        Checksum.
```

<u>S0 - RECORD</u>

0A + 00 + 00 + 63 + 68 + 34 + 2E + 4F + 55 + 54 = 22 F

LS BYTE
OF SUM

LS BYTE = $2F
1'S COMPLEMENT OF $2F = $D0 CHECKSUM VALUE

<u>S1 - RECORD</u>

19 + C4 + 00 + BD + . . . 26 + EB + 3F = 840

LS BYTE
OF SUM

LS BYTE = $40
1'S COMPLEMENT OF $40 = $BF CHECKSUM VALUE

<u>S9 - RECORD</u>

03 + 00 + 00 = 03

LS BYTE = $03
1'S COMPLEMENT OF $03 = $FC CHECKSUM VALUE

FIGURE 4.10 Examples of how checksum sum value is determined. All values are in hexadecimal.

Checksum

The checksum is determined first by adding all the bytes in the record length, address, and code/data fields, then obtaining the one's complement of the least significant byte (LS byte) of the sum. Figure 4.10 shows how the checksum can be hand calculated for each of the S-records in Figure 4.9. Remember all values are hexadecimal.

4.22

DOWNLOADING AN S-RECORD FILE

It is the S-record that is downloaded from your personal computer to the microcontroller's RAM. For our applications, this RAM is on the EVB. The step-by-step procedure that you use may differ from that given below because of the communication package, the serial port used, and/or the baud rate. In developing the programs for this text, the authors tested the downloading procedures using both KERMIT and PROCOMM communication packages, serial ports 1 and 2 on IBM-compatible computers, as well as baud rates of 4800 and 9600.

Assume that your assembled files have been created in a directory called HC11\WORK on the C drive of an IBM-compatible computer and KERMIT is the communications package. The following steps show how an S-record file is downloaded using the KERMIT communication package.

4.22.1. Accessing KERMIT

Type KERMIT

```
C:\HC11\WORK> KERMIT <ENTER>
KERMIT>
```

At this time you may set the port and baud rate to be different from the default settings.

Example 4.11:

Consider the default settings are port 1 and 4800 baud and you wish to select (a) port 2 and 9600 baud, (b) port 1 and 9600 baud.

Solution:

After the KERMIT prompt, type your settings:

```
(a)  KERMIT> SET PORT 2 <ENTER>
     KERMIT> SET BAUD 9600 <ENTER>
(b)  KERMIT> SET BAUD 9600 <ENTER>
```

Note: In part (b) only the baud rate had to be changed. Any time the system is reinitialized or you EXIT from KERMIT, the communication settings may revert back to the default settings and have to be reset according to Example 4.11.

4.22.2. Connecting to the EVB

After the port and baud rate have been selected, type C after the next KERMIT prompt

```
KERMIT> C <ENTER>
```

The cursor appears in the upper left-hand corner. Press switch S1 on the EVB and the monitor's message statement is displayed:

```
Bit User Fast Friendly Aid to Logical Operation
```

Press the Return or Enter key and the BUFFALO prompt (>) appears on the next line.

If you press the S1 key and unrecognizable characters appear, the baud rate is wrong. Jump to step 4(4.22.4) and then after getting back to KERMIT set the correct baud rate using the procedure given in step 1. If nothing happens, check the cable connections between the PC and the EVB and then start at step 1 again.

4.22.3. Preparing the EVB to Receive an S-Record

After the BUFFALO prompt type the LOAD T command.

```
> LOAD T <ENTER>
```

   LOAD T may be abbreviated as LO T. The EVB is ready to receive an S-record file. It is now necessary to go back to KERMIT and download the S-record file.

4.22.4. Disconnecting from the EVB

To get back to the files on the PC and KERMIT, the following steps are necessary. Hold down the control key and press] now press C.

```
> <CTRL> ] <ENTER>
C <ENTER>
```

Now KERMIT and the prompt appear again as

```
KERMIT>
```

4.22.5. Downloading the S-Record File

The S-record is downloaded to the EVB by using the DOS TYPE command and the name of the file.

```
KERMIT> TYPE (file name).S>COM1
```

   Note: When you type in the file name, use the extension S as shown. If you are using port 2, then type COM2 instead of COM1.

4.22.6. Reconnecting to the EVB

This step is the same as section 4.22.2.

```
KERMIT> C <ENTER>
```

Press switch S1 on the EVB and once again the monitor's message statement appears:

```
Bit User Fast Friendly Aid to Logical Operation
```

Press the Return or Enter key and the BUFFALO prompt (>) is displayed.

4.22.7. Checking the Downloaded Program

To be sure that the program has been downloaded into memory, use the BUFFALO command ASM and the starting address used in the ORG directive. For example, if the starting address is $C400, then > ASM C400 <ENTER>. The first instruction of your program should now be displayed. If it isn't, check the connections between the PC and EVB and repeat the downloading procedure.

PROBLEMS

1. What does the term BUFFALO stand for?
2. How many commands are available to the user of the BUFFALO monitor program?
3. Power is applied to the EVB board and the RESET button is pressed. What is displayed on the screen?
4. How do you terminate a command line? What happens after a command line is terminated?
5. What is the function of the RM command?
6. How do you modify the existing program counter location $C200 to $D122?
7. What keystrokes must be given to see the results of loading the new program counter location of Problem 6?
8. List the keystrokes necessary to modify register X to contain 127 decimal.
9. Can the SPACE BAR and ENTER keys be used interchangeably to modify the contents of MCU registers?
10. How many lines of memory will be displayed after the following command lines and where does the display start?
    (a) >MD C100
    (b) >MD C100 C110
    (c) >MD
11. Write the command line to load all ones in memory locations $D200 to $D210.
12. Write the command line necessary to display the results of Problem 11.
13. The following command line is typed BF FF00 FF20 00. Explain the screen message.
14. Use the BUFFALO commands to move 64 bytes of information from $C100 to $D100.
15. Use the BUFFALO commands to display the five memory locations beginning at $D200.
16. Load the memory locations $D400 to $D403 to contain the ASCII hex values for AMDS.
17. Explain the differences between the ASM and MD commands.
18. Give the format for the GO command.

19. What will cause a program, once started with a GO command, to stop?
20. Write the command steps to enter the program shown in Figure 4.3 at location $C300 and then use the trace command through $C30A.
21. Write the commands to set a breakpoint at location $C30A.
22. Write the command to set breakpoints at $C303, $C306, and $C307.
23. What command line will display the breakpoints in Problems 21 and 22?
24. Show how the breakpoint at location $C30A in Problem 21 is removed.
25. Show how all the breakpoints in Problem 22 are removed.
26. Explain the following command line:

$$P \quad <ENTER>$$

27. Show the command line needed to execute a subroutine starting at address $D200.
28. The following message has been stored in a buffer starting at location $D100: "Input TEMPERATURE." Show how to output this message to a monitor.
29. What does the ASCII character $04 indicate?
30. Show how the following BCD values can be sent to a monitor as 0.11A.
    D100 00
    D101 01
    D102 01
31. Write a short program (using the INCHAR utility subroutine) to monitor the keyboard, waiting for the input character V. If the character is entered, branch to a software interrupt to display the CPU register. If any other character is entered, branch back to the start and continue monitoring the keyboard.
32. Explain why the first byte in the vector jump table must always be a JMP (jump) instruction.
33. Define (a) assembler and (b) cross-assembler programs.
34. Give several advantages of using a cross-assembler.
35. List the four fields of an assembler line statement and explain each.
36. Use an assembly directive to start an application program at location $C200.
37. When is the END directive not necessary?
38. Use an assembly directive to fill a memory buffer labeled INPUT with 01, 02, 03, 04.
39. Use the RMB directive to reserve 36 bytes of memory labeled DATA
40. Assume you are using the communication package KERMIT. Set the baud rate to 4800 and access to port 1 after the KERMIT prompt is obtained.
41. Assume you will use KERMIT for communication between the PC and EVB.
    (a) What keystrokes will access KERMIT?
    (b) How do you connect the PC (drive C) to the EVB?
    (c) How do you prepare the EVB to receive an S-record?
    (d) How do you disconnect from the EVB?
    (e) How do you download the S-record file?
    (f) How do you reconnect to the EVB?

CHAPTER 5

Interfacing Analog Signals To the M68HC11

5.0

INTRODUCTION

This chapter describes how to interface analog signals to the microcontroller. Physical variables such as temperature and pressure are analog in nature. This analog signal must first be converted to a digital value before it can be processed by the CPU. The conversion is done by the MCU's analog-to-digital converter (ADC).

We begin this chapter by considering the characteristics and specifications of the M68HC11's analog-to-digital converter. Then we will address the issue of acquiring and outputting data in a five-step sequence: (1) writing to the ADC's control-status register (ADCTL) to initialize the unit and to begin conversion; (2) accessing the data from a result register; (3) storing the information in memory; (4) converting the data from binary to decimal; and (5) displaying the decimal result on the screen.

For our first problem, the input analog signal is within the range of the MCU's analog-to-digital converter, 0 to 5.12V. Then we will study how to interface signals that are outside this range. To solve this problem, you will learn that an *Analog Interface* (AI) must be designed consisting of (1) a *transducer* that converts a physical quantity such as temperature or pressure into an electrical quantity like current or voltage, and (2) a *signal conditioning circuit* (SCC) that provides the actual conversion and scaling to *fit* the transducer's output signal to the ADC's input range. A list of circuits and hardware equations are given and they will be used in the design procedure for the AI examples in Chapters 7 through 10. These hardware equations are given in this chapter to aid in learning the analog design procedure in the applications chapters.

5.1

ANALOG-TO-DIGITAL CONVERTERS

5.1.1 Input Range and Resolution

Two basic specifications for an ADC are "analog input range" and "resolution." Input range for an M68HC11 microcontroller is 0 to 5.12V. The analog interface must scale the transducer signal to fit within this range. This topic is covered in sections 5.9 to 5.12.

Resolution for the M68HC11 is 8 bits. This specification means that the ADC has (1) 8 digital outputs as shown in Figure 5.1(a) and (2) 2^8 or 256 possible binary output values from 00000000 to 11111111. "Resolution" also gives a measure of accuracy.

Figure 5.1(b) is a graph for the output-input characteristic of a simple 3-bit ADC. It shows that a *change in value of 1 input-volt is required to change the output by one bit*. This is the fundamental definition of resolution and can be evaluated from the basic ADC specifications as:

$$\text{Resolution} = \frac{\text{Analog input range}}{2^n} \qquad (5.1)$$

where n is the number of bits.

Example 5.1:

What is resolution of the M68HC11 ADC?

Solution:

The 8-bit M68HC11 has an input range of 0 to 5.12V. From Equation (5.1):

$$\text{Resolution} = \frac{5.12\text{V}}{2^8} = \frac{20\text{mV}}{1\text{ bit}}$$

This means the input must change by 20mV to change the digital output code by 1 bit.

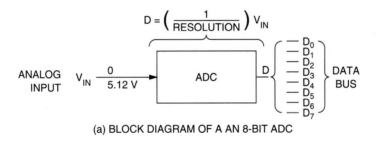

$$D = \left(\frac{1}{RESOLUTION} \right) V_{IN}$$

(a) BLOCK DIAGRAM OF A AN 8-BIT ADC

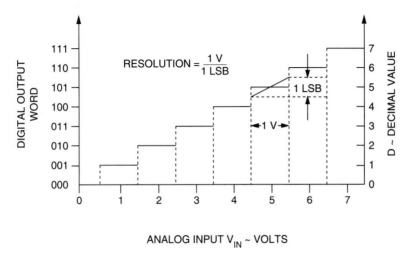

(b) DIGITAL OUTPUT CODE VERSUS ANALOG INPUT VOLTAGE
FOR AN IDEAL 3-BIT ADC. RESOLUTION IS 1 V PER BIT.

FIGURE 5.1 Block diagram of an 8-bit ADC in (a), and 3-bit output-input characteristic in (b).

5.1.2 Quantization Error

In Figure 5.1(b), the digital output code is 001 for input voltages between 0.5 and 1.5V. This unavoidable uncertainty is called quantization error and equals ±1/2 LSB (least significant bit), or ±10mV for the M68HC11. It is inherent in all ADCs and can be reduced only by dividing the analog input into more partitions for better resolution. This means increasing n in Eq. (5.1). A/D converters with 8, 10, 12, 14, 16, 20, and 24 bits are available, but the M68HC11 uses an 8-bit on-board converter because this resolution is sufficient for most applications that use a microcontroller.

5.1.3 ADC Hardware Equation

The output-input characteristic equation of an ADC can be described mathematically by a linear equation in the standard form of $y = mx + b$ where:

y = dependent output variable (digital code)

m = slope or conversion gain = $\left(\dfrac{1}{\text{resolution}} \right)$

x = independent input variable (analog input)

$b = y$-axis intercept or offset (usually zero for an ADC)

The ADC hardware equation for Figure 5.1 is:

$$D = \left(\frac{1}{\text{resolution}} \right)(V_{\text{in}}) \tag{5.2}$$

where D = decimal value of the digital output word.

Example 5.2:

The input voltage to the ADC in Example 5.1 is 2.56 volts. Find the decimal value of its digital output.

Solution:

From Eq. (5.2) and Example 5.1:

$$D = \left(\frac{1 \text{ bit}}{20\text{mV}} \right) \times 2.56\text{V} = 128$$

Converting decimal 128 into straight binary yields 10000000.

Thus, if a temperature of 25.6°C is converted into 2.56V by a transducer and a signal conditioning circuit, this measurement will be stored by the microcontroller as 10000000 (80 hex).

The programming instructions necessary to acquire and store data from the ADC are given in the next few sections.

5.2

PORT E

Chapter 1 introduced the package styles and pin assignments for the M68HC11. The EVB system uses this chip housed in a plastic leaded chip carrier (PLCC) package. As shown in Figure 1.3, port E is pins 43–50. These port pins have been extended to the EVB I/O connector and have the same pin numbering scheme (43–50) on port P1, thereby making it easy for users to check their designs from a prototype to a finished product. The EVB I/O connector is shown in Figure I.4.

Port E is an 8-bit input port and may be used as general purpose input lines for digital logic levels and/or for analog voltage signals. This port has been designed so that you may (1) use it for all digital inputs, (2) use it for all analog inputs, or (3) use some pins for digital inputs and the remaining ones for analog inputs. In this text, we will use port E to input analog signals which in turn are connected to the MCU's A/D converter. However, you may have an application to use this port to input digital information. Whether your application is inputting digital data or analog signals you need to know how the CPU can "read" data from port E.

5.3

PORT E MEMORY MAP LOCATIONS

Motorola uses a memory map scheme for all their I/O (input/output) devices. This means that the registers within an I/O device can be addressed as easily as any memory location without the need for any special I/O instructions. Figure 5.2 shows the address locations and how to visualize port E registers for the M68HC11 on the EVB. Since port E is configured only as an input port, there is no data direction control register associated with it as there is for ports A, B, and C which were introduced in Chapter 1 and covered again in Chapter 6.

Location $100A is used to store the data when port E is being used to input digital voltage levels. Thus, if the CPU "reads" location $100A, it has obtained

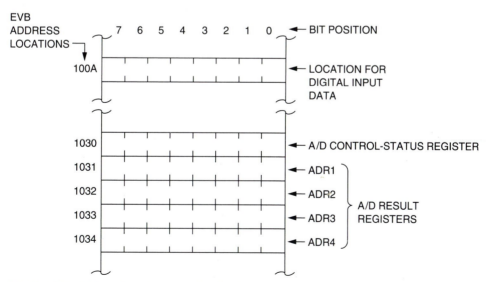

FIGURE 5.2 Address locations associated with port E.

the digital data that was on pins 43 to 50 of the MCU. Although we are primarily interested in using port E for inputting analog signals, let's first study two examples showing how digital signals may be "read" by the CPU.

Example 5.3:

The following binary pattern is at port E on an EVB system. Show the programming steps required to store the data at location $D000.

50 48 46 44   49 47 45 43   ← Pin numbers
 1   0   1   0   1   1   0   1   ← Digital input data
 └──────┬──────┘ └──────┬──────┘
        A   B   ← Hexadecimal

Solution:

Since port E for reading digital data does not have to be initialized, a load and store operation is all that is needed.

```
LDAA  $100A    CPU reads the data from Port E
STAA  $D000    CPU stores AB(hex) at location $D000
```

Example 5.4:

Write a program to read 20 bytes of digital data from port E and store it beginning at location $D000. Assume a timing loop delay of approximately 65μs (see Examples 3.19 and 3.20) is adequate between read operations.

Solution:

Since the data is to be stored at sequential memory locations, let's use the X register for indexing. Accumulator A is used for reading the data, while accumulator B is used for the time delay count and location $DC00 is used as a temporary register for holding the number of times port E must be read. The flow chart and instructions shown in Figure 5.3 illustrate the steps involved.

5.4

A/D REGISTERS

Figure 5.2 shows the address locations and how to visualize the M68HC11's A/D result registers. Unlike using port E for digital inputs, there is a control register when the port is being used for analog signals. The control register is not for programming the direction of the I/O lines (port E lines are always inputs) but rather how the port will be used. This topic will be covered in the next section.

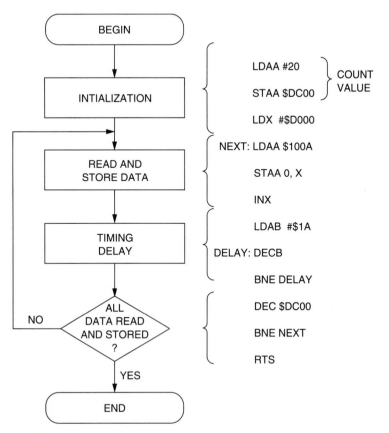

FIGURE 5.3 Solution to Example 5.4.

The actual analog-to-digital conversion is accomplished by an on-board A/D converter (see section 5.1) and the result is put into one of the four result registers (ADR1–ADR4). Therefore, the user only has to write instructions for the CPU to read a result register to obtain the digital equivalent of an analog input signal. Although the microcontroller has 8 A/D channels, the result from a group of 4 channels (0–3 or 4–7) can be stored in the result registers at any one time. Another way of using the result registers is to store four results from a single channel. Both methods are discussed in the following sections.

5.4.1 A/D Control-Status Register (ADCTL)

The MCU on the EVB has an 8-bit register at location $1030 that is the A/D's control and status register (ADCTL) as shown in Figures 5.2 and 5.4. Bits 0–5 are the control bits and may be read from or written to. Bit 6 is not used and is always read as a logic 0. Bit 7 is a status bit and can only be read. Data written to this bit is ignored. The function of each bit or group of bits is now discussed.

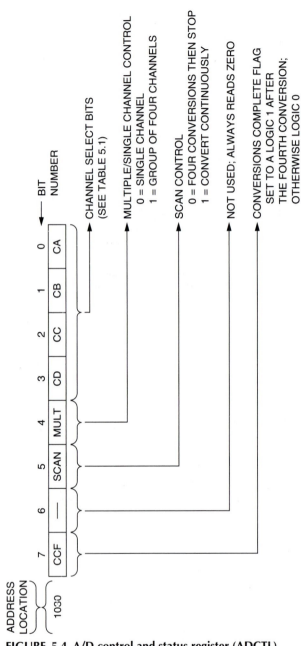

FIGURE 5.4 A/D control and status register (ADCTL).

138

5.4.2 Conversion Complete Flag (CCF)—Bit 7

The CCF bit (bit 7) is a read-only status flag. It is set automatically by the MCU after the A/D completes the fourth conversion and the results are stored in the result registers. This bit is cleared each time the ADCTL register is written to. Also, any time the ADCTL register is written to, a new conversion sequence begins immediately. Note: A conversion operation begins immediately after writing to the ADCTL register. Also, by writing to the ADCTL register the programmer stops any conversion in progress and begins a new one. If the MCU is programmed for the continuous scan mode (bit 5 = logic 1), then the CCF bit *may* remain set and the result registers are updated automatically.

5.4.3 Scan Control (SCAN)—Bit 5

This bit (bit 5) is also known as continuous scan control. It allows the programmer to choose between a single conversion sequence and a continuous sequence. When the SCAN bit is a logic 0, the A/D is in the single conversion mode, thereby performing four conversions and filling the four result registers. No more conversions are performed at this time.

When the SCAN bit is a logic 1, the A/D is in its continuous conversion mode. Conversions are performed in a round-robin fashion and the result registers are continuously updated.

5.4.4 Multiple/Single Channel Control (MULT)—Bit 4

Bit 4 of the ADCLT register is used to select between a single-channel conversion or a four-channel conversion. When this bit is a logic 0, single-channel conversion is selected. The A/D selects a single channel (according to the binary pattern in the CD-CC-CB-CA bits) and performs four consecutive conversions placing the digital data into the result registers. The first conversion goes into ADR1, the second conversion goes into ADR2, and so forth. See Figure 5.2 for the locations of these registers.

When bit 4 is set to a logic 1, the A/D performs a single conversion on each channel in the group selected by the CD and CC bits (bits CB and CA are ignored). Table 5.1 shows which group is selected when bit 4 is a logic 1 and the register that stores the data for each channel. Note: Binary patterns in the CD-CA bits for 8 to 11 are reserved and for 12 to 15 are for factory testing and are not shown in Table 5.1.

5.4.5 Channel Select Bits (CD, CC, CB, CA)—Bits 3–0

These four bits select the channel or channels to be used for the A/D conversion. See Table 5.1. Although the MCU's internal multiplexer is capable of selecting one of sixteen possible channels, users of the device only have access to 8

■■■■ **TABLE 5.1   Channel Selection When Bit 4 = 1**

CD	CC	CB	CA	Port E	Result Register
0	0	0	0	PE0	ADRI
0	0	0	1	PE1	ADR2
0	0	1	0	PE2	ADR3
0	0	1	1	PE3	ADR4
0	1	0	0	PE4	ADR1
0	1	0	1	PE5	ADR2
0	1	1	0	PE6	ADR3
0	1	1	1	PE7	ADR4

channels (PE0–PE7). Note: If you are using the 48-pin dual-in-line package version of the MCU there are only four external channels available (PE0–PE3). The full 8 channels are available on the EVB's I/O connector. (However, PE0 on the EVB comes jumpered to a 10kΩ pull-down resistor.) When the MULT is set to a logic 1, a group of four input channels is selected by the CD and CC bits. Channel select bits CB and CA have no effect for this condition. The following examples show how to program the ADCTL register for different applications.

Example 5.5:

Write the programming steps to initialize the A/D control-status register so that the conversions will be continuous only for channel #1.

Solution:

The first step is to determine the binary pattern that you want to store in the ADCTL register.

```
7 6 5 4 3 2 1 0 ← Bit position of ADCTL register
X X 1 0 0 0 0 1 ← Binary pattern using Figure 5.4
    2     1       ← Hex value
```

Let's consider the Xs (don't care) as logic 0s for programming purposes.

```
        LDAA   #$21     A/D control word
        STAA   $1030    Initialize ADCTL register
```

Remember, bits 6 and 7 cannot be written to, only read from.

Example 5.6:

What programming steps are needed to initialize the ADCTL register so that the A/D will convert continuously group 0? That is, the four input channels of PE0, PE1, PE2, and PE3.

Solution:

Let's follow the same procedure as in Example 5.5.

7 6 5 4 3 2 1 0 ← Bit position of ADCTL register

X X 1 1 0 0 X X ← Binary pattern using Figure 5.4

  3   0   ← Hex value

Once again the Xs are considered logic 0s and the programming steps are

```
LDAA  #$30    A/D control word
STAA  $1030   Initialize ADCTL register
```

5.5

A/D RESULT REGISTERS (ADR1–ADR4)

The result(s) of an analog-to-digital conversion are stored in one of the A/D result registers shown in Figure 5.2. Their addresses are from $1031 to $1034. These registers hold the result of an 8-bit conversion and are read-only registers. The CCF status bit is set to a logic 1 after all four result registers are filled. As new conversions are completed in the A/D, they are transferred automatically to a result register during nonread timing cycles of the CPU. This ensures that the CPU only reads valid data after a conversion is completed. Although an A/D result register may be read at any time, you may want to be sure the ADC has sufficient time to make a conversion. That is, the time between the ADCTL register being written to and when a valid conversion is in an A/D result register. Figure 5.5 is a plot of the timing diagram for a sequence of four A/D conversions. As shown, the ADC requires 32 clock cycles to update one result register or a total of 128 clock cycles to update the four registers. On the EVB, an 8MHz crystal is connected to the MCU. This frequency is four times greater than the MCU's bus frequency (known as E clock—the letter E does not refer to port E). Thus, the MCU's E clock is 2.0 MHz and a single clock cycle is 0.5 μs. If we use a clock cycle of 0.5 μs and Figure 5.5, an A/D result register can be updated every 16 μs or 64 μs for the four registers.

You may use the MCU's interval timer to set the interrupt flag bit after 64 μs or use a timing delay loop. Since the interval timer is not covered until the next chapter and you have already used timing loops, the following example uses a delay loop before the CPU reads the ADC result registers.

Example 5.7:

Write a program to initialize the A/D to convert the analog signals at four channels (PE0–PE3) and stop. The resultant digital data is then to be stored in memory from $D000 to $D003.

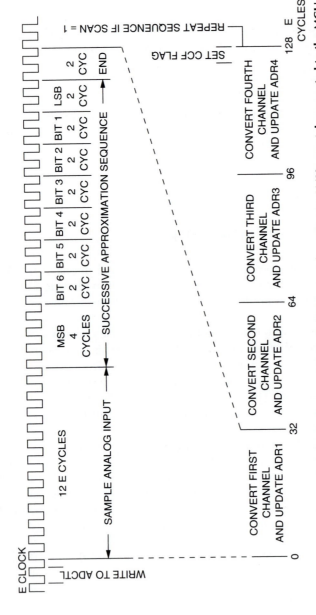

FIGURE 5.5 Timing diagram for four analog-to-digital conversions. For an 8MHz crystal connected to the MCU, the time for one E clock cycle is 0.5μs. (Courtesy of Motorola, Inc.)

Solution:

A flow chart and corresponding instructions are given in Figure 5.6. The hexadecimal value needed to initialize the A/D converter for this application is 10_{hex} (x x 0 1 0 0 x x). Accumulator A is used to read and store the data, while accumulator B is used for the timing delay loop. For a delay of approximately 64μs, accumulator B should be initialized with a value of 26_{dec} because each delay loop takes 2.5μs to complete, thereby yielding a delay of 65 μs. Memory location $DC00 is used as a temporary register and is initialized with a count value of four for the four A/D result registers.

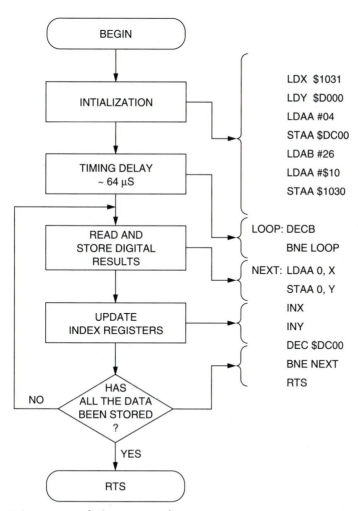

FIGURE 5.6 Solution to Example 5.7.

5-6

PRACTICAL CONSIDERATIONS FOR INPUTTING ANALOG SIGNALS TO THE M68HC11

5.6.1 A/D Reference Voltages

The MCU's analog-to-digital converter circuitry requires two reference input voltages. They are a low voltage reference V_{RL}, pin 51, and a high voltage reference, V_{RH}, pin 52. These pins are for the PLCC package and are the same pin numbers on the EVB's I/O connector. Motorola recommends that these pins be connected to V_{DD} and V_{SS} through a low-pass filter as shown in Figure 5.7(a). The circuit of Figure 5.7(a) is not mounted on the EVB; however, the EVB system does come with a $0.1\mu F$ capacitor connected between V_{RH} and V_{RL} as shown in Figure 5.7(b). Although the A/D does work if V_{RL} (pin 51 on the EVB) is connected to ground (pin 1 on the EVB), as shown in Figure 5.7(b), the authors used the recommended low-pass filter to the I/O connector as shown in Figure 5.7(c).

5.6.2 Limiting A/D Input Current

If port E pins are being used to input analog signals, some precautions must be taken so that the ADC's inputs are not permanently damaged. An electrical model of an A/D input is given in Figure 5.8(a). The model shows the protection device as an equivalent zener diode, so that when a positive analog input exceeds the threshold value, the diode avalanches. If this occurs, the input current must be limited by external circuitry. With no external circuit protection, an A/D input also can be permanently damaged by applying a negative voltage especially from a low impedance source. As an example, if −1V is applied from a low impedance source, the diode conducts in the forward direction and there is no current-limiting resistance; hence the input can easily be destroyed.

The manufacturer recommends that the input current should not exceed 25mA as a good design procedure. Figures 5.7(b), 5.7(c), and 5.8(b) show an external resistor, R, connected in series with an A/D input pin. A resistor value of between $1k\Omega$ and $10k\Omega$ yields best results. A value greater than $10k\Omega$ may cause measurement errors because of the leakage current flowing through it. Let's study two examples to illustrate the point that the range of $1k\Omega$ to $10k\Omega$ is a good design choice.

Example 5.8:

Assume an A/D's full-range input is 5.12V. If R in Figure 5.8(b) is $10k\Omega$ and the worst-case input leakage current of 400nA flows, what will be the input offset voltage?

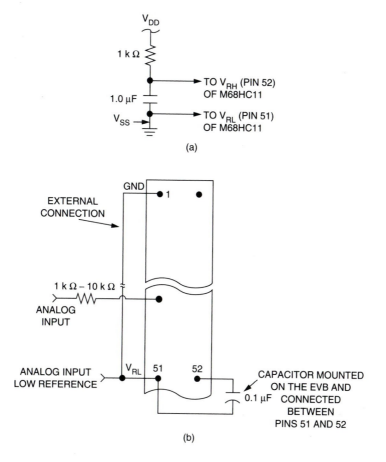

(a)

(b)

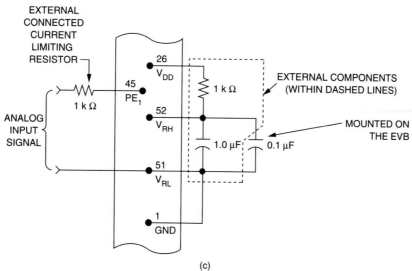

(c)

FIGURE 5.7 (a) Manufacturer's recommended low-pass filter, (b) minimum connections, (c) EVB system connections used by the authors.

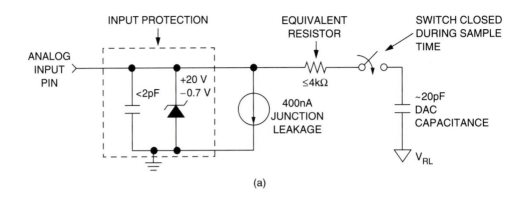

(a)

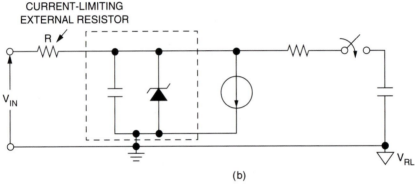

(b)

FIGURE 5.8 (a) Electrical model of an A/D input pin (Courtesy of Motorola, Inc.); (b) Adding a current-limiting external resistor.

Solution:

For an input range of 5.12V each binary count equals

$$\frac{5.12V}{256} = 20mV$$

or $20mV = 1LSB$. The leakage current produces an error of

$$(400nA)(10k\Omega) = 4\ mV$$

or, in terms of LSB

$$\frac{4mV}{20mV/LSB} = 0.2LSB$$

From this example, we see that it is possible to double R to $20k\Omega$ and still not reach an error of 0.5LSB. However, an R value much greater than $10k\Omega$ is asking for trouble because of errors not accounted for by resistance tolerances, temperature changes, noise, etc.

Example 5.9:

Assume you are connecting an A/D input to a signal conditioning circuit (this will be done in sections 5.9 to 5.12) and you accidentally touch the A/D input to the circuit's –15V power supply line. If R in Figure 5.8(b) is 1kΩ, will the input current be less than 25mA?

Solution:

The negative voltage forward biases the diode, causing the voltage drop across R to be

$$\frac{(15 - 0.7)\ V}{1k\Omega} = 14.3mA$$

Hence, the A/D's input is well protected. Although it is possible to calculate a theoretical minimum value for R, it is best not to use it. It is better to be safe than sorry.

In conclusion, too large a value of R results in conversion errors, while too low a value of R results in permanent damage.

5.7

MEASURING A KNOWN VOLTAGE

In this section, we shall set a known dc voltage and use the MCU's analog-to-digital converter section to read its value, thereby learning how the A/D stores its results and how data can be read by the CPU. The input voltage in the test circuit of Figure 5.9 is adjusted to 2.0V. The 1kΩ resistor limits the current and prevents a low impedance voltage source from being connected directly to an input pin on port E, pin PE_1. Pin 45 on the EVB's I/O connector is wired to port PE_1 (which is also pin 45 on the MCU). The input reference low line for the MCU's analog-to-digital converter is V_{RL} (pin 51) and is connected to the ground pin (pin 1) on the EVB. For convenience, the authors connected a 10kΩ potentiometer as shown in Figure 5.9 and adjusted the wiper arm for $V_{in} = 2.0V$.

Example 5.10:

If V_{in} in Figure 5.9 is set at 2.0V, what would be the expected binary value stored in the MCU's A/D register?

Solution:

From section 5.1, we learned that the MCU's converter has a resolution of 20mV/bit. Therefore, the count value stored in the A/D register is $2.0V/20mV = 100_{dec} = 64_{hex}$ or a binary value of 01100100.

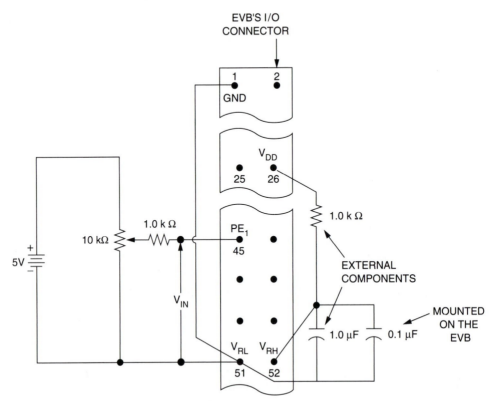

FIGURE 5.9 Setting up a known dc voltage at PE$_1$.

Remember that the EVB's monitor program will display the data on a CRT screen in a hexadecimal format because it is easier for humans to read than a string of binary digits.

Example 5.11:

Write the programming steps to initialize the MCU's A/D control-status register and to read port PE$_1$. Store the result in memory location $D500. What BUFFALO commands are needed to single trace through the instructions and display the result in memory?

Solution:

To initialize the A/D control-status register, assume that you select the continuous scan control mode for a single channel and use port PE$_1$ (pin 45) as the input line (channel 1). Referring to Figure 5.4 the binary pattern written for the (ADCTL) control register is

$$x \ x \ 1 \ 0 \ 0 \ 0 \ 0 \ 1 = 21_{hex}$$

Assume that the starting address of the program is at memory location $C500.

```
$C500   LDAA   #$21    A/D control word
        STAA   $1030   Initialize ADCTL register
        LDAA   $1031   Read channel #1
        STAA   $D500   Store the data
```

Note: Register locations $1032, $1033, or $1034 could also have been read because the A/D converter is in the single channel mode.

To use the single-trace (T) BUFFALO command, the program counter must first be set at $C500_{hex}$. To do this use the RM (register modify) command and set the program counter to $C500_{hex}$. Now type T4 <ENTER>. The four instructions will be executed and the contents of the CPU registers will be displayed for each instruction. Note the contents of accumulator A for the last two displays is the converted value. The memory display command (MD D500) will show you that the result has been stored at location $D500. By using the trace command, the A/D has sufficient time to convert the analog signal. If you use the GO command (G C500), the A/D does not have enough time to make the conversion. A time delay is needed.

Example 5.12:

Modify Example 5.11 to provide sufficient time for A/D's conversion.

Solution:

A time delay must be inserted after the control-status register is initialized and before the channel #1 register is read. A software time delay program can be used as explained in Example 5.7 and given in Figure 5.6.

```
$C500   LDAA   #$21    A/D control word
        STAA   $1030   Initialize ADCTL register
        LDAB   #$26    Initialize count value for time delay
Delay:  DECB
        BNE    Delay   Time delay ~ 65µs
        LDAA   $1031   Read channel #1
        STAA   $D500   Store the data
        SWI            Software interrupt to display CPU
                       registers
```

Since the A/D only requires 64µs for four conversions, the time delay is sufficient. Therefore, the initial count value loaded into accumulator B is 26_{hex}. Chapter 6 will show how to initialize and use the MCU's on-board timer, thereby eliminating software timing delay loops for some applications. However, this timing delay loop only requires three lines of code and for many applications is the easiest solution.

5.8

MEASURING AN ANALOG SIGNAL AND DISPLAYING A DECIMAL VALUE

Up to this point, we have applied a known voltage to channel #1 and have been able to store its binary value into memory. In the later application chapters, the input voltage will vary due to some physical change, but our technique to initialize the ADCTL register and read the converted digital value will not change. After the digital value has been stored, the application might require the data to be processed by the CPU and then output the result as a decimal number to a monitor or printer. In Chapter 3, you learned how to write a program to convert from binary to BCD. In Chapter 4, you learned how to use a BUFFALO utility subroutine to output data to a monitor. Let's use this knowledge to output the result of an A/D conversion to a monitor in decimal form.

Example 5.13:

What programming steps are needed to measure any input voltage in Figure 5.9 within the range from 0 to 5.12V and output its decimal value to the monitor?

Solution:

The flowchart in Figure 5.10 helps us to visualize what has to be done for this example and those basic building blocks that have been studied previously. Let's assume that after the ADCTL has been initialized the A/D result register stores all logic 1s or FF_{hex} (maximum input voltage). Since each bit has a weight of 20mV, the input digital data will be multiplied by 14_{hex} (20_{dec}). The decimal point will be inserted before the data is outputted.

Hexadecimal			Decimal Equivalent
FF	←	Input data	255
× 14	←	Equal to 20_{dec}	× 20
13EC	←	Result in accumulator D	5100

In the following program, the hexadecimal value $13EC ($5100_{dec}$) is temporarily stored at location $D100 and then converted to a 5-digit BCD number by the BINDEC subroutine studied in Example 3.24. The result of this conversion is stored in memory beginning at location $DB00, as shown in Figure 5.11(b). Now the Utility Subroutines stored in the EPROM may be used to output the result to the screen. The decimal point and the abbreviation for volts, V, are included as part of the ouput instructions as shown in Figure 5.11(c).

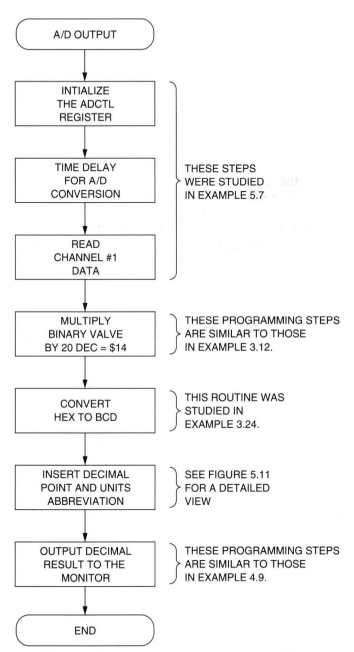

FIGURE 5.10 A flowchart showing the steps required for Example 5.13.

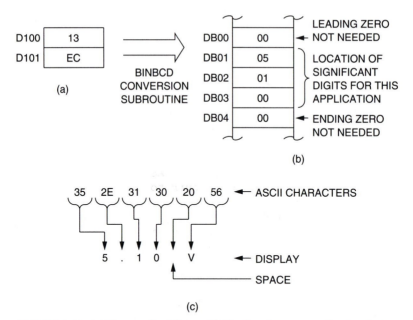

FIGURE 5.11 (a) The result of the multiplication is temporarily stored at locations $D100 and $D101. **(b)** The results of the binary-to-BCD (BINBCD) conversion subroutine are stored in a memory buffer starting at $DB00. **(c)** The significant digits are converted to an ASCII character and sent to the screen using BUFFALO's utility subroutines. See Example 5.13.

This input/output data program (I/ODATA) was written using a cross-assembler on a PC and downloaded into the EVB's RAM. However, the one-line BUFFALO assembler may be used to enter the instructions. In that case, do not use the directives ORG and END. Also do not use labels, such as DELAY; absolute addresses must be used and all values are to be in hex without the $ symbol.

```
           ORG $C500          Assembler directive
I/ODATA:   LDAA #$21          A/D control word
           STAA $1030         Initialize ADCTL register
           LDAB #$26          Time delay count
DELAY:     DECB               Time delay loop
           BNE DELAY          Branch if Acc. B ≠ 0
           LDAA $1031         Read A/D register
           LDAB #$14          Load multiplier $14 (20₁₀)
           MUL                Multiply (Input data) x $14 → D
           STD $D100          Store product temporarily
           JSR BINBCD         Jump to conversion subroutine
           LDAA $DB01         Load first significant number
           JSR $FFB5          Convert to ASCII and output
```

```
              LDAA #$2E        Decimal point is inserted
              JSR $FFB8        Output ASCII character
              LDAA $DB02       Load second value
              JSR $FFBB        Convert to ASCII and output
              LDAA $DB03       Load third value
              JSR $FFB5        Convert to ASCII and output
              LDAA #$20        Space character is inserted
              JSR $FFB8        Output ASCII character
              LDAA #$56        Abbreviation for volts (V) is
                               inserted
              JSR $FFB8        Output ASCII character
              JMP $E0B2        Return to BUFFALO's monitor program

BINBCD:       LDD $D100        Load 16-bit number to be converted
              LDX #10000       Load divisor 10,000 (2710hex)
              IDIV             Integer divide
              XGDX             Save remainder in X register
              STAB $DB00       Store quotient in memory buffer
              XGDX             Return remainder back to D
              LDX #1000        Load divisor 1,000 (3E8hex)
              IDIV             Integer divide
              XGDX             Save remainder in X register
              STAB $DB01       Store quotient in memory buffer
              XGDX             Return remainder back to D
              LDX #100         Load divisor 100 (64hex)
              IDIV             Integer divide
              XGDX             Save remainder in X register
              STAB $DB02       Store quotient in memory buffer
              XGDX             Return remainder back to D
              LDX #10          Load divisor 10 (Ahex)
              IDIV             Integer divide
              XGDX             Save remainder in X register
              STAB $DB03       Store quotient in memory buffer
              XGDX             Return remainder back to D
              STAB $DB04       Store quotient in memory buffer
              RTS              Return from subroutine
              END              Assembler directive
```

Remember the BINDEC was studied in Example 3.24 but is reproduced here for our convenience. This subroutine converts the 16-bit binary value stored at $D100 and $D101 to a 5-digit BCD value. The converted values are stored in memory beginning at location $DB00. Note: This subroutine does not save the contents of the CPU registers; you may want to modify it for other applications.

To this point we have learned the programming steps necessary to (1) configure Port E for measuring analog signals, and (2) acquire data for voltages that are within the 0 to 5.12V range of the ADC.

The next issue is how to condition signals that are *outside* the ADC range and bring them into the 0 to 5.12V range. This topic is known as Analog Interfacing (AI), and in the following sections seven signal conditioning circuits (SCC's) are presented with their hardware equations, each solving a common interface problem.

ANALOG INTERFACE

The block diagram of an analog interface in Figure 5.12 shows a transducer block and a signal conditioning circuit (SCC) block. The transducer circuit converts a physical variable such as pressure or temperature into an electrical quantity such as voltage, current, or resistance. Then the SCC converts and scales the transducer's output into a voltage range suitable for the ADC.

The output-input performance of the transducer and SCC can each be described by an equation. Transducer equations are given or derived for each transducer when it is used in subsequent application chapters. These equations are necessary to predict the electrical quantity and its *range* of values delivered to the SCC input.

The output range of a SCC usually matches or is slightly less than the analog input range of the ADC. Thus, the SCC must scale its input (transducer's output) range to an output range that fits the ADC. A SCC *design equation* will be derived from the SCC input-output range data. The task of designing hardware to implement the design equation is briefly introduced in section 5.13. A more thorough *design procedure* is introduced in Chapter 7 and presented again in each of the following application chapters (8 through 10).

The design procedure uses a direct comparison of the *design equation* with a hardware equation that describes the output-input characteristics of a SCC. Understanding the design procedure is easier if the designer can select from a collection of signal conditioning circuits with known hardware equations. These equations can be thought of as design tools, and four such equations with their hardware are presented in the next section.

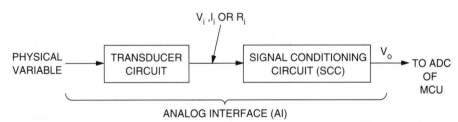

FIGURE 5.12 The analog interface consists of a transducer circuit and a signal conditioning circuit.

5.10

INTRODUCTORY SCCS AND HARDWARE EQUATIONS

5.10.1 Introduction

The lowest cost SCCs use only one op amp. Two versions are presented in this section to illustrate the ideas of gain and offset as they pertain to circuit hardware.

5.10.2 Inverting Adder

A two-channel inverting adder circuit forms an inexpensive SCC as in Figure 5.13(a). Suppose the designer connects the transducer's output to input V_1. Then V_1 is defined to be the independent variable (x) and is plotted on the x-axis of the output-input characteristic shown in Figure 5.13(b). A *hardware equation* for this SCC is written in a standard form:

$$V_o = -\frac{R_F}{R_1} V_1 - \frac{R_F}{R_2} V_2 \tag{5.3a}$$

or

$$y = m x + b$$

Equation (5.3a) describes the SCC's output-input characteristic and is graphed in Figure 5.13(b). The graph's slope, m, is negative and set by the ratio of R_F to R_1. Note that slope m is analogous to the voltage gain of channel 1.

$$\text{Gain (term)} = -\frac{R_F}{R_1} = \text{slope} = m \tag{5.3b}$$

The y-axis intercept b corresponds to a dc offset:

$$\text{Offset (term)} = b = -\frac{R_F}{R_2} V_2 \tag{5.3c}$$

where V_2 is a constant.

5.10.3 Single Op Amp Subtractor

A single op amp subtractor forms the SCC in Figure 5.14a. If the transducer's output is connected to V_1 (independent variable x) the hardware equation is expressed by:

$$V_o = \left(\frac{R_F + R_1}{R_1}\right)V_1 - \frac{R_F}{R_1}V_2 \tag{5.4a}$$

which is of the form

$$y = m x + b$$

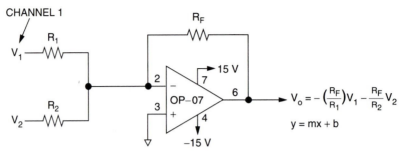

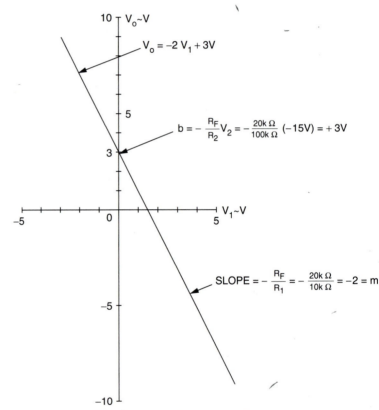

(a) INVERTING ADDER SIGNAL CONDITIONING CIRCUIT

$$V_o = -\left(\frac{R_F}{R_1}\right)V_1 - \frac{R_F}{R_2}V_2$$

$$y = mx + b$$

$V_o \sim V$

$V_o = -2\,V_1 + 3V$

$$b = -\frac{R_F}{R_2}V_2 = -\frac{20k\,\Omega}{100k\,\Omega}\,(-15V) = +3V$$

$V_1 \sim V$

$$\text{SLOPE} = -\frac{R_F}{R_1} = -\frac{20k\,\Omega}{10k\,\Omega} = -2 = m$$

(b) OUTPUT - INPUT GRAPH OF THE SCC IN (a) IF $R_F = 20\ k\,\Omega$, $R_1 = 10\ k\,\Omega$, $R_2 = 100\ k\,\Omega$, $V_2 = -15$ V AND, V_1 IS CONNECTED TO THE INDEPENDENT INPUT VARIABLE (TRANSDUCER OUTPUT)

FIGURE 5.13 The two-input inverting adder in (a) has the output-input characteristic shown in (b).

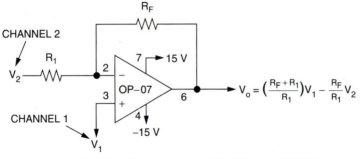

(a) SINGLE OP AMP SUBTRACTOR SIGNAL CONDITIONING CIRCUIT

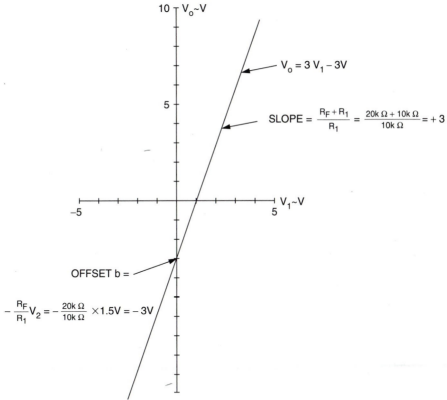

(b) OUTPUT - INPUT GRAPH OF THE SCC IN (a) IF $R_F = 20$ k Ω, $R_1 = 10$ k Ω, $V_2 = +1.5$ V, AND V_1 IS CONNECTED TO THE INPUT VARIABLE

FIGURE 5.14 The single op amp subtractor in (a) has the output-input characteristic shown in (b).

The transducer's output, V_1, is multiplied by a positive gain:

$$\text{Gain (term)} = \frac{R_F + R_1}{R_1} = \text{slope} = m \tag{5.4b}$$

For the component values given in Figure 5.14(b), gain = +3.
The offset term is determined by:

$$\text{Offset (term)} = b = -\frac{R_F}{R_1} V_2 \tag{5.4c}$$

If V_2 is chosen to be positive 1.5V, the offset will be negative 3V (–3V) as shown in Figure 5.14(b). Compare this value with the positive 3V offset in Figure 5.13(b).

Note that a designer has the option to connect the transducer's output to V_2 rather than V_1 in Figure 5.14(a). Since V_2 is now the independent variable (x-axis), the hardware equation must be written as:

$$V_o = -\frac{R_F}{R_1} V_2 + \frac{R_F + R_1}{R_1} V_1 \tag{5.5}$$

which again is in the form

$$y = m \, x + b$$

The input impedance of channel 1 in Figure 5.14(a) can be approximated to a very large value (often assumed to be the ideal value of ∞) of resistance and R_1 sets the input impedance on channel 2.

5.10.4 Loading and Sign Changing

Equations (5.3a) and (5.4a) are valid only when signal sources V_1 and V_2 have negligible internal impedance. Current is drawn from any input signal connected via an input resistor to the inverting terminal of an op amp with negative feedback. The resulting voltage drop across the signal source's internal resistance loads down the signal source. To eliminate this loading effect, connect a voltage follower between the signal source and input resistor of the SCC. For example, suppose that in Figure 5.13(a), source V_1 has an internal resistance R_0. Add the follower circuit as in Figure 5.15(a). The high-input resistance of the (+) input of an op amp eliminates loading.

Now suppose you want to change the sign of a term in a hardware equation like the V_1 term in Eq. (5.3a) for Figure 5.13. Simply add an op amp inverter between input V_1 and R_1 as in Figure 5.15(b). An op amp inverter circuit has a feedback resistor equal to its input resistor. In Figure 5.15(b), if we replace the equal inverter resistors R by resistors with general values R_3 and R_4, the resulting circuit is called a subtractor. Its hardware equation is:

$$V_o = \left(\frac{R_3}{R_4}\right)\left(\frac{R_F}{R_1}\right) V_1 - \frac{R_F}{R_2} V_2 \tag{5.6}$$

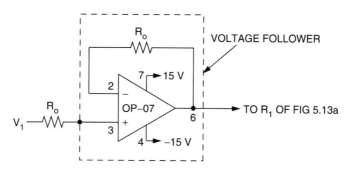

(a) HIGH INPUT IMPEDANCE OF A VOLTAGE FOLLOWER
ELIMINATES LOADING BY R_1 OF FIGURE 5.13(a)

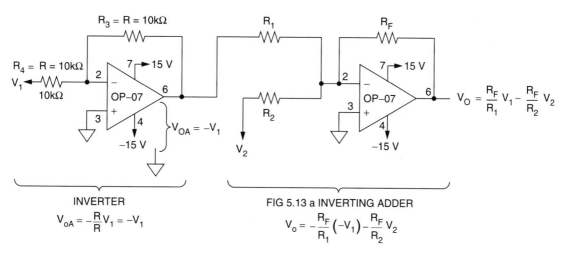

(b) OP AMP A MULTIPLIES V_1 BY -1 (INVERTS) SO THAT
$V_{oA} = -V_1$, OP AMP B MULTIPLIES $-V_1$ BY $-R_F/R_1$ TO YIELD
A NET POSITIVE GAIN TERM AT V_O OF R_F/R_1

FIGURE 5.15 The voltage follower in (a) eliminates the effects of output impedance within voltage sources V_1 or V_2 in Figure 5.13(a). The sign of any term in the hardware equation can be changed by inserting an inverter as in (b).

5.10.5 Two Op Amp Adder

A hardware equation that has both a positive gain term and offset term results when an inverter is connected to the single op amp subtractor of Figure 5.14(a). The resultant circuit is shown in Figure 5.16. Op amp A amplifies V_2 by $-R_3/R_4$ and op amp B amplifies the result by $-R_1/R_2$. Op amp B also amplifies V_1 by a gain of $(1+ R_1)/R_2$. The adder's hardware equation is:

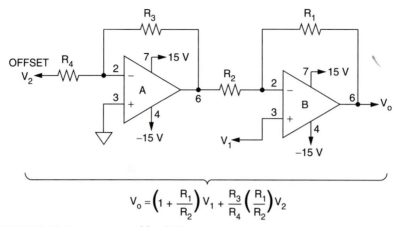

$$V_o = \left(1 + \frac{R_1}{R_2}\right)V_1 + \frac{R_3}{R_4}\left(\frac{R_1}{R_2}\right)V_2$$

FIGURE 5.16 Two op amp adder SCC.

$$V_o = \left(\frac{1 + R_1}{R_2}\right)V_1 + \left(\frac{R_3}{R_4}\right)\left(\frac{R_1}{R_2}\right)V_2 \qquad (5.7)$$

which is in the form of

$$y = m\,x + b$$

5.11

CURRENT-TO-VOLTAGE CONVERTER SCC

Some transducers output a current that is proportional to an input physical variable. For example, in Chapter 7 we will employ an IC temperature-to-current converter, the AD590. This transducer's current output must be converted to a voltage suited to the microcontroller's A/D converter. We will need an I-to-V converter SCC and hardware equation to design the analog interface.

An I-to-V converter SCC is shown in Figure 5.17 and has the hardware equation:

$$V_o = (R_F)\,I - \frac{R_F}{R_1}V_1 \qquad (5.8)$$

which is again of the form

$$y = mx + b$$

Current I flows through R_F to drive V_o positive by a voltage $(R_F)I$. This voltage

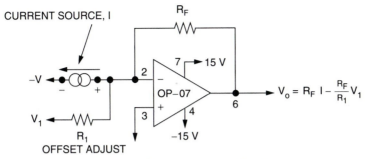

FIGURE 5.17 Current-to-voltage converter with offset.

is above the virtual ground at the op amp's (–) input. [To generate a –(R$_F$)I term, reverse direction of the current source.] V$_1$ is inverted and amplified by the ratio of R$_F$ to R$_1$ to develop any required offset term. If a positive offset is needed, reverse the polarity of V$_1$. Operation of this circuit will be further explained in the design example of Chapter 7.

5.12

DIFFERENTIAL AMPLIFIERS

5.12.1 Introduction

The final two SCCs to be presented are (1) a two op amp differential amplifier, and (2) the superior instrumentation amplifier. A differential amplifier amplifies the difference between two signals and gives a single-ended output (the output voltage is measured with respect to ground). The differential gain must be adjustable by only a single resistor.

5.12.2 Two Op Amp Differential Amplifier

The two op amp differential amplifier in Figure 5.18 has three possible input terminals. Positive input voltage , V$_{+in}$, negative input voltage, V$_{-in}$, and reference input voltage, V$_R$. The differential gain A is given by:

$$A = 2 + \frac{2R}{R_G} \tag{5.9a}$$

The four R resistors must be within 1%. Gain is adjusted by varying only resistor R$_G$.

Reference voltage V$_R$ is transmitted through both op amps with unity gain and is used to set the offset term in the hardware equation:

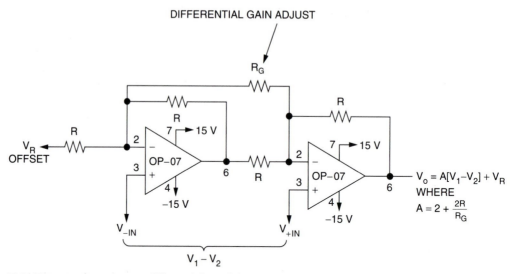

FIGURE 5.18 Two op amp differential amplifier. All four R resisters must be equal. Typically, R = 10kΩ, 1%. V_{+in} and V_{-in} are connected to amplify the output of a bridge circuit.

$$V_o = A\,(V_{+in} - V_{-in}) + V_R \qquad\qquad (5.9b)$$

which is in the form of

$$y = m\,x + b$$

where A is given by Eq. (5.9a).

Example 5.14:

Design an amplifier with a differential gain of 100 and 2.5V offset voltage.

Solution:

Select the SCC of Figure 5.18, since the differential inputs present high impedances at the op amp (+) input terminals. Connect a 2.5V low impedance source to input V_R to generate the offset.

Now choose 10kΩ, 1.0% resistors for the four R resistors. Find R_G from Eq. (5.9a).

$$100 = 2 + 2\,\frac{10k\Omega}{R_G}$$

and

$$R_G = \frac{10k\Omega}{49} = 204\Omega$$

5.12.3 AD524 Instrumentation Amplifier

The circuit symbol shown in Figure 5.19(a) is for the versatile 16-pin AD524 precision instrumentation amplifier manufactured by Analog Devices. Pins 1 and 2 are the differential V_2 (negative) and V_1 (positive) inputs, respectively. Differential gain A is easily pin-programmed for values of 1, 10, 100, or 1,000 by a jumper

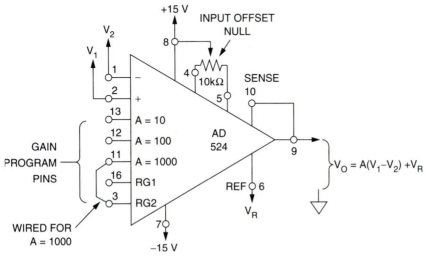

(a) AD524 PRECISION, PIN-PROGRAMMABLE, INSTRUMENTATION AMPLIFIER

CONNECT PIN NO.	TO	PIN NO.	FOR	GAIN (A) EQUAL TO
3		NONE		1
3		13		10
3		12		100
3		11		1000

(b) CONNECTIONS FOR PROGRAMMING GAINS OF 1, 10, 100, 1000

$$R_G \cong \frac{40k\Omega}{A-1} = R_G$$

(c) METHOD TO OBTAIN INTERMEDIATE GAINS FROM 1 TO 1000

FIGURE 5.19 The AD524 precision instrumentation amplifier has pinouts shown in (a). Differential gain A may be programmed for fixed gains of 1, 10, 100, or 1000 by jumper wires as in (b) or intermediate values as in (c).

wire, as shown in Figure 5.19(b). For example, jumper pin 3 to pin 11 for a differential gain of 1000.

Reference pin 6 is a third input, and low impedance source V_R, shown in Figure 5.19(a), sees a gain of unity. Thus, the hardware equation for the AD524 SCC is:

$$V_o = A(V_1 - V_2) + V_R \tag{5.10}$$

where A is set by the jumper. Intermediate values of A can be set by installing a gain setting resistor R_G between pins 3 and 16 as shown in Figure 15.19(c). To establish a particular gain A, calculate the required value of R_G from

$$R_G \cong \frac{40k\Omega}{A-1} \tag{5.11}$$

An application for the AD524 is illustrated by an example.

Example 5.15:

Design a hardware circuit to implement the desired design equation:

$$V_o = 25 (V_{TA} - V_{TB}) + 2.5V$$

Solution:

(a) Find a hardware equation such as Eq. (5.10) that is similar to the design equation and compare equations:

$$V_o = A (V_1 - V_2) + V_R$$

Comparing equations tells the designer to:

    (b) Wire V_{TA} to V1 input pin 2
    (c) Wire V_{TB} to V2 input pin 1
    (d) Wire a low impedance source of +2.5V to V_R input pin 6, and finally
    (e) Establish a gain of A = 25 by finding a value for R_G from Equation (5.11):

$$R_G \cong \frac{40k\Omega}{25-1} \cong \frac{40k\Omega}{24} = 1667\Omega$$

Note that R_G should be a potentiometer, since Eq. (5.11) is only an approximation and trim is always required.

5.13 SUMMARY OF HARDWARE EQUATIONS AND SCCS

The analog interface design procedure presented in application Chapters 7 through 10 will be easier to follow if there is a designer's "tool" selection readily available. Each tool consists of a signal conditioning circuit (SCC) and its associated hardware equation. The selection is listed by hardware equation number as it appears in this chapter.

1. Inverting Adder—Figure 5.13(a)

$$V_o = -\left(\frac{R_F}{R_1}\right)V_1 - \left(\frac{R_F}{R_2}\right)V_2 \qquad (5.3a)$$

2. Single Op Amp Subtractor—Figure 5.14(a)

$$V_o = \left(\frac{R_F + R_1}{R_1}\right)V_1 - \left(\frac{R_F}{R_1}\right)V_2 \qquad (5.4a)$$

3. Inverting Adder plus Inverter—Figure 5.15(b)

$$V_o = \left(\frac{R_3}{R_4}\right)\left(\frac{R_F}{R_1}\right)V_1 - \left(\frac{R_F}{R_2}\right)V_2 \qquad (5.6)$$

4. Two op amp Adder—Figure 5.16

$$V_o = \left(\frac{1 + R_1}{R_2}\right)V_1 + \left(\frac{R_3}{R_4}\right)\left(\frac{R_1}{R_2}\right)V_2 \qquad (5.7)$$

5. Current-to-Voltage Converter—Figure 5.17

$$V_o = R_F I - \left(\frac{R_F}{R_1}\right)V_1 \qquad (5.8)$$

6. Two Op Amp Differential Amplifier—Figure 5.18

$$V_o = A\left(V_{+in} - V_{-in}\right) + V_R \qquad (5.9b)$$

$$\text{where } A = 2 + \frac{2R}{R_G} \qquad (5.9a)$$

7. AD524 Instrumentation Amplifier —Figure 5.19.

$$V_o = A(V_1 - V_2) + V_R \qquad (5.10)$$

$$R_G \cong \frac{40k\Omega}{A-1} \qquad (5.11)$$

The circuits presented in sections 5.10 to 5.12 will allow us to scale a transducer's output voltage or current to a range acceptable for the microcontroller's A/D converter.

Example 5.16:

Design an analog interface to accept the terminal voltage of a NiCd battery that is expected to vary from 1.3V to 1.8V during a normal charge discharge cycle. Scale this signal to use the approximate full scale, 0 to 5.0V ADC range at PE_1 (pin #45) of the EVB board.

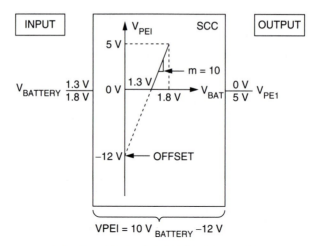

(a) PLOT OF OUTPUT VERSUS INPUT FOR THE SCC
REQUIRED TO INTERFACE A NiCd BATTERY TO THE
M68HC11

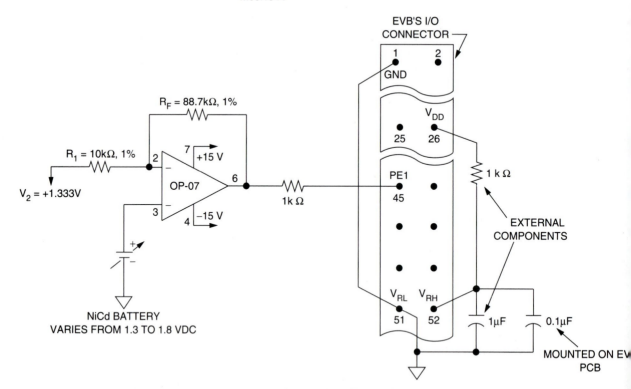

(b) A SINGLE OP AMP SUBTRACTOR IS USED
FOR THIS SCC DESIGN

FIGURE 5.20 Interfacing a NiCd battery to PE$_1$ of the M68HC11 microcontroller.

Solution:

The output vs. input characteristics of this problem are shown graphically in Figure 5.20(a), and the SCC design equation that results from this plot is given as

$$V_o = 10 \, V_{battery} - 12V \tag{5-12}$$

(See Chapter 7 for a complete discussion of how to solve an SCC design equation from plotted output vs. input data).

From Eq. (5.12) we note that a positive gain and negative offset is required to interface the battery to the ADC. Since the single op amp subtractor (Figure 5.14(a)) has a similar hardware equation, Equation (5.4a), we choose it for our interface.

Compare design and hardware equations to yield the following:

$$V_{PE1} = 10V_{battery} - 12V$$

$$V_o = \left(\frac{R_F}{R_1} + 1 \right) V_1 - \frac{R_F}{R_1} V_2$$

a) Connect the SCC output (V_o) to the EVB input (PE_1). See Figure 5.20(b).
b) Wire the NiCd ($V_{battery}$) to pin 3 of the op amp (V_1).
c) Set the gain to +10 by choosing $R_1 = 10k\Omega$, 1% and $R_F = 90k\Omega$
d) Compare offset terms.

$$-12V = -\frac{R_F}{R_1} V_2$$

Solving for V_2 yields

$$V_2 = \frac{-12V}{-R_F/R_1} = \frac{-12V}{-90k\Omega/10k\Omega} = +1.333V$$

Example 5.16 is presented here as a sample illustration of interfacing. A more detailed and complete coverage of this topic will studied in Chapter 7 and continues through all four application chapters.

Problems

1. Define resolution for an analog-to-digital converter.
2. What is the input range for the M68HC11 ADC's?
3. Find the resolution of a 12-bit ADC with an input range of 10 volts.
4. Explain quantization error and tell how it can be improved.
5. Find the digital output, in straight binary, for the following inputs applied to the M68HC11 ADC input.
   (a) 0V, (b) 1V, (c) 2V, (d) 3V, (e) 4V, (f) 5V, and (g) 6V.

6. Convert the answers given in problem 5 from straight binary to hexadecimal.
7. Explain the input/output options available on port E of the M68HC11 microcontroller.
8. When port E is used to acquire digital input data, it is stored in memory location _____.
9. Write the instructions to acquire digital data from port E and store it in memory loacation $C256.
10. At what location is the control register when using port E to input analog data?
11. How many result registers are available at port E and where are they located?
12. The CCF bit at location $1030 is a write-only bit. (True/False)
13. A conversion begins 512μs after writing to the ADCTL register. (True/False)
14. What logic level must be the logic state of the scan bit (bit 5) of $1030 to establish continuous conversions.?
15. Explain the function of MULT (bit 4) of the ADCTL register.
16. Write the instructions to initialize the A/D control register to continuously scan channel 2.
17. If the EVB crystal frequency is set at 4MHz, find how long it takes to make (a) **a** one channel conversion, and (b) a 4-channel conversion.
18. Compute the expected error in terms of fractions of an LSB if the M68HC11 A/D is used with a 4.99kΩ, 1% input limiter.
19. Compute the minimum value of A/D input resistor if the maximum reverse voltage is -12V and the current must not exceed 25mA.
20. Solve for the digital value in hex for each analog signal below. Assume a standard 20mV/bit resolution.
    (a) 20mV, (b) 1V, (c) 2.56V, (d) 5V, (e) 5.10V, (f) 5.12V
21. Write the hardware equation for Figure 5.13(a) if V_2 is used as the dependent input.
22. Refer to Figure 5.13. Solve for R_F, R_2, and V_2 for the following equations (assume $R_1 = 10$kΩ).
    (a) $V_o = -3.5V_1 + 6V$,   b) $V_o = -2V_1 - 2V$
    (c) $V_o = -1.75V_1 - 8V$,   d) $V_o = -10V_1 + 1.5V$
23. Refer to Figure 5.14. Design this SCC for the following equations (assume $R_F = 100$kΩ).
    (a) $V_o = 5V_1 + 5V$ (b) $V_o = 15V_1 - 2V$
    (c) $V_o = +3V_2 + 5V$ (d) $V_o = 6V_2 - 2.5V$
24. Refer to Figure 5.15. Design this SCC for the following equations. Assume RF = 100kΩ and find all unknown resistor values and V_2.
    (a) $V_o = +6V_1 - 3V$ (b) $V_o = +3.3V_1 + 3.3V$
    (c) $V_o = +2.5V_1 + 0V$ (d) $V_o = +1.5V_1 - 8V$
25. Refer to Figure 5.16. Design this SCC for the following equations (assume $R_4 = R_3 = 10$kΩ).
    (a) $V_o = 2V_1 - 2V$ (b) $V_o = +3.3V_1 + 3.3V$
    (c) $V_o = 1.8V_1 - 2.722V$ (d) $V_o = 14V_1 - 3V$

26. Refer to Figure 5-17. Design this SCC for the following equations. Show direction of current source I for each.
    (a) $V_o = 10k\Omega(I) - 2.732V$ (b) $V_o = -20k\Omega(I) + 3V$
    (c) $V_o = 25k\Omega(I) + 1V$ (d) $V_o = -10k\Omega(I)$

27. Refer to Figure 5.18. Design this SCC for the following equations. Assume the resistor values are $10k\Omega$ and find R_G and V_R.
    (a) $V_o = 80(V_1 - V_2) + 8V$ (b) $V_o = 5(V_1 - V_2) - 2.5V$
    (c) $V_o = 16.67(V_1 - V_2) + 0V$ (d) $V_o = 22(V_1 - V_2)$

28. Refer to Figure 5.19. Design this SCC for the following equations. Include a drawing of your designs.
    (a) $V_o = 10(V_A - V_B) - 2V$ (b) $V_o = 33.3(V_X - V_Y) + 5V$

CHAPTER 6

Output Peripherals and Software Control

6.0

INTRODUCTION

Output peripherals such as indicator lamps, motors, relays, or solenoids are activated by high currents and voltages that greatly exceed the capability of any microcontroller's output control line. For this reason, control devices are required to interface between peripherals and MCU output port lines. Some typical interface and control circuits are introduced in this chapter. In order to drive these circuits, however, you must first acquire knowledge of the MCU's I/O ports and the necessary programming steps to use them. A general introduction to the MCU's I/O ports was given in Chapter 1, but a detailed method of testing and using them is given in this chapter.

Often output peripherals are turned on and off for a specified period. This chapter also introduces how to use the M68HC11 timer unit for specific applications. Although most of the applications in this chapter deal with output and timing functions, it may be necessary to measure a pulse width or be able to count events before turning on or off an output device. Therefore, this chapter also introduces an input capture function.

6.1

I/O PORTS

Chapter 1 introduced the M68HC11's five input/output (I/O) ports labeled A through E. Each port has eight I/O pins, except port D which only has six. To provide as much versatility as possible, Motorola designed each port for dual functions either for general purpose I/O applications or for an alternate I/O use. An example of this dual function capability is port E studied in Chapter 5. It may be used as a general purpose input port for digital signals or be used as an input port to accept analog signals which are routed to the MCU's A/D converter.

Some of the port's I/O pins are only inputs, others only outputs, and still others are bidirectional. A bidirectional I/O line refers to one that may be configured by the user as either input or output depending on the application. As you will study, the configuration is done by software. Table 6.1 summarizes the M68HC11's I/O ports and the alternate function of each pin.

TABLE 6.1   Functions of MCU's I/O Lines

Port	Bit(s)	General Purpose for Digital Use	Alternate Function
A	0–2	Input	Input capture
	3–6	Output	Output compare
	7	Bidirectional	Pulse accumulator
B	0–7	Output	Address*
C	0–7	Bidirectional	Address/data multiplexed*
D	0	Bidirectional	Rx data
	1	Bidirectional	Tx data
	2	Bidirectional	Master in/slave out
	3	Bidirectional	Master out/slave in
	4	Bidirectional	Serial clock
	5	Bidirectional	Slave select
E	0–7	Input	Analog inputs

*When the MCU is configured for extended mode

6.2

TESTING AN I/O PORT

The BUFFALO commands of MM (memory modify) and MD (memory display) can be used to learn how data is read from or written to an I/O port. The MM command can also be used to configure those ports that have bidirectional capability.

6.2.1 Reading Data from an I/O Port

Consider that you wish to learn how port E receives digital data. Note: For this application port E is being used to receive digital data, not an analog signal. Therefore, the A/D registers (ADR1–ADR4) are not used. If no connections are made to port E (IC pins 43–50), the inputs will be read as logic 0s. From Figure 1.7 the digital input register for port E is $100A. Using the MD command, this port is read as

```
> MD 1000 100A <ENTER>

1000 XX XX XX XX XX XX XX XX XX XX 00 XX XX XX XX XX
                                   ‾‾‾‾‾
                                   port E data
```

where XX represents data from other bytes in the display string. Remember the MD command displays data on 16-bit boundaries.

Example 6.1:

A jumper wire is connected from V_{DD} (pin 26) to PE3 (IC pin 49). What data is read from port E?

Solution:

The received binary pattern is

```
7 6 5 4 3 2 1 0   Port E bit positions
0 0 0 0 1 0 0 0   Binary data
‾‾‾‾‾‾‾ ‾‾‾‾‾‾‾
   0       8      Hex value
```

Using the MD command yields

```
> MD 1000 100A <ENTER>

1000 XX XX XX XX XX XX XX XX XX XX 08 XX XX XX XX XX
```

Therefore, any digital data received on port E pins can be received by the CPU by reading location $100A. In a program the instruction could be LDAA $100A.

6.2.2 Writing Data to an I/O Port

The MM command can be used to learn how data is sent to an I/O port. For this discussion let's use port B since this port's lines are always configured as digital output lines. From Figure 1.7, port B is location $1004. Therefore, any binary pattern written to this address can be measured at port B (pins 35–42 on the MCU and EVB) by using a logic probe, voltmeter, or DC coupled oscilloscope.

Example 6.2:

The following binary pattern is to be sent to port B to control external peripheral equipment. Show how the MM command can be used to test this application.

```
7 6 5 4 3 2 1 0   Port B bit positions
0 1 1 0 1 0 1 0   Binary pattern
   6       A      Hex value
```

Solution:

The format to use the MM command is

> MM 1004 < ENTER>

1004 XX 6A <ENTER>

Now use a logic probe or voltmeter to check the logic states of pins 35–42.

```
7   6   5   4   3   2   1   0  ← Port B bit positions
35  36  37  38  39  40  41  42 ← Port B pin numbers
L   H   H   L   H   L   H   L  ← Logic state
```

Refer to Figure I.4 for the location of port pins on the EVB's P1 connector if you run a test of this example.

Example 6.3:

What programming steps are necessary to send the binary pattern of Example 6.2 to port B?

Solution:

Only load and store instructions are required, such as

```
LDAA #$6A
STAA $1004
```

The data is latched at port B after the store instruction is executed.

6.2.3 Bidirectional Port Lines

All I/O lines of ports C and D can be configured as bidirectional lines. Each of these ports has a special register, called a data direction register (DDR), assigned to it. The binary pattern written to the DDR configures the corresponding I/O line, either to be an input or an output line. A logic 0 programs the line as an input and a logic 1 programs the line as an output. Figure 6.1 shows four examples of a binary pattern stored in port C's data direction register, and the arrows on the port register show the direction of data flow. Note: The binary pattern in the data direction register only determines the direction that data will flow on the corresponding port line and not the logic state of the line.

Example 6.4:

Show how the MM command can be used to configure DDRC so that the lowest numbered I/O lines of port C are input and the highest numbered I/O lines are output as shown in Figure 6.1(c).

Solution:

From Figure 6.1(c) the binary pattern is 11110000 or F0$_{hex}$. From Figure 1.7, the location of DDRC is $1007. Using the MM command, the format is

> `> MM 1007 <ENTER>`

> `1007 XX F0 <ENTER>`

Note: XX represents old data before F0 is loaded. To check that this binary pattern has been stored at $1007, use the MD command.

> `> MD 1000 1007 <ENTER>`

> `1000 XX XX XX XX XX XX XX F0 XX XX XX XX XX XX XX XX`

At address $1007 the data is F0.

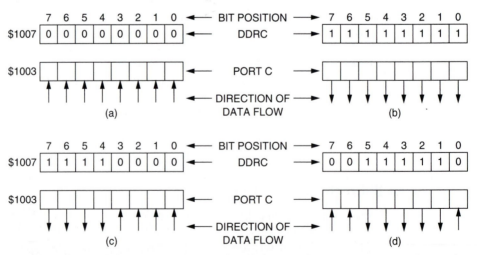

FIGURE 6.1 Examples of how a binary pattern in the data direction register configures the port's I/O lines.

Example 6.5:

Write the programming steps necessary to configure all of port C as output lines and bring all the lines to a low logic state.

Solution:

Upon system reset all of port C lines are inputs. This happens because the reset condition forces all bits in the data direction register to be zeros. Thus, after reset the I/O lines are left in a known condition from which you can design. This application requires two write operations—one to the DDR and then to the port register. Refer to Figure 1.7 for the address of DDRC and port C.

```
LDAA  #$FF   \  DDRC is loaded with logic 1s
STAA  $1007  /
LDAA  #$00   \  A low logic state appears on
STAA  $1003  /  all port C I/O lines
```

If you enter this program and execute it, use a logic probe and test the state of each line. Once data is written to an output line it is latched there until new data is written over it. Hence, it is easy to turn on (or off) peripheral equipment and leave it on (or off) for an indefinite length of time.

6.2.4 Port CL

Port C has another register associated with it called port C latch (PORT CL at address $1005). The difference between port C and port CL is on the input captures and output writes. A normal read of port C as previously discussed returns the current logic state that exists on any line configured as an input line. In addition to these normal I/O functions, there is a separate 8-bit parallel latch (address $1005) that stores the data on port C whenever an active edge is detected on the STRA input pin (IC pin 4). Write operations to port CL drive the data out port C and generate a handshake signal on the STRB pin (IC pin 6). Normal writes to port C do not trigger a handshake signal.

Keeping an output signal on an output line for a specified length of time requires using software timing delay loops or the MCU's timer unit. In Chapter 3 we studied timing loops; we now turn our attention to the MCU's timing system.

6.3

MCU'S MAIN TIMING SYSTEM

All of the MCU's timing signals are derived from its E clock signal which is one-quarter of the crystal frequency. The EVB's crystal frequency is 8MHz and the E clock is 2MHz or a fundamental (E Clock) timing clock period of 500ns. Therefore, an instruction that takes four clock cycles requires (4 × 500ns) 2μs to be executed on the EVB. Not only does the E clock signal determine an instruction execution time, but it controls all other timing aspects within the MCU.

6.3.1 Prescaler Unit and Timer Counter Register

The E clock is the input to a prescaler which has divide ratios that may be set to 1, 4, 8, or 16. The output of the prescaler drives a 16-bit free-running timer counter (TCNT) as shown in Figure 6.2. The prescaler factors are set by the binary pattern in bits 0 and 1 of the timer mask register 2 (TMSK2) as shown in Figure 6.3. However, the prescaler's rate can only be changed once and this must be within the first 64 clock cycles after reset. Then the rate remains fixed until the next reset. If you are using a system such as the EVB, you do not have access to the bus within the first 64 clock cycles. Therefore, on the EVB, the prescaler factor is set by the monitor program to one. You may check this by using the MM command and try to change bits 0 and 1 of the TMSK2 register which is at location $1024.

```
>MM 1024 <ENTER>          Use MM command
1024  00 03 <ENTER>       Try to change bits 0 and 1
rom -                     You have tried to access a nonuser register
>
>MM 1024 <ENTER>          Check result
1024  00                  Bits 0 and 1 have not changed
```

Note: Only bits 0 and 1 of TMSK2 register set the prescaler rate. Bits 4–7 may be changed, bits 2 and 3 are always a logic 0.

Figure 6.4 shows the address of the TCNT registers within the memory map scheme. These registers are read-only registers and can be read as a 16-bit value

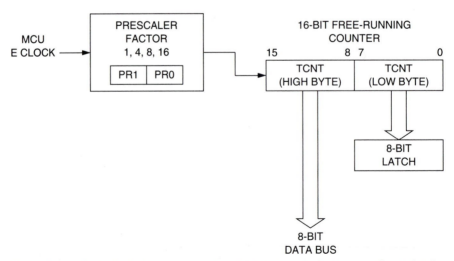

FIGURE 6.2 The E clock drives a prescaler which in turn is the input to the 16-bit free-running timer counter (TCNT).

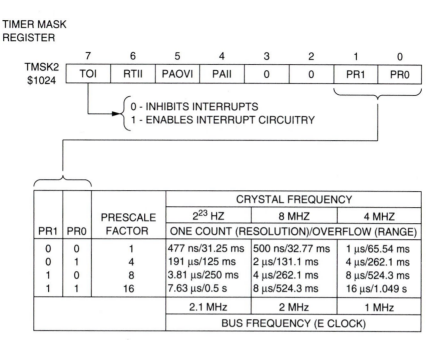

TIMER MASK
REGISTER

TMSK2
$1024

	7	6	5	4	3	2	1	0
	TOI	RTII	PAOVI	PAII	0	0	PR1	PR0

0 - INHIBITS INTERRUPTS
1 - ENABLES INTERRUPT CIRCUITRY

		PRESCALE FACTOR	CRYSTAL FREQUENCY		
PR1	PR0		2^{23} HZ	8 MHZ	4 MHZ
			ONE COUNT (RESOLUTION)/OVERFLOW (RANGE)		
0	0	1	477 ns/31.25 ms	500 ns/32.77 ms	1 µs/65.54 ms
0	1	4	191 µs/125 ms	2 µs/131.1 ms	4 µs/262.1 ms
1	0	8	3.81 µs/250 ms	4 µs/262.1 ms	8 µs/524.3 ms
1	1	16	7.63 µs/0.5 s	8 µs/524.3 ms	16 µs/1.049 s
			2.1 MHz	2 MHz	1 MHz
			BUS FREQUENCY (E CLOCK)		

TIMER FLAG
REGISTER

TFLG2
$1025

	7	6	5	4	3	2	1	0
	TOF	RTIF	PAOVF	PAIF	0	0	0	0

0 - BY WRITING A ONE TO THIS BIT
1 - AUTOMATICALLY SET ON ROLL OVER

FIGURE 6.3 Bits PR1 and PR0 in the TMSK2 register set the prescale factor. TFLG2 is the status register. On reset, all bits in both TMSK2 and TFLG2 are cleared to logic 0.

by a LDD $100E instruction. When this instruction is executed, the low byte is latched (see Figure 6.2) while the high byte is moved to accumulator A. Then the low byte is automatically moved to accumulator B. The latch ensures that the low byte and high byte belong to the same count value. Otherwise, it is quite possible that in the interval while the high byte is being read, the counter could be incremented once or several times.

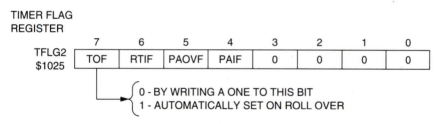

TCNT
$100E

	7	6	5	4	3	2	1	0	
	Bit 15	–	–	–	–	–	–	Bit 8	HIGH ORDER BYTE

TCNT
$100F

	7	6	5	4	3	2	1	0	
	Bit 7	–	–	–	–	–	–	Bit 0	LOW ORDER BYTE

FIGURE 6.4 The timer counter (TCNT) register.

6.4

TIMER OVERFLOW

As previously discussed, the output of the prescaler drives the 16-bit free-running timer counter. The counter is incremented on each clock signal it receives. The count starts at $0000 on reset and counts up to $FFFF and then rolls over to $0000. This rollover causes bit 7 of the timer flag register 2 (TFLG2) to be set. This register is shown in Figure 6.3 and bit 7 is called the timer overflow flag (TOF) bit. This bit, along with the timer overflow interrupt enable (TOI) bit, which is bit 7 of the timer mask register 2 (TMSK2), can be used for polled operation or hardware generated-interrupts. If the TOI bit is a logic 0, interrupt overflow is inhibited; hence polled operation. Polled operation means that the user's software routine is continuously monitoring the TOF bit to determine when it is set and then usually branching to a service routine. A logic 1 in the TOI bit causes an interrput request every time the TOF bit is set (that is, when TCNT count rolls over from $FFFF to $0000). The TOF bit is cleared by writing a logic 1 to it. This must be done before leaving the interrupt service routine; otherwise the TOF bit remains set, generating another interrupt immediately, which would not be a user's intention. Note: Writing a zero to the TOF does not clear it.

Example 6.6:

Write instructions to set the TOI bit and clear the TOF bit.

Solution:

The TOI bit is set by a logic 1 and the TOF bit is cleared by a logic 1. Therefore, these bits require a logic 1 to be written to their respective positions. Logic 0s should be written to the other bit positions; this causes no logic state change at these positions. Since both the TOI and TOF bits are located at bit position 7 as shown in Fig. 6.3, the binary pattern is 10000000 = 80_{hex}. If the cross-assembler is being used, the instruction sequence can be

```
LDAA  #%10000000
STAA  TMSK2
STAA  TFLG2
```

where TMSK2 equates to address $1024 and TFLG2 equates to address $1025. The LDAA #%10000000 instruction could also have been written as LDAA #$80.

When the PR1 and PR0 bits of the TMSK2 register are logic 0s, the rollover in the TCNT register occurs every 32.77ms. This value is determined by the fact that there are 65,536 counts from $0000 and back to $0000 and the counter is incremented by one every 0.5μs. This is the condition on the EVB because the monitor program configures the PR1 and PR0 bits to logic 0s and the user can not change it. It is quite possible to write a time delay program that uses the contents of the TCNT register and/or knowledge that the TOF bit has been set. However, we will forego this problem at this time and concentrate on the MCU's real time interrupt (RTI) function that will be used to generate time delays and is used in application Chapters 7 and 10. The TCNT will be used again in section 6.6 with another register to generate a square wave .

6.5

REAL TIME INTERRUPT FUNCTION

Chapter 3 showed how a software routine may be used to generate a timing delay. For short delays in the microsecond range, this method requires only a few lines of code and is easy to incorporate into a program. Timing delays, based on software, execute the same set of instructions until a count value equals zero. Since the execution of each instruction requires a fixed number of clock cycles, an inherent delay is created. For longer time delays, it is best to use the microcontroller's real time interrupt (RTI) function.

Use of the RTI function requires knowledge of specific bit locations in three registers. The registers are the pulse accumulator (PACTL) register; the timer mask register 2 (TMSK2); and the timer flag register 2 (TFLG2). These registers, the bits of interest, and their memory map location are shown in Figure 6.5. The two bits, RTR1 and RTR0, in the PACTL register are known as the real time interrupt rate select bits. These bits determine the rate at which interrupts can be generated by the RTI circuitry as given in Figure 6.5 for different frequencies. These bits can be written to at any time, even for the EVB system, unlike the prescaler bits, PR1 and PR0, previously discussed.

The real time interrupt flag (RTIF) bit (bit 6 of TFLG2 register) is set to a logic 1 at the end of each RTI period. If your application requires generating a hardware interrupt request each time the RTIF bit is set, then the real time enable (RTII) bit (bit 6 of the TMSK2 register) must be a logic 1. If you are using polled operation, then the RTII bit is cleared to a logic 0. A summary is given in Figure 6.5.

The steps involved to generate a real time hardware interrupt are:

1. Select the desired rate, by using the RTR1 and RTR0 bits.
2. Set bit 6 (RTIF bit) of the TMSK2 register.
3. Clear bit 6 (RTIF bit) of the TFLG2 register. Note: This bit is cleared by writing a one to it, not a zero.
4. Wait for an interrupt request to occur. This may be done by using a branch always instruction back to itself. For example:

```
WAIT: BRA WAIT
```

5. After the interrupt occurs, and the interrupt service routine is executed, bit 6 (RTIF bit) of the TFLG2 must be cleared again in order to receive the next real time interrupt.

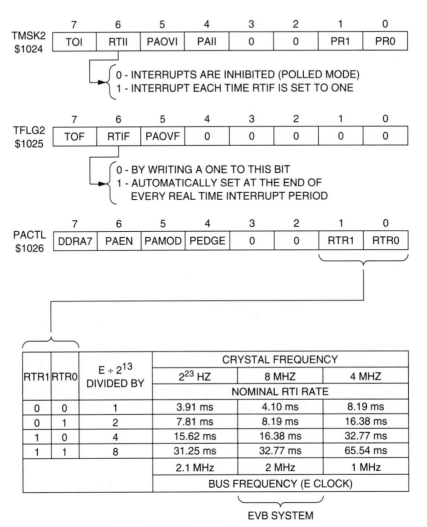

FIGURE 6.5 RTII, RTIF, RTR1, and RTR0 bits control how the real time interrupt system is being used. All bits in the three registers are cleared to logic 0 on reset. (Courtesy of Motorola, Inc.)

If you are using the EVB system, the pseudo interrupt RTI vector must also be initialized before the previous steps are executed. These pseudo interrupt vectors were introduced in section 4.17 and the vector jump table is given in Table 4.4. The addresses for the pseudo vectors for a real time interrupt are $00EB–$00ED.

Note that when a logic 1 is written to bit 6 of either TMSK2 or TFGL2 register, a logic 0 should be written to all other bits of these registers. This ensures that the logic state of the other bits does not change. You will see this in the following example.

Example 6.7:

Write the programming steps necessary to generate a 5-second time delay using the EVB system. Use an interrupt-driven program. After the delay, programming execution returns to the EVB monitor program (BUFFALO prompt is displayed).

Solution:

Before writing the actual instructions, let's draw a flow chart to help visualize the steps necessary to accomplish this task. See Figure 6.6. As shown in the flow chart of Figure 6.6, a timer counter must be initialized. The count value depends on the duration of time delay and the divide by ratio configured by the RTR1 and RTR0 bits. Let's choose a 32.77ms interval between interrupts. Thus, the count value is

$$\frac{5s}{32.77ms} = 153 = 99_{hex}$$

The program listing is shown in Figure 6.7.

The next example shows how to modify Example 6.7 to control the timing interval between toggle states of port B lines.

Example 6.8:

Toggle all of port B lines every 2 seconds. Start with logic 0s on the four lowest numbered lines (PB3–PB0) and logic 1s on the highest numbered lines (PB7–PB4). Repeat the sequence for 10 counts and then program execution returns to the EVB monitor program (BUFFALO prompt).

Solution:

A flow chart showing how to incorporate the toggle function for port B with the time delay routine is given in Figure 6.8. The program listing is given in Figure 6.9.

6.6

OUTPUT-COMPARE FUNCTION

Port A can be used either for (a) general purpose I/O, (b) output-compare, (c) input-capture, or (d) pulse-accumulator applications. Figure 6.10 is a partial view of the MCU's block diagram showing port A. This section introduces the output-compare functions because they use the MCU's main timer unit already described and are useful in generating waveforms to drive output peripheral interface circuits. The registers associated with the output-compare functions for basic I/O applications are timer output control registers (TOC1–TOC5), timer mask

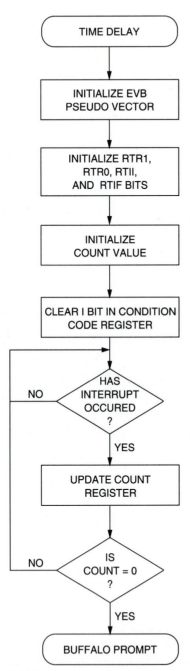

FIGURE 6.6 Flow chart to generate a time delay using the real time interrupt function

```
LINE    S  PC     OPCO  OPERANDS  S  LABEL    MNEMO  OPERANDS  COMMENT
00001                                         NAM    EXAMPLE 6.7        5 SECOND TIME DELAY
00002
00003                              * * * * * * * * * * * * * * * * * * * * * * * * * * * * * * * * * * * * * * * * *
00004                              *                                           REGISTER EQUATES              *
00005                              *      THESE LOCATIONS ARE FIXED ADDRESSES IN THE MEMORY MAP.            *
00006                              * * * * * * * * * * * * * * * * * * * * * * * * * * * * * * * * * * * * * * * * *
00007
00008   P  0000    00EB         A  RTIVEC   EQU    $00EB     PSEUDO VECTOR LOCATION ON THE EVB.
00009   P  0000    1024         A  TMSK2    EQU    $1024     MAIN TIMER INTERRUPT MASK REGISTER 2.
00010   P  0000    1025         A  TFLG2    EQU    $1025     TIMER INTERRUPT FLAG REGISTER 2.
00011   P  0000    1026         A  PACTL    EQU    $1026     PULSE ACCUMULATOR CONTROL REGISTER.
00012   P  0000    E0B2            BUFFALO  EQU    $E0B2     STARTING LOCATION OF THE BUFFALO PROMPT.
00013
00014                              * * * * * * * * * * * * * * * * * * * * * * * * * * * * * * * * * * * * * * * * *
00015                              *                                           BUFFER LOCATION              *
00016                              *      THESE BUFFER LOCATIONS IS USED TO STORE TEMPORARY DATA IN RAM.  THE   *
00017                              *      STARTING ADDRESS IS $DA00.                                           *
00018                              * * * * * * * * * * * * * * * * * * * * * * * * * * * * * * * * * * * * * * * * *
00019
00020   A  DA00                                ORG    $DA00     ASSEMBLER DIRECTIVE
00021
00022   A  DA00    02           A  TDREG    RMB    2         HOLDS THE COUNT VALUE FOR THE TIME DELAY LOOP.
00023                              * * * * * * * * * * * * * * * * * * * * * * * * * * * * * * * * * * * * * * * * *
00024                              *      TDELAY: THIS ROUTINE GENERATES A 5 SECOND TIME DELAY AND THEN       *
00025                              *      PROGRAM EXECUTION RETURNS TO THE EVB MONITOR PROGRAM AND THE        *
00026                              *      BUFFALO PROMPT IS DISPLAYED.                                        *
00027                              *      THE STACK POINTER IS RESET TO $004A TO INSURE A STACK OVERFLOW      *
00028                              *      DOES NOT OCCUR IF THE PROGRAM IS EXECUTED SEVERAL TIMES.            *
00029                              * * * * * * * * * * * * * * * * * * * * * * * * * * * * * * * * * * * * * * * * *
00030
00031   A  C600                                ORG    $C600     ASSEMBLER DIRECTIVE
00032
00033   A  C600 86  7E           A  TDELAY:  LDAA   #$7E      \   INITIALIZE THE PSEUDO VECTOR ADDRESSES
00034   A  C602 97  EB           A           STAA   RTIVEC    I  ON THE EVB FOR THE REAL TIME INTERTUPT
00035   A  C604 CC  C61F         A           LDD    #CT       I  FUNCTION.
00036   A  C607 DD  EC           A           STD    RTIVEC+1  /
00037
00038   A  C609 86  03           A           LDAA   #$03      \  SET THE RTRI AND RTR0 BITS
00039   A  C60B B7  1026         A           STAA   PACTL     /  FOR A DIVIDE BY 8 RATIO.
00040
00041   A  C60E 86  40           A           LDAA   #%01000000  \   SET THE RTII BIT AND
00042   A  C610 B7  1024         A           STAA   TMSK2     I  CLEAR THE RTIF BIT.
00043   A  C613 B7  1025         A           STAA   TFLG2     /
00044
00045   A  C616 CC  0099         A           LDD    #153      \  STORE THE COUNT VALUE AT A LOCATION
00046   A  C619 FD  DA00         A           STD    TDREG     /  CALLED TDREG (TIME DELAY REGISTER).
00047
00048   A  C61C 0E                            CLI              CLEAR INTERRUPT MASK BIT.
00049   A  C61D 20  FE     C61D WAIT:         BRA    WAIT      THE CPU IS WAITING FOR AN INTERRUPT.
00050
```

FIGURE 6.7 Program listing for Example 6.7

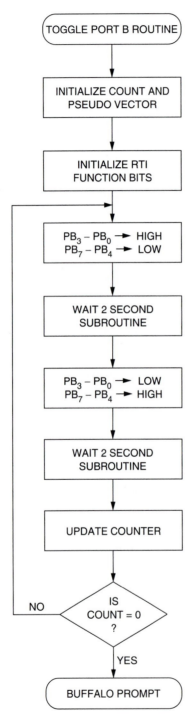

FIGURE 6.8 Flow chart for Example 6.8.

```
LINE   S PC     OPCO  OPERANDS  S LABEL     MNEMO  OPERANDS  COMMENT
00001
00002                                         NAM      EXAMPLE 6.8 TOGGLE PORT B I/O LINES EVERY 2 SECONDS.
00003                             * * * * * * * * * * * * * * * * * * * * * * * * * * * * * * * * * * * * * * * * *
00004                             *                         REGISTER EQUATES                                      *
00005                             *    THESE LOCATIONS ARE FIXED ADDRESSES IN THE MEMORY MAP.                     *
00006                             * * * * * * * * * * * * * * * * * * * * * * * * * * * * * * * * * * * * * * * * *
00007  P 0000   00EB            A RTIVEC   EQU    $00EB     PSEUDO VECTOR LOCATION ON THE EVB.
00008  P 0000   1024            A TMSK2    EQU    $1024     MAIN TIMER INTERRUPT MASK REGISTER 2.
00009  P 0000   1025            A TFLG2    EQU    $1025     TIMER INTERRUPT FLAG REGISTER 2.
00010  P 0000   1026            A PACTL    EQU    $1026     PULSE ACCUMULATOR CONTROL REGISTER.
00011  P 0000   E0B2            A BUFFALO  EQU    $E0B2     STARTING LOCATION OF THE BUFFALO PROMPT.
00012  P 0000   1004            A PORTB    EQU    $1004     ADDRESS OF PORT B.
00013                             * * * * * * * * * * * * * * * * * * * * * * * * * * * * * * * * * * * * * * * * *
00014                             *                         BUFFER LOCATIONS                                      *
00015                             *    THESE BUFFER LOCATIONS ARE USED TO STORE TEMPORARY DATA IN RAM.  THE *
00016                             *    STARTING ADDRESS IS D600 HEX.                                              *
00017                             * * * * * * * * * * * * * * * * * * * * * * * * * * * * * * * * * * * * * * * * *
00018
00019  A D600                                 ORG    $D600
00020
00021  A D600   02              A TDREG    RMB    2         STORES THE TIME DELAY COUNT.
00022  A D602   01              A INTCNT   RMB    1         STORES THE NUMBER OF LOOPS.
00023
00024                             * * * * * * * * * * * * * * * * * * * * * * * * * * * * * * * * * * * * * * * * *
00025                             *    THIS ROUTINE TOGGLES PORT B'S I/O LINES EVERY 2 SECONDS.                   *
00026                             *                  *      *      *      *      *                                *
00027                             *    THE STACK POINTER IS RESET TO LOCATION $004A SO A USER STACK OVERFLOW      *
00028                             *    DOES NOT OCCUR.  REMEMBER FROM CHAPTER 4 THAT THE USER STACK AREA          *
00029                             *    BEGINS AT ADDRESS $004A.                                                   *
00030                             * * * * * * * * * * * * * * * * * * * * * * * * * * * * * * * * * * * * * * * * *
00031
00032  A C680                                 ORG    $C680     ASSEMBLER DIRECTIVE
00033
00034  A C680 8E 004A           A           LDS    #$004A  INITIALIZE THE STACK POINTER
00035
00036  A C683 86 0A             A BEGIN:    LDAA   #10            \  INITIALIZE THE INTERVAL
00037  A C685 B7 D602           A           STAA   INTCNT         /  COUNTER FOR 10 LOOPS.
00038
00039  A C688 86 7E             A TDELAY:   LDAA   #$7E           \  INTIALIZE THE PSUEDO VECTOR ADDRESSES
00040  A C68A 97 EB             A           STAA   RTIVEC         |  ON THE EVB FOR THE REAL TIME INTERRUPT
00041  A C68C CC C6C0           A           LDD    #CONT          |  FUNCTION
00042  A C68F DD EC             A           STD    RTIVEC+1       /
00043
00044  A C691 86 03             A           LDAA   #%00000011     \  SET THE RTR1 AND RTR0 BITS
00045  A C693 B7 1026           A           STAA   PACTL          /  FOR A DIVIDE BY 8 RATIO.
00046
00047  A C696 86 40             A           LDAA   #%01000000     \  SET THE RTII BIT AND
00048  A C698 B7 1024           A           STAA   TMSK2          |  CLEAR THE RTIF BIT.
00049  A C69B B7 1025           A           STAA   TFLG2          /
00050
00051  A C69E 86 0F             A REPEAT:   LDAA   #$0F           \  LINES PB0-PB3 GO HIGH AND
00052  A C6A0 B7 1004           A           STAA   PORTB          /  LINES PB4-PB7 GO LOW.
```

FIGURE 6.9 Program listing for Example 6.8

```
LINE    S  PC    OPCO  OPERANDS  S  LABEL    MNEMO  OPERANDS  COMMENT
00053   A  C6A3  8D    12           C6B7     BSR    T2
00054
00055   A  C6A5  86    F0        A           LDAA   #$F0      \   LINES PB0-PB3 GO LOW AND
00056   A  C6A7  B7    1004      A           STAA   PORTB     /   LINES PB4-PB7 GO HIGH.
00057   A  C6AA  8D    0B           C6B7     BSR    T2
00058
00059   A  C6AC  7A    D602      A           DEC    INTCNT    DECREMENT THE INTERVAL COUNT VALUE.
00060   A  C6AF  27    03           C6B4     BEQ    T1        IF COUNT = 0, BRANCH TO T1.
00061   A  C6B1  7E    C69E      A           JMP    REPEAT    JUMP BACK TO THE LABEL REPEAT.
00062
00063   A  C6B4  7E    E0B2      A  T1:       JMP    BUFFALO   JUMP TO THE EVB MONITOR PROGRAM.
00064
00065   A  C6B7  CC    003D      A  T2:       LDD    #61       \   STORE THE COUNT VALUE AT A LOCATION
00066   A  C6BA  FD    D600      A           STD    TDREG     /   CALLED TDREG (TIME DELAY REGISTER).
00067
00068   A  C6BD  0E                           CLI              CLEAR INTERRUPT MASK BIT.
00069   A  C6BE  20    FE           C6BE  WAIT:  BRA    WAIT      THE CPU IS WAITING FOR AN INTERRUPT.
00070
00071   A  C6C0  FC    D600      A  CONT:     LDD    TDREG     \
00072   A  C6C3  83    0001      A           SUBD   #1        |   CHECK TO SEE IF THE ROUTINE HAS
00073   A  C6C6  FD    D600      A           STD    TDREG     |   LOOPED 61 TIMES TO GIVE A TOTAL
00074   A  C6C9  1A83  0000      A           CPD    #0        |   TIME DELAY OF ~ 2 SECONDS.
00075   A  C6CD  26    04           C6D3     BNE    CLRFLG    /
00076
00077   A  C6CF  8E    0048      A           LDS    #$0048    RESET THE SP TO RETRIEVE THE RTS ADDRESS.
00078   A  C6D2  39                           RTS
00079
00080   A  C6D3  86    40        A  CLRFLG:   LDAA   #%01000000  \   CLEAR THE RTIF BIT IN THE
00081   A  C6D5  B7    1025      A           STAA   TFLG2     /   TFLG2 REGISTER.
00082   A  C6D8  3B                           RTI              RETURN FROM INTERRUPT.
00083
00084                                         END    $C680     ASSEMBLER DIRECTIVE.
```

TOTAL NUMBER OF ERRORS: 0
TOTAL NUMBER OF WARNINGS: 0
TOTAL NUMBER OF LINES: 84

NUMBER OF BYTES IN SECTION ASCT: 92

NUMBER OF BYTES IN PROGRAM: 92

			CROSS REFERENCE TABLE		
NAME	ATTRB	S	VALUE	P:LINE	LINE 1....N
BEGIN		A	C683	2:36	
BUFFALO	EQU	A	E0B2	2:11	63
CLRFLG		A	C6D3	3:80	75
CONT		A	C6C0	3:71	41
INTCNT		A	D602	2:22	37 59

			CROSS REFERENCE TABLE			
NAME	ATTRB	S	VALUE	P:LINE	LINE 1....N	
PACTL	EQU	A	1026	2:10	45	
PORTB	EQU	A	1004	2:12	52 56	
REPEAT		A	C69E	2:51	61	
RTIVEC	EQU	A	00EB	2:7	40 42	
T1		A	C6B4	3:63	60	
T2		A	C6B7	3:65	53 57	
TDELAY		A	C688	2:39		
TDREG		A	D600	2:21	66 71	73
TFLG2	EQU	A	1025	2:9	49 81	
TMSK2	EQU	A	1024	2:8	48	
WAIT		A	C6BE	3:69	69	

FIGURE 6.9 *(continued)*

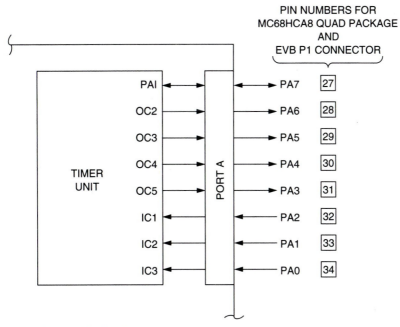

FIGURE 6.10 Block Diagram of port A

register 1 (TMSK1), timer flag register 1 (TFLG1), and timer control register 1 (TCTL1). Each of the timer output control registers is 16 bits. Figure 6.11 shows the TOCx registers and Figure 6.12 shows the TMSK1 and TFLG1 registers. Bits 0, 1, and 2 in both the TMSK1 and TFLG1 registers are used for input-capture functions (see section 6.11) and not for output-compare functions. The TCTL1 register and the bit patterns to configure the output-compare lines of OC2–OC5 are shown in Figure 6.13.

Example 6.9:

What binary pattern must be stored in the timer control 1 register to toggle port line A6 on successful compares?

Solution:

Port line A6 is driven by the output-compare 2 circuitry. (See Figure 6.10.) Using Figure 6.13, the binary pattern must be 0 1 0 0 0 0 0 0. The sequence of instructions are

```
LDAA #$40
STAA $1020
```

7	6	5	4	3	2	1	0		
Bit 15	–	–	–	–	–	–	Bit 8	$1016	TOC1
Bit 7	–	–	–	–	–	–	Bit 0	$1017	
Bit 15	–	–	–	–	–	–	Bit 8	$1018	TOC2
Bit 7	–	–	–	–	–	–	Bit 0	$1019	
Bit 15	–	–	–	–	–	–	Bit 8	$101A	TOC3
Bit 7	–	–	–	–	–	–	Bit 0	$101B	
Bit 15	–	–	–	–	–	–	Bit 8	$101C	TOC4
Bit 7	–	–	–	–	–	–	Bit 0	$101D	
Bit 15	–	–	–	–	–	–	Bit 8	$101E	TOC5
Bit 7	–	–	–	–	–	–	Bit 0	$101F	

FIGURE 6.11 The M68HC11's output-compare registers (Courtesy of Motorola, Inc.)

An OCxF status bit in the timer flag register 1 (TFLG1) is set whenever the value in the corresponding TOCx register matches the value in the MCU's free-running counter (TCNT). Figure 6.14 helps to visualize the internal circuitry for the compare operation. For example, the user loads a timer output control register such as TOC2 and when TOC2 equals TCNT, the OC2F bit is set. Remember from section 6.3 the TCNT count is incremented on every clock pulse from the prescaler.

The OCxI bits in the timer mask register 1 (TMSK1) select whether or not a hardware interrupt request will be generated when a match occurs.

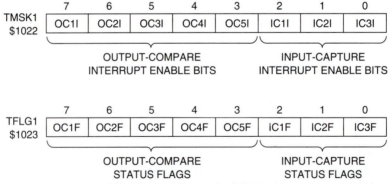

FIGURE 6.12 Control bits for enabling and inhibiting interrupt requests for output-compare and input-capture functions are written to the TMSK1 register. Status information is read from the TFLG1 register. All bits of both registers are cleared to logic zeros on reset.

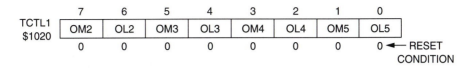

OMx	OLx	CONFIGURATION
0	0	DOES NOT AFFECT OCx PIN (OC1 STILL MAY)
0	1	TOGGLE OCx PIN ON SUCCESSFUL COMPARE
1	0	CLEAR OCx PIN ON SUCCESSFUL COMPARE
1	1	SET OCx PIN ON SUCCESSFUL COMPARE

FIGURE 6.13 The bit pairs provide for automatic pin actions to occur on OC2 (pin 28), OC3 (pin 29), OC4 (pin 30), and OC5 (pin 31).

A logic 0 in an OCxI bit inhibits an interrupt, hence polled operation is being used. A logic 1 in an OCxI bit enables the interrupt hardware.

An OCxF flag is cleared by writing a logic 1 to the bit position in the TFLG1 register. This is the same procedure used to clear the TOF bit in the TFLG2 register. The OCxF bit should be cleared before leaving the interrupt service routine. Otherwise, another interrupt will be automatically generated.

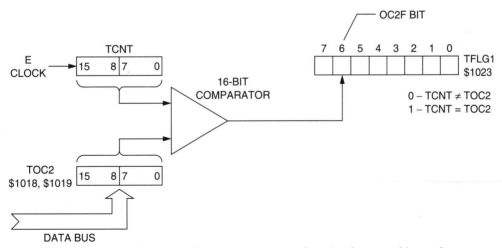

FIGURE 6.14 The OC2F bit is set when TCNT = TOC2; otherwise the OC2F bit equals zero.

Example 6.10:

Show programming steps to clear the OC2F bit.

Solution:

A straightforward method is to use a load and store sequence. Since the OCF2 bit is position 6 in the TFLG1 register, then the binary pattern to clear it is 01000000 = $40 and the programming steps are:

```
LDAA #$40
STAA $1023
```

If you are using the EVB assembler, do not include the $ symbol. If you are using the cross-assembler, include it. The cross-assembler also permits the binary pattern to be entered directly as

```
LDAA #%01000000
STAA $1023
```

One of the first tests of the output-compare function is to generate a square wave and measure it on an oscilloscope. The basic operation is to toggle an OC line when the TCNT register value equals the value loaded into the TOCx register. The program can be written for either polled or interrupt-driven operation. Let's write a program for an interrupt driven application.

Example 6.11:

Write an interrupt-driven program to generate a square wave with a period of 2ms at PA6 (pin 28).

Solution:

The PA6 line should toggle every 1ms due to an interrupt. Since PA6 is specified, our application requires using OC2 (see Figure 6.10). If the EVB system is being used, the pseudo vector for OC2 is at locations $00DC–$00DE (see Table 4.4) and it must be initialized. Figure 6.15 is a flow chart to assist in visualizing the logical sequence of events. Since a square wave has equal high and low times, the count value that must be loaded into TOC2 can be determined by

$$\frac{1/2 \text{ period}}{\text{E clock}} = \text{Count value in decimal}$$

For our example we obtain

$$\frac{1\text{ms}}{0.5\mu\text{s}} = 2000_{\text{dec}} = 7D0_{\text{hex}}$$

To make a general solution, use the MM (memory modify) command to enter the count value before the program is executed. Let's choose locations $D6E0 and $D6E1 to hold the count value.

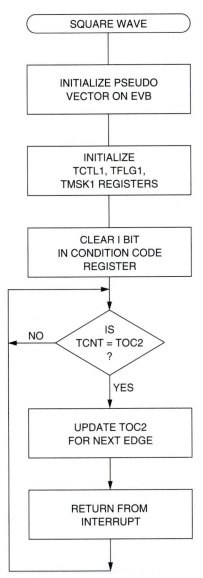

FIGURE 6.15 A flow chart for generating the square wave of Example 6.11

Figure 6.15 shows the logical sequence of events to be accomplished. The program listing for this example is given in Figure 6.16. This program is similar to one given in Motorola's M68HC11 reference manual. The program was written on an IBM-compatible computer, assembled, and downloaded. Remember the count value must be loaded into $D6E0 and $D6E1

```
LINE     S  PC     OPCO  OPERANDS  S  LABEL        MNEMO  OPERANDS  COMMENT
00001
00002                                              NAM     EXAMPLE 6-11 SQUARE WAVE USING OUTPUT COMPARE FUNCTION.
00003
00004                                  * * * * * * * * * * * * * * * * * * * * * * * * * * * * * * * * * * * * * *
00005                                  *                              REGISTER EQUATES                          *
00006                                  *    THESE LOCATIONS ARE FIXED ADDRESSES IN THE MEMORY MAP.              *
00007                                  * * * * * * * * * * * * * * * * * * * * * * * * * * * * * * * * * * * * * *
00008    P  0000   00DC           A  OC2VEC  EQU    $00DC   PSEUDO VECTOR LOCATION ON THE EVB.
00009    P  0000   1018           A  TOC2    EQU    $1018   TIMER OUTPUT COMPARE REGISTER 2.
00010    P  0000   1020           A  TCTL1   EQU    $1020   TIMER CONTROL REGISTER 1.
00011    P  0000   1022           A  TMSK1   EQU    $1022   TIMER MASK REGISTER 1.
00012    P  0000   1023           A  TFLG1   EQU    $1023   TIMER FLAG REGISTER 1.
00013
00014                                  * * * * * * * * * * * * * * * * * * * * * * * * * * * * * * * * * * * * * *
00015                                  *                              BUFFER LOCATIONS                          *
00016                                  *    THESE BUFFER LOCATIONS ARE USED TO STORE TEMPORARY DATA IN RAM.  THE  *
00017                                  *    STARTING ADDRESS IS D6E0 HEX.                                       *
00018                                  * * * * * * * * * * * * * * * * * * * * * * * * * * * * * * * * * * * * * *
00019
00020    A  D6E0                                    ORG     $D6E0
00021
00022    A  D6E0   02             A  TDC     RMB    2       STORES THE TIME DELAY COUNT.
00023
00024
00025                                  * * * * * * * * * * * * * * * * * * * * * * * * * * * * * * * * * * * * * *
00026                                  *    THIS FOLLOWING ROUTINE GENERATES A 2ms SQUARE WAVE ON PORT LINE PA6  *
00027                                  *    USING THE OUTPUT COMPARE FUNCTION, OC2.                             *
00028                                  *                              * * * * *                                 *
00029                                  *    THE STACK POINTER IS SET TO LOCATION $004A                          *
00030                                  * * * * * * * * * * * * * * * * * * * * * * * * * * * * * * * * * * * * * *
00031
00032    A  C6E0                                    ORG     $C6E0   ASSEMBLER DIRECTIVE
00033
00034    A  C6E0   8E    004A      A           LDS     #$004A  INITIALIZE THE STACK POINTER AT $004A.
00035
00036    A  C6E3   86    7E        A           LDAA    #$7E    \   INTIALIZE THE PSUEDO VECTOR ADDRESSES
00037    A  C6E5   97    DC        A           STAA    OC2VEC  |   ON THE EVB FOR THE REAL TIME INTERRUPT
00038    A  C6E7   CC    C6FA      A           LDD     #INTROUT|   FUNCTION.
00039    A  C6EA   DD    DD        A           STD     OC2VEC+1/
00040
00041    A  C6EC   86    40        A           LDAA    #%01000000 \
00042    A  C6EE   B7    1020      A           STAA    TCTL1   |   SET OC2 FOR TOGGLE MODE, SET OC2I,
00043    A  C6F1   B7    1022      A           STAA    TMSK1   |   AND CLEAR OC2F.
00044    A  C6F4   B7    1023      A           STAA    TFLG1   /
00045
00046    A  C6F7   0E                          CLI             CLEAR I BIT IN CONDITION CODE REGISTER.
00047    A  C6F8   20    FE        C6F8 WAIT:  BRA     WAIT    WAIT FOR INTERRUPT.
00048
00049    A  C6FA   FC    D6E0      A  INTROUT: LDD     TDC     LOAD VALUE FROM TIME DELAY REGISTER.
00050    A  C6FD   F3    1018      A           ADDD    TOC2    \ UPDATE TOC2 REGISTER FOR NEXT EDGE.
00051    A  C700   FD    1018      A           STD     TOC2    /
00052
```

FIGURE 6.16 Program listing for Example 6.11

LINE	S	PC	OPCO	OPERANDS	S	LABEL	MNEMO	OPERANDS	COMMENT
00053	A	C703	86	40	A		LDAA	#%01000000	\ CLEAR THE OC2F BIT BEFORE LEAVING
00054	A	C705	B7	1023	A		STAA	TFLG1	/ INTERRUPT SERVICE ROUTINE.
00055	A	C708	3B				RTI		RETURN FROM INTERRUPT.
00056									
00057							END	$C6E0	ASSEMBLER DIRECTIVE.

TOTAL NUMBER OF ERRORS: 0
TOTAL NUMBER OF WARNINGS: 0
TOTAL NUMBER OF LINES: 57

NUMBER OF BYTES IN SECTION ASCT: 43

NUMBER OF BYTES IN PROGRAM: 43

CROSS REFERENCE TABLE

NAME	ATTRB	S	VALUE	P:LINE	LINE 1....N	
INTROUT		A	C6FA	2:49	38	
OC2VEC	EQU	A	00DC	2:8	37	39
TCTL1	EQU	A	1020	2:10	42	
TDC		A	D6E0	2:22	49	
TFLG1	EQU	A	1023	2:12	44	54
TMSK1	EQU	A	1022	2:11	43	
TOC2	EQU	A	1018	2:9	50	51
WAIT		A	C6F8	2:47	47	

FIGURE 6.16 *(continued)*

before the program is executed. The MM format is

> MM D6E0 <ENTER>

D6E0 XX 07 <SP> XX D0 <ENTER>

To observe the results, connect an oscilloscope to pin 28 (PA6) of the P1 connector on the EVB. The program can be stopped at any time by pressing the EVB's reset switch and new values may be loaded into $D6E0 and $D6E1 which is the location of the TDC (time delay counter) register.

In addition to OC2–OC5, the M68HC11 has another output-compare function, OC1, and its operation is different, as shown in the next section.

6.7
OUTPUT-COMPARE 1 FUNCTION

Output-compare 1 (OC1) has a special feature which allows the user to control up to five output pins (PA7–PA3) when the contents of TCNT register matches the contents of TOC1 register. Figure 6.17 shows the two registers that are used for OC1 to control pin action into the TOC1 register shown in Figure 6.11. As

	7	6	5	4	3	2	1	0
OC1M $100C	OC1M7	OC1M6	OC1M5	OC1M4	OC1M3	0	0	0

	7	6	5	4	3	2	1	0
OC1D $100D	OC1D7	OC1D6	OC1D5	OC1D4	OC1D3	0	0	0

PA7	PA6	PA5	PA4	PA3	
27	28	29	30	31	◄——— PIN NUMBERS

FIGURE 6.17 Output-compare 1 (OC1) registers. Both registers are cleared to logic 0 on reset.

seen in Figure 6.17 the register bits (7–3) correspond to an MCU pin. The least significant three bits are always read as a logic 0. For a port A pin to be affected by the OC1 function, a logic 1 must be written to the corresponding bit in the OC1M (output-compare 1 mask) register.

The binary value in the OC1D (output-compare 1 data) register determines whether the port A pin goes to high or low logic state. For example, if the OC1D bit is a logic 1, the corresponding port A line goes high when a match occurs. If the OC1D bit is a logic 0, the corresponding port A line goes low when a match occurs.

Example 6.12:

What programming steps are necessary to use the OC1 function to set PA3, PA4, and clear PA5 and PA6 when a match occurs between TCNT and TOC1? PA7 is not being used.

Solution:

A logic 1 must be written to those bits in OC1M register that are being used and a logic 1 must be written to those bits in OC1D register to cause the port pin to go high. The binary patterns are

```
7  6  5  4  3  2  1  0  ← Bit position
0  1  1  1  1  0  0  0  ← OC1M binary pattern
0  0  0  1  1  0  0  0  ← OC1D binary pattern
X  L  L  H  H  X  X  X  ← Logic state at port A
```

The instructions are

```
LDAA #%01111000
STAA $100C
LDAA #%00011000
STAA $100D
```

If you are using the EVB's one-line assembler to enter the instructions, convert the binary patterns to hexadecimal and do not use the $ symbol.

PA7 is configured differently than the four other pins. PA6–PA3 are output only pins, but PA7 is bidirectional. Therefore, if PA7 is to be used with the OC1 function, it must be configured as an output pin. This is done by writing a logic 1 into DDRA7 (bit 7 of the PACTL register) as shown in Figure 6.5.

Example 6.13:

What programming steps must be included in Example 6.12 to use PA7 as an output line?

Solution:

The DDRA7 is set by

```
LDAA #%10000000
STAA $1026
```

These instructions would be inserted before the instructions given in Example 6.12.

6.8

FORCED OUTPUT COMPARE

This compare feature provides a method of changing the logic states on output-compare pins without waiting for an output-compare match to occur. To use this feature, write a logic 1 to the corresponding bit in the timer compare force (CFORC) register (see Figure 6.18). This logic 1 causes the compare action as if a match between the TCNT and TOCx registers happened but there is no interrupt. For each write operation, this forced action occurs only once and then the logic 1 disappears. Therefore, a new write operation is necessary for another forced action. A read of CFORC register always yields logic 0s. Note: You can write to more than one CFORC bit at time.

	7	6	5	4	3	2	1	0
CFORC $100B	FOC1	FOC2	FOC3	FOC4	FOC5	0	0	0
	PA7 27	PA6 28	PA5 29	PA4 30	PA3 31		PORT NUMBERS PIN NUMBERS	

FIGURE 6.18 Timer compare force (CFORC) register provides a method to set or clear a port A output line without waiting for a match between TCNT and TOC$_x$ registers. On reset, all bits are cleared to a logic 0. (Courtesy of Motorola, Inc.)

Example 6.14:

Consider the following binary pattern is stored in timer control 1 (TCTL1) register.

```
7 6 5 4 3 2 1 0 ← Bit postion
0 1 1 0 1 1 0 0 ← Contents of TCTL1 register
```

What would occur on PA6–PA3 on the next clock cycle to the free-running counter? PA7 is configured as an input line. The binary pattern stored in the CFORC register is 01111000.

Solution:

The contents of the TCTL1 register configure PA6–PA3 as given in Figure 6.13 and shown below:

Bits Positions	Binary Value	Configuration	
7 6	0 1	Toggle	PA6
5 4	1 0	Clear	PA5
3 2	1 1	Set	PA4
1 0	0 0	No effect	PA3

The configuration column shows the action that happens on pins PA6–PA3.

6.9

INTRODUCTION TO PERIPHERAL INTERFACE DEVICES

Sections 6.1 to 6.8 were devoted to the software and command instructions needed to control I/O lines on the MCU. We now direct our attention to the peripheral interface devices needed to allow low-power MCU control line logic levels to control high power.

All the following interface devices can be tested at the bench separately. However, a better method is to wire the device's input to an I/O pin such as PB1 (pin 41) and use the MM and MD BUFFALO commands for test simulation.

6.9.1 7407 Hex Buffer/Driver

An open-collector buffer/driver such as the hex 7407 can be used to control loads of up to 1 watt. The 7407 acts as a buffer for driving TTL inputs or as a high voltage open-collector driver to interface with relays, lamps, or optoisolator circuits.

The schematic drawing and logic symbol for one-sixth of a 7407 are shown in Figures 6.19(a) and (b). When PB1 (pin 41) of the microcontroller is driven to a logic 0 (below 0.8V), the input to the 7407 is brought low, Q_1 turns on to reduce

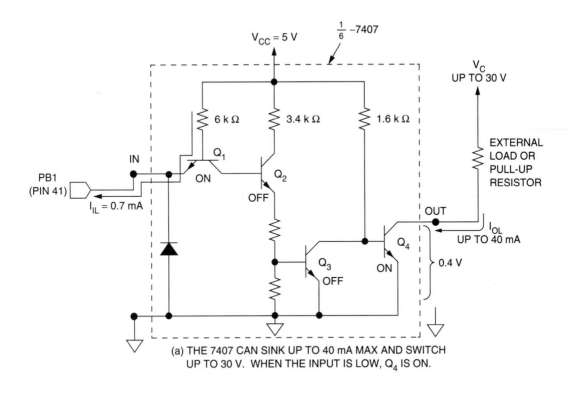

(a) THE 7407 CAN SINK UP TO 40 mA MAX AND SWITCH
UP TO 30 V. WHEN THE INPUT IS LOW, Q_4 IS ON.

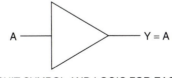

(b) CIRCUIT SYMBOL AND LOGIC FOR EACH GATE

FIGURE 6.19 Approximate circuit schematic for one gate of a 7407hex buffer/driver with open-collector high-voltage output in (a) and circuit symbol in (b)

Q_2 emitter current to zero which turns off Q_3. Output transistor Q_4 conducts a base current of almost 3mA, which is more than enough to support a collector current at the maximum rated output sink current of 40mA. Thus, a low input from the MCU gives a low output level at high current capacity.

When a 7407 gate input is brought high to a logic 1 level (above 2V), the base-collector diode of Q_1 conducts to turn on Q_2 which drives Q_3 into saturation. Q_4 is cut off and the output exhibits an open circuit (not shown in Figure 6.19(a)). As shown in Figure 6.19(a), the output can switch up to 30V. Thus, a high input signal causes the buffer output to go high to external voltage V_C.

For higher output current capacity of up to 500mA and high-voltage outputs up to 55V, consult the data sheets for the 75416 series of dual peripheral drivers.

6.9.2 Low Voltage Applications

Figure 6.20(a) shows how an indicating LED (light-emitting diode) is controlled by the MCU. The LED has a typical on voltage of 2.0V when conducting a forward current I_F of approximately 20mA. Resistor R is calculated from:

$$R = \frac{V_{CC} - 2.0V}{I_F} \tag{6.1}$$

When load current requirements exceed the 40mA limit of one 7407, the open-collector outputs of two or more 7407 gates can be *wire-ORed* together. See Figure 6.20(b), where two gate outputs sink the 50mA relay operating current. Of course, inputs of the wire-ORed gates must also be connected together. If the

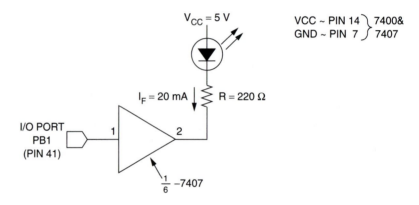

(a) THE LED IS ON WITH A HIGH INPUT AND OFF
FOR A LOW INPUT

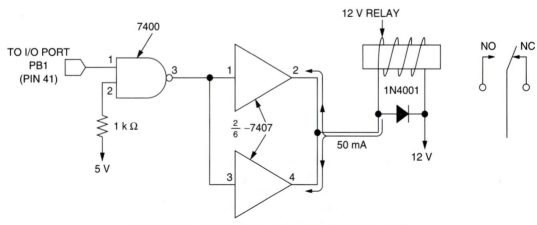

(b) OPEN-COLLECTOR 7407 OUTPUTS ARE CONNECTED
TOGETHER (WIRE-OR) TO DOUBLE CONTROL CURRENT CAPACITY.
A LOW INPUT OPERATED THE RELAY.

FIGURE 6.20 A single 7407 gate controls an LED in (a), and two wire-OR gates control a relay in (b).

MCU's I/O port cannot furnish increased gate input current, add another 7407 with 1kΩ pull-up resistor or one 7400 NAND gate as shown.

6.10

INTERFACING AC LOADS

6.10.1 Introduction

It is sound engineering practice to provide electrical isolation between low-power MCU circuitry and high-power AC loads. Sensitive gate power triacs are the most common devices used to control line voltages of 115V or 230V with load currents up to 8A. A MCU can control and also be electrically isolated from a power triac by an *optocoupler*.

There are two types of optical couplers that can interface the MCU to a power triac: the triac driver and the zero-crossing triac driver. A triac driver such as the MOC3011 or 3021 turns on a power triac immediately upon command by the MCU. A zero-crossing triac driver such as the MOC3031 or 3041 turns on a power triac only if line voltage is near zero (actually between +25V and –25V).

6.10.2 Characteristics of Triac Drivers

The schematic drawing for both types of triac drivers is identical and shown in Figure 6.21. All devices are made of a galliam arsenide infrared emitter (LED) which can optically excite and activate a detector-driver chip. The MOC3031 and 3041 also include zero-crossing circuitry, a distinction not apparent on the schematic of Figure 6.21. All LEDs are activated by a forward current of about 15mA (10mA for the 3011) with a forward voltage drop of approximately 1.2V.

All triac drivers can withstand a maximum repetitive surge current load of 1.2A. When activated, the drivers can directly control loads of up to 100mA and

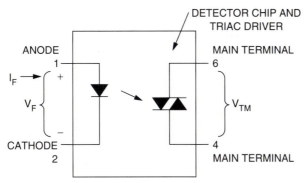

FIGURE 6.21 6-pin triac driver schematic for both zero-crossing and non-zero-crossing types.

exhibit an on-voltage of $V_{TM} = 3.0V$ maximum. When the main terminal current drops below holding current I_H, all drivers turn off. When off, the MOC 3011 and 3031 will block 250V and are used to control 115V AC lines. The MOC 3021 and 3041 will block 400V and can control 230V lines. Driver characteristics are summarized below:

Optocouplers

Triac Driver	I_F	Load Voltage	I_H
MOC3011	10mA	115VAC	100μA
MOC3021	15mA	230VAC	100μA
Zero-Crossing Triac Driver			
MOC3031	15mA	115VAC	200μA
MOC3041	15mA	230VAC	200μA

6.10.3 Snubber Circuit

Triacs and non-zero-crossing triac drivers can be turned on accidentally by an abrupt rise of voltage across their main terminals. The maximum rate of rise is specified by a triac's dv/dt rating and is typically 10V/μs. The worst case voltage change from a 230V or 115V line would occur if power is applied at peak voltages of 340V and 170V, respectively. A resistor-capacitor snubber circuit is connected across the power triac (or across the triac driver in direct drive) to reduce rate of rise below the dv/dt rating. The snubber RC circuit should have a time constant T of:

$$T = \frac{V_{peak}}{dv/dt} \tag{6.2}$$

If a dv/dt rating of 100V/μsec is applied to the triac;

$T = 3.4μs$ for 340V; $T = 1.7μs$ for 170V

Zero-crossing triac drivers have very high dv/dt ratings and and do not need snubbers.

6.10.4 Application of a Non-Zero-Crossing Driver

A typical application for a MOC3021 is shown in Figure 6.22(a). If the load is inductive, snubber circuit R_2 and C is required. Because the MOC3021 can be turned on when C is charged to peak line voltage of 340V, R_1 must be added to limit driver surge current to 1.2A. Calculate the valve of R_1 from:

$$R_1 = \frac{V_{peak}}{I_{surge}} = \frac{340}{1.2A} = 300\Omega \tag{6.3}$$

If dv/dt of the triac is 1V/μs, then from Eq. (6.2)

$$T = \frac{340V}{1V/\mu sec} = 340\mu s$$

Assume the triac requires a gate current of 15mA when line voltage is at 40V. Then $R_1 + R_2$ is found from

$$R_1 + R_2 = \frac{40V}{15mA} = 2700\Omega$$

Since $R_1 = 300\Omega$, pick $R_2 = 2400\Omega$ and find C from:

$$T = 340\mu s = R_2 C = (2400\Omega)C$$
$$C = 0.15\mu F$$

If the load is resistive, remove R_2 and C.

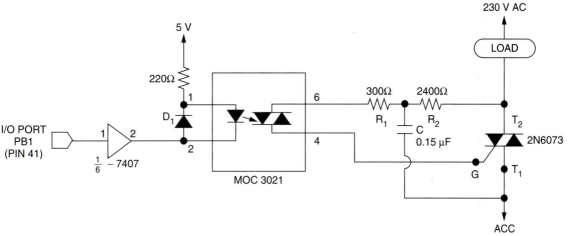

(a) INTERFACING AN AC LOAD WITH A NON-ZERO-CROSSING
    TRIAC DRIVER. D_1 PROTECTS THE LED AGAINST ACCIDENTAL
    REVERSE BIAS.

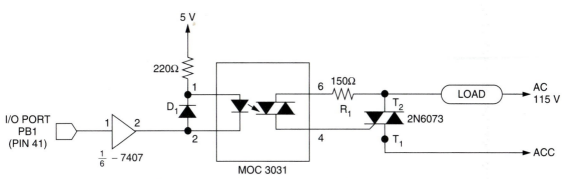

(b) ZERO-CROSSING TRIAC DRIVERS DO NOT NEED
    SNUBBER CIRCUITS BECAUSE OF A HIGH $\frac{dv}{dt}$ RATING.

FIGURE 6.22 Application of non-zero-crossing optocoupler in (a) and zero-crossing triac driver in (B)

6.10.5 Application of Zero-Crossing Triac Drivers

The MOC3031 and 3041 are zero-crossing triac drivers whose operating characteristics are given in section 6.10.2. Their dv/dt rating is so high that they do not need a snubber circuit as shown in Figure 6.22(b). However, their companion power triac may need a snubber depending on the load.

Zero-crossing triac drivers are preferred when controlling inductive loads or incandescent lamps because drivers are inhibited from turning on if line voltage is above +25V or below −25V. When power is applied to an incandescent lamp, the initial cold resistance of the filament is a tenth or less than the operating hot resistance. For example, a 115V 200W lamp has a hot resistance of about 70Ω and a cold resistance less than 10Ω. If the lamp is switched on at peak line voltage (170V), the filament surge current is 17A. A zero-crossing driver will restrict cold surge current to a maximum of $25V/10\Omega = 2.5A$.

In both Figures 6.22(a) and (b), main terminals T_1 and T_2 of the power triac exhibit a voltage drop of about 1V when the triac conducts load current. Thus, the triac driver and any snubber circuit are protected by essentially a short circuit across T_1 and T_2. The triacs turn off when load current drops below the holding current rating of 50 to 100mA.

6.11
■■■■■

INPUT-CAPTURE FUNCTIONS

As mentioned in the introduction of this chapter, some applications that have the MCU controlling output devices first require knowing something about the time an input event occurred. Therefore, this section introduces another feature of the M68HC11 microcontroller, its input capture functions which are associated with port A.

PA0, PA1, and PA2 are input only pins. They can be used for general purpose applications or for its alternate feature of input-capture. Each input-capture function has a 16-bit register, edge detector, and interrupt request circuitry associated with it. The three 16-bit timer input-capture (TICx) registers are shown in Figure 6.23. The association of port A pins and an input-capture number is shown in Figure 6.10 (IC1 ← PA2, IC2 ← PA1, and IC3 ← PA0).

The edge detector circuitry is programmable to detect positive or negative going edges. Edge control for each pin is configured by the binary pattern stored in the TCTL2 (timer control 2) register as shown in Figure 6.24. Thus, the programmer has control on the edge polarity for a capture to occur. When an active edge occurs, the time of the capture is copied from the TCNT register into the TICx register.

Example 6.15:

What binary pattern must be written to TCTL2 register to capture the time for a rising edge on PA0? The input-capture function is not being used for PA1 and PA2.

		7	6	5	4	3	2	1	0
TIC1	$1010	Bit 15	–	–	–	–	–	–	Bit 8
	$1011	Bit 7	–	–	–	–	–	–	Bit 0

		7	6	5	4	3	2	1	0
TIC2	$1012	Bit 15	–	–	–	–	–	–	Bit 8
	$1013	Bit 7	–	–	–	–	–	–	Bit 0

		7	6	5	4	3	2	1	0
TIC3	$1014	Bit 15	–	–	–	–	–	–	Bit 8
	$1015	Bit 7	–	–	–	–	–	–	Bit 0

FIGURE 6.23 Timer input-capture registers

Solution:

From Figure 6.24 and the fact that PA0 is associated with input-capture function IC3, the binary pattern is

```
7 6 5 4 3 2 1 0   ←Bit position
0 0 0 0 0 0 0 1   ←Binary pattern in TCTL2
```

The instructions to accomplish this task are

```
LDAA #%00000001 (or LDAA #$01)
STAA $1021
```

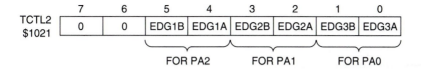

	7	6	5	4	3	2	1	0
TCTL2 $1021	0	0	EDG1B	EDG1A	EDG2B	EDG2A	EDG3B	EDG3A

FOR PA2   FOR PA1   FOR PA0

EDGxB	EDGxA	CONFIGURATION
0	0	CAPTURE DISABLED
0	1	CAPTURE ON RISING EDGES ONLY
1	0	CAPTURE ON FALLING EDGES ONLY
1	1	CAPTURE ON ANY EDGE (RISING OR FALLING)

FIGURE 6.24 The bit pattern in the TCTL2 register selects which edge (if any) will be detected. This register is cleared upon reset; thus, all input-capture functions are disabled. (Courtesy of Motorola, Inc.)

6.11.1 Enable and Status Bits

The programmer has the option of using polled or interrupt operation to jump to a service routine whenever an input capture occurs. Polled or interrupt driven requests are selected by the logic state in the TMSK1 (timer mask 1) register. A logic 0 indicates polled operation and a logic 1 is for interrupt requests. See Figure 6.25.

When an input capture occurs, the corresponding bit in the TFLG1 (timer flag 1) register is set. As with other flag bits in the MCU, the ICxF bit in the TFLG1 register is cleared either upon reset or by writing a logic 1 into the bit. The ICxF bit must be cleared before leaving the input-capture service routine; otherwise it would appear that another capture has occurred.

Example 6.16:

What instructions are needed to cause an interrupt request for an active edge on PA1 and PA2 but polled operation for an active edge on PA0?

Solution:

First determine the binary pattern that must be written to the TMSK1 register.

```
7 6 5 4 3 2 1 0   ←Bit position
0 0 0 0 0 1 1 0   ←TMSK1 binary pattern
```

The instructions are

```
LDAA #%00000110 (or LDAA #$06)
STAA $1022
```

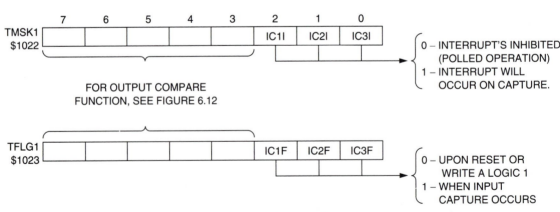

FIGURE 6.25 The logic state in the ICxI bits enable or inhibit an interrupt request whenever an input capture occurs. An ICxF bit is set when an input capture occurs. All bits in both registers are cleared upon reset.

Input-capture functions are used in applications that require measurements of pulse width, period of a waveform, or time between event intervals. Before writing a program it is best to sketch out the task you are attempting to do and identify the registers and binary patterns that will be written to them. Figure 6.26 shows this idea to measure the time duration of a short pulse width. The difference between TOC3 and TOC2 is the number of counts that occurred in the TCNT register between edge changes. Knowing the rate at which the TCNT register is being incremented, the time duration of the pulse width can be calculated.

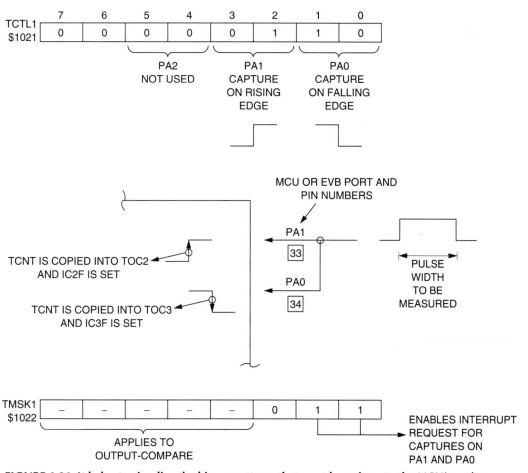

FIGURE 6.26 It helps to visualize the binary patterns that must be written to the MCU's registers before attempting to write a program.

PROBLEMS

1. How many input/output ports are available on the M68HC11 MCU and how are they labeled?
2. What are the two uses of port E on the M68HC11?
3. Explain what a bidirectional I/O port is and give one M68HC11 example.
4. A logic 1 is applied to all inputs of port E. (a) Write a BUFFALO command line to read this port. (b) Show the results (Note: Refer to Example 6.1).
5. PE7 is driven high and PE6 to PE0 are all at logic 0. You do a MD 1000 100A <ENTER>. Indicate the display.
6. Write the command lines necessary to configure port B with the following binary pattern:

$$1\ 1\ 1\ 1\ 0\ 0\ 1\ 0.$$
PB7   PB0

7. Repeat problem 6.6 for the following binary pattern:

$$0\ 1\ 0\ 1\ 1\ 0\ 1\ 1$$
PB7   PB0

8. What logic level must be written to a DDR to configure the corresponding port line as an (a) input and (b) output?
9. Use the MM command to configure the DDRC register for (a) all input port lines and (b) all output port lines.
10. Write the programming steps necessary to configure all of port D as output lines and bring all the lines to a logic low. Note: Refer to Figure 1.7 for the address of DDRD and port D.
11. The E clock signal of a typical MCU is running at 1.8MHz. If an instruction takes 3 clock cycles, how long is the instruction execution time?
12. What are the divide ratios of the E clock prescaler?
13. (a) What is the default value of the prescaler used on the EVB board? (b) Can this value be changed? Why?
14. Explain polling.
15. What does a logic 1 in the TOI bit of the TMSK2 register cause?
16. The real time flag (RTIF) bit of the TFLG2 register is set to a logic 1 at the end of each RTI period. (True/False?)
17. Determine the count value for a 1-second delay if the interval betwen interrupts is 8.19ms.
18. List the four (4) functions possible with port A.
19. What is the maximum current and voltage controllable by 1/6 of a 7407 open-collector buffer/driver?
20. Limit the LED on current in Figure 6.20(a) to 10mA by recalculating R.

21. Explain the difference between MOC3011 and MOC3031 power triacs.
22. What are the typical I_F and V_F specifications of a MOC3011 power triac?
23. Explain why a snubber circuit is not used with a zero-crossing triac?
24. Determine the value of C needed in series with a 10Ω resistor to design a triac snubber circuit with a time constant of 1.7μs for 170V.

CHAPTER 7

Designing a Temperature Measuring System with Microcontroller Display

7.0

INTRODUCTION

An overall block diagram of a temperature measuring system using a microcontroller is presented in Figure 7.1(a). The analog section of this system is an interface that converts the physical variable, temperature, into an electrical signal suitable for the MCU's analog-to-digital converter. The microcontroller section consists of the EVB hardware and a program to obtain the digital data from the A/D converter, convert the binary data to degrees Celsius, and display the result on a monitor.

Figure 7.1(b) shows that the analog interface consists of a transducer circuit plus a signal conditioning circuit. Design and operation of the analog section can be characterized by an *analog interface equation* that is obtained from the statement of the problem (see section 7.1). This chapter introduces a *procedure* that shows how to *design* such a system. The procedure begins by examining the block diagram as shown in Figure 7.1(b).

The interface will be designed by a three-step procedure. First, a suitable transducer is selected to convert the input physical variable into an electrical signal. Then the *transducer circuit's output-input equation* is derived either from manufacturer's data sheets or from measured data. The data is used to determine the

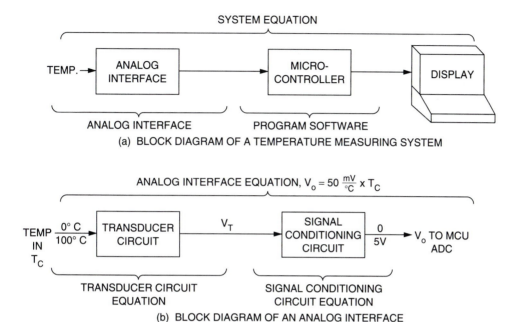

SYSTEM EQUATION

TEMP. → ANALOG INTERFACE → MICRO-CONTROLLER → DISPLAY

ANALOG INTERFACE

PROGRAM SOFTWARE

(a) BLOCK DIAGRAM OF A TEMPERATURE MEASURING SYSTEM

ANALOG INTERFACE EQUATION, $V_o = 50\ \frac{mV}{°C} \times T_C$

TEMP IN T_C — $\frac{0°\ C}{100°\ C}$ → TRANSDUCER CIRCUIT — V_T → SIGNAL CONDITIONING CIRCUIT — $\frac{0}{5V}$ → V_o TO MCU ADC

TRANSDUCER CIRCUIT EQUATION

SIGNAL CONDITIONING CIRCUIT EQUATION

(b) BLOCK DIAGRAM OF AN ANALOG INTERFACE

FIGURE 7.1 The block diagram of a microcontroller-based temperature measuring system in (a) consists of an analog section and a digital section. The analog section is represented by the block diagram in (b). Values shown come from the design example that follows.

transducer's output at upper and lower limits for corresponding input limits. Second, the two output limits are then used to derive the *signal conditioning circuit's (SCC) design equation*. Third, a standard signal conditioning circuit, whose *hardware equation* has the same general form as the SCC design equation, is chosen from the selection given in Chapter 5. Component values for the signal conditioning circuit are then calculated by direct comparison between the design and hardware equations (math-to-hardware conversion).

After the analog circuit has been designed, the program to be executed by the microcontroller will be developed and tested. This software design is presented in sections 7.7 through 7.9. Before any design begins, it is necessary to have an understanding of the problem you want the system to solve, and this is given next.

7.1

STATEMENT OF THE PROBLEM

Design a system to measure temperature in an exhaust duct and display the measurements on a computer screen at 30-second intervals for a period of 5 minutes. The anticipated temperature range is 0 to 100°C.

7.1.1 Solution

An M68HC11 microcontroller unit is selected to provide A/D conversion, binary-to-decimal conversion, timing functions, and control of the screen display. The MCU, software, and display make up the digital portion of the system. Remember the MCU has an on-board A/D converter and timer. The input range of the A/D is 0 to 5.12V.

We now have enough information from the statement of the problem and the input range of the MCU's A/D converter to begin the design by deriving the analog interface equation.

7.2

DERIVING AN ANALOG INTERFACE EQUATION

7.2.1 Introduction

This section is presented for two reasons. First, it presents the idea that a linear system's performance can be described mathematically. Second, it shows how to derive the output-input performance equation of any linear system, required signal conditioning circuit, or transducer circuit. This section also defines certain instrumentation terminology such as *range* and *span* to explain the terms of slope, sensitivity, and conversion gain.

7.2.2 Deriving the Systems Performance Equation

A block diagram of our design system is drawn in Figure 7.2(a). Temperature T_C is the input variable and is plotted on the x-axis of the graph (independent variable). The desired output display, D, is plotted on the y-axis because it is the dependent variable. Definition of the term *range* is obvious. Range identifies the upper and lower limits of the variable. Input range and output range are both equal to 0 to 100°C.

Span is defined as the difference between upper and lower limits of a range. In Figure 7.2(a), output span is $\Delta y = (100 - 0)°C = 100°C$. Input span $\Delta x = (100 - 0)°C = 100°C$. The terms *system gain, conversion gain,* or *sensitivity* convey the same meaning. They are evaluated by calculating the slope, m, of the output-input graph. By definition:

$$m = \text{gain} = \text{sensitivity} = \frac{\Delta y}{\Delta x} = \frac{\text{span out}}{\text{span in}} \tag{7.1}$$

In Figure 7.2(a), slope m is evaluated from:

$$m = \text{system sensitivity} = \frac{\Delta y}{\Delta x} = \frac{(100 - 0)°C}{(100 - 0)°C} = 1°C \text{ per } °C = 1$$

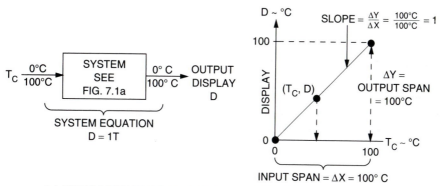

(a) THE TEMPERATURE MEASURING SYSTEM HAS AN INPUT RANGE
OF $T_C = 0$ TO 100° C AND AN OUTPUT RANGE OF 0 TO 100° C. SYSTEM
SENSITIVITY IS UNITY AND THE SYSTEM EQUATION IS OUTPUT = 1 x T

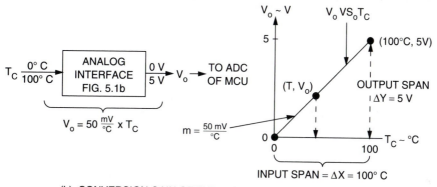

(b) CONVERSION GAIN OF THE INTERFACE IS CALCULATED FROM
THE SLOPE OF OUTPUT-INPUT CHARACTERISTIC CURVE.

FIGURE 7.2 The system equation is derived from its output-input characteristic in (a). The analog interface equation is derived from its output-input characteristic in (b).

The system equation can now be derived and forced into the standard form of a straight line:

$$y = mx + b \qquad (7.2)$$

where:

y = dependent output variable (display D)
x = independent input variable (temperature T)
m = slope of the output vs. input graph (y vs. x)
b = the y-axis intercept or *offset* (i.e. when x = 0)

The derivation begins by locating any (x,y) operating point on the graph in Figure 7.2(a) at coordinates (T_C, D). Write the slope in general terms as:

$$\text{slope} = \frac{\Delta y}{\Delta x} = \frac{D-0}{T_C-0} = \frac{D}{T_C}$$

Equate the general slope with the value of slope

$$m = \frac{D}{T_C} = 1$$

Rearranging this equation so that it corresponds to the standard form yields

$$y = mx$$

$$D = \left(\frac{1\,°C}{°C}\right) \times T_C \tag{7.3}$$

where units of $T_C = °C$ and the display units are also $°C$. For example, if input $T_C = 25°C$, output D will show 25 $°C$. The offset term is zero in Eq. (7.3) because the straight line passes through the origin. See Figure 7.2(a).

7.3

THE ANALOG INTERFACE EQUATION

Draw a block diagram of the analog interface as shown in Figure 7.2(b). Show the input range for T_C. Choose a convenient output range of 0 to 5.0V for the M68HC11 MCU A/D converter's input capacity of 5.12V. Lay out input T_C on the x-axis and output V_o on the y-axis. Plot and draw a line between *end points* at coordinates (0°C, 0V) and (100°C, 5V). This forms a graph of the analog interface output-input characteristic. Its equation is derived in the next example.

Example 7.1:

Derive an analog interface equation for the output-input characteristic shown in Figure 7.2(b). Calculate conversion gain of the interface.

Solution:

Evaluate the output span = $(5 - 0)V = 5V = \Delta V_o$. Evaluate the input span = $(100 - 0)°C = \Delta T_C = 100°C$. Calculate the slope (conversion gain) from Eq. (7.1):

$$\text{conversion gain} = \frac{\Delta V_o}{\Delta T_C} = \frac{5V}{100°C} = 50\,\frac{mV}{°C} = \text{slope}$$

An equation of the graph's slope is determined by locating a general operating point at coordinates (T_C, V_o) as shown in Figure 7.2(b).

$$\frac{\Delta V_o}{\Delta T_C} = \frac{V_o - 0V}{T_C - 0°C} = \frac{V_o}{T_C} = \text{slope in general terms}$$

Equate the general slope to the conversion gain given in Example 7.1:

$$\frac{V_o}{T_C} = 50 \frac{mV}{^\circ C}$$

Solving for the output V_o yields the analog interface equation in the standard form:

$$V_o = \frac{50mV}{^\circ C} \times T_C$$

7.4

DESIGNING THE ANALOG INTERFACE

7.4.1   Introduction

The analog interface consists of a transducer circuit and a signal conditioning circuit, as shown in Figure 7.1(b). It can be designed using the three-step procedure given in section 7.0. As a refresher, the procedure is summarized: (1) derive the transducer equation; (2) derive the signal conditioning circuit design equation; and (3) compare the SCC design equation with a carefully chosen signal conditioning circuit's hardware equation to complete the design.

7.4.2 The Transducer Equation, Step 1

Recall that the problem (section 7.1) is to measure temperature in an exhaust duct. This infers that the transducer will be located some distance from its signal conditioning circuit. We therefore choose the AD590 IC temperature transducer because it generates an output current proportional to absolute input temperature. A current signal is independent of the length of an insulated twisted wire pair. A transducer with a voltage output, however, would be subject to voltage drops between it and the signal conditioning circuit, which may be up to hundreds of feet away.

Figure 7.3(a) shows pinouts of the AD590 along with its thermal resistance and thermal time constant in still air. The circuit symbol is drawn in Figure 7.3(b). The manufacturer (Analog Devices, Inc.) specifies that the AD590 has a nominal temperature coefficient (conversion gain) of $1\mu A/^\circ K$, so its transducer equation is:

$$I_T = \frac{1\mu A}{^\circ K} \times T_K \tag{7.4a}$$

We substitute into Equation (7.4a) for T_K from the temperature conversion equations:

$$T_K = T_C + 273.2^\circ C \text{ and } T_C = \frac{5}{9}(T_F - 32^\circ F)$$

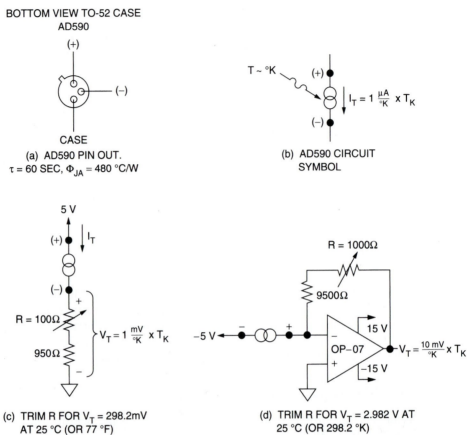

(a) AD590 PIN OUT.
$\tau = 60$ SEC, $\Phi_{JA} = 480$ °C/W

(b) AD590 CIRCUIT SYMBOL

(c) TRIM R FOR $V_T = 298.2$mV AT 25 °C (OR 77 °F)

(d) TRIM R FOR $V_T = 2.982$ V AT 25 °C (OR 298.2 °K)

FIGURE 7.3 The AD590 temperature transducer has the pinout shown in (a) and circuit symbol in (b). Output current is proportional to absolute temperature in degrees Kelvin (°K). Self-heating and tolerance errors are trimmed by the current-to-voltage converter circuits of (c) and (d).

to obtain the transducer equations:

$$I_T = \frac{1\mu A}{°K} T_K \tag{7.4a}$$

$$I_T = \frac{1\mu A}{°C}(T_C) + 273.2\mu A \tag{7.4b}$$

$$I_T = \frac{0.555\mu A}{°F}(T_F) + 255.4\mu A \tag{7.4c}$$

The nominal transducer equations above may be different for your transducer due to manufacturing tolerance limits. See Figure 7.3(c) for trimming techniques. The transducer equation for *any* linear transducer can be determined by measurements of two operating points. See Example 7.2.

Example 7.2:

Output currents from the AD590 are measured as $I_T = 298\mu A$ and $323\mu A$ at 25°C and 50°C respectively. Derive its transducer equation.

Solution:

Lay out input temperature T_C on the x-axis and output current I_T on the y-axis to plot measured data points at coordinates (25°C, 298μA) and (50°C, 323μA). See Figure 7.4. To graph I_T vs. T_C characteristic, connect these points. Evaluate the slope or Tempco (temperature coefficient) from Equation (7.1):

$$\frac{\Delta y}{\Delta x} = \frac{\Delta I_T}{\Delta T_C} = \frac{(323 - 298)\mu A}{(50 - 25)°C} = \frac{25\mu A}{25°C} = \frac{1\mu A}{°C}$$

Write the general slope $\dfrac{\Delta y}{\Delta x} = \dfrac{I_T - 298\mu A}{T_C - 25°C}$

Equate slopes and solve for I_T in standard form:

$$\frac{I_T - 298\mu A}{T_C - 25°C} = \frac{1\mu A}{°C} \qquad \text{or} \qquad I_T - 298\mu A = \frac{1\mu A}{°C}T_C - 25\mu A$$

$$I_T = \frac{1\mu A}{°C} \times T_C + 273\mu A \tag{7.5}$$

The equation for your transducer is important *because it is used to predict its output range* for the design problem.

Example 7.3:

Calculate the output current range of the transducer in Example 7.2 for (a) an input range of the problem, 0 to 100°C, (b) an operating range of the AD590, $-55°C$ to $+150°C$.

Solution:

Substitute values for T_C to evaluate I_T in Equation (7.5). The results are:

(a) $I_T = 273\mu A$ at 0°C and 373μA at 100°C.
(b) $I_T = 218\mu A$ at $-55°C$ and 423μA at 150°C.

The second part of the analog interface is the signal conditioning circuit.

7.4.3 Signal Conditioning Circuit Design Equation, Step 2

What must the signal conditioning circuit (SCC) do to interface or convert the transducer's output range of 273 to 373μA (Examples 7.2 and 7.3a) into the 0 to 5V range (section 7.3, Figures 7.1(b) and 7.2(b)) required by the MCU's A/D converter? The answer to this question is clearly described by the *signal conditioning circuit design equation*.

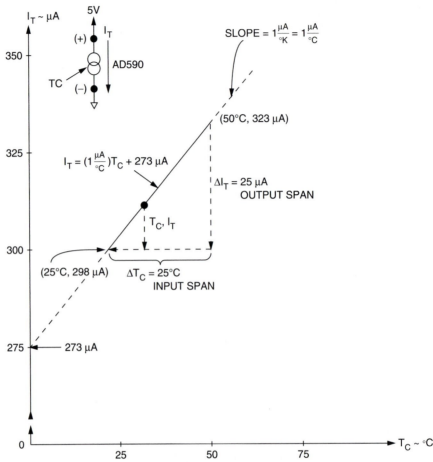

(A) THE AD590'S TRANSDUCER EQUATION IS DERIVED FROM A
GRAPH OF ITS I_T VS. T_C CHARACTERISTIC AS IN EXAMPLE 7.2

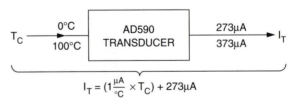

(B) BLOCK DIAGRAM OF THE TESTED TRANSDUCER. VALUES
FOR THE INPUT, AND OUTPUT RANGES OF THE DESIGN
PROBLEM ARE CALCULATED FROM THE DESIGN EQUATION,
SEE EXAMPLE 7.3

**FIGURE 7.4 The equation for any linear transducer can be derived from any two
measured operating points in (a). The transducer's output range can then be
calculated as in (b) for any given input range.**

Begin to derive the SCC design equation by drawing a block diagram of the analog interface in Figure 7.5(a). Enter values for the (a) temperature input range, $T_C = 0$ to 100°C, (b) corresponding transducer output range $I_T = 273$ to 373 μA, and (c) corresponding SCC output range $V_o = 0$ to 5V. For completeness and sound engineering practice, also show both analog interface and transducer equations.

Next assign SCC input I_T to the x-axis and SCC output V_o to the y-axis in Figure 7.5(b). Plot (x,y) operating points for the range limits at coordinates (273μA,0V) and (373μA,5V). Connect them with a solid line to graph the required output-input performance of the SCC design equation. Derive the design equation from the graph as follows:

(a) Evaluate slope from Eq. (7.1):

$$m = \frac{\Delta V_o}{\Delta I_T} = \frac{(5-0)V}{(373-273)\mu A} = \frac{5V}{100\mu A} = 50,000 \ \frac{V}{A} = 50k\Omega$$

The units for slope, m, are ohms (volts per amp).

(b) Locate a general (x,y) point (I_T, V_o) to get the general slope:

$$m = \frac{(V_o - 0)V}{(I_T - 273)\mu A} = \frac{V_o}{(I_T - 273)\mu A}$$

(c) Equating slopes, we obtain the general form $y = mx + b$:

$$\frac{V_o}{(I_T - 273)\mu A} = 50k\Omega$$

$$V_o = 50k\Omega \, (I_T - 273)\mu A$$

To obtain the SCC design equation:

$$V_o = (50k\Omega) \, I_T - 13.65V \tag{7.6}$$

The SCC design equation is very important because it clearly and simply "tells" how to design hardware to implement this equation. (It minimizes the need for intuition or broad analog design experience.) Equation (7.6) states that input current I_T must be converted to a voltage by passing it through a 50kΩ resistor and then *offsetting* the result by −13.65V. Therefore, look for hardware that is a current-to-voltage converter circuit with an inverting adder or offset feature. It will be easy to identify because its *signal conditioning circuit hardware equation* will have the *same* general form as the SCC design equation.

7.4.4   Designing SCC Hardware, Step 3

From the SCC circuits presented in Chapter 5 we select a trial current-to-voltage converter circuit with offset as given in Figure 7.6(a). Write its output-input (hardware) equation: Note: Figure 7.6(a) is similar to Fig. 5.17.

SCC Hardware Equation: $V_o = R_F I_T - \dfrac{R_F V}{R}$ $\tag{7.7}$

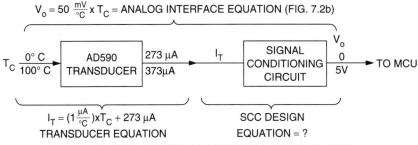

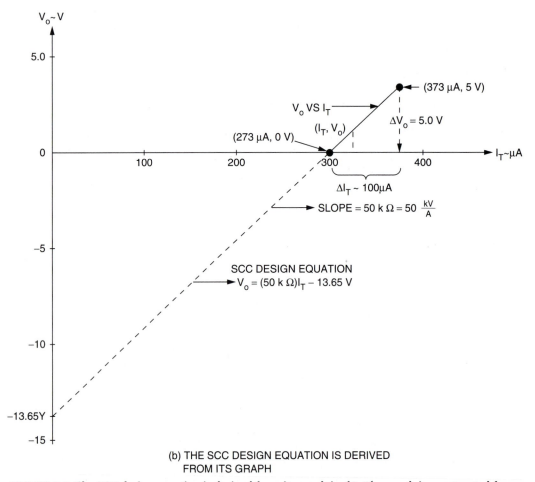

$$I_T = (1 \frac{\mu A}{\degree C})\times T_C + 273 \ \mu A$$
TRANSDUCER EQUATION

SCC DESIGN
EQUATION = ?

(a) THE SCC MUST CONVERT AN INPUT RANGE OF 273μA TO
373 μA INTO AN OUTPUT RANGE OF 0 TO 5V. END POINTS
OF THE RANGE ARE PLOTTED IN (b) TO GRAPH THE REQUIRED
SCC DESIGN EQUATION.

(b) THE SCC DESIGN EQUATION IS DERIVED
FROM ITS GRAPH

FIGURE 7.5 The SCC design equation is derived from its graph in (b). The graph is constructed from range data shown on the block diagram of the SCC in (a).

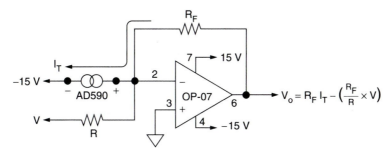

(a) THIS TRIAL SCC HARDWARE CIRCUIT HAS AN OUTPUT-
INPUT EQUATION WITH THE SAME FORM AS THE SCC
DESIGN EQUATION (7.6)

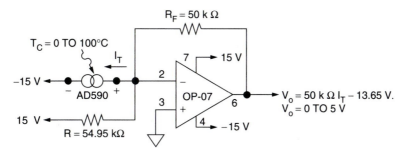

(b) IDEALIZED SIGNAL CONDITIONING CIRCUIT AND THE
AD590 MAKE UP THE ANALOG INTERFACE.

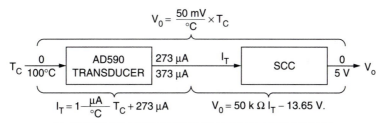

(c) BLOCK DIAGRAM OF THE ANALOG INTERFACE IN (b)

**FIGURE 7.6 A trial hardware circuit is selected in (a). Its hardware
equation is compared with the SCC design equation to find component
values for the analog interface in (b). A block diagram of the interface is
given in (b).**

Write the required design equation from Equation (7.6).

SCC Design Equation: $V_o = (50k\Omega)I_T - 13.65V$

Note that each equation must be in the standard form, $y = mx + b$ or $y = gain$
$term$ times $input$ $variable$ plus $offset$ $term$. A technique to design component

values to implement Eq. (7.6) becomes obvious by comparing it term-by-term to Eq. (7.7).

Step 1. Equate the gain terms:

$R_F \times I_T = (50k\Omega)I_T$, solve for R_F:
$R_F = 50k\Omega$

Note: R_F could be adjusted to *trim the slope* in Figure 7.2(b) and Eq. (7.6).

Step 2. Equate the offset terms:

Substitute the value of R_F obtained in step 1, and equating the offset terms of Eqs. (7.6) and (7.7) yields:

$$-\frac{(50k\Omega)\ V}{R} = -13.65V \tag{7.8}$$

There are two unknowns, V and R. V must be positive to satisfy the equality. For economy, choose the op amp's positive supply voltage; then $V = +15V$. Substitute into Eq. (7.8) and solve for R.

$$-\frac{50k\Omega(15V)}{R} = -13.65V$$

$$R = 50k\Omega \left(\frac{15V}{13.65V} \right) = 54.95k\Omega$$

The idealized values for the SCC are shown in Figure 7.6(b). $R_F = 50k\Omega$, R = 54.95kΩ, and V = 15.0V. A block diagram for the completed analog interface is given in Figure 7.6(c) and includes the actual transducer, SCC, and analog interface equations. Compare this figure with those pointing the way to its successful design—Figures 7.1 through 7.5.

Example 7.4:

Calculate (a) I_T and (b) V_o for the analog interface in Figures 7.6(b) and 7.6(c) if $T_C = 50°C$.

Solution:

(a) From Equation (7.5):

$$I_T = \frac{1\mu A}{°C} \times 50°C + 273\mu A = 50\mu A + 273\mu A = 323\mu A$$

(b) From Eq. (7.6):

$$V_o = (50k\Omega)(323\mu A) - 13.65V = 16.15V - 13.65V = 2.5V$$

Check against analog interface Eq. (7.3):

$$V_o = 50 \frac{\mu V}{°C} \times 50°C = 2.5V$$

7.5

▬▬▬

TRANSDUCER SELF-HEATING ERROR

7.5.1 Cause and Effect

The AD590, like all semiconductor temperature transducers, requires power to sense its own thermal environment. Current through and voltage across the AD590 develops an internal power P_D. P_D is all converted into heat energy that self-heats the transducer above the ambient temperature T_A by a temperature increase ΔT. The amount of self-heating is given by:

$$\Delta T = \theta_{JA} P_D \qquad (7.9a)$$

where θ_{JA} = thermal resistance junction-to-ambient in °C/W or °C/mW and

$$P_D = I_T V_{AD590} \qquad (7.9b)$$

where V_{AD590} = voltage drop across the AD590. Actual internal junction temperature T_J of the AD590 that determines I_T is:

$$T_J = T_A + \Delta T \qquad (7.9c)$$

The effect of self-heating is illustrated by an example.

Example 7.5:

Thermal resistance θ_{JA} = 480°C/W for the AD590 in Figure 7.6(b). Calculate its temperature rise due to self-heating in ambient temperatures of 0°C and 100°C.

Solution:

From Eq. (7.5), I_T = 273µA at 0°C and 373µA at 100°C. From Eq. (7.9b), with V_{AD590} = 15V:

P_D = 273µA × 15V = 4.1mW at 0°C and
P_D = 373µA × 15V = 5.6mW at 100°C

ΔT is found from Equation (7.9a):

$$\Delta T = 480 \, \frac{°C}{W} \times 4.1mW = 2.0°C \text{ at } 0°C$$

$$\Delta T = 480 \, \frac{°C}{W} \times 5.6mW = 2.7°C \text{ at } 100°C$$

7.5.2 Minimizing Self-heating Errors

Self-heating can be reduced by reducing either thermal resistance or power dissipated. See Eq. (7.9(a)). Thermal resistance can be reduced by properly mounting the transducer on a heat sink to increase its mass. However, this action will increase the transducer's time constant and slow its response. Thermal resistance can also be reduced by immersion in a fluid or forcing air by it with a fan. Neither reduction technique is appropriate to our problem of measuring exhaust temperature.

The only way left to reduce self-heating in a current source like the AD590 is to reduce its terminal voltage. The AD590 needs at least 4V across it for proper operation. Thus, the −15V supply voltage in Figure 7.6(b) could be replaced with a −5V IC voltage source, to reduce V, P_D, and ΔT by one-third. Since only a −15V source is available, we will add a dissipating resistor, R_D, in series with the AD590 to "drop" 10V out of the −15V supply voltage.

A value for R_D is calculated by assigning it to drop 10V when I_T is highest at 100°C or 373μA.

$$R_D = \frac{10V}{373\mu A} = 25k\Omega$$

Now R_D absorbs 10V × 373μA = 3.7mW away from the AD590 that now develops only 5V × 373μA = 1.8mW. The AD590 self-heats by only 1.8mW × 480°C/W = 0.9°C. This error can easily be trimmed out by the calibration procedure shown in the next section.

7.6

CALIBRATION PROCEDURE

7.6.1   Need for Calibration

Calibration error is defined as the difference between actual temperature and indicated temperature. Let us examine possible sources of error in the analog interface circuit of Figure 7.6(b).

Bias currents (±1nA) and input offset voltage of 30μV for the OP-07 op amp are negligible in this application. If R_F is a 50kΩ, 1% resistor, the 50mV/°C slope of the analog interface equation can be off by ±1%. An AD590L can have a ±3°C error over its rated performance range of −55°C to 150°C. This error and self-heating error is reasonably constant and can be trimmed out with a slope adjustment using R_F. Resistor R is nowhere near a standard 10% value and its 15V stable regulated supply voltage can be high or low by ±0.5V to affect the offset voltage. The net effect of all these possible error sources can be minimized by modifying the circuit of Figure 7.6(b) so that it can be calibrated.

7.6.2   Circuit Modifications

The interface circuit of Figure 7.6(b) will be modified so that it can be (a) calibrated, and (equally important) (b) tested. Section 7.5.2 showed that self-heating by the AD590 could be reduced by about two-thirds if we add a 25kΩ series heat-dissipating resistor, R_D. Refer to Figure 7.7. Add a 10kΩ, 1% resistor R_{D2} and a

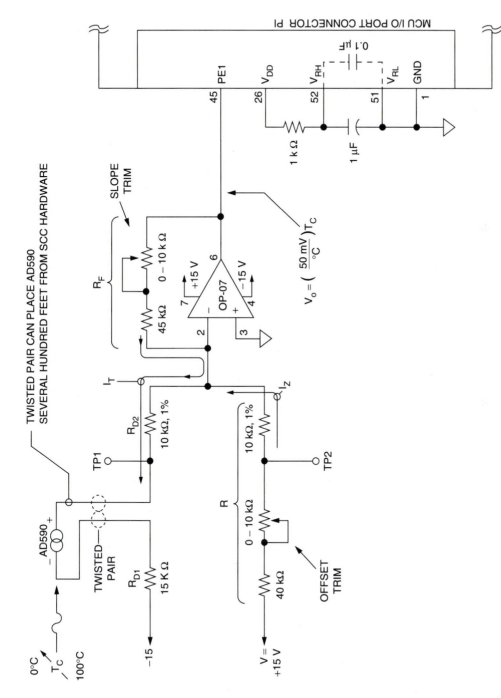

FIGURE 7.7 The analog interface in Figure 7.6(b) is modified by (a) adding heat transfer resistor R_{D1} and I_T, measuring resistor R_{D2}, (b) substituting a 10kΩ variable resistor and a 10kΩ, 1% resistor for a portion of R to null the circuit, and (c) changing R_F to allow slope or full-scale calibration.

223

15kΩ, 5% resistor R_{D1} to make up the necessry 25kΩ. Test point 1 can be brought out to allow for testing AD590 current I_T. Pin 2 of the op amp is at virtual ground, so I_T is measured by measuring the voltage at TP1 and calculating I_T from:

$$I_T = \frac{|V_{TP1}|}{10k\Omega} \tag{7.10a}$$

T_C will then be indicated as:

$$T_C = (I_T - 273\mu A) \times \frac{1°C}{\mu A} \tag{7.10b}$$

The 54.95kΩ resistor R of Figure 7.6(b) is replaced by a 40kΩ, 5%, 10kΩ, 1% for TP2 and 10kΩ variable resistor as in Figure 7.7. Feedback resistor R_F is made adjustable by substituting a 45kΩ ±5% resistor and a 10kΩ variable resistor.

7.6.3   Calibration Procedure

One typical calibration procedure encountered in the literature proceeds as follows:

1. With sensor at $T_C = 0°C$, trim R for $V_o = 0V$(null adjust).
2. With sensor at $T_C = 100°C$, adjust R_F for full-scale output of $V_o = 5.0V$ (slope or sensitivity adjust).
3. Repeat 1 and 2 as required, until both points are fixed.

This advice is useless if you do not have a precision, variable temperature chamber and unlimited time. A faster, more practical calibration procedure employs the following principles:

(a) *Assume* that the AD590 is at $T_C = 0°C$. I_T will then equal 273μA from Eq. (7.4b). Then if current I_Z is adjusted to 273μA, both I_T and I_Z will sum to zero. No current flows through R_F, making its value irrelevant and V_o will equal 0V. I_Z will equal 273μA when voltage at TP2 is

$$V_{TP2} = 273\mu A \times 10k\Omega = 2.73V$$

Thus adjusting the offset 10kΩ variable resistor for $V_{TP2} = 2.73V$ "nulls," "zeroes," or establishes a correct offset for the analog interface.

(b) Measure temperature T_C.

V_o should equal 50mV/°C times T_C. Adjust R_F until V_o equals this value (slope adjustment).

The new calibration procedure now is:

(a) Trim R until $V_{TP2} = 2.732V$.
(b) Trim R_F until $V_o = (50mV/°C) \times T_C$.

With the analog interface completed we next turn to the l software design to implement the remaining requirements of the problem given in Section 7.1.

7.7

SOFTWARE DESIGN

Before we start to write the program for this application, let's review the statement of the problem so that we may list and understand what has to be done. From section 7.1, the key software tasks of this application are:

1. Measure a temperature at 30-second intervals for 5 minutes;
2. The temperature range is from 0 to 100°C;
3. Display the temperature readings on a monitor.

From this listing, we see that there are routines we have already written and used in previous chapters. For example, we can use a timing delay routine from Chapter 6, a measurement reading routine for the MCU's A/D converter from Chapter 5, and display data routines using the EVB utility subroutines from Chapter 4. These routines, plus additional ones, are required to solve the software design portion for this application. One of the additional routines is to scale the digital input data to degrees Celsius. Another routine is to round off the temperature to the nearest tenth of a degree. Although this last routine is not strictly required (from the statement of the problem), it may be nice to include.

Most application programs usually begin by initializing counters and clearing any memory locations that will be used as temporary registers or buffers. Now our list of tasks to be done is longer and more complete. We need to put them in logical order and see if they accomplish all the requirements stated in the original statement of the problem.

A way to visualize and interconnect these tasks is by using a flow chart. Figure 7.8 shows an overall flow chart for this application. The column titled *application routines* lists the labels used in section 7.7. This should allow the reader to easily refer to the next section to check the actual line code for that portion of the application.

The following subsections follow the flow chart of Figure 7.8 and the reader should refer to section 7.8 for the instructions of each routine.

7.7.1   Initialize the Interval Counter

In the statement of the problem described in section 7.1, and reviewed in section 7.7, the MCU was being used to take measurements at 30-second intervals for a period of 5 minutes. Thus, there must be 2 measurements every minute for 5 minutes, or a total of 10 measurements. Although either accumulator A or B could be used to store the count value, the accumulators will be used in the main part of the program. Therefore, let's choose a temporary RAM location and label

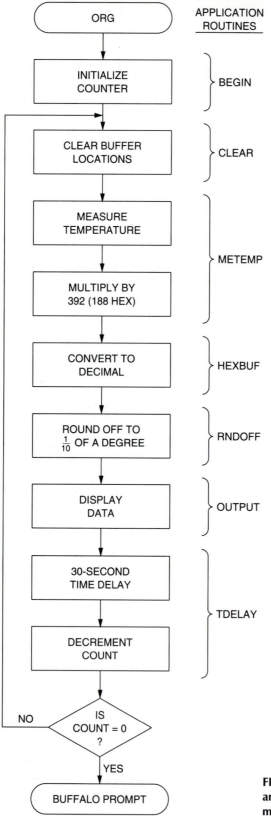

FIGURE 7.8 Flow chart for obtaining and displaying data of a temperature measuring system.

it INTCNT, for interval count, to store the value. We will use the assembler directive RMB (reserve memory byte) to assign a RAM location. Now the counter register location can be initialized as

```
LDAA    #10         Count value
STAA    INTCNT      Store count value in a register labeled
                    INTCNT (location $D70F)
```

These are the first two lines of code of the application program given in section 7.8.

7.7.2   Clear Memory Buffers

When power is applied, random data appears in the RAM locations. Although this random data is overwritten when a location is used, there are some locations that we want to be sure contain logic 0s before we start or when we loop through the program. For this reason, let's include a short routine that clears all the memory buffer locations before we use them each time. However, the INTCNT location cannot be cleared because it is keeping a record of how many temperature readings must still be taken. *Be sure not to clear this location.* The actual number of locations and the starting location to be cleared are usually not known until you have finished the program, at which time you return to this routine and enter the number and the starting location. For now the authors will tell you that the total number of locations used for temporary data for this application is 15 and the first location is labeled ADBUFF. Refer to section 7.8, and the routine labeled CLEAR, and see how a short looping program stores logic 0s in the buffer locations ($D700–$D70E).

7.7.3   METEMP Routine

This routine is an expanded version of using the MCU's A/D converter introduced in Chapter 5. In this application, the METEMP routine accomplishes five tasks. They are: (1) initialize the A/D control register (ADCTL), (2) execute a short time delay program so that the A/D has enough time to complete a conversion, (3) read the digital value from an A/D storage register, (4) scale the digital value to degrees Celsius, and (5) store the scaled value in a 3-byte buffer. Although this routine accomplishes many tasks, it only requires 12 instructions. Let's see how each task is done.

A/D CNTL Register

In Chapter 5, you learned the programming steps necessary to set up the analog-to-digital converter's control register for a variety of applications. In our present temperature monitoring system, let's select the continuous scan mode and use channel 1 for the input signal from the signal conditioning circuit. See Figure 7.9. This information allows us to determine the binary pattern that must be stored in the A/D control (ADCTL) register at location $1030. Also from Chapter 5, we learned that the binary pattern sent to bits 0–3 selects the channel. Bit 4 is the multiple or single channel control bit; a logic 0 selects single control. Bit 5 is the scan control bit; a logic 1 selects the continous convert mode. Bit 6 is not used by the ADCTL register, but since the CPU puts a logic state on all data bus lines during a write operation let's choose a logic 0 for bit 6. Bit 7 is a status bit and thus can only be read. Any data sent to this bit is never stored. But once again, the programmer needs to account for each bit in order to write the line of code that initializes the A/D converter. From Figure 7.9, the binary pattern 00100001 = 21_{hex} and the programming steps are:

```
LDAA  #$21    Control word in hex.
STAA  ADCTL   Store the control word at location labeled
              ADCTL (ADCTL is location $1030).
```

A/D Time Delay

These few lines of code provide a delay loop so that the microcontroller's A/D converter has sufficient time to convert the analog signal to digital. This concept was introduced in Chapter 3 (Examples 3.19 and 3.20), and also used in Chapter 5. A register is loaded with a count value which is decremented once each time through the loop and only when the count equals zero does the program execution continue. Since the CPU requires a certain amount of time to execute each

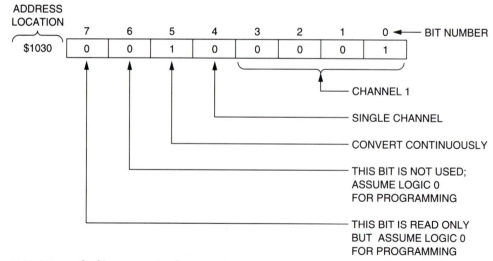

FIGURE 7.9 The binary pattern that must be sent to ADCTL, location 1030_{hex}, to initialize the converter section of the MCU ($0010001 = 21_{hex}$).

instruction, a timing delay is created. The lines of code for a sufficient time delay loop are:

```
        LDAB  #$26   Initialize accumulator B with the count.
DELAY:  DECB         Decrement acumulator B.
        BNE   DELAY  If count =/= 0, branch back to DELAY.
```

Read A/D Register

Since we have programmed the A/D's control register (ADCTL) for single-channel operation and the continuous convert mode, the four A/D registers (locations $1031–$1034) are being continuously updated. Remember, the A/D converter section does the update on nonread cycles so the data is always valid. In this application, it is possible to read any of the four registers because the incoming analog signal from a temperature monitoring system does not change quickly. For programming purposes let's choose register 1, which is location $1031 (or label ADR1). To temporarily store data so that it can be used later, let's choose a location labeled ADBUFF. The programming steps to read the A/D converter and move the data to a temporary memory location are:

```
    LDAA ADR1    Read the contents of A/D register 1.
    STAA ADBUFF  Store the binary data temporarily.
```

Refer to section 7.8 and note that the assembler directive EQU has been used to set ADR1 equal to $1031 and the directive RMB has set ADBUFF equal to $D700.

Multiply by 392 (188_{hex})

This temperature measuring system is being designed for a range from 0 to 100°C. The analog interface circuitry (sections 7.2 to 7.6) signal conditioned this temperature range for 0 to 5.00V, which is the approximate full range of the MCU's A/D converter. Since the converter is an 8-bit unit, there are $2^8 = 256$ counts which range from 0 to 255_{dec}. Thus at 0°C the count is 0_{dec} (00_{hex}) and at 100°C the count is 255_{dec} (FF_{hex}). Each count or bit represents

$$\frac{100°C}{255} = 0.392°C/bit$$

The A/D register is read, data is temporarily stored, and then multiplied by 0.392°C/bit. The result is the temperature in degrees Celsius, which then can be displayed. The value of 0.392 causes a small error due to rounding off. At 100°C the error is 0.04°C. Since this is much less than the sensitivity of the transducer, it will not be a major practical concern in most designs.

Since 0.392 (392×10^{-3}) is a constant, it can become a fixed value in the program. The multiplying instruction in the CPU operates on binary numbers and the program must contain the hexadecimal equivalent of 392 or 188_{hex}. As shown in the flow chart of Figure 7.8, the remaining program steps convert the product back to decimal, move the decimal point, and display the final answer. The handling of the location of the decimal point and the display of the answer are given in section 7.7.6. This section describes the steps involved in multiplying the digital input data (DID) by 188_{hex}. The procedure is

$$Product = DID \times 188 \tag{7.11a}$$

which can be written as

$$Product = DID (100) + DID (88) \tag{7.11b}$$

Since the range of the digital input data is from 00_{hex} to FF_{hex}, Eq. (7.11b) shows how quickly the product of DID $\times$ 188 can be obtained. The first term, DID (100) = DID 00, is nothing more than the digital input data expressed as a 16-bit number with the least significant 8 bits all logic 0s. This is easily accomplished by reserving two bytes and storing the result of the A/D register 1 (ADR1) in the high byte with the low byte all logic 0s. This 2-byte buffer is labeled ADBUFF.

The second term of Eq. (7.11b) is only an 8-bit by 8-bit multiplication which can be accomplished by the MUL instruction. Let's do an example showing how the product is obtained using Eqs. (7.11a and b) before referring to actual programming steps.

Example 7.6:

Show that Eq. (7.11b) yields the same result as Eq. (7.11a) for the following digital input data: (a) FF_{hex}, b) 05_{hex}.

Solution:

(a) Applying Equation (7.11a) yields

$$
\begin{array}{r}
188 \\
\times\, FF \\
\hline
16F8 \\
16F8 \\
\hline
18678 \leftarrow \text{Hex value}
\end{array}
$$

Applying Equation (7.11b) we obtain

$$FF(188) = \underbrace{FF(100)}_{FF00} + \underbrace{FF\,(88)}_{}$$

$$
\begin{array}{r}
88 \\
\times\, FF \\
\hline
8778 \\
+FF00 \\
\hline
18678 \leftarrow \text{Hex value}
\end{array}
$$

Thus, the same hexadecimal value is obtained. Figure 7.10 shows the contents of ADBUFF and the MCU's register. Note that $18678_{hex} = 99,960_{dec}$. A conversion routine is given in Section 7.7.4. Since the decimal point will be

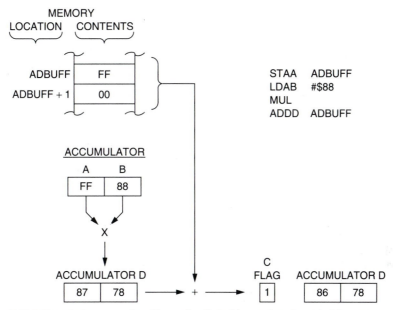

FIGURE 7.10 An example of how the digital input data is scaled by 392 (188_{hex}) mV/bit in four instructions. The decimal point will be included at a later programming step.

moved three places to the left, the final answer will be 99.96. Remember that the digital input data value of FF_{hex} is for a measured temperature of 100°C. The reason for the difference of 0.04 has been previously discussed. However, another routine has been included as part of this application program to round off the final answer to the nearest tenth of a degree, so the result of 99.96 will be rounded off to 100°C. See section 7.7.4.

(b) From Eq. (7.11a):

$$(5) \times (188) = 7A8_{hex}$$

From Eq. (7.11b)

$$(5) \times (188) = \underbrace{5(100)}_{500} + \underbrace{5(88)}_{88}$$

$$\begin{array}{r} 88 \\ \times 5 \\ \hline 2A8 \\ + 500 \\ \hline 7A8 \end{array}$$

The last six lines of code of the METEMP routine in section 7.8 show how the digital input data is multiplied by 188_{hex} and stored in a memory buffer labeled HEXBUFF . Three bytes of RAM, labeled HEXBUF, are reserved to store the answer. Note: the multiplication of the digital input data by 100 is accomplished by

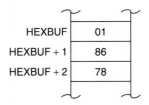

HEXBUF	01
HEXBUF + 1	86
HEXBUF + 2	78

FIGURE 7.11 The answer of Figure 7.10 is stored in a RAM buffer labeled HEXBUF. In this application, the physical addresses are $D702–$D704.

the STAA ADBUFF instruction. The reason is that the ADBUFF is two bytes and the contents of accumulator A is stored in the high byte with low byte preloaded with logic 0s.

The last instruction, ROL HEXBUF, saves the carry flag because, depending on the DID value, there may be a carry as a result of the ADDD ADBUFF instruction. Figure 7.11 shows how the answer of part (a) of this example is stored in HEXBUF. Refer to the routine labeled MTEMP in section 7.8 for the instructions and comments.

7.7.4   HEXBCD Routine

In Chapter 3, we used a general program that converted a 16-bit number to an unpacked binary coded decimal (BCD) value. That program is fast and will be used as part of the application programs of Chapters 8 and 10. However, it cannot be used to convert a 24-bit number to BCD and this is what is needed for this application. The procedure described in this section can be modified for any binary to BCD conversion. This conversion routine comes from a program published by Motorola in their M68HC11 Reference Manual. It is based on subtraction and uses a counter to record the number of times the subtraction result is positive. If the result is negative, an addition is done to restore the value and the count value is decremented by 1 and saved. Then the counter is reset to perform the next sequence of subtractions.

The program begins by setting a counter to 1 and then subtracting the greatest power of ten (see Table 7.1) from the number to be converted. If the result is positive (C flag = 0), the counter is incremented and another subtraction is done. If the result is negative (C flag = 1), the number is restored and the count value −1

TABLE 7.1   Highest Power-of-Ten Used for Converting from Binary to BCD

Numbers of Bits	Power-of-Ten	
	Decimal	Hexidecimal
8	100	64
16	10,000	2710
24	10,000,000	989680

is stored. The procedure continues to the next lower power of ten. Figure 7.12 illustrates how this procedure is used to convert the 8-bit number FF_{hex} to 255_{dec}. Remember $64_{hex} = 100_{dec}$ and $0A_{hex} = 10_{dec}$. The C flag for subtraction operations is known as the borrow flag or borrow bit.

The general routine for converting a 24-bit number to an 8-byte unpacked BCD value is given in section 7.8 under the label of HEXBCD. The number to be converted comes from a memory buffer labeled HEXBUF and the result is stored in a memory buffer labeled BCDBUF. A memory map guide is shown in Figure 7.13. As you will see in sections 7.8 and 7.9, the BCDBUF follows the HEXBUF in RAM. A flow chart for the HEXBCD routine is given in Figure 7.14.

7.7.5   RNDOFF Routine

This routine is used in this application and in Chapter 8. In this chapter, it is used to round off the temperature to the nearest tenth of a degree. In the next chapter, it is used to round off the total cost of a product to the nearest cent.

```
                                              COUNT
                                    COUNT     VALUE
                                    VALUE     STORED
            FF  –  64  =  9B          1
            9B  –  64  =  37          2
            37  –  64  =  D3          3  –  1  =  2
                          ⨆

          NEGATIVE RESULT
            C FLAG = 1

      RESTORE VALUE BY ADDING
            D3 + 64 = [1]37

                      IGNORE CARRY

          37  –  0A  =  2D          1
          2D  –  0A  =  23          2
          23  –  0A  =  19          3
          19  –  0A  =  0F          4
          0F  –  0A  =  05          5
          05  –  0A  =  FB          6  –  1  =  5
                        ⨆

        NEGATIVE RESULT
          C FLAG = 1

    RESTORE VALUE BY ADDING
          FB + 0A = [1] 05 ➝ STORE RESULT ➝ 5

                  IGNORE CARRY              BCD
                                           VALUE
```

FIGURE 7.12 Example showing the steps to convert FF_{hex} to BCD using a subtraction procedure.

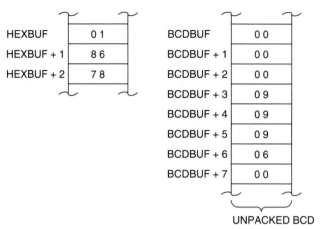

HEXBUF	0 1
HEXBUF + 1	8 6
HEXBUF + 2	7 8

BCDBUF	0 0
BCDBUF + 1	0 0
BCDBUF + 2	0 0
BCDBUF + 3	0 9
BCDBUF + 4	0 9
BCDBUF + 5	0 9
BCDBUF + 6	0 6
BCDBUF + 7	0 0

UNPACKED BCD

FIGURE 7.13 The HEXBCD routine converts a 24-bit number to an 8-byte unpacked BCD result. The physical addresses for the BCDBUF in this application are $D705–$D70C.

Figure 7.15(a) shows the contents of BCDBUF for an input temperature of 100°C (FF × 188 = 18678_{hex} = 99960_{dec}). The roundoff routine checks the next to the least significant byte. If it is greater than 5, a round up of one tenth of a degree occurs; otherwise the value remains unchanged. Figure 7.15 shows the contents of BCDBUF before and after the round up occurs. Note that the least two significant bytes are not outputted and therefore they do not have to be cleared. Figure 7.16 shows the flow chart of the RNDOFF routine. The subroutine RNDUP (round up) are the instructions that add the one tenth of a degree. Now refer to the application program in section 7.8 for the line code and comments for the RNDOFF and RNDUP routines.

7.7.6   OUTPUT Routine

This routine outputs the temperature and suppresses leading zeros. The format for the temperature display of 100°C is

Temperature: 100.0 degrees Celsius

The EVB utility subroutines (OUTA, OUTRHLF, and OUTSTRG) studied in Chapter 4 are used to output messages, temperature values, and the decimal point. This routine does not output the least two significant digits in the BCDBUF. The programming steps are given in section 7.8 under the label OUTPUT.

7.7.7   TDELAY Routine

The statement of the problem required that the temperature measurements are to be taken at 30-second intervals. This requires the program to contain a 30-second

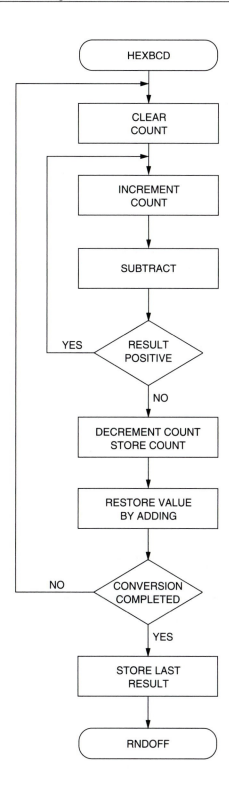

FIGURE 7.14 Flow chart for converting a binary number to BCD using the subtraction technique.

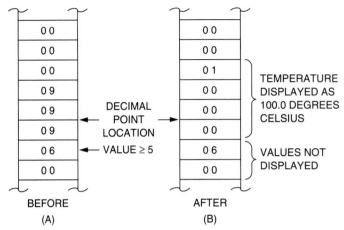

FIGURE 7.15 An example of how the temperature is stored in the BCDBUF before and after a round-up of one-tenth degree.

time delay routine. In Chapter 6, we studied how to program the MCU's timer unit to create real time interrupts. The routine studied in Chapter 6 is modified and used in this application. The lines of code are given in section 7.8 under the heading of TDELAY.

This routine also includes lines of code that decrement the interval counter. If the count equals zero, CPU execution returns to the BUFFALO prompt. If the count is not equal to zero, CPU execution jumps to the beginning of the program to take the next temperature reading.

7.8

APPLICATION PROGRAM

The actual program instructions were assembled on an IBM-compatible computer and downloaded into RAM on the EVB. There are several reasons for using a cross-assembler for your application program. Some of the reasons are easy editing, ability to add comments, use of assembler directives, and in particular the ability to save the program on disk. As described in Chapter 4, to download a program after it has been assembled as S-records, a communication program is needed such as KERMIT or PROCOMM. Remember, comments are not included as part of the S-record and therefore are not downloaded into the RAM on the EVB. After the program is loaded in the EVB RAM, program execution is accomplished by the microcontroller's CPU. The microcomputer (IBM or compatible) is used only as a monitor to display temperature.

This application program begins with equate tables, reserve memory byte tables, and the messages to be displayed. The ORG $C700 assembler directive

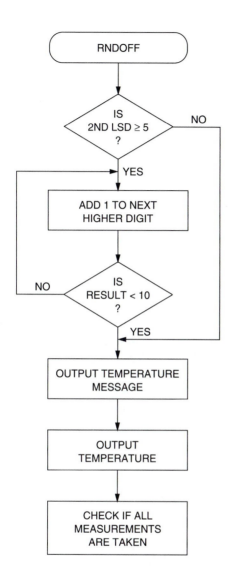

FIGURE 7.16 Flow chart for the RNDOFF and RNDUP routines for the temperature measurement application.

indicates that the program will be stored in the EVB RAM starting at location C700$_{hex}$. Other origin directives, ORG $D000, ORG $D700, and ORG $D720, are the starting locations of a memory buffer and messages, respectively.

After the program is downloaded into the EVB RAM, you may execute it by using the G (GO) command. The format is

>G C700 <ENTER>

Note: You do not have to connect the entire signal conditioning circuit to test the software. If you would like to vary the voltage at port E1 to simulate different temperature readings, use the procedure in Chapter 5 and shown in Figure 5.9. If no connections are made, the CPU reads all logic 1s (FF$_{hex}$) from the A/D register 1. Therefore, if you test the application program under these condtions, the temperature displayed will be 100°C.

```
LINE  S PC    OPCO OPERANDS  S LABEL    MNEMO OPERANDS COMMENT
00001                                   NAM   Temperature measurements using the AD590
00002
00003                        ***********************************************************************
00004                        *                     EVB Utility Subroutine Addresses               *
00005                        *   The EVB utility subroutines introduced in Chapter 4 allow the user *
00006                        *   to perform certain input/output functions. They are called by a   *
00007                        *   JSR instruction to the applicable address.                        *
00008                        *********************************************************************** *
00009 P 0000   ffb5   A OUTRHLF   EQU   $FFB5     Convert right nibble to ASCII and output.
00010 P 0000   ffb8   A OUTA      EQU   $FFB8     Output character in accumulator A.
00011 P 0000   ffc7   A OUTSTRG   EQU   $FFC7     Output message string until $04 include leading <CR> <LF>.
00012 P 0000   ffca   A OUTSTRGO  EQU   $FFCA     Output message string until $04 no leading <CR> <LF>.
00013
00014                        ***********************************************************************
00015                        *                     Register Equates                               *
00016                        *   These locations are fixed addresses in the memory map.            *
00017                        ***********************************************************************
00018 P 0000   00eb   A RTIVEC    EQU   $00EB     Pseudo vector location on the EVB.
00019 P 0000   1024   A TMSK2     EQU   $1024     Main timer interrupt mask register 2.
00020 P 0000   1025   A TFLG2     EQU   $1025     Timer interrupt flag register 2.
00021 P 0000   1026   A PACTL     EQU   $1026     Pulse accumulator control register.
00022 P 0000   1030   A ADCTL     EQU   $1030     A/D control register.
00023 P 0000   1031   A ADR1      EQU   $1031     A/D register #1.
00024 P 0000   e0b2   A BUFFALO   EQU   $E0B2     Starting location of the BUFFALO prompt.
00025
00026                        ***********************************************************************
00027                        *                     Buffer Locations                               *
00028                        *   These buffer locations are used to store temporary data in RAM.  The *
00029                        *   starting address is D700 hex.                                     *
00030                        ***********************************************************************
00031 A d700                           ORG   $D700     Assembler directive
00032 A d700   02     A ADBUFF    RMB   2         Stores the A/D input.
00033 A d702   03     A HEXBUF    RMB   3         Stores the digital input x 392 deg/bit.
00034 A d705   08     A BCDBUF    RMB   8         Stores the result of the 24 bit to BCD conversion.
00035 A d70d   02     A TDREG     RMB   2         Stores the time delay count.
00036 A d70f   01     A INTCNT    RMB   1         Stores the number of temperature samples to be taken.
00037
00038                        ***********************************************************************
00039                        *                     24 Bit Equivalent Values                       *
00040                        *   These values are used for the 24 bit binary to BCD conversion     *
00041                        *   subroutine.  Each decimal value is stored as a 24 bit number.     *
00042                        ***********************************************************************
00043 A d720                           ORG   $D720     Assembler directive
00044 A d720   989680 A CON10M    FCB   $98,$96,$80 Hex equivalent of 10,000,000.
00045 A d723   0f4240 A           FCB   $0F,$42,$40 Hex equivalent of 1,000,000.
00046 A d726   0186a0 A           FCB   $01,$86,$A0 Hex equivalent of 100,000.
00047 A d729   002710 A           FCB   $00,$27,$10 Hex equivalent of 10,000.
00048 A d72c   0003e8 A           FCB   $00,$03,$E8 Hex equivalent of 1,000.
00049 A d72f   000064 A           FCB   $00,$00,$64 Hex equivalent of 100.
00050 A d732   00000a A           FCB   $00,$00,$0A Hex equivalent of 10.
00051 A d735   d735   A CONEND    EQU   *
00052
00053                        ***********************************************************************
00054                        *                     Display Messages                               *
00055                        *   The following messages are outputted with the temperature so the  *
00056                        *   data can be easily interpreted.                                   *
00057                        *                     * * * * *                                       *
00058                        *   The messages are stored in memory beginning at location $D000.    *
00059                        ***********************************************************************
00060
```

```
LINE   S PC    OPCO OPERANDS  S LABEL    MNEMO OPERANDS COMMENT
00061  A d000                            ORG   $D000     Assembler directive
00062
00063  A d000  54            A MSTEMP    FCC   'Temperature: '
00064  A d00d  04            A           FCB   $04       End-of-message mark.
00065  A d00e  20            A MSDEG     FCC   ' degrees Celsius'
00066  A d01e  04            A           FCB   $04       End-of-message mark.
00067
00068
00069
00070                        ***********************************************************************
00071                        *   The application program for this chapter begins at address C700 hex.   *
00072                        *                           * * * * *                                  *
00073                        *   The first two lines of code initialize the counter INTCNT for the     *
00074                        *   number of samples to be taken.  The next seven lines of code clear all *
00075                        *   the temporary buffer locations that are used to store data.            *
00076                        ***********************************************************************
00077
00078  A c700                            ORG   $C700     Assembler directive
00079
00080  A c700  86   0a       A BEGIN:    LDAA  #10       \ Initialize the interval counter
00081  A c702  b7   d70f     A           STAA  INTCNT    / for 10 temperature measurements.
00082
00083  A c705  18ce d70e     A CLEAR:    LDY   #ADBUFF+14 Initialize the Y register.
00084  A c709  c6   0f       A           LDAB  #15       Initialize the count value.
00085  A c70b  4f                        CLRA            #0            Clear accumulator A.
00086  A c70c  18a7 00       A C1:       STAA  00,Y      Clear buffer location.
00087  A c70f  1809                      DEY             Change pointer to next location.
00088  A c711  5a                        DECB            Decrement count value.
00089  A c712  26   f8   c70c            BNE   C1        If count =/= 0, branch to C1.
00090
00091
00092
00093                        ***********************************************************************
00094                        *   This portion of the application program initializes the             *
00095                        *   microcontroller's A/D control register, introduces a time delay for  *
00096                        *   the A/D conversion, measures the temperature at port E1, multiplies  *
00097                        *   the digital input data (DID) by 188 hex (392 degrees per bit), and   *
00098                        *   stores the result in the buffer labeled HEXBUF.                      *
00099                        ***********************************************************************
00100
00101
00102
00103
00104
00105  A c714  86   21       A METEMP:   LDAA  #$21      ADCTL control word.
00106  A c716  b7   1030     A           STAA  ADCTL     Initialize the A/D control register.
00107
00108  A c719  c6   26       A           LDAB  #$26      Initialize time delay count.
00109  A c71b  5a                DELAY:  DECB            Decrement time count.
00110  A c71c  26   fd   c71b           BNE   DELAY     If count =/= 0, branch to DELAY.
00111
00112  A c71e  b6   1031     A           LDAA  ADR1      Read A/D register #1.
00113  A c721  b7   d700     A           STAA  ADBUFF    Store the DID value in A/D buffer.
00114  A c724  c6   88       A           LDAB  #$88      Load the constant value 88 hex.
00115  A c726  3d                        MUL             Multiply A x B ---> D.
00116  A c727  f3   d700     A           ADDD  ADBUFF    Add DID(100) value.
00117
00118  A c72a  fd   d703     A STORE:    STD   HEXBUF+1  Store accumulator D.
00119  A c72d  79   d702     A           ROL   HEXBUF    Carry flag is saved.
00120
00121
00122                        ***********************************************************************
00123                        *   This portion of the application program converts a 24 bit number    *
00124                        *   stored in HEXBUF to an 8 byte unpacked BCD value.  The BCD value     *
00125                        *   is stored in a buffer labled BCDBUF.                                 *
00126                        ***********************************************************************
00127
00128  A c730  18ce d705     A HEXBCD:   LDY   #BCDBUF   Initialize the Y register.
00129  A c734  ce   d720     A           LDX   #CON10M   Initialize the X register.
00130  A c737  5f                NEXDGT: CLRB
00131  A c738  5c                LOOP1:  INCB            Increment once per subtract.
00132  A c739  b6   d704     A           LDAA  HEXBUF+2 \ Load, subtract,
```

```
LINE   S PC    OPCO OPERANDS S LABEL    MNEMO OPERANDS COMMENT
00133  A c73c  a0   02       A          SUBA  2,X      | and update low
00134  A c73e  b7   d704     A          STAA  HEXBUF+2 / byte.
00135  A c741  b6   d703     A          LDAA  HEXBUF+1 \ Load, subtract,
00136  A c744  a2   01       A          SBCA  1,X      | and update middle
00137  A c746  b7   d703     A          STAA  HEXBUF+1 / byte.
00138  A c749  b6   d702     A          LDAA  HEXBUF   \ Load, subtract,
00139  A c74c  a2   00       A          SBCA  0,X      | and update high
00140  A c74e  b7   d702     A          STAA  HEXBUF   / byte.
00141
00142  A c751  24   e5       c738       BCC   LOOP1    If borrow flag is set, subtract again.
00143
00144  A c753  b6   d704     A ADD:      LDAA  HEXBUF+2 \ Load, add, and
00145  A c756  ab   02       A          ADDA  2,X      | restore last low
00146  A c758  b7   d704     A          STAA  HEXBUF+2 / byte value.
00147  A c75b  b6   d703     A          LDAA  HEXBUF+1 \ Load, add, and
00148  A c75e  a9   01       A          ADCA  1,X      | restore last middle
00149  A c760  b7   d703     A          STAA  HEXBUF+1 / byte value.
00150  A c763  b6   d702     A          LDAA  HEXBUF   \ Load, add, and
00151  A c766  a9   00       A          ADCA  0,X      | restore last high
00152  A c768  b7   d702     A          STAA  HEXBUF   / byte value.
00153
00154  A c76b  c0   01       A          SUBB  #1
00155  A c76d  18e7 00       A          STAB  0,Y      Store BCD value.
00156
00157  A c770  1808          A          INY            Increment Y pointer to next location.
00158  A c772  08                       INX            \ Increment X pointer to
00159  A c773  08                       INX            | next conversion value.
00160  A c774  08                       INX            /
00161
00162  A c775  8c   d735     A          CPX   #CONEND  Check to see if conversion is complete.
00163  A c778  26   bd       c737       BNE   NEXDGT   If not done branch back to NEXDGT.
00164
00165  A c77a  f6   d704     A          LDAB  HEXBUF+2 \ Store least significant value.
00166  A c77d  18e7 00       A          STAB  0,Y      /
00167
00168              ******************************************************************
00169              *  This routine determines how the least significant value should be   *
00170              *  rounded off.  If the least significant digit is equal to or greater *
00171              *  than 5, then a round up of a 1/10 of degree occurs, otherwise there *
00172              *  is no round up.                                                      *
00173              ******************************************************************
00174
00175  A c780  ce   d70b     A RNDOFF:   LDX   #BCDBUF+6 \
00176  A c783  a6   00       A          LDAA  00,X     | Check the value in location BCDBUF+6.
00177  A c785  81   05       A          CMPA  #5       | Branch if accumulator A < 5.
00178  A c787  2d   14       c79d       BLT   OUTPUT   /
00179
00180  A c789  09                       RNDUP:  DEX    Change X pointer.
00181  A c78a  a6   00       A          LDAA  00,X     Load accumulator A.
00182  A c78c  0d                       SEC            Set carry flag (C = 1).
00183  A c78d  89   00       A          ADCA  #0       Add accumulator A + carry + 0.
00184  A c78f  19                       DAA            Decimal adjust.
00185  A c790  81   10       A          CMPA  #$10     \ Branch to R1 if adjusted
00186  A c792  2d   07       c79b       BLT   R1       / value is less than 10.
00187  A c794  80   10       A          SUBA  #$10     Subtract 10 from accumulator A.
00188  A c796  a7   00       A          STAA  00,X     Store result.
00189  A c798  7e   c789     A          JMP   RNDUP    Jump to RNDUP.
00190  A c79b  a7   00       A R1:       STAA  00,X     Store result.
00191
00192              ******************************************************************
00193              *  The following program steps output the temperature message and the  *
00194              *  temperature value stored in the BCDBUF.  Leading zeros are suppressed. *
00195              ******************************************************************
00196
00197  A c79d  ce   d000     A OUTPUT:   LDX   #MSTEMP  Initialize X register.
00198  A c7a0  bd   ffc7     A          JSR   OUTSTRG  Output the temperature message.
00199  A c7a3  ce   d707     A          LDX   #BCDBUF+2 Initialize X register.
00200  A c7a6  a6   00       A          LDAA  00,X     \
00201  A c7a8  81   00       A          CMPA  #0       |
00202  A c7aa  27   0c       c7b8       BEQ   OUT1     |
00203  A c7ac  bd   ffb5     A          JSR   OUTRHLF  |
00204  A c7af  08                       INX            | Check for leading zeros
00205  A c7b0  a6   00       A          LDAA  00,X     | and output hundreds,
```

```
LINE  S PC   OPCO OPERANDS  S LABEL     MNEMO OPERANDS COMMENT
00206 A c7b2 bd   ffb5      A           JSR   OUTRHLF  | tenths, and units values.
00207 A c7b5 7e   c7c2      A           JMP   OUT2     |
00208
00209 A c7b8 08             OUT1:       INX            |
00210 A c7b9 a6   00        A           LDAA  00,X     |
00211 A c7bb 81   00        A           CMPA  #0       |
00212 A c7bd 27   03   c7c2             BEQ   OUT2     |
00213 A c7bf bd   ffb5      A           JSR   OUTRHLF  |
00214 A c7c2 08             OUT2:       INX            |
00215 A c7c3 a6   00        A           LDAA  00,X     |
00216 A c7c5 bd   ffb5      A           JSR   OUTRHLF  /
00217 A c7c8 86   2e        A           LDAA  #$2E     \  Insert decimal point.
00218 A c7ca bd   ffb8      A           JSR   OUTA     /
00219 A c7cd 08                         INX            \
00220 A c7ce a6   00        A           LDAA  00,X     | Output one-tenth value.
00221 A c7d0 bd   ffb5      A           JSR   OUTRHLF  /
00222 A c7d3 ce   d00e      A           LDX   #MSDEG   \  Initialize X register.
00223 A c7d6 bd   ffca      A           JSR   OUTSTRGO /  Output MSDEG message.
00224
00225                                   *******************************************************************************
00226                                   * This portion of the routine is a built in 30 second time delay.  It    *
00227                                   * is similar to the procedure described in Example 6-7.                  *
00228                                   *                        * * * * *                                      *
00229                                   * The stack pointer is reset to location $004A so a user stack overflow  *
00230                                   * does not occur.  Remember from Chapter 4 that the user stack area      *
00231                                   * begins at address $004A.                                              *
00232                                   *******************************************************************************
00233
00234 A c7d9 86   7e        A TDELAY:   LDAA  #$7E     \  Initialize the pseudo vector addresses
00235 A c7db 97   eb        A           STAA  RTIVEC   |  on the EVB for the real time interrupt
00236 A c7dd cc   c7f8      A           LDD   #CONT    |  function.
00237 A c7e0 dd   ec        A           STD   RTIVEC+1 /
00238
00239 A c7e2 86   03        A           LDAA  #$03     \  Set the RTRI and RTRO bits
00240 A c7e4 b7   1026      A           STAA  PACTL    /  for a divide by 8 ratio.
00241
00242 A c7e7 86   40        A           LDAA  #$40     \  Set the RTII bit and
00243 A c7e9 b7   1024      A           STAA  TMSK2    |  clear the RTIF bit.
00244 A c7ec b7   1025      A           STAA  TFLG2    /
00245
00246 A c7ef cc   0392      A           LDD   #914     \  Store the count value at a location
00247 A c7f2 fd   d70d      A           STD   TDREG    /  called TDREG (time delay register).
00248
00249 A c7f5 0e             CLI                        Clear interrupt mask bit.
00250 A c7f6 20   fe   c7f6 WAIT:       BRA   WAIT     The CPU is waiting for an interrupt.
00251
00252 A c7f8 fc   d70d      A CONT:     LDD   TDREG    \
00253 A c7fb 83   0001      A           SUBD  #1       |  Check to see if the routine has
00254 A c7fe fd   d70d      A           STD   TDREG    |  looped 914 times to give a total
00255 A c801 1a83 0000      A           CPD   #0       |  time delay of approximately 30 seconds.
00256 A c805 26   0e   c815             BNE   CLRFLG   /
00257
00258
00259
00260
00261 A c807 8e   004a      A           LDS   #$004A   Reset the user stack pointer in the EVB.
00262 A c80a 7a   d70f      A           DEC   INTCNT   Decrement the interval count value.
00263 A c80d 27   03   c812             BEQ   T1       If count = 0, branch to T1.
00264 A c80f 7e   c705      A           JMP   CLEAR    Jump back to the beginning of the program.
00265
00266 A c812 7e   e0b2      A T1:       JMP   BUFFALO  Jump to the Buffalo prompt.
00267
00268 A c815 86   40        A CLRFLG:   LDAA  #$40     \  Clear the RTIF bit in the
00269 A c817 b7   1025      A           STAA  TFLG2    /  TFLG2 register.
00270 A c81a 3b             RTI                        Return from interrupt.
00271
00272                                   END
00273
00274
```

```
Total number of errors: 0
Total number of warnings: 0
Total number of lines: 274


Number of bytes in section ASCT: 351

Number of bytes in program: 351
              CROSS REFERENCE TABLE
NAME     ATTRB S VALUE P:LINE LINE1....N

ADBUFF       A d700 2:32      83 113 116
ADCTL    EQU A 1030 2:22     106
ADD          A c753 4:144
ADR1     EQU A 1031 2:23     112
BCDBUF       A d705 2:34     128 175 199
BEGIN        A c700 3:80
BUFFALO  EQU A e0b2 2:24     266
C1           A c70c 3:86      89
CLEAR        A c705 3:83     264
CLRFLG       A c815 7:268    256
CON10M       A d720 2:44     129
CONEND   EQU A d735 2:51     162
CONT         A c7f8 6:252    236
DELAY        A c71b 4:109    110
HEXBCD       A c730 4:128
HEXBUF       A d702 2:33     118 119 132 134 135 137 138 140 144 146 147 149 150 152 165
INTCNT       A d70f 2:36      81 262
LOOP1        A c738 4:131    142
METEMP       A c714 4:105
MSDEG        A d00e 3:65     222
MSTEMP       A d000 3:63     197
NEXDGT       A c737 4:130    163
OUT1         A c7b8 6:209    202
              CROSS REFERENCE TABLE
NAME     ATTRB S VALUE P:LINE LINE1....N

OUT2         A c7c2 6:214    207 212
OUTA     EQU A ffb8 2:10     218
OUTPUT       A c79d 5:197    178
OUTRHLF  EQU A ffb5 2:9      203 206 213 216 221
OUTSTRG  EQU A ffc7 2:11     198
OUTSTRGO EQU A ffca 2:12     223
PACTL    EQU A 1026 2:21     240
R1           A c79b 5:190    186
RNDOFF       A c780 5:175
RNDUP        A c789 5:180    189
RTIVEC   EQU A 00eb 2:18     235 237
STORE        A c72a 4:118
T1           A c812 7:266    263
TDELAY       A c7d9 6:234
TDREG        A d70d 2:35     247 252 254
TFLG2    EQU A 1025 2:20     244 269
TMSK2    EQU A 1024 2:19     243
WAIT         A c7f6 6:250    250
```

7.9

TESTING AND DEBUGGING THE APPLICATION PROGRAM

The testing and debugging of the application program require using some of the monitor commands in BUFFALO. All of the monitor commands were introduced in Chapter 4. Those commands that we will use now for troubleshooting the software for this application program are:

- BR—Breakpoint set
- G—Execute program
- MD—Memory display
- MM—Memory modify
- P—Proceed/continue from breakpoint
- RM—Register modify

Some of these commands will be used more than others. When troubleshooting hardware circuitry, you select the piece of equipment that will give the most information. Similarly, when debugging a program, select a command that will give you the most information. Note: Troubleshooting hardware requires other hardware (other electronic equipment); troubleshooting software requires other software. Note: The monitor commands are themselves programs.

7.9.1   Testing the BEGIN and CLEAR Routines

This application program does not use many subroutines. Therefore, the application program may be easiest to debug selecting points to insert a breakpoint. Remember from Chapter 4, when a breakpoint(s) is inserted, the program is executed up to the breakpoint and stops. The CPU registers are displayed and the MD command may be used to display the contents of memory.

Example 7.7:

Use the BR and MD commands to check the BEGIN and CLEAR routines of the application program given in section 7.8.

Solution:

Refer to section 7.8. The last instruction in the CLEAR routine is BNE Cl. A breakpoint is inserted at the address of the next instruction, which is location $C714. The format for inserting the breakpoint is:

```
> BR C714 <ENTER>

> C714 0000 0000 0000 (Breakpoint inserted)
```

Now use the G (GO) command.

```
> G C700 <ENTER>
```

The first nine lines of code are executed and the CPU registers are displayed. Use the MD command to check memory.

```
> MD D700 D700 <ENTER>

D700   00 00 00 00 00 00 00 00 00 00 00 00 00 00 00 0A
```

Note: The 16th byte contains 0A (10$_{dec}$), the value of the interval counter.

If you use the RMB table at the beginning of the application program, you may check to see which bytes will be used for the different buffers. For example, ADBUFF is 2 bytes and starts at $D700. Therefore, it uses $D700 and $D701.

7.9.2   Testing the METEMP Routine

The application program may be tested from the beginning through the METEMP routine. First, let's remove the breakpoint at $C714 and insert it after the METEMP routine. The format to remove a breakpoint is:

```
> BR - <ENTER>

> 0000 0000 0000 0000
```

Example 7.8:

Insert a breakpoint after the METEMP routine and check the results.

Solution:

The instruction following the METEMP routine is at address $C730, which will be the location to insert the breakpoint.

```
> BR C730 <ENTER>

> C730 0000 0000 0000
```

Remember from section 7.7.3 that the METEMP routine not only stores the contents of the A/D register 1 in the ADBUFF, but also multiplies the value by 188$_{hex}$ and then stores the product in the locations labeled HEXBUF ($D702–$D704).

If you are testing the application program and there are no connections to port E1 of the EVB, then the data read into the A/D register 1 will be all logic 1s (FF$_{hex}$). Now use the G command.

```
> G C700 <ENTER>
```

Program execution stops when the breakpoint is encountered. Use the MD command to check the contents of the ADBUFF and HEXBUF.

```
> MD D700 D700 <ENTER>

> D700 FF 00  01 86 78 00 00 00 00 00 00 00 00 00 00 0A
          ‿‿    ‿‿‿‿‿‿‿
        ADBUFF   HEXBUF
```

If you have not connected the entire signal conditioning circuit to test the software but would like to vary the voltage at port E1 to simulate different temperature readings, use the procedure in Chapter 5 and shown in Figure 5-9.

7.9.3 Testing the HEXBCD Routine

To check the HEXBCD routine, we can add another breakpoint. It is not necessary to remove the breakpoint at $C730. The procedure is:

```
> BR C780 <ENTER>

> C730 C780 0000 0000
```

Address $C780 is the memory address of the instruction following the HEXBUF routine. Now use the G command.

```
> G C700 <ENTER>
```

Program execution stops after the METEMP routine. Use the P command to proceed.

```
> P <ENTER>
```

Program execution continues and stops after the HEXBCD routine. Use the MD command to check the results.

```
> MD D700 D700 <ENTER>

> D700 FF 00 XX XX XX 00 00 00 09 09 09 06 00 00 00 0A
       ADBUFF   HEXBUF            BCDBUF
```

Note that the contents of the BCDBUF are unpacked BCD values. Also note that the HEXBCD routine alters the contents of the HEXBUF. This alteration does not cause a problem because the HEXBUF is not used again until the next temperature reading.

If you would like to check just the HEXBCD routine for any value stored in HEXBUF, use the MM command to enter data. First remove the breakpoint at $C730. This operation may be done by:

```
>BR -C730 <ENTER>

0000 C780 0000 0000
```

The breakpoint at $C780 has not been removed.

Example 7.9:

Use the HEXBCD routine to convert FF FF FF to its decimal equivalent.

Solution:

Although this value far exceeds the A/D conversion register, it does show that the HEXBCD routine is capable of converting a 24-bit number to an 8-byte unpacked BCD value. Use the MM command to enter the hexadecimal number at addresses $D702–$D704.

> `MM D702 <ENTER>`

> `D702 XX FF <space bar> XX FF <space bar> XX FF <ENTER>`

The XX represents a previous byte of data. You may use the MD command to check that the data has been entered.

> `MD D700 D700 <ENTER>`

> `D700 XX XX FF FF FF XX . . .`

If a breakpoint has already been inserted after the HEXBCD routine, at address $C780 use the G command. If not, use the BR command and enter the breakpoint and then the G command. Since we only want to execute the HEXBCD routine, the G command is entered as:

> `G C730 <ENTER>`

Note the starting address of the HEXBCD routine is $C730. Check the conversion result by using the MD command.

> `MD D700 D700 <ENTER>`

> `D700  FF 00 XX XX XX 01 06 07 07 07 02 01 05 00 00 0A`

                     HEXBUF   BCDBUF

Remember the HEXBCD routine alters the contents of the HEXBUF.
   The other routines in this application program may be tested in a similar fashion.

PROBLEMS

1. Write the analog interface equation for each of the following measurement systems:

(a) 0 to 100°C input, 0 to 5V output
(b) 0 to 212°F input, 0 to 5V output
(c) 0 to 25 pounds input, 0 to 5V output
(d) 0 to 10psig input, 0 to 5V output

2. Use Eq. (7.4a) to determine transducer current I_T at (a) 298.2°K and (b) 398.2°K.

3. Use Eq. (7.4b) to determine transducer current I_T at (a) 0°C and (b) 100°C.

4. Use Eq. (7.4c) to determine transducer current I_T at (a) 32°F and (b) 212°F.

5. Write the SCC design equation for each of the following conditions:

(a) 273.2 to 373.2µA input, 0 to 5V output
(b) 255.4 to 373.2µA input, 0 to 5V output
(c) 218 to 423µA input, 0 to 5V output

6. Design the current-to-voltage converter shown in Figure 7.6(a) for the following SCC design equations:

(a) $V_o = (10k\Omega)I_T - 2.732V$
(b) $V_o = (100\Omega)I_T + 2.554V$
(c) $V_o = (25k\Omega)I_T - 10V$

7. Calculate the self-heating of an AD590 operated at 25°C and with a $V_{AD590} = 4V$.

8. Refer to Figure 7.9 and create the binary pattern to select PE2 for single conversion of a single channel.

9. Using section 7.7.1 as a guide, write code to establish a value to make one measurement per second for one hour and store in it an appropriate temporary RAM location (labeled INTCNT).

10. Refer to section 7.7.2 on clearing memory buffers. Rewrite the code beginning at location $C705 to clear ADBUFF if your application requires only 9 locations of RAM starting at $D600.

11. Refer to the A/D time delay portion of section 7.7.2. Modify the A/D converter's time delay loop for approximately 16µS. (Note that the M68HC11 operates at a rate of 2µs/count.)

12. Refer to the Read A/D register portion of section 7.7.2. Comment on each code line:

```
ADR2     EQU    $1032
         ORG    $D100
ADBUFF   RMB    2
LDAA     ADR2
STAA     ADBUFF
```

13. Show that Eq. (7.11b) yields the same results as Eq. (7.11a) for the following data: (a) 01_{hex}, (b) $0F_{hex}$, (c) $F0_{hex}$.

14. Write a test procedure to check the contents of the ADBUFF before the HEX value is converted to decimal. (Note: Insert a breakpoint at the correct location.)

CHAPTER

Weight
with a

8.0

INTRODUC

Load cells are
differential el
type strain ga
mechanical se
volts. The tra
volts (2 to 3m
ditioning circ
tial gain.

Commercia
ounces to ton
ry to correct t

In this chap
terface will be
conditioning
a M68HC11 m

*The basic measu

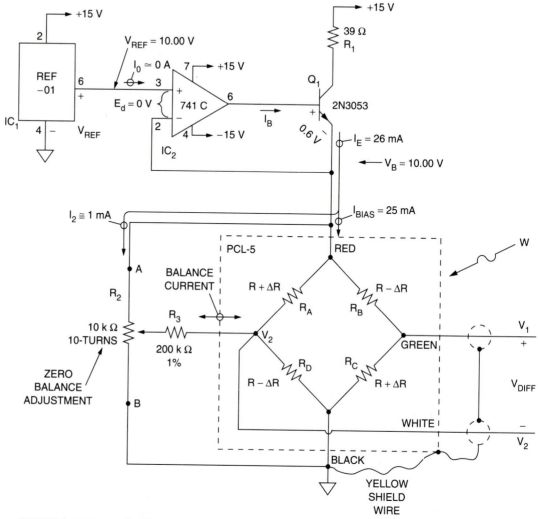

FIGURE 8.5 TA practical load cell biasing circuit with zero balance adjustment

Example 8.5:

For the conditions shown on Figure 8.5, determine the power dissipated by Q_1 to drive a PLC-5 load cell.

Solution:

The voltage drop across R_1 is $V_{R1} = I_C R_1 \cong I_E R_1 \cong 26mA(39\Omega) \cong 1V$. $V_{CE} = 15V - V_B - V_{R1} = 15V - 10V - 1V = 4V$. Power dissipation is then $P_{Q1} = V_{CE} \cdot I_C = 4V (26mA) = 0.104$ watts.

A 2N3053 mounted in a TO-5 case can easily handle this level of power dissipation without an external heatsink.

8.3.3   Zero Balance Adjustment

Load cell manufacturers often include a *Zero Balance* figure of merit on their specifications, which is an indication of how closely the strain-gage arms are matched in resistance. For our PLC-5 transducer this figure of merit is ±5% of FSO.

Example 8.6:

Determine the maximum imbalance of a PLC-5 load cell.

Solution:

From Example 8.2, FSO = 21.21mV; then FSO (±5%) = 21.21mV(±0.05) = ±1.06mV.

We conclude that V_{diff} in Figure 8.5 can be out of zero balance by about ±1mV with no load applied.

R_2 and R_3 in Figure 8.5 null out these zero balance errors. Select a good quality 10-turn linear potentiometer for R_2 and minimize pot loading by choosing R_3 to be greater than 10 times R_2. The values of R_2 and R_3 determine the maximum balancing current that can be injected into or extracted from node V_2.

Balancing action can be observed in Figure 8.5 by measuring the differential output, V_{diff}, with a differential reading digital multimeter (DMM) capable of 5-place accuracy. $V_{diff} = V_1 - V_2$. With *no* load on the transducer, adjust R_2 until $V_{diff} = 0V$.

8.3.4   Writing the Transducer Equation

To integrate a PLC-5 load cell into a precision weight measurement system, a 4 oz (0.25 lb) aluminum table is added to the upper foldback arm and a stable base is secured to the lower structure of Figure 8.3(a). (A picture of the complete system is shown in Figure 8.10.) The table is necessary to build our system, but it introduces a permanent *table offset* voltage to the output of Figure 8.5.

Example 8.7:

Determine V_{diff} in Figure 8.5 for a 0.25 lb table.

Solution:

From Example 8.3, bridge sensitivity is m = 4.242mV/lb. Therefore, the table offset voltage V_{off} or the b term in the general transducer equation becomes

$$V_{off} = b = 4.242mV/lb \times 0.25\ lb = 1.06mV$$

Figure 8.6 shows the block diagram of the transducer which includes the PLC-5 load cell, and a 0.25 lb table. Now write the transducer equation in the standard form

$$y = mx + b$$

by inspection as

$$V_{diff} = V_1 - V_2 = (4.242\text{mV/lb})\, W + 1.06\text{mV} \tag{8.5}$$

where W is the weight placed on the table for measurements.

Example 8.8:

Determine the differential output voltage limits of the transducer for weights of (a) 0 lbs and (b) 5 lbs.

Solution:

Using Eq. (8.5)

a) $V_1 - V_2 = (4.242\text{mV/lb})\, 0\text{ lb} + 1.06\text{mV} = 1.06\text{mV}$
b) $V_1 - V_2 = (4.242\text{mV/lb})\, 5\text{ lb} + 1.06\text{mV} = 22.27\text{mV}$

Note: The 1.06mV offset voltage created by the table could have been eliminated by a readjustment of R_2. However, adjustments of R_2 have been reserved only for zero balance. The transducer's table offset will be removed in the next sections with the signal conditioning circuit (SCC).

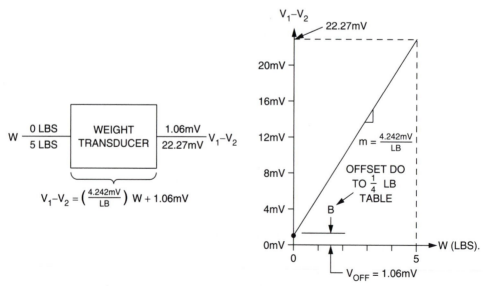

FIGURE 8.6 Transducer equation and graph of Figure 8.5 with a 1/4 lbs table added to the load cell

8.3.5 Writing the SCC Design Equation

The task in this section is to write a signal conditioning circuit design equation. It will describe what the SCC must do to the the output of the transducer to interface it to the 0 to 5V input range of the MCU's A/D converter. See Figure 8.7.

We begin to derive the SCC design equation by drawing a block diagram of the analog interface as shown in Figure 8.7(a). On the drawing the entered values

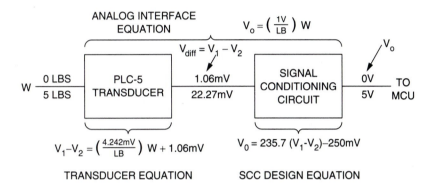

$$V_o = \left(\frac{1V}{LB}\right) W$$

$$V_{diff} = V_1 - V_2$$

$$V_1 - V_2 = \left(\frac{4.242mV}{LB}\right) W + 1.06mV$$

TRANSDUCER EQUATION

$$V_0 = 235.7 \, (V_1 - V_2) - 250mV$$

SCC DESIGN EQUATION

(a) THE SCC MUST CONVERT A DIFFERENTIAL INPUT
VOLTAGE RANGE OF 1.06mV TO 22.27mV INTO A SINGLE-
ENDED OUTPUT VOLTAGE RANGE OF 0 TO 5V

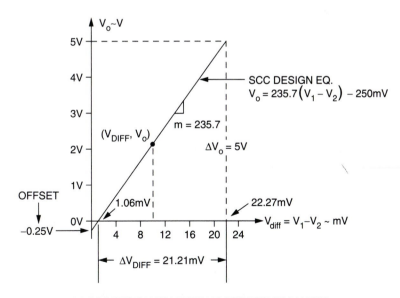

$$V_o = 235.7 \left(V_1 - V_2\right) - 250mV$$

(b) SCC DESIGN EQUATION IS DERIVED FROM THIS
GRAPH (SECTION 8.3.5).

FIGURE 8.7 The SCC design equation is derived from the data plotted in (b)

are for (a) input weight range, W, from 0 to 5 lbs, (b) corresponding transducer output range, V_{diff} from 1.06mV to 22.27mV; and (c) required SCC output range, V_o from 0 to 5V to interface with the MCU's A/D converter.

Next, assign SCC input $(V_1–V_2)$ to the x-axis and SCC output (V_o) to the y-axis as shown in Figure 8.7(b). Plot data at the end points (1.06mV, 0V) and (22.27mV, 5V). Connect these points with a straight line to plot the required performance of the SCC design equation.

Evaluate slope, or the circuit's differential gain from

$$m = \text{differential gain} = \frac{\Delta V_o}{\Delta V_{diff}}$$

$$= \frac{(5 - 0)V}{(22.27 - 1.06)mV} = 235.7$$

Now locate a general point (V_{diff}, V_o) to equate slope terms:

$$235.7 = \frac{V_o - 0V}{V_{diff} - 1.06mV}$$

Multiply both sides by the denominator, which yields

$$235.7 (V_{diff} - 1.06mV) = V_o - 0V$$

The SCC design equation in standard form is then

$$V_o = 235.7 (V_{diff}) - 250mV \tag{8.6}$$

From Eq. (8.6) we conclude that the differential output voltage ($V_{diff} = V_1 - V_2$) from Figure 8.5, must first be amplified by a differential gain of 235.7, converted to a single-ended voltage, V_o, and then this result must be offset by –250mV. The design of hardware to perform these tasks is considered next.

8.4

SIGNAL CONDITIONING CIRCUIT: HARDWARE DESIGN

8.4.1   Basic SCC Hardware

To implement Eq. (8.6), choose an instrumentation amplifier (IA) such as the AD524C from Analog Devices, Inc. This device, housed in a single 16-pin DIP, provides a differential gain and differential-to-single-ended voltage conversion. Its output voltage can also be superimposed on a reference voltage, V_{ref}, to provide for the offset voltage needed in our design. Figure 8.8(a) shows this basic signal conditioning circuit (SCC). Its hardware equation is

$$V_o = A_{diff} (V_{pos} - V_{neg}) + V_{ref} \tag{8.7}$$

Note: See section 5.12.3 to review this SCC.

From Eq. 8.6

$$V_o = 235.7 \, (V_1 - V_2) - 250mV$$

Now compare Eq. (8.7) with Eq. (8.6) for both offset and gain terms in each equation.

Equate Offset Terms $V_{ref} = -250mV$

By inspection we see that a negative 250mV dc offset voltage must be applied to the reference terminal (pin 6) of the IA.

Equate Gain Terms $A_{diff} = 235.7$

The IA's differential gain must be set to 235.7. A_{diff} for the AD524C IA is adjustable, and set by R_G according to the expression

$$R_g \cong \frac{40k\Omega}{A_{diff} - 1} \tag{8.8}$$

Example 8.9:

Solve for the value of gain control resistor R_G to set A_{diff} to 235.7.

Solution:

Use Eq. (8.8)

$$R_G \cong \frac{40k\Omega}{A_{diff} - 1} \cong \frac{40k\Omega}{235.7-1} \cong 170\Omega$$

In practice, R_G must be a potentiometer. A 250Ω 10-turn pot should be chosen and adjusted for gain.

A practical design is given in Figure 8.8(b). Note that correct wiring of the transducer's bridge outputs to the SCC's inputs is possible by comparing

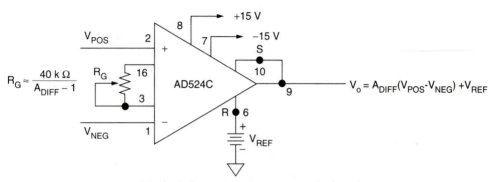

(a) A COMMERCIAL INSTRUMENTATION AMPLIFIER (IA)

FIGURE 8.8 A commercial IA can be used to signal condition a load cell weight system

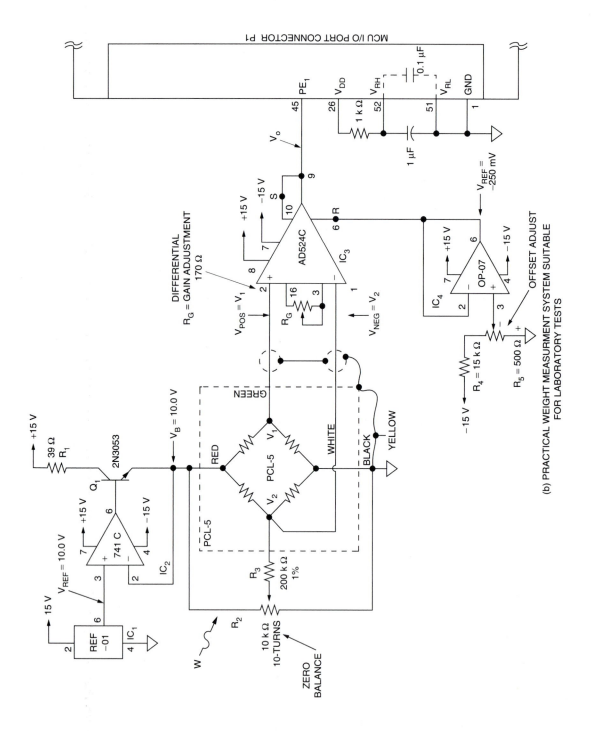

(b) PRACTICAL WEIGHT MEASURMENT SYSTEM SUITABLE FOR LABORATORY TESTS

input terms between the hardware and design equation. V_1 of the bridge must be connected to V_{pos} and V_2 of the bridge must be connected to V_{neg}.

Good common mode rejection (CMR) is possible with IC_3 only if the reference voltage applied to pin 6 is supplied from a low impedance source. To create this negative offset voltage, use the wiper of R_5 and buffer it with a voltage follower (IC_4).

Begin calibration of Figure 8.8(b) by monitoring V_o of IC_3 with a precision DMM. With no weight on the load cell, and the table removed, adjust R_2 for $V_o = 0V$. Replace the table and adjust the offset pot R_5 to once again set V_o equal to 0V. Finally adjust for full scale by loading the table with a precision 5-lb weight and adjust the gain trim pot R_G for a V_o equal to 5.00V. This calibration procedure need be done only once because there is no interaction between trim pots.

Figure 8.8(b) is a good choice for testing load cells in a controlled laboratory situation. However, if it is to be used in a noisy industrial or commerical environment, a few practical modifications must be included.

8.4.2 Practical SCC Hardware for Industrial Usage

One of the more challenging problems to the practicing engineer is preventing noise from coupling into a design. Circuits that work predictably well in a sterile laboratory are not always reliable in a noisy industrial or commercial environment. Figure 8.8(b) is just such a circuit. If the electronics has to be located several feet from the load cell, a shielded cable is needed to interface the low-level bridge output to the IA's inputs. However, even with careful shield grounding, 60 Hz power line noise can be introduced into the low-level bridge signal and amplified along with the transducer output.

Figure 8.9 is a practical solution to the problem of front-end noise. IC_3 is reconfigured for a differential gain of only 10.0 by removing R_G and strapping pins 3 and 13 together. This modest gain amplifies both signal and noise and is the output of IC_3 labeled as V_o'. The low-pass filter of R_6 and C_1 set a high-frequency cutoff of about 5Hz. Therefore, Vo" contains the differential bridge output but the 60Hz noise is attenuated at a rate of $-20dB/decade$ above 5Hz.

To re-establish the proper SCC design equation, IC_5, a noninverting amplifier, is added to the signal path. Gain trim is made by adjusting R_9 for an amplifier gain of 23.57 to reset the overall signal path gain to $10(23.57) = 235.7$.

8.4.3 Interfacing to the 68HC11 MCU

An industrial prototype of Figure 8.9 is shown photographed in Figure 8.10. The output of the analog interface circuitry is wired to the MCU's PE_1 port at pin 45. MCU's analog low reference terminal at pin 51 is wired to the high-quality ground of the ±15V power supply on the breadboarding system.

In the next sections, software will be presented to solve the weight measurement problem given at the beginning of this chapter.

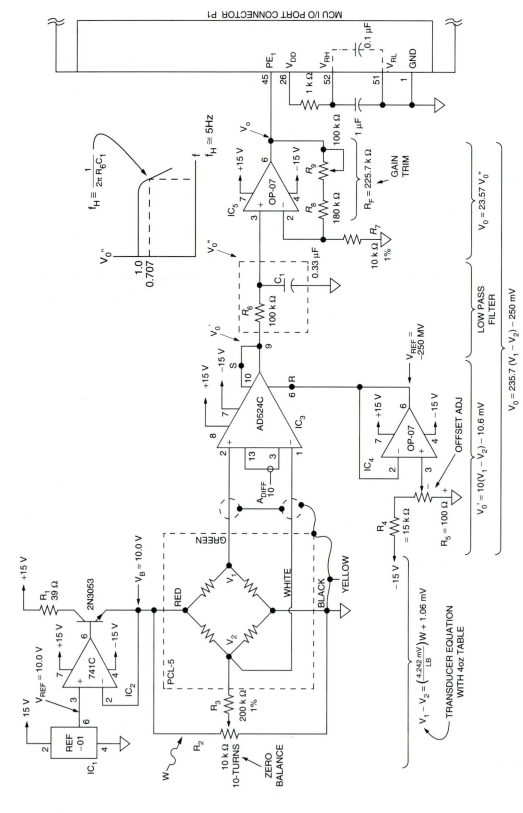

FIGURE 8.9 Low-pass filter R_6, C_1 removes 60Hz power line noise from the low-level bridge signal

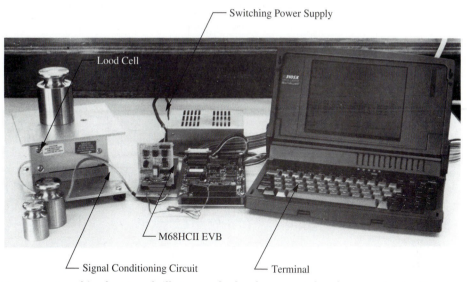

FIGURE 8.10 This photograph illustrates the hardware interface between load cell, EVB, and computer terminal

8.5
■■■

SOFTWARE DESIGN

Programmers of microcomputer-based products must clearly understand the entire system. They must work closely with their colleagues who are doing the analog circuit design so that they understand what has and has not been done by the input signal conditioning circuitry and what output is desired. From the statement of the problem given in section 8.1, the software routines for this application must accomplish six major tasks:

1. identify a valid part number;
2. obtain the part's price from a memory buffer;
3. read the weight from an A/D register;
4. calculate the total cost (price × weight);
5. round off the sale price to the nearest penny;
6. display the final sale price on a terminal.

This chapter's application uses many of the routines studied in previous chapters as well as some new ones. Some of the EVB utility subroutines studied in Chapter 4 will also be used to input and output data. Thus, it is unnecessary to write separate programs for these tasks. Routines that you have previously used successfully will save a considerable amount of time in the overall development cycle toward a finished product. These previously used routines may be linked together to solve a new application problem. For our present application, previ-

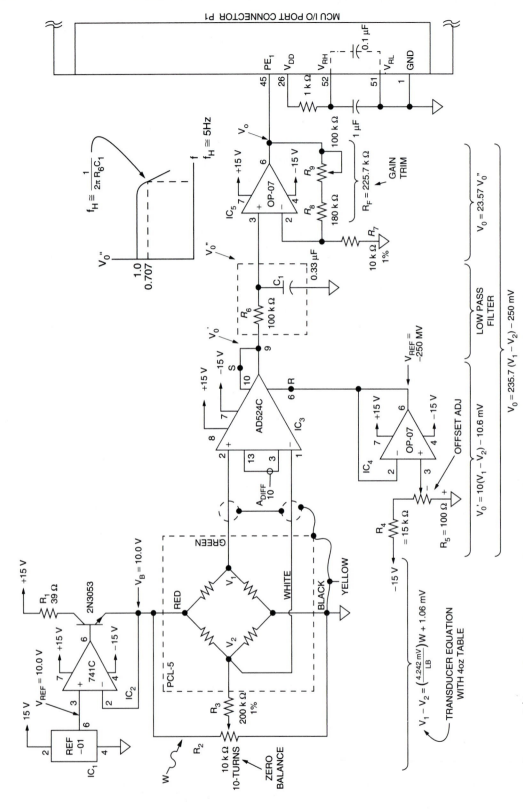

FIGURE 8.9 Low-pass filter R_6, C_1 removes 60Hz power line noise from the low-level bridge signal

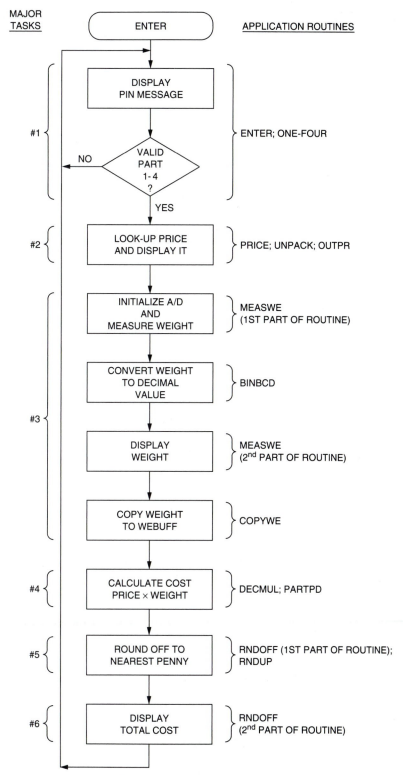

Figure 8.11 Overall flow chart of the application program and the corresponding routines used for each part.

Ideally, we would like the operator to enter a valid part number (1-4) and then press the <Return> or <Enter> key. Let's list some possible errors and design the software to handle them. Examples of operator error could be an invalid part number (any number other than 1–4), pressing a valid part number twice (such as 11—thereby creating an invalid part number), pressing a letter key, pressing a key other than the <Enter> key after entering a part number. We could think of other possible errors, but these typical errors illustrate enough examples for now. Task #1 in Figure 8.11 now can be designed for the functions necessary to handle the input conditions. Figure 8.12 is a flow chart showing a possible path for these input conditions. For our application, the instructions are for the operator to press the <Enter> key after entering the part number. Figure 8.12 shows that if the second character is not a delimiter, the initial message is displayed again. If the second character is a delimiter, then the first entered character is checked to be sure it is a valid part number. (Remember from Chapter 4 a delimiter is a carriage return or whitespace.) The flow chart shows the path to be taken for valid and invalid entered part numbers. It is possible to redraw the flow chart to check for part numbers before checking for the delimiter. This problem is left as an exercise for the student.

With the flow chart of Figure 8.12 as a guide, lines of code can now be written. Remember that EVB utility subroutines are used to input and output data. The student may want to review the function of the EVB utility subroutines labeled INCHAR, DCHEK, OUTCRLF, and OUTSTRO from Chapter 4. Now the reader should be able to follow the application routines in section 8.6 labeled ENTER and ONE-FOUR.

8.5.2   PRICE and UNPACK Routines

The PRICE-UNPACK routines are used to obtain a valid part's price, stored in a look-up table as a packed BCD value, and put it as an unpacked BCD value into a memory buffer labeled PRBUFF (price buffer). Data stored in the PRBUFF are the multiplicand values which will be used in the DECMUL routine. The conversion from packed to unpacked BCD numbers is accomplished by using accumulator D and left shift operations. Figure 8.13 gives an example of how this task is accomplished. Each price value from the table is four BCD numbers. Therefore, a loop is set up so that two packed BCD values are converted and then the next two are converted. The individual lines of code labeled PRICE and UNPACK in section 8.6 should now be studied to see how this task can be done.

8.5.3   OUTPR Routine

The routine labeled OUTPR outputs the price per pound message and then the part's price. Since each price is stored as four BCD numbers, the price of some parts may have a zero as the most significant digit (MSD). The software routine can be written to check the MSD and not display it if it is a zero, thereby suppressing any leading zero. The remaining digits are displayed and a decimal

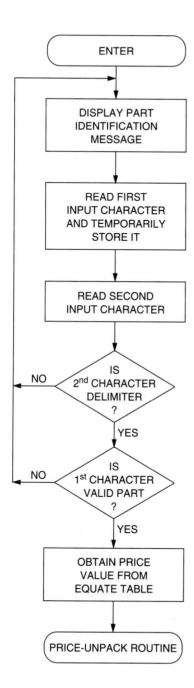

FIGURE 8.12 A flow chart for the ENTER and ONE-FOUR routines

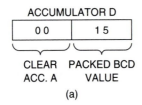

ACCUMULATOR D

0 0	1 5

CLEAR   PACKED BCD
ACC. A   VALUE

(a)

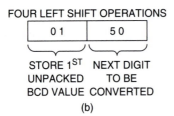

FOUR LEFT SHIFT OPERATIONS

0 1	5 0

STORE 1ST   NEXT DIGIT
UNPACKED   TO BE
BCD VALUE CONVERTED

(b)

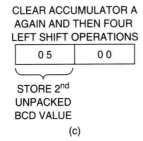

CLEAR ACCUMULATOR A
AGAIN AND THEN FOUR
LEFT SHIFT OPERATIONS

0 5	0 0

STORE 2nd
UNPACKED
BCD VALUE

(c)

FIGURE 8.13 The UNPACK routine converts two packed BCD values to two unpacked values by using accumulator D and left shift operations

point is inserted. As an example, a price stored as 0925 is displayed as $9.25 and a price of 0060 is displayed as $0.60.

A flow chart for this routine is shown in Figure 8.14. A check of the line code of the OUTPR routine in section 8.6 shows that the price to be displayed is taken from the PRBUFF (price buffer). It has been stored there as four unpacked BCD numbers and can be outputted easily using EVB utility subroutines. The OUT-RHLF utility subroutine converts the BCD value to ASCII before sending it to the serial port. The ASCII character for a decimal point or period is $2E_{hex}$ and this is included in the program and outputted using the OUTA utility subroutine. The dollar sign ($) is included as part of the message and does not have to be outputted separately.

8.5.4   WECOST Routine

The routine labeled WECOST stands for weight and cost. It is primarily a collection of subroutines. Some of them have been used in other chapters and each subroutine has been written to accomplish a particular task. By collecting the subroutines in this way, you can see what remains to be accomplished in the rest

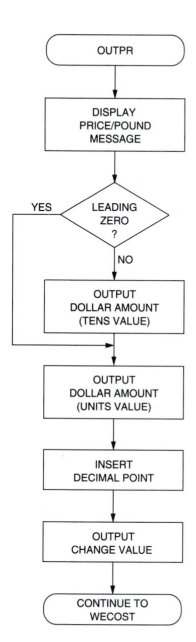

FIGURE 8.14 A flow chart illustrating the OUTPR
(output price) routine

of the application program. Also in section 8.7 you will see how the BUFFALO CALL command can be used to test the subroutines separately. This debugging technique is extremely helpful to locate programming errors.

8.5.5   MEASWE Routine

The label MEASWE stands for measurement of the weight. This routine includes the programming steps that initialize the microcontroller's A/D control register (ADCTL), introduce a time delay, read and output the weight value along with a weight message. The instructions to initialize the A/D include a time delay, read an A/D register, and multiply the binary number by 20mV (the value of each bit in an A/D register, i.e., 1 LSB) were studied in Chapter 5 and in particular in Example 5.13. The multiplied value must be converted to BCD to be displayed on a screen and to be used in the decimal multiplication routine. Therefore, a binary to BCD conversion routine is required. Fortunately, we have already solved this problem in Chapter 3 as Example 3.24 and have also used it in Example 5.13. This conversion routine is labeled BINBCD. Figure 8.15 is a flow chart showing the steps involved for the MEASWE routine. The BINBCD program is a subroutine in the MEASWE routine. The results of the BINBCD routine are stored in a memory buffer labeled DBUFF (data buffer). Now refer to the routines labeled MEASWE and BINBCD in section 8.6 for the actual line code and additional comments.

8.5.6   COPYWE Routine

The routine labeled COPYWE copies the weight from the BCD buffer (DBUFF) to WEBUFF (weight buffer). The reason this is necessary is because the BINBCD and DECMUL were written separately. The BINBCD routine of Example 3.24 stores its results in one buffer (DBUFF) and the DECMUL obtains its values from another buffer (WEBUFF). The decimal multiplication (DECMUL) routine uses the contents of the WEBUFF as multiplier values. The few lines of code in the COPYWE routine copies the data from one memory area to another. The reader should check the lines of code in the COPYWE routine to see how the X and Y registers are used to transfer data easily.

8.5.7   DECMUL Routine

The DECMUL is a decimal multiplication routine. It is an expanded version of the multiplication routine of Example 3.25. A review of Example 3.25 shows that memory locations are used to hold the multiplicand and multiplier values as well as store the product. For this application, the multiplicand value is the part's price and is stored in a buffer called PRBUFF (price buffer). The multiplier value is the weight and is stored in a buffer called WEBUFF (weight buffer). The product of price times weight is the total cost and is stored in a buffer called TCBUFF (total cost buffer).

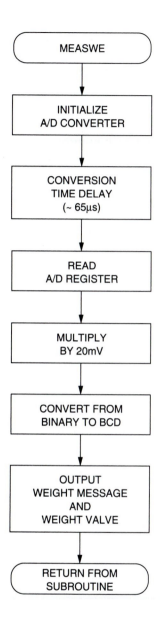

FIGURE 8.15 Flow chart illustrating the steps used in the MEASWE routine

Thus, the DECMUL routine multiplies the price value stored in the PRBUFF by the weight value stored in the WEBUFF. The product is the total cost or sale price and is stored in the buffer labeled TCBUFF. In addition to these memory buffers, this routine uses several memory locations to temporarily hold counter and pointer values. They are:

• MDPNTR—multiplicand pointer
• MRPNTR—multiplier pointer

- TCPNTR—total cost pointer
- MDCNT—multiplicand counter
- MRCNT—multiplier counter

The actual memory locations for these registers and buffers are given in section 8.6 and shown in Figure 8.19.

The flow chart for the DECMUL routine is shown in Figure 8.16. The PARTPD is a subroutine that adds the partial products after each multiplication step and keeps the data in the TCBUFF current. Refer to Section 8.6 for additional comments and the code for this routine.

8.5.8   RNDOFF Routine

The roundoff (RNDOFF) routine checks the value of the three least significant digits in the TCBUFF to determine if a round up of one cent should occur. If a round up is to occur, program execution jumps to the round up (RNDUP) subroutine and then the final sale price is outputted to the display. If a round up is not to occur, then the final answer is outputted immediately. Figure 8.17 gives an example of typical data that could exist in the TCBUFF before and after a round up of one cent occurs. Note: The decimal point is always five places from the bottom (3 places are due to the A/D's conversion of 20 mV/bit and 2 places are due to the price per pound value). Thus, the contents of the last three locations in TCBUFF ($D32D–$D32F) are never displayed. They are only checked to determine if a round up should occur. If the last three digits are a number greater than 500, round up by one cent; otherwise do not round up. In practice, only the contents of location $D32D (PRBUFF + 13) has to be checked to determine if it is greater than or equal to 5.

Figure 8.18 shows the flow chart of the RNDOFF routine. Remember the round up (RNDUP) subroutine is the program that adds one cent to the subtotal. The last part of the RNDOFF routine also includes the steps to output the total cost message and the final sale price. Now refer to the application program in section 8.6 for the actual line code.

8.6

APPLICATION PROGRAM

This application program was written using a cross-assembler on an IBM-compatible computer and downloaded into RAM on the EVB. Remember the advantages of a cross-assembler are that labels can be used, programs can be edited easily, comments can be included, equate tables can be used, output messages can be added, and the program can be saved as a file on a hard and/or floppy disk.

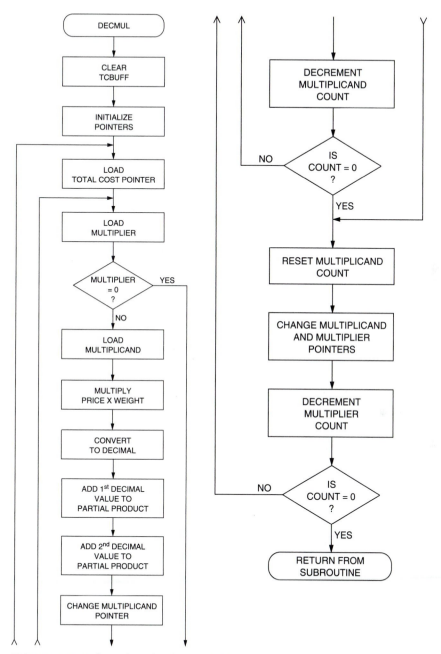

FIGURE 8.16 A flow chart for the DECMUL routine

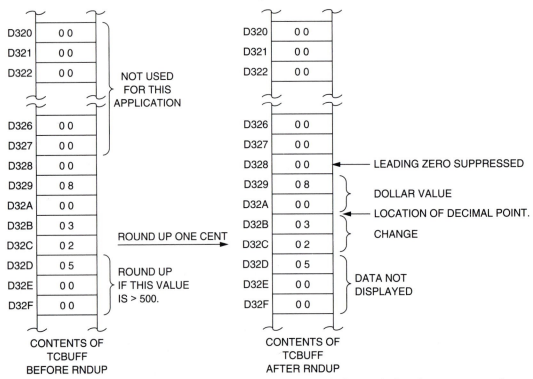

FIGURE 8.17 Example of how a result is stored in the TCBUFF before and after the RNDUP routine. The total cost will be displayed as $80.33.

After the program is downloaded, the PC is then used only as a dumb terminal for inputting part numbers via the keyboard and for displaying the output information on the terminal. It is the microcontroller's central processing unit that is used to execute the application program.

The following application program begins with a listing of the equate values grouped according to functions, e.g., EVB utility subroutines, part numbers, price values, temporary register and buffer locations, and also a listing of the messages to be displayed. For this application, the authors have used an equate table to set fixed addresses for those memory locations used as temporary registers and buffers. We could have used the RMB (reserve memory bytes) assembler directive and allowed the assembler to find memory space as was done in Chapter 7. The reason for not using the assembler directive for this application program is so that the reader can refer to previous examples and see that the subroutines are identical and the same temporary locations are being used. For another application, the RMB directive may be used. Figure 8.19 is a memory map guide showing the addresses used and typical contents.

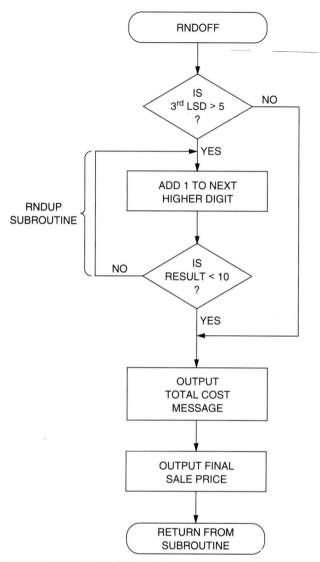

FIGURE 8.18 Flow chart for the RNDOFF and RNDUP routines

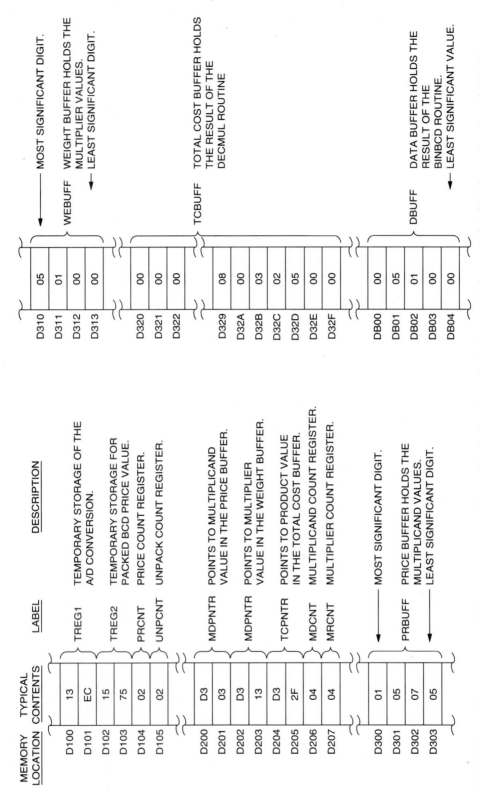

FIGURE 8.19 Memory map guide for temporary register and buffer locations. Typical contents for a weight of 5.1 lbs and a price of $15.75.

```
LINE  S PC    OPCO OPERANDS S LABEL   MNEMO OPERANDS COMMENT
00001                               NAM   Weight Measurements with a Load Cell
00002                        ***************************************************************
00003                        *             EVB Utility Subroutine Addresses                *
00004                        * Utility subroutines allow the user to perform a variety of   *
00005                        * input/output tasks and are described in Chapter 4.  They are *
00006                        * stored in ROM and may be used by executing a JSR instruction  *
00007                        * to the applicable address.                                   *
00008                        ***************************************************************
00009
00010
00011 P 0000  ffa6      A DCHEK    EQU   $FFA6      Check delimiter character.
00012 P 0000  ffb5      A OUTRHLF  EQU   $FFB5      Convert right nibble to ASCII and output.
00013 P 0000  ffb8      A OUTA     EQU   $FFB8      Output character in accumulator A.
00014 P 0000  ffc4      A OUTCRL   EQU   $FFC4      Output <carriage return> <line feed>.
00015 P 0000  ffc7      A OUTSTRG  EQU   $FFC7      Output message string until $04 include leading <CR> <LF>.
00016 P 0000  ffc4      A OUTCRLF  EQU   $FFC4      Output carriage return followed by a line feed.
00017 P 0000  ffca      A OUTSTRGO EQU   $FFCA      Output message string until $04 no leading <CR> <LF>.
00018 P 0000  ffcd      A INCHAR   EQU   $FFCD      Input ASCII character and echo back.
00019
00020
00021
00022                        ***************************************************************
00023                        *               Part Identification Numbers                   *
00024                        * These identification numbers are stored in ASCII format because *
00025                        * input data from a keyboard is received as an ASCII character. *
00026                        * Therefore, an ASCII to decimal conversion is not necessary for *
00027                        * this application.                                            *
00028                        ***************************************************************
00029
00030
00031 P 0000  0031      A PIN1     EQU   $31        ASCII value for part number 1.
00032 P 0000  0032      A PIN2     EQU   $32        ASCII value for part number 2.
00033 P 0000  0033      A PIN3     EQU   $33        ASCII value for part number 3.
00034 P 0000  0034      A PIN4     EQU   $34        ASCII value for part number 4.
00035
00036
00037
00038                        ***************************************************************
00039                        *                   Price Part Equates                        *
00040                        * The price of each part is stored as four BCD values including a *
00041                        * leading zero where necessary.  When the price is displayed the *
00042                        * leading zero will be suppressed.   A dollar symbol and decimal *
00043                        * point will be inserted at the appropriate locations.         *
00044                        ***************************************************************
00045
00046
00047 P 0000  0450      A PRICE1   EQU   $0450      Price of part 1 is  $4.50
00048 P 0000  0925      A PRICE2   EQU   $0925      Price of part 2 is  $9.25.
00049 P 0000  0320      A PRICE3   EQU   $0320      Price of part 3 is  $3.20.
00050 P 0000  1575      A PRICE4   EQU   $1575      Price of part 4 is $15.75.
00051
00052
00053
00054
00055
00056                        ***************************************************************
00057                        *           Temporary Register and Buffer Equates             *
00058                        * These memory locations are used to hold data temporarily.  It is *
00059                        * possible to allow an assembler directive to set the locations. *
00060                        * However, the locations are the same as they have been in previous *
00061                        * examples and therefore they are set by using this equate table. *
00062                        * Refer to Figure 8-19 as a memory map guide.                   *
00063                        ***************************************************************
00064
00065 P 0000  d100      A TREG1    EQU   $D100      Stores the product of the DECMUL routine.
00066 P 0000  d102      A TREG2    EQU   $D102      Stores the price as a packed BCD value.
00067 P 0000  d104      A PRCNT    EQU   $D104      Holds a count for the PRICE routine.
00068 P 0000  d105      A UNPCNT   EQU   $D105      Holds a count for  the UNPACK routine.
00069 P 0000  d200      A MDPNTR   EQU   $D200      Location of multiplicand pointer.
00070 P 0000  d202      A MRPNTR   EQU   $D202      Location of multiplier pointer.
00071 P 0000  d204      A TCPNTR   EQU   $D204      Location of total cost pointer.
00072 P 0000  d206      A MDCNT    EQU   $D206      Location of multiplicand count.
```

```
LINE  S PC    OPCO OPERANDS  S LABEL    MNEMO OPERANDS  COMMENT
00073 P 0000  d207           A MRCNT    EQU   $D207     Location of multiplier count.
00074 P 0000  d300           A PRBUFF   EQU   $D300     Starting address of price buffer.
00075 P 0000  d310           A WEBUFF   EQU   $D310     Starting address of weight buffer.
00076 P 0000  d320           A TCBUFF   EQU   $D320     Starting address of total cost buffer.
00077 P 0000  db00           A DBUFF    EQU   $DB00     Starting address of a data buffer.
00078
00079
00080                          ******************************************************************
00081                        *                       Display Messages                          *
00082                        * Display messages start at address $D000.                        *
00083                          ******************************************************************
00084
00085 A d000                            ORG   $D000
00086
00087 A d000  45             A MSPIN    FCC   'Enter the part identification number: '
00088 A d026  04             A          FCB   $04       End-of-message mark.
00089 A d027  50             A MSPPLB   FCC   'Price per pound: $'
00090 A d039  04             A          FCB   $04       End-of-message mark.
00091 A d03a  57             A MSWEI    FCC   'Weight: '
00092 A d042  04             A          FCB   $04       End-of-message mark.
00093 A d043  70             A MSLBS    FCC   'pounds'
00094 A d049  04             A          FCB   $04       End-of-message mark.
00095 A d04a  54             A MSTCOST  FCC   'Total Cost: $'
00096 A d057  04             A          FCB   $04       End-of-message mark.
00097
00098                          ******************************************************************
00099                        * ENTER:  This routine outputs an initial message to the screen,  *
00100                        * waits for a key closure and checks for a valid part number      *
00101                        * before continuing.  If an invalid number is entered, the        *
00102                        * original message is displayed again.  Figure 8-12 shows a        *
00103                        * flowchart of this routine.                                       *
00104                          ******************************************************************
00105
00106 A c800                            ORG   $C800     Assembler directive
00107
00108 A c800  ce   d000      A ENTER:   LDX   #MSPIN    Initialize X register.
00109 A c803  bd   ffca      A          JSR   OUTSTRGO  Output pin number message.
00110 A c806  bd   ffcd      A          JSR   INCHAR    Check for an input character.
00111 A c809  16             A          TAB             A ---> B Temporarily store input character.
00112 A c80a  bd   ffcd      A          JSR   INCHAR    Check for next input character.
00113 A c80d  bd   ffa6      A          JSR   DCHEK     Check for <CR> or whitespace.
00114 A c810  27   06   c818 A          BEQ   E1        If Z = 1, branch to E1.
00115 A c812  bd   ffc4      A          JSR   OUTCRLF   Output <CR> and <LF>.
00116 A c815  7e   c800      A          JMP   ENTER     Jump back to ENTER.
00117
00118
00119 A c818  c1   31        A E1:      CMPB  #PIN1     Check for part number 1.
00120 A c81a  27   0f   c82b A          BEQ   ONE       If Z = 1, branch to ONE.
00121 A c81c  c1   32        A          CMPB  #PIN2     Check for part number 2.
00122 A c81e  27   11   c831 A          BEQ   TWO       If Z = 1, branch to TWO.
00123 A c820  c1   33        A          CMPB  #PIN3     Check for part number 3.
00124 A c822  27   13   c837 A          BEQ   THREE     If Z = 1, branch to THREE.
00125 A c824  c1   34        A          CMPB  #PIN4     Check for part number 4.
00126 A c826  27   15   c83d A          BEQ   FOUR      If Z = 1, branch to FOUR.
00127 A c828  7e   c800      A          JMP   ENTER     Jump back to ENTER.
00128
00129
00130
00131                          ******************************************************************
00132                        * ONE - FOUR:  After a part has been identified, its price is      *
00133                        * obtained from the equate table and loaded into accumulator D.    *
00134                        * Then a jump to the PRICE routine occurs.                         *
00135                          ******************************************************************
00136
00137 A c82b  cc   0450      A ONE:     LDD   #PRICE1   Load the price for part number 1.
00138 A c82e  7e   c843      A          JMP   PRICE     Jump to routine labeled PRICE.
00139 A c831  cc   0925      A TWO:     LDD   #PRICE2   Load the price for part number 2.
00140 A c834  7e   c843      A          JMP   PRICE     Jump to routine labeled PRICE.
00141 A c837  cc   0320      A THREE:   LDD   #PRICE3   Load the price for part number 3.
00142 A c83a  7e   c843      A          JMP   PRICE     Jump to routine labeled PRICE.
00143 A c83d  cc   1575      A FOUR:    LDD   #PRICE4   Load the price for part number 4.
00144 A c840  7e   c843      A          JMP   PRICE     Jump to routine labeled PRICE.
```

```
LINE   S PC   OPCO OPERANDS  S LABEL    MNEMO OPERANDS COMMENT
00145
00146
00147                        *****************************************************************
00148                        *   PRICE - UNPACK:  The PRICE routine and the UNPACK subroutine *
00149                        *   unpack the BCD price value and stores the result into the PRBUFF *
00150                        *   (price buffer).  PRBUFF values are the multiplicand values used *
00151                        *   in the DECMUL (decimal multiplication) routine.                *
00152                        *                                          * * * * *              *
00153                        *   Figure 8-13 gives an example of how the UNPACK operation is done. *
00154                        *****************************************************************
00155
00156
00157
00158   A c843 fd   d102    A PRICE:    STD   TREG2    Store price in temporary register.
00159   A c846 86   02      A          LDAA  #2       \ Initialize price counter
00160   A c848 b7   d104    A          STAA  PRCNT    / with a value of 2.
00161   A c84b ce   d300    A          LDX   #PRBUFF  Initialize X register.
00162   A c84e 18ce d102    A          LDY   #TREG2   Initialize Y register.
00163   A c852 18e6 00      A PR1:      LDAB  00,Y     Load packed BCD value into acc. B.
00164   A c855 bd   c865    A          JSR   UNPACK   Jump to UNPACK subroutine.
00165   A c858 7a   d104    A PR2:      DEC   PRCNT    Decrement price count.
00166   A c85b 27   05    c862         BEQ   PR3      If count = 0, branch to PR3.
00167   A c85d 1808                    INY            Change Y pointer.
00168   A c85f 7e   c852    A          JMP   PR1      Jump to point PR1.
00169   A c862 7e   c878    A PR3:      JMP   OUTPR    Jump to OUTPR routine.
00170
00171   A c865 86   02      A UNPACK:   LDAA  #2       \ Initialize unpack counter
00172   A c867 b7   d105    A          STAA  UNPCNT   / with a value of 2.
00173   A c86a 4f           UN1:       CLRA           Clear accumulator A.
00174   A c86b 05                      LSLD           \
00175   A c86c 05                      LSLD           | Convert packed BCD value to
00176   A c86d 05                      LSLD           | an unpacked BCD value.
00177   A c86e 05                      LSLD           /
00178   A c86f a7   00      A          STAA  00,X     Store unpacked value in PRBUFF.
00179   A c871 08                      INX            Change X pointer to next location.
00180   A c872 7a   d105    A          DEC   UNPCNT   Decrement price counter.
00181   A c875 26   f3    c86a         BNE   UN1      If count =/= 0, branch to UN1.
00182   A c877 39                      RTS            Return from subroutine to  PR2.
00183
00184                        *****************************************************************
00185                        *   OUTPR:  The following routine outputs the price per pound   *
00186                        *   message and the part's price which has been stored previously *
00187                        *   in the PRBUFF (price buffer).  Also any leading zero is      *
00188                        *   suppressed and a decimal point is inserted.                  *
00189                        *                                          * * * * *            *
00190                        *   A flowchart for this routine is shown in Figure 8-14.        *
00191                        *****************************************************************
00192
00193   A c878 ce   d027    A OUTPR:    LDX   #MSPPLB  Initialize X register.
00194   A c87b bd   ffca    A          JSR   OUTSTRGO Output price per pound message.
00195   A c87e ce   d300    A          LDX   #PRBUFF  Initialize X register.
00196   A c881 a6   00      A          LDAA  00,X     Load first unpacked BCD value.
00197   A c883 81   00      A          CMPA  #00      Check for a leading zero.
00198   A c885 27   03    c88a         BEQ   OPR1     If leading zero ignore it.
00199   A c887 bd   ffb5    A          JSR   OUTRHLF  If no leading zero output the value.
00200   A c88a 08           OPR1:      INX            Change to next PRBUFF location.
00201   A c88b a6   00      A          LDAA  00,X     Load second unpacked BCD value.
00202   A c88d bd   ffb5    A          JSR   OUTRHLF  Output the value.
00203   A c890 86   2e      A          LDAA  #$2E     ASCII character for decimal point.
00204   A c892 bd   ffb8    A          JSR   OUTA     Output decimal point.
00205   A c895 08                      INX            Change to next PRBUFF location.
00206   A c896 a6   00      A          LDAA  00,X     Load third unpacked BCD value.
00207   A c898 bd   ffb5    A          JSR   OUTRHLF  Output the value.
00208
00209
00210   A c89b 08                      INX            Change to next PRBUFF location.
00211   A c89c a6   00      A          LDAA  00,X     Load fourth unpacked BCD value.
00212   A c89e bd   ffb5    A          JSR   OUTRHLF  Output the value.
00213   A c8a1 7e   c8a4    A          JMP   WECOST   Jump to weight/cost routine.
00214
00215
00216
```

```
LINE   S PC    OPCO OPERANDS  S LABEL    MNEMO OPERANDS COMMENT
00217          ****************************************************************
00218                          *  WECOST:  The first four subroutines, MEASWE, COPYWE, DECMUL,  *
00219                          *  RNDOFF, are a major part of this application program and may be  *
00220                          *  studied as separate units by placing known values into those  *
00221                          *  temporary locations used by the subroutines.       * * * * *  *
00222                          *                                               * * * * *        *
00223                          *  The JSR OUTCRLF routines insert extra line spaces before the  *
00224                          *  application program is used again.                             *
00225                          ****************************************************************
00226
00227   A c8a4 bd   c8bc     A WECOST:   JSR    MEASWE   Subroutine to measure weight.
00228   A c8a7 bd   c926     A W1:       JSR    COPYWE   Subroutine to copy weight.
00229   A c8aa bd   c93b     A W2:       JSR    DECMUL   Decimal multiplication subroutine.
00230   A c8ad bd   c9d5     A W3:       JSR    RNDOFF   Round-off subroutine.
00231   A c8b0 bd   ffc4     A W4:       JSR    OUTCRLF  \
00232   A c8b3 bd   ffc4     A           JSR    OUTCRLF  | Extra line spaces.
00233   A c8b6 bd   ffc4     A           JSR    OUTCRLF  /
00234   A c8b9 7e   c800     A           JMP    ENTER    Return to ENTER.
00235
00236
00237
00238                          ****************************************************************
00239                          * MEASWE:  This subrouine performs 5 functions: (1) initializes the *
00240                          * the A/D control register, (2) introduces a time delay so that the *
00241                          * A/D can make the conversion, (3) outputs the weight message,      *
00242                          * (4) outputs the measured  weight after it has been converted to   *
00243                          * BCD, and (5) outputs the pound message.                           *
00244                          *                                               * * * * *          *
00245                          * A flowchart of this routine is shown in Figure 8-15.             *
00246                          ****************************************************************
00247
00248   A c8bc 86   21       A MEASWE:   LDAA   #$21     A/D control word.
00249   A c8be b7   1030     A           STAA   $1030    Initialize ADCTL register.
00250   A c8c1 c6   26       A           LDAB   #$26     Initialize time delay count.
00251   A c8c3 5a            DELAY:      DECB            Decrement time delay count.
00252   A c8c4 26   fd    c8c3           BNE    DELAY    If count =/= 0, branch to DELAY.
00253   A c8c6 b6   1031     A           LDAA   $1031    Read A/D register.
00254   A c8c9 c6   14       A           LDAB   #20      Load multiplier 20 dec (14 hex).
00255   A c8cb 3d            MUL                          Multiply  input data x 20 ---> D.
00256   A c8cc fd   d100     A           STD    TREG1    Store product temporarily.
00257   A c8cf bd   c8fb     A           JSR    BINBCD   Jump to  conversion subroutine.
00258
00259
00260
00261
00262   A c8d2 ce   d03a     A M1:       LDX    #MSWEI   Initialize X register.
00263   A c8d5 bd   ffc7     A           JSR    OUTSTRG  Output weight message.
00264   A c8d8 b6   db01     A           LDAA   DBUFF+1  Load first significant number.
00265   A c8db bd   ffb5     A           JSR    OUTRHLF  Convert to ASCII and output.
00266   A c8de 86   2e       A           LDAA   #$2E     Decimal point is inserted.
00267   A c8e0 bd   ffb8     A           JSR    OUTA     Output ASCII character.
00268   A c8e3 b6   db02     A           LDAA   DBUFF+2  Load second value.
00269   A c8e6 bd   ffb5     A           JSR    OUTRHLF  Convert to ASCII and output.
00270   A c8e9 b6   db03     A           LDAA   DBUFF+3  Load third value.
00271   A c8ec bd   ffb5     A           JSR    OUTRHLF  Convert to ASCII and output.
00272   A c8ef 86   20       A           LDAA   #$20     Space character is inserted.
00273   A c8f1 bd   ffb8     A           JSR    OUTA     Output ASCII character.
00274   A c8f4 ce   d043     A           LDX    #MSLBS   Initialize X register.
00275   A c8f7 bd   ffca     A           JSR    OUTSTRGO Output pound message.
00276   A c8fa 39            RTS                          Return from subroutine to point W1.
00277
00278                          ****************************************************************
00279                          * BINDEC:  This subroutine converts the 16 bit binary value stored *
00280                          * at TREG1 ($D100 and $D102) to a five digit BCD value. The        *
00281                          * converted values are then stored in memory buffer  DBUFF          *
00282                          * ($DB00 - $DB04) as unpacked BCD values.                           *
00283                          *                                               * * * * *          *
00284                          * This subroutine was studied in Example 3-24. The labels  TREG1   *
00285                          * and DBUFF were not used in Example 3-24 only the absolute         *
00286                          * addresses; otherwise the progams are identical.                   *
00287                          ****************************************************************
00288
```

```
LINE  S PC   OPCO OPERANDS S LABEL   MNEMO OPERANDS COMMENT
00289 A c8fb fc   d100     A BINBCD: LDD   TREG1    Load 16 bit number to be converted
00290 A c8fe ce   2710     A         LDX   #10000   Load divisor 10,000 (2710hex).
00291 A c901 02                      IDIV           Integer divide.
00292 A c902 8f                      XGDX           Save remainder in X register.
00293 A c903 f7   db00     A         STAB  DBUFF    Store quotient in memory buffer.
00294 A c906 8f                      XGDX           Return remainder back to D.
00295 A c907 ce   03e8     A         LDX   #1000    Load divisor 1,000 (3E8hex).
00296 A c90a 02                      IDIV           Integer divide.
00297 A c90b 8f                      XGDX           Save remainder in X register.
00298 A c90c f7   db01     A         STAB  DBUFF+1  Store quotient in memory buffer.
00299 A c90f 8f                      XGDX           Return remainder back to D.
00300 A c910 ce   0064     A         LDX   #100     Load divisor 100 (64hex).
00301 A c913 02                      IDIV           Integer divide.
00302 A c914 8f                      XGDX           Save remainder in X register.
00303 A c915 f7   db02     A         STAB  DBUFF+2  Store quotient in memory buffer.
00304 A c918 8f                      XGDX           Return remainder back to D.
00305 A c919 ce   000a     A         LDX   #10      Load divisor 10 (A hex).
00306 A c91c 02                      IDIV           Integer divide.
00307 A c91d 8f                      XGDX           Save remainder in X register.
00308 A c91e f7   db03     A         STAB  DBUFF+3  Store quotient in memory buffer.
00309 A c921 8f                      XGDX           Return remainder back to D.
00310 A c922 f7   db04     A         STAB  DBUFF+4  Store quotient in memory buffer.
00311 A c925 39                      RTS            Return from subroutine to point M1.
00312
00313                       ****************************************************************
00314                       *  COPYWE:  This subroutine copies the least signifacant four BCD  *
00315                       *  weight values stored at  DBUFF+1 to DBUFF+4 ($DB01 - $DB04) to  *
00316                       *  the multiplier buffer which is labeled WEBUFF (weight buffer).  *
00317                       *  For this application, the most significant BCD value stored at  *
00318                       *  DBUFF ($DB00) is always 0 and therefore not copied.             *
00319                       ****************************************************************
00320
00321 A c926 ce   db01     A COPYWE: LDX   #DBUFF+1 Initialize X register.
00322 A c929 18ce d310     A         LDY   #WEBUFF  Initialize Y register.
00323 A c92d c6   04       A         LDAB  #4       Number of values to be copied.
00324 A c92f a6   00       A NEXT:   LDAA  00,X     \ Copy a byte.
00325 A c931 18a7 00       A         STAA  00,Y     /
00326 A c934 08                      INX            \ Change pointers.
00327 A c935 1808                    INY            /
00328 A c937 5a                      DECB           Decrement count.
00329 A c938 26   f5  c92f           BNE   NEXT     If count =/= 1, branch back to NEXT.
00330 A c93a 39                      RTS            Return from subroutine to point W2.
00331
00332                       ****************************************************************
00333                       *  DECMUL:  This subroutine multiplies the price per pound stored  *
00334                       *  in the PRBUFF (price buffer) by the weight stored in the WEBUFF  *
00335                       *  (weight buffer).  The product which is the total cost will be    *
00336                       *  stored in the TCBUFF (total cost buffer).                        *
00337                       *                              * * * * *                            *
00338                       *  Memory locations $D200 to $D207 are used to hold address         *
00339                       *  pointers and count values.  See Figure 8-19.                     *
00340                       *                              * * * * *                            *
00341                       *  This routine is an expanded version of the decimal               *
00342                       *  multiplication program of Example 3-25.                           *
00343                       *                              * * * * *                            *
00344                       *  A flowchart of this routine is shown in Figure 8-16.             *
00345                       ****************************************************************
00346
00347 A c93b 18ce d320     A DECMUL: LDY   #TCBUFF  Initialize Y register.
00348 A c93f c6   10       A         LDAB  #16      Initialize count value.
00349 A c941 4f                      CLRA
00350 A c942 18a7 00       A DM1:    STAA  00,Y     \   Clear partial product buffer
00351 A c945 1808                    INY            |   (TCBUFF) which is 16 bytes
00352 A c947 5a                      DECB           |   in length beginning at
00353 A c948 26   f8  c942           BNE   DM1      /   $D320.
00354
00355 A c94a cc   d303     A         LDD   #PRBUFF+3  \
00356 A c94d fd   d200     A         STD   MDPNTR     |
00357 A c950 cc   d313     A         LDD   #WEBUFF+3  |
00358 A c953 fd   d202     A         STD   MRPNTR     |
00359 A c956 cc   d32f     A         LDD   #TCBUFF+15 |  Initialize pointers and counters.
00360 A c959 fd   d204     A         STD   TCPNTR     |
00361 A c95c 86   04       A         LDAA  #04        |
```

```
LINE  S PC    OPCO OPERANDS  S LABEL     MNEMO OPERANDS  COMMENT
00362 A c95e  b7   d206      A           STAA  MDCNT     |
00363 A c961  86   04        A           LDAA  #04       |
00364 A c963  b7   d207      A           STAA  MRCNT     /
00365
00366 A c966  18fe d204      A DM2:       LDY   TCPNTR    Initialize Y register.
00367 A c96a  fe   d202      A DM3:       LDX   MRPNTR    Initialize X register.
00368 A c96d  e6   00        A           LDAB  00,X      Load multiplier value.
00369 A c96f  c1   00        A           CMPB  #00       Check for multiplier equal to zero.
00370 A c971  27   23        c996        BEQ   CONT      If multiplier = 0, branch to CONT (continue).
00371 A c973  fe   d200      A           LDX   MDPNTR    Initialize X register.
00372 A c976  a6   00        A           LDAA  00,X      Load multiplicand value.
00373 A c978  3d                         MUL             Multiply A x B --> D.
00374 A c979  ce   000a      A           LDX   #10       Load divisor 10dec = $0A.
00375 A c97c  02                         IDIV            Convert binary product to decimal.
00376 A c97d  17                         TBA             Transfer B --> A.
00377 A c97e  bd   c9b9      A           JSR   PARTPD    Jump to partial product subroutine.
00378
00379 A c981  8f                         XGDX            Move quotient to D register.
00380 A c982  17                         TBA             Transfer B --> A.
00381 A c983  1809                       DEY             Decrement Y register.
00382 A c985  bd   c9b9      A           JSR   PARTPD    Jump to partial product subroutine.
00383 A c988  fc   d200      A           LDD   MDPNTR    \
00384 A c98b  83   0001      A           SUBD  #1        | Decrement multiplicand pointer.
00385 A c98e  fd   d200      A           STD   MDPNTR    /
00386 A c991  7a   d206      A           DEC   MDCNT     Decrement multiplicand counter.
00387 A c994  26   d4        c96a        BNE   DM3       If count =/= 0, branch to DM3.
00388 A c996  86   04        A CONT:      LDAA  #4        \  Reset multiplicand counter.
00389 A c998  b7   d206      A           STAA  MDCNT     /
00390 A c99b  cc   d303      A           LDD   #PRBUFF+3 \
00391 A c99e  fd   d200      A           STD   MDPNTR    |
00392 A c9a1  fc   d202      A           LDD   MRPNTR    |
00393 A c9a4  83   0001      A           SUBD  #1        |  Set buffer pointers for next
00394 A c9a7  fd   d202      A           STD   MRPNTR    |  decimal multiplication.
00395 A c9aa  fc   d204      A           LDD   TCPNTR    |
00396 A c9ad  83   0001      A           SUBD  #1        |
00397 A c9b0  fd   d204      A           STD   TCPNTR    /
00398 A c9b3  7a   d207      A           DEC   MRCNT     Decrement multiplier count.
00399 A c9b6  26   ae        c966        BNE   DM2       If count =/= 0, branch to DM2.
00400 A c9b8  39                         RTS             Return from subroutine to point W3.
00401
00402
00403
00404                         ****************************************************************
00405                         *  PARTPD:  This subroutine adds the partial products thereby  *
00406                         *  updating the result in the TCBUFF.  At the end of the DECMUL *
00407                         *  program, the total cost is stored in the buffer.             *
00408                         *            * * * * *                                          *
00409                         *  Note: The contents of the Y register remain unchanged upon   *
00410                         *  returning to the DECMUL program.                             *
00411                         ****************************************************************
00412
00413
00414
00415
00416
00417 A c9b9  183c           PARTPD:     PSHY            Save Y register.
00418 A c9bb  0c                         CLC             Clear C flag.
00419 A c9bc  18a9 00        A PP1:       ADCA  $00,Y     Add partial product + acc. A + C flag.
00420 A c9bf  19                         DAA             Decimal adjust.
00421 A c9c0  81   10        A           CMPA  #$10      Compare acc. A with 10hex.
00422 A c9c2  2d   0b        c9cf        BLT   PP2       If A < 10hex, branch to PP2.
00423 A c9c4  84   0f        A           ANDA  #$0F      Mask out upper nibble.
00424 A c9c6  18a7 00        A           STAA  00,Y      Store result.
00425 A c9c9  4f                         CLRA            Clear accumulator A.
00426 A c9ca  0d                         SEC             Set C flag.
00427 A c9cb  1809                       DEY             Decrement Y pointer.
00428 A c9cd  20   ed        c9bc        BRA   PP1       Branch to update partial product.
00429 A c9cf  18a7 00        A PP2:       STAA  00,Y      Store result.
00430 A c9d2  1838                       PULY            Retrieve Y register.
00431 A c9d4  39                         RTS             Return to DECMUL subroutine.
00432
```

```
LINE   S PC    OPCO OPERANDS  S LABEL    MNEMO OPERANDS COMMENT
00433                           *******************************************************************
00434                           *  RNDOFF: This subroutine determines how the least significant    *
00435                           *  values should be rounded-off.  If the least significant digits  *
00436                           *  are greater than 500 then a round up of one cent occurs;        *
00437                           *  otherwise the calculated total price remains unchanged. See     *
00438                           *  Figure 8-17 for an example.                                     *
00439                           *                     * * * * *                                    *
00440                           *  This subroutine also outputs the total cost message and the     *
00441                           *  total cost of the parts.                                        *
00442                           *******************************************************************
00443
00444  A c9d5 ce  d32d     A RNDOFF:  LDX   #TCBUFF+13 \
00445  A c9d8 a6  00       A          LDAA  00,X       | Check the value in location $D32D.
00446  A c9da 81  05       A          CMPA  #5         | Branch if accumulator A < 5.
00447  A c9dc 2d  03  c9e1 A          BLT   OUTPUT     |
00448  A c9de bd  ca1e     A          JSR   RNDUP      /
00449  A c9e1 ce  d04a     A OUTPUT:  LDX   #MSTCOST Initialize X register.
00450  A c9e4 bd  ffc7     A          JSR   OUTSTRG Output total cost message.
00451  A c9e7 ce  d328     A          LDX   #TCBUFF+8 Initialize X register.
00452  A c9ea a6  00       A          LDAA  00,X       \
00453  A c9ec 81  00       A          CMPA  #0         |
00454  A c9ee 27  0c  c9fc A          BEQ   OUT1       |
00455  A c9f0 bd  ffb5     A          JSR   OUTRHLF    |
00456  A c9f3 08           A          INX              |
00457  A c9f4 a6  00       A          LDAA  00,X       |
00458  A c9f6 bd  ffb5     A          JSR   OUTRHLF    |
00459  A c9f9 7e  ca06     A          JMP   OUT2       | Check for leading zeros
00460  A c9fc 08             OUT1:    INX              | and output dollar value.
00461  A c9fd a6  00       A          LDAA  00,X       |
00462  A c9ff 81  00       A          CMPA  #0         |
00463  A ca01 27  03  ca06 A          BEQ   OUT2       |
00464  A ca03 bd  ffb5     A          JSR   OUTRHLF    |
00465  A ca06 08             OUT2:    INX              |
00466  A ca07 a6  00       A          LDAA  00,X       |
00467  A ca09 bd  ffb5     A          JSR   OUTRHLF    /
00468
00469
00470  A ca0c 86  2e       A          LDAA  #$2E       \  Insert decimal point.
00471  A ca0e bd  ffb8     A          JSR   OUTA       /
00472  A ca11 08           A          INX              \
00473  A ca12 a6  00       A          LDAA  00,X       |
00474  A ca14 bd  ffb5     A          JSR   OUTRHLF    | Output change value.
00475  A ca17 08           A          INX              |
00476  A ca18 a6  00       A          LDAA  00,X       |
00477  A ca1a bd  ffb5     A          JSR   OUTRHLF    /
00478  A ca1d 39           A          RTS   Return from subroutine to point W4.
00479  A ca1e 09             RNDUP:   DEX   Change X pointer.
00480  A ca1f a6  00       A          LDAA  00,X   Load accumulator A.
00481  A ca21 0d           A          SEC   Set carry flag (C=1).
00482  A ca22 89  00       A          ADCA  #0    Add 1 to accumulator A.
00483  A ca24 19           A          DAA   Decimal adjust.
00484  A ca25 81  10       A          CMPA  #$10  \ Branch to R1 if adjusted
00485  A ca27 2d  07  ca30 A          BLT   R1    / value is less than 10.
00486  A ca29 80  10       A          SUBA  #$10  Subtract 10 from accumulator A.
00487  A ca2b a7  00       A          STAA  00,X  Store result.
00488  A ca2d 7e  ca1e     A          JMP   RNDUP  Jump to RNDUP.
00489  A ca30 a7  00     A R1:        STAA  00,X  Store result.
00490  A ca32 39           A          RTS   Return from subroutine to OUTPUT.
00491
00492                                 END   $C800  Assembler directive
00493
00494
00495
00496
00497
00498
00499
00500
00501
00502
00503
00504
00505
```

```
LINE  S PC   OPCO OPERANDS  S LABEL    MNEMO OPERANDS COMMENT
00506
00507
00508
00509
00510
00511
00512
00513


Total number of errors: 0
Total number of warnings: 0
Total number of lines: 513
Number of bytes in section ASCT: 651

Number of bytes in program: 651

              CROSS REFERENCE TABLE
NAME      ATTRB S VALUE P:LINE LINE1....N

BINBCD        A c8fb  7:289      257
CONT          A c996  9:388      370
COPYWE        A c926  8:321      228
DBUFF    EQU  A db00  3:77       264  268  270  293  298  303  308  310  321
DCHEK    EQU  A ffa6  2:11       113
DECMUL        A c93b  8:347      229
DELAY         A c8c3  6:251      252
DM1           A c942  8:350      353
DM2           A c966  9:366      399
DM3           A c96a  9:367      387
E1            A c818  4:119      114
ENTER         A c800  4:108      116  127  234
FOUR          A c83d  4:143      126
INCHAR   EQU  A ffcd  2:18       110  112
M1            A c8d2  7:262
MDCNT    EQU  A d206  3:72       362  386  389
MDPNTR   EQU  A d200  3:69       356  371  383  385  391
MEASWE        A c8bc  6:248      227
MRCNT    EQU  A d207  3:73       364  398
MRPNTR   EQU  A d202  3:70       358  367  392  394
MSLBS         A d043  3:93       274
MSPIN         A d000  3:87       108
MSPPLB        A d027  3:89       193
MSTCOST       A d04a  3:95       449
MSWEI         A d03a  3:91       262
NEXT          A c92f  8:324      329
ONE           A c82b  4:137      120
OPR1          A c88a  5:200      198
OUT1          A c9fc 10:460      454
OUT2          A ca06 10:465      459  463
OUTA     EQU  A ffb8  2:13       204  267  273  471
OUTCRL   EQU  A ffc4  2:14
OUTCRLF  EQU  A ffc4  2:16       115  231  232  233
OUTPR         A c878  5:193      169
OUTPUT        A c9e1 10:449      447
OUTRHLF  EQU  A ffb5  2:12       199  202  207  212  265  269  271  455  458  464  467  474  477
OUTSTRG  EQU  A ffc7  2:15       263  450
OUTSTRGO EQU  A ffca  2:17       109  194  275
PARTPD        A c9b9 10:417      377  382
PIN1     EQU  A 0031  2:31       119
PIN2     EQU  A 0032  2:32       121
PIN3     EQU  A 0033  2:33       123
PIN4     EQU  A 0034  2:34       125
PP1           A c9bc 10:419      428
PP2           A c9cf 10:429      422
PR1           A c852  5:163      168
PR2           A c858  5:165
PR3           A c862  5:169      166
PRBUFF   EQU  A d300  3:74       161  195  355  390
PRCNT    EQU  A d104  3:67       160  165
PRICE         A c843  5:158      138  140  142  144
PRICE1   EQU  A 0450  2:47       137
```

```
                     CROSS REFERENCE TABLE
     NAME   ATTRB S VALUE P:LINE LINE1....N
     PRICE2  EQU  A 0925  2:48       139
     PRICE3  EQU  A 0320  2:49       141
     PRICE4  EQU  A 1575  2:50       143
     R1           A ca30 11:489      485
     RNDOFF       A c9d5 10:444      230
     RNDUP        A ca1e 11:479      448  488
     TCBUFF  EQU  A d320  3:76       347  359  444  451
     TCPNTR  EQU  A d204  3:71       360  366  395  397
     THREE        A c837  4:141      124
     TREG1   EQU  A d100  3:65       256  289
     TREG2   EQU  A d102  3:66       158  162
     TWO          A c831  4:139      122
     UN1          A c86a  5:173      181
     UNPACK       A c865  5:171      164
     UNPCNT  EQU  A d105  3:68       172  180
     W1           A c8a7  6:228      228
     W2           A c8aa  6:229      229
     W3           A c8ad  6:230      230
     W4           A c8b0  6:231      231
     WEBUFF  EQU  A d310  3:75       322  357
     WECOST       A c8a4  6:227      213
```

8.7

TESTING AND DEBUGGING THE APPLICATION PROGRAM

To troubleshoot a sensor and signal conditioning circuit requires a voltmeter and an oscilloscope. The testing and debugging of an application program requires other programs such as the command routines studied in Chapter 4. The monitor commands in BUFFALO that are helpful for software troubleshooting are:

- BR—Breakpoint set
- CALL—Execute subroutine
- G—Execute program
- MD—Memory display
- MM—Memory modify
- P—Proceed/continue from breakpoint
- RM—Register modify
- T—Trace

Each one of these commands is not necessary for every problem, but we now have a set of programs that can be used and we can choose those that will give us the most information.

8.7.1 Using the CALL Command

Much of this chapter's application program has been written using subroutines. This was done so that the MM, CALL, and MD commands could be used to check results. If a subroutine is using counters and data from a memory buffer, we can use the MM command to load known values into memory and then execute the CALL command. The MD command is used to display the answer so it can be checked against expected results.

Example 8.10:

Show how the MM, CALL, and MD commands are used to check the BIN-BCD subroutine.

Solution:

The BINBCD subroutine converts a 16-bit binary value stored at locations $D100 and $D101 to 5 bytes of unpacked BCD values. The results of the conversion are stored in a data buffer (DBUFF) whose address range is $DB00–$DB04. Remember when you are using BUFFALO commands you must use absolute addresses, not labels.

Use the MM command to put a known binary value into $D100 and $D101. Assume that we want to convert FFFF to BCD. Refer to section 4.9 as a refresher on the use of the MM command.

```
>MM D100 <ENTER>

>D100 XX FF <space bar> XX FF <ENTER>
```

where XX represents the present data that happens to be at locations D100 and D101 before the new data is entered. Check to be sure the value FFFF has been stored by using either the MD command or the MM command again. Remember the MD command (MD D100) displays 9 lines of data. You are interested only in the first 2 bytes of the first line. It should be FFFF.

If the entire application program has been entered, as shown in section 8.6, the starting address of the BINBCD subroutine is $C8FB. To execute this routine using the CALL command, type

```
> CALL C8FB <ENTER>
```

After the program is executed, the command displays the status of the CPU registers at the time the RTS instruction is encountered, except for the program counter (P) register. The P register will contain the starting address of the BINBCD subroutine.

Now use the MD command to check the contents of the data buffer (locations $DB00–$DB04).

```
> MD DB00 <ENTER>

>DB00 06 05 05 03 05 . . .
```

This is the unpacked BCD value of 65,535.

Remember the MD command displays 9 lines and each line contains 16 bytes. The results we need are the first 5 bytes of the first line.

8.7.2 Using the Break Command

Other parts of the application program are best checked by using the BR (BREAK) and G (GO) commands.

Example 8.11:

Show how to test the first five lines of code of the ENTER routine (from LDX #MSPIN to JSR INCHAR).

Solution:

The instruction immediately following the second JSR INCHAR instruction is located at address $C80D. This is the address to insert a breakpoint.

```
>  BR C80D  <ENTER>

>C80D 0000 0000 0000
```

Now use the G (Go) command.

```
>  G C800  <ENTER>
```

The first two lines of code are executed but the INCHAR utility subroutine waits for someone to enter a part number. Enter a valid part number (1–4) and press <Enter>. Now the contents of the CPU registers are displayed. The ASCII value of the part number you entered is in accumulator B and the ASCII value of a carriage return (0D) is held in accumulator A.

8.7.3 Using the Trace Command

The T (trace) command may be the best technique for debugging other parts of the program. This command allows you to single-step through the instructions. Usually the T command is not used if you have loops that are repeated a number of times (greater than 10) or where you encounter a jump to one of the utility programs. The reason for not using the T command in these situations is that you may not gain any more information by executing the same loop over again or by single stepping through a utility program. It is best to insert a breakpoint after the loop or utility program, as was done in Example 8.11, and then use the T command.

Example 8. 12:

Show how to use the T command to check the PRICE and UNPACK routines.

Solution:

These routines convert the packed BCD values held at TREG2 (location $D102) and at TREG2 +1 (location $D103) to four unpacked BCD values and store the result in PRBUFF (locations $D300–$D303). Use the MM (memory modify) command to preload a known value into $D102 and $D103. Let's choose the price of part number 4, $15.75.

```
>  MM  D102  <ENTER>

>D102  XX  15  <space bar>  XX  75  <ENTER>
```

From the program printout, the starting address of the PRICE routine is $C843. Use the RM (register modify) command to set the CPU's program counter.

```
>  RM  <ENTER>

>P - XXXX Y- XXXX X-XXXX A-XX B-XX C-XX S-XXXX

>P XXXX C843  <ENTER>

>  T  <RETURN>
```

This command executes an instruction each time the <ENTER> key is pressed. Since the contents of the CPU registers are displayed after each instruction is executed, you see what has happened. After single stepping through the UNPACK routine twice and the contents of the P register is $C862, stop. Now use the MD command to check the contents of PRBUFF.

```
>  MD  D300  <ENTER>
>  D300  01  05  07  05  .  .  .
```

This is the price of part number 4 stored in the price buffer as unpacked BCD values.

PROBLEMS

1. A load cell specified with an R_{in} = 350Ω is powered with a bridge bias of 5.00V. Find (a) I_{Bias} and (b) power dissipated in the transducer.
2. The following specifications are provided for a load cell: RC = 25 lbs, RO = 3mV/V. If a bridge bias of 5.00V is chosen, solve for (a) FSO and (b) transducer sensitivity.

3. Repeat problem if RC = 2 lbs and RO remains at 3 mV/V.
4. Write the analog interface equation for a weight system that accepts 0 to 100 lbs and outputs 0 to 1 V. Give your answer in the standard form of $y = mx + b$.
5. Graph a weight system that outputs 0 to 250mV for an input of 0 to 25 grams. Write the analog interface equation for this system in the standard form of $y = mx + b$.
6. Recalculate the conditions of Example 8.5 changing R_1 from 39Ω to 22Ω. Does the power dissipated in Q_1 increase, decrease, or remain the same?
7. If the zero balance of R_2 in Figure 8.5 is chosen to be 50kΩ, what should you choose as minimum value for resistor R_3?

QUESTIONS

Hardware

1. What is the typical sensitivity of a foil-type load cell in units of millivolts/volt of rated load?
2. Define the active length of a strain gage and indicate how it is measured.
3. What is the typical unstrained resistance of a foil-type strain gage?
4. The sensing axis of a strain gage is orientated 90° to the stress axis of a beam to form a load cell. (True/False)
5. Explain the effect on gage length (L) and resistance (R) if a load cell is placed first under tension and then under compression.
6. The PLC-5 bridge bias is limited to 10.0V to minimize self-heating. (True/False)
7. Explain the advantages of providing four strain gages with complementary resistance swings, as shown in Figure 8.3.
8. Refer to Figure 8.5. Will the voltage at node V_2 increase or decrease as the wiper of R_2 moves (a) toward point A and (b) towards point B?
9. A load cell with a sensitivity of 3.5mV/oz is equipped with a 3-oz table. Refer to Examples 8.7 and 8.8 and write the transducer equation in the standard form of $y = mx + b$.
10. The load cell and table used in a platform weight system (0 to 500 oz) is expressed by $V_{diff} = [(2mV/oz) \times W] + 4.5mV$. Write the SCC design equation to interface it to the 0 to 5V range of the M68HC11 microcomputer.
11. Solve for V_{ref} and R_G to configure Figure 8.8(a) for the following SCC design equations:
    (a) $V_o = 53.5 (V_{pos} - V_{neg}) + 1.05V$
    (b) $V_o = 185 (V_{diff}) - 42mV$
    (c) $V_o = 10 [V(+) - V(-)] + 700mV$

Software

11. Using the flow chart shown in Figure 8.12 as a guide, develop a new flow chart that (a) accepts valid part numbers ranging from 0 to 999, and (b) displays "invalid part number" followed by "Enter correct part identification number: ___"

12. Write code to convert from packed to unpacked BCD numbers, if the price range requires 6 BCD numbers.

13. Modify the OUTPR flow chart illustrated in Figure 8.14 and discussed in section 8.5.4 to include values up to $1,000.

14. Modify the line code in the subroutine titled MEASWE for a time delay of 30µs.

15. Modify the flow chart of Figure 8.18 to round up if the last three digits are greater than 499.

16. Write code to accomplish problem 15. Use the code written in the RNDOFF subroutine as a guide.

CHAPTER 9

Measuring Pressure
with Semiconductor Sensors

9.0

INTRODUCTION

Pressure measurements have become commonplace and the scope of applications has widened to a point that measuring pressure is now embedded in such diverse systems as automotive, medical, environmental, and industrial processes. This is due in part to the availability of low-cost reliable semiconductor-based transducers. Further, the number and variety of applications will increase as the microprocessor is added to automate control of pressure in various processes.

A typical semiconductor-type pressure sensor structure begins with a silicon diaphragm, micromachined chemically to form a seismic cavity. See Figures 9.1(a) and (b). Four piezo-resistive strain gage resistors are diffused into the diaphragm and interconnected to form a Wheatstone bridge. The piezo-resistive elements are then coated with a silicon dioxide (SiO_2) insulating layer for protection and the diaphragm is electrostatically bonded to a Pyrex constraint (support). The single-crystal nature of silicon makes the diaphragm literally stronger than steel, with no pressure hysteresis at zero differential pressure, and excellent output linearity. However, semiconductors are sensitive to ambient temperature. For this reason manufacturers supply sensors complete with temperature compensating thermistors.

Figure 9.1(c) shows an energized Wheatstone bridge and when an input pressure is applied to the sensor, the diaphragm deflects, creating a differential output voltage (V_{diff}) that is directly proportional to input pressure. The output

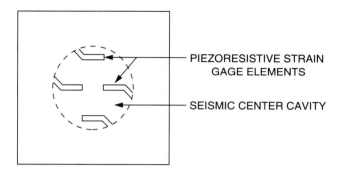

(a) TOP VIEW OF A RECTANGULAR PRESSURE SENSOR DIE

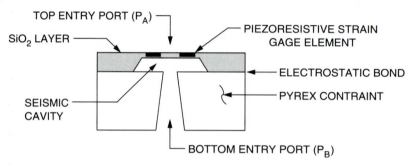

(b) SIDE VIEW OF PRESSURE SENSOR MOUNTED ON
A PYREX SUPPORT

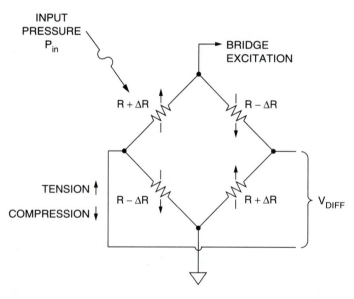

(c) PIEZORESISTIVE ELEMENTS OF A PRESSURE SENSOR
WIRED TO FORM A WHEATSTONE BRIDGE

FIGURE 9.1 Basic elements of a semiconductor-type pressure sensor

voltage–input pressure relationship is extremely linear since opposite arms of the bridge are simultaneously in *tension* or *compression*.

This chapter shows how to design electronics to interface a commercial pressure sensor to the M68HC11 MCU to solve a typical process control problem.

9.1

STATEMENT OF THE PROBLEM

A semiconductor device manufacturer, plagued with contamination difficulties in a wet-film photo resist image area, has isolated the problem to dust caused by a missing filter inside one of the clean room's air supply ducts. Apparently, the old filter was removed on the last routine maintenance check, but a new replacement filter was never installed. To prevent this costly problem from ever reoccurring again, the manufacturer has decided to install an automatic monitoring system for all air supply dust filters.

Figure 9.2 illustrates conceptually a solution to this problem. Measure and evaluate the differential pressure across the air duct filter with a semiconductor pressure sensor. The sensor's differential output voltage will be signal conditioned and applied directly to the MCU's A/D. Three possible conditions could exist: the first is a missing filter, the second is a clogged filter, and the third is a clean, properly installed filter.

For condition one, the differential pressure between port B (high-pressure side) and port A (low-pressure side) would be zero and an error message "MISSING FILTER" is to be displayed on the process control computer terminal. For condition two, a clogged filter, a differential pressure greater than 0.8psid (pounds per square inch differential) would exist and the message "REPLACE CLOGGED FILTER" is to be displayed. For our system a clean, new filter exhibits a differential pressure drop of 0.2psid, gradually increasing as the filter traps dust and becomes clogged. For condition three, pressure readings between 0.2 and 0.8psid display "AIR FILTER OK." Finally, the air ducts are located up to 1200 feet from the MCU control room. Pressures measured at the filters must be converted into electrical signals and transmitted accurately over these long distances through a noisy industrial environment.

9.2

SEMICONDUCTOR PRESSURE SENSORS

9.2.1 Types of Pressure References

All pressures are measured differentially. That is, the measured value is made with respect to a reference pressure. Semiconductor sensors are designed to respond to three types of pressure measurements: (a) *absolute* pressure, (b) *gage*

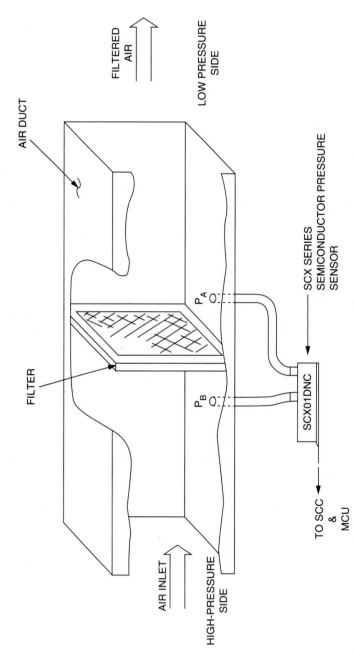

FIGURE 9.2 A semiconductor pressure sensor is used to detect the differential pressure on both sides of an air filter

pressure and (c) *differential* pressure. Figure 9.3 illustrates each type of pressure measurement.

Absolute pressure sensors measure input pressures with respect to a total vacuum or zero pressure. See Figure 9.3(a). Port B is sealed to create a near perfect vacuum. Port A becomes the active or working measuring port of the sensor. Barometric or atmospheric pressure measurements are made with this type of sensor. Thus, it is the fundamental device for the meteorological sciences. At sea level a slight dimpling of the seismic cavity indicates a positive pressure on port A with respect to its vacuum reference.

Gage pressure sensors measure input pressures with respect to an atmospheric pressure reference. See Figure 9.3(b). Usually port B is the active port for gage pressure and port A is vented (exposed) to the atmosphere as the reference. The most familiar type of gage pressure is automobile tire pressure. Pressure within the tire is measured with respect to how much it is above atmospheric pressure. Another type of gage pressure measurement is vacuum pressure; for example, measuring the pressure within an automobile vacuum hose to know how far it is below atmospheric pressure.

Differential pressure sensors measure the difference in pressure between two independently variable pressures. See Figure 9.3(c). Differential pressure measurements are the general form of the more specific gage pressure measurements. Usually port B is connected to the higher pressure side of the system and port A watches the lower pressure side. Our design problem requires this type of differential measurement sensor.

9.2.2 Units for Pressure Measurement

Historically, atmospheric or barometric pressure is measured with a barometer. As shown in Figure 9.4(a), a barometer can be made by filling a graduated tube

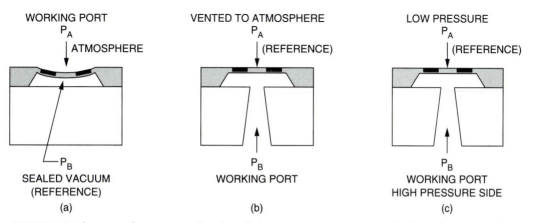

FIGURE 9.3 There are three types of semiconductor pressure sensors: (a) absolute, (b) gage, and (c) differential.

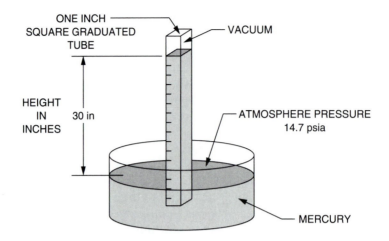

(a) ATMOSPHERIC PRESSURE MEASURED WITH A
MERCURY BAROMETER. TYPICALLY A SEA LEVEL VALUE
OF 14.7 psia IS GIVEN.

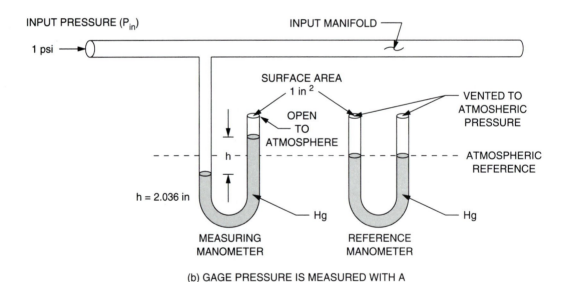

(b) GAGE PRESSURE IS MEASURED WITH A
MANOMETER

FIGURE 9.4 Using barometers and manometers to measure atmospheric and gage pressure

one inch square in cross section with mercury (Hg). The tube is then inverted and the open end placed in a container. Assume that the height of the mercury stabilizes at 30 inches. The volume of Hg within the tube is 30in. x 1in. x 1in. = 30in^3 and its weight (if measured) is 14.7 pounds. Therefore, the atmospheric pressure supporting the column must be 14.7 *pounds per square inch absolute* (14.7psia).

If the liquid within the tube is changed from mercury (Hg) to water (H_2O) and the dimension changed from inches to centimeters (cm) or millimeters (mm), a wide selection of scales can be constructed for the barometer configuration shown in Figure 9.4(a). Table 9.1 lists the conversion between some common pressure scales.

TABLE 9.1   Conversion Constants between Pressure Scales

	in Hg	in H_2O	mm Hg	cm H_2O
1 psi	2.036	27.68	51.75	70.308

Historically gage pressure was measured with a U-shaped tube filled with a fluid such as mercury. It is called a manometer and a typical configuration is shown in Figure 9.4(b). Initially with Pin = 0, a barometric reference line is established with a reference manometer and the measuring manometer is filled to exactly the same liquid height. A pressure of 1 psi is then applied to the input manifold. Its open end is exposed to an atmospheric pressure of 14.7 psi.

The effect of 1.0 psi input pressure can now be measured in terms of inches by measuring the displacement distance h. For mercury at 1 psid, h equals 2.036 inches. From Table 9.1, 1 psid = 2.036 in Hg. By changing the liquid from Hg to H_2O or the dimensions from inches to cm (or mm), we can recreate the scale conversions of Table 9.1 shown for atmospheric pressure.

If the open end of the manometers of Figure 9.4(b) are connected to different pressures, the measurement is a differential reading and units of psid should be assigned. While tube-type barometers and manometers are useful as a tutorial to explain pressure units, they are fragile, impractical transducers. In the next sections we will look at a series of practical semiconductor-based pressure sensors.

9.2.3 SCX C Series Semiconductor Pressure Sensors

The SCX C series of semiconductor pressure sensors, illustrated in Figure 9.5, is produced by SenSym of Sunnyvale, California. This type of sensor is a good choice for noncorrosive fluids used in medical equipment, pneumatic controls, and HVAC (*Heating Ventilating and Air Conditioning*) systems. The sensors in this series can measure all three types of pressure and are available in ranges from 0 to 1 psi (SCX01) to 0 to 100 psi (SCX100). SCX C series transducers are packaged in a corrosion resistant nylon case with two mounting holes. Pressure ports are designed to accept standard 0.175 inch (ID) plastic tubing secured with a plastic cable tie as shown in Figure 9.5(a).

In Figure 9.5(b), the pressure sensor chip is coated with a protective coating of silicon gel and provided with an RTV seal. Access to the sensor through port A is therefore compatible with most noncorrosive fluids. All fluids inert to glass (silicon) are compatible media to port B. For this reason, port B is most often chosen as the working port for gage pressure measurement with port A vented to the atmosphere.

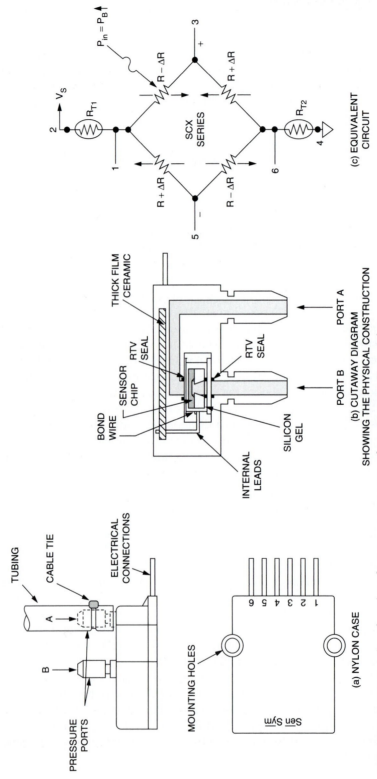

FIGURE 9.5 SCX C series of semiconductor pressure sensor from SenSym Corporation

An SCX C series pressure is excited by applying dc power between pins 2 and 4 as shown in Figure 9.5(c). If the pressure applied to port B is increased, the differential output voltage (V_{diff}) across the sensor will cause pin 3 to be more positive than pin 5.

$$\mathbf{V_{diff}} = (V_3 - V_5) \uparrow (P_B \uparrow) \tag{9.1a}$$

If, however, the input connections are reversed and port A is made to increase in pressure, then

$$\mathbf{V_{diff}} = (V_5 - V_3) \uparrow (P_A \uparrow) \tag{9.1b}$$

and the voltage at pin 5 will be more positive than pin 3.

Finally, SCX C series sensors are internally calibrated (by laser trimming) and temperature compensated (with thermistors R_{T1} and R_{T2}) to give an accurate stable output over an environment that ranges from 0 to 70°C.

9.2.4 Pressure Sensor Specifications

A data sheet for the SCX01DNC differential pressure sensor is given in Figure 9.6. These specifications along with the equivalent circuit of Figure 9.5(c) are used to illustrate how the transducer equation is derived from the sensor's specifications.

Supply Voltage, V_s

A maximum bridge supply voltage of $30V_{dc}$ can be applied between pins 2 and 4; however, all data sheet values are given with $V_s = 12.0V_{dc}$. (See note 1 of Figure 9.6). Selecting a bridge bias greater than 12.0V has the advantage of increased sensitivity but the disadvantage of increased self-heating.

Input Impedance, R_{in}

The input impedance, R_{in}, between pins 2 and 4 (see note 6) is typically $4.0k\Omega$.

Example 9.1:

Use the SCX01DNC data sheet values and $V_s = 10.0V$ to determine (a) bridge supply current, and (b) bridge power dissipation.

Solution:

(a) $I_{supply} = V_s/R_{in} = 10.0V/4k\Omega = 2.5mA$.
(b) $P_{bridge} = V_s I_{supply} = 10.0V(2.5mA) = 25mW$.

Note that this power consumption requirement is 10% of that demanded by a typical foil-type strain-gage bridge (see Chapter 8). An inexpensive $10.0V_{dc}$ reference like the REF-01 is an excellent power source for this type of bridge circuit.

PRESSURE SENSOR CHARATERISTICS

SCX C Series

STANDARD PRESSURE RANGES

PART NUMBER	OPERATING PRESSURE	PROOF PRESSURE*	FULL-SCALE PLAN
SCX01DNC	0-1 psid	20 psid	18 mV
SCX05DNC	0-5 psid	20 psid	60 mV
SCX15ANC	0-15 psia	30 psia	90 mV
SCX15DNC	0-15 psid	30 psid	90 mV
SCX30ANC	0-30 psia	60 psia	90 mV
SCX30DNC	0-30 psid	60 psid	90 mV
SCX100ANC	0-100 psia	150 psia	100 mV
SCX100DNC	0-100 psid	150 psid	100 mV

*Maximum pressure above which causes permanent sensor failure.

Maximum Ratings (For All Devices)

Supply Voltage, V_S	$+30V_{DC}$
Common-mode Pressure	50 psig
Lead Temperature	
(Soldering, 10 seconds)	300°C

Environmental Specifications (For All Devices)

Temperature Range	
Compensated	0 to 70°C
Operating	−40°C to +85°C
Storage	−55°C to +125°C
Humidity Limits	0 to 100%RH

SCX01DNC PERFORMANCE CHARACTERISTICS (NOTE 1)

CHARACTERISTIC	MIN	TYP	MAX	UNIT
Operating Pressure Range		–	1	psid
Sensitivity	–	18	–	mV/psi
Full-scale Span (Note 2)	17.00	18.00	19.00	mV
Zero Pressure Offset	−1.0	0	+1.0	mV
Combined Linearity and Hysteresis (Note 3)	–	±0.2	±1.0	%FSO
Temperature Effect on Span (0-70°C) (Note 4)	–	±0.4	±2.0	%FSO
Temperature Effect on Offset (0-70°C) (Note 4)	–	±0.20	±1.0	mV
Repeatability (Note 5)	–	±0.2	±0.5	%FSO
Input Impedence (Note 6)	–	4.0	–	kΩ
Output Impedance (Note 7)	–	4.0	–	kΩ
Common-mode Voltage (Note 8)	5.7	6.0	6.3	V_{DC}
Response Time (Note 9)	–	100	–	μsec
Long Term Stability of Offset and Span (Note 10)	–	±0.1	–	%FSO

Specification Notes: (For All Devices)

Note 1: Reference Conditions: Unless otherwise noted: Supply Voltage, $V_S = 12V_{DC}$, $T_A = 25°C$, Common-mode Line Pressure = 0psig, Pressure Applied to Port B. For absolute devices only, pressure is applied to Port A and the output polarity is reversed.

Note 2: Span is the algebraic difference between the ouput voltage at full-scale pressure and the output at zero pressure. Span is ratiometric to the supply voltage.

Note 3: See Definition of Terms.
Hysteresis - the maximum output difference at any point within the operating pressure range for increasing and decreasing pressure.

Note 4: Maximum error band of the offset voltage and the error band of the span, relative to the 25°C reading.

Note 5: Maximum difference in output at any pressure with the operating pressure range and temperature within 0°C to +70°C after:
(a) 1,000 temperature cycles, 0°C to +70°C
(b) 1.5 million pressure cycles, 0 psi to full-scale span.

Note 6: Input impedance is the impedance between pins 2 and 4.

Note 7: Output impedance is the impedance between pins 3 and 5.

Note 8: This is the common-mode voltage of the output arms (Pins 3 and 5) for $V_S = 12\ V_{DC}$.

Note 9: Response time for a 0 psi to full-scale span pressure step change, 10% to 90% rise time.

Note 10: Long term stability over a one year period.

FIGURE 9.6 Data sheet for the SCX01DNC differential pressure sensor from SenSym (Courtesy of SenSym Corporation)

Operating Pressure Range and Full-scale Span

See lines 1 and 2 of the SCX01DNC performance characteristics in Figure 9.6. When the maximum operating range pressure of 1 psid is applied to port B of an SCX01DNC sensor, it produces a typical full-scale span of 18mV (see note 2 of Figure 9.6). That is to say, the differential output voltage between pins 3 and 5 is 18mV positive, $V_{diff} = (V_3 - V_5)$. In actual tests, the full-scale span may vary by ± 1mV.

Data sheet sensitivity (S_d) is given as 18mV/psid (line 2) when tested at $V_s = 12.0V_{dc}$. Since sensitivity is ratiometric to the supply voltage V_s, it can be corrected for any bridge supply voltage by the following equation:

$$S_c = \frac{V_s}{12V} \cdot S_d \tag{9.2}$$

Example 9.2:

> Ratiometrically correct the sensitivity of an SCX01DNC sensor for a bridge supply of $10.0V_{dc}$.

> **Solution:**

> Use Eq. (9.2). The corrected sensitivity, S_c, becomes

> $$S_c = \frac{(10V)}{12V} \, 18\text{mV/psid} = 15\text{mV/psid}$$

Zero Pressure Offset

While the typical value of output voltage, for zero input pressure, is given on the data sheet as 0mV, it can range between ± 1mV. Therefore, a zero adjustment technique, similar to that discussed in Chapter 8, is required.

Note that data sheet specifications on linearity, hysteresis, long-term stability, and temperature contribute only second-order effects. Thus, they need not be considered here.

9.3
■■■

ANALOG INTERFACE EQUATION

An analog interface equation can be written for the problem presented in section 9.1. Refer to Figure 9.7. The input pressure that ranges from 0 to 1 psid must be signal conditioned to interface to the 0–5V range of the MCU's A/D converter. The analog interface equation is derived by calculating slope or system sensitivity from:

$$\text{System Sensitivity} = m = \frac{\text{span out}}{\text{span in}} = \frac{\Delta V_o}{\Delta P_{in}} \tag{9.3}$$

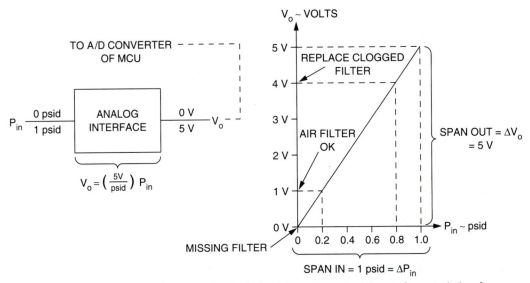

FIGURE 9.7 The analog interface equation is derived from the output-input characteristics shown

Example 9.3:

Solve for system sensitivity using the graph shown in Figure 9.7.

Solution:

From Eq. (9.3); m = 5V/1psid = 5V/psid. Note that at an input pressure of 0 psid, the output must be 0 volts. The system has no offset term. Therefore, write the analog interface equation in standard form by inspection as:

$$y = mx + b$$

$$V_o = \left(\frac{5V}{psid} \right) P_{in} + 0V \tag{9.4}$$

Example 9.4:

Determine the magnitude of voltage (V_o) into the MCU that will display (a) "MISSING FILTER," (b) "REPLACE CLOGGED FILTER," and (c) "AIR FILTER OK."

Solution:

Use Eq. (9.4) and section 9.2.

(a) For Pin = 0psid, then $V_o = \left(\dfrac{5V}{psid} \right) 0psid = 0V$

(b) For Pin > 0.8psid, then $\qquad V_o = \left(\dfrac{5V}{psid}\right) 0.8psid = 4V$

(c) 0.2< Pin < 0.8psid, then $\qquad V_o = \left(\dfrac{5V}{psid}\right) 0.2psid > 1V \text{ but} < 4V$

9.4
▬▬

DESIGNING A PRESSURE SENSOR INTERFACE

9.4.1 Bridge Bias

A practical bridge bias circuit for the SCX01DNC pressure sensor is shown in Figure 9.8(a). The necessary bridge supply voltage V_S, of 10.0V, is derived directly from a low-cost reference chip (IC_1) that is capable of delivering upwards of 10mA at its output, pin 6. Example 9.1 shows that the bridge requires a supply current of 2.5mA. Adding a 10kΩ zero pressure offset adjustment potentiometer increases the current demanded from the REF-01 to about 3.5mA.

9.4.2 Zero Pressure Offset Adjustment

We conclude from the data sheet presented in section 9.2.4 that the typical value of pressure sensor output voltage, V_{diff}, for Figure 9.8(a) should be 0mV when zero pressure is applied to the SCX01DNC. However, this offset voltage can range between ± 0.833mV (ratiometrically corrected data sheet values) of 0mV. R_1 and R_2 must be added to form an offset adjustment for zero pressure. Zeroing action for this type of balancing circuitry was discussed in section 8.4.2. For the values given in Figure 9.8(a) an adjustment span of about ±1.3mV is possible to compensate for the expected zero pressure offset of ±0.833mV.

In practice, we adjust zero pressure offset resistor, R_1, until the differential voltage, V_{diff}, is 0V when the pressure applied to port B is 0 psid.

9.4.3 Writing the Transducer Equation

The transducer circuitry of Figure 9.8(a) consists of an SCX01DNC differential pressure sensor, a bridge supply, and a zero pressure offset adjustment, R_1 as shown in a block diagram form of Figure 9.8(b) along with the transducer graph. The transducer equation for Figure 9.8(a) can be written by inspection in the form

$$y = mx + b$$

$$V_{diff} = V_3 - V_5 = \left(\frac{15mV}{psid}\right) Pin + 0mV \tag{9.5}$$

Note: The ratiometrically corrected sensitivity was determined in Example 9.2 and the 0mV offset adjustment in section 9.4.2.

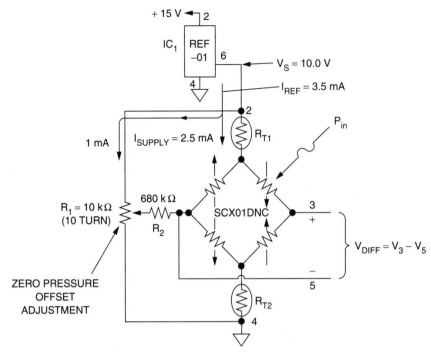

(a) PRESSURE SENSOR BIASING WITH ZERO PRESSURE OFFSET
ADJUSTMENT

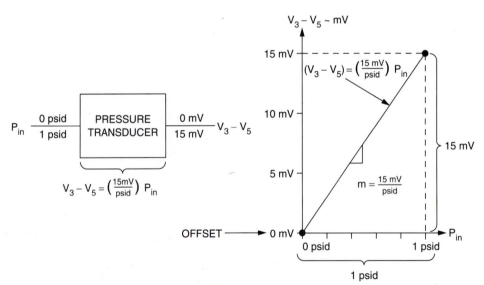

(b) TRANSDUCER EQUATION AND GRAPH WITH THE ZERO
PRESSURE OFFSET SET TO 0 mV

FIGURE 9.8 Differential pressure transducer circuitry and transducer equation

Example 9.5:

Determine the differential output voltage limits of Figure 9.8(a) when pressures of a) 0psid and b) 1psid are applied.

Solution:

Using Eq. (9.5)

(a) $V_{diff} = V_3 - V_5 = \left(\dfrac{15mV}{psid} \right) 0psid = 0mV$

(b) $V_{diff} = V_3 - V_5 = \left(\dfrac{15mV}{psid} \right) 1psid = 15mV$

A performance graph of transducer output vs. input is shown in Figure 9.8(b).

9.4.4 Writing the SCC Design Equation

From section 9.4.1, you learned the pressure sensor with a differential output voltage $(V_3 - V_5)$ range of 0 to 15mV must interface with the 0 to 5V range of the MCU's A/D converter. Also from the problem statement of section 9.1, the signal must pass through a noisy and hostile industrial environment over a distance of 1200 feet to a microcontroller. Thus, the MCU is located remotely from the air ducts.

The first task is to convert the transducer's differential output voltage into a current for signal transmission. Current-mode transmitted signals have the advantages of (a) immunity to noise, (b) elimination of voltage drop errors due to line resistance, and (c) minimal crosstalk between signal lines. Transmission of accurate information is possible with a single pair of twisted wires, thus eliminating the need for expensive shielded cable. At the receiver end (the A/D converter of MCU), the current must be converted back into a voltage and scaled for the A/D converter.

Figure 9.9(a) illustrates a block diagram of the SCC. The differential voltage-to-current converter accepts the 0–15mV transducer signal. Now choose a convenient output current range of 0 to 1mA for transmission. The current-to-voltage converter at the MCU converts the current back to a voltage V_o which is scaled to 0 to 5V for the MCU's A/D converter.

Differential Voltage-to-Current Converter

The performance graph for the differential voltage-to-current converter is constructed in Figure 9.9(b). To determine its design equation first find its conversion gain by evaluating slope m:

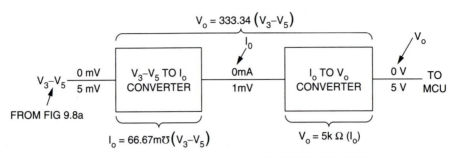

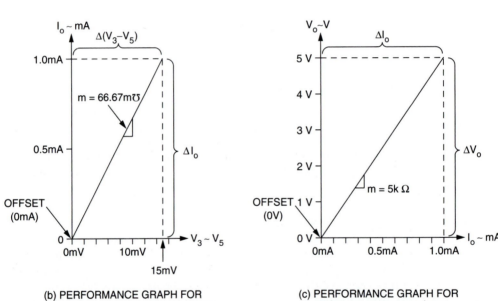

(a) THE BLOCK DIAGRAM OF A CURRENT TRANSMITTER
FOLLOWED BY A CURRENT-TO-VOLTAGE CONVERTER

(b) PERFORMANCE GRAPH FOR
THE (V_3-V_5)-TO-I_o CONVERTER

(c) PERFORMANCE GRAPH FOR
THE I_o-TO-V_o CONVERTER

FIGURE 9.9 A signal conditioning cirtcuit to transmit current over long distances in a noisy electrical environment

$$m = \frac{\Delta I_o}{\Delta(V_3 - V_5)} = \frac{(1-0)\text{mA}}{(15-0)\text{mV}} = 66.67\text{m}\mho$$

By inspecting the graph of Figure 9.9(b), note that the offset term is 0mA. Now write the design equation for the first circuit by inspection as

$$I_o = 66.67\text{m}\mho\,(V_3 - V_5) \tag{9.6}$$

This expression is implemented in the next section.

Current-to-Voltage Converter

Figure 9.9(c) shows the performance graph needed to convert the current output of the previous circuit into a voltage scaled for acceptance by the MCU's A/D converter. To find the design equation first solve for conversion gain.

$$m = \frac{\Delta V_o}{\Delta I_o} = \frac{(5-0)V}{(1-0)mA} = 5k\Omega$$

Again note that Figure 9.9(c) has no offset term. The design equation can be written by inspection as:

$$V_o = 5k\Omega \, (I_o) \tag{9.7}$$

Example 9.6:

Determine the complete design equation for Figure 9.9(a).

Solution:

Substitute Eq. (9.6) into Eq. (9.7) and solve for V_o.

$$V_o = 5k\Omega \, [\, 66.67m\mho \, (V_3{-}V_5)]$$
$$V_o = 333.34 \, (V_3{-}V_5) \tag{9.8}$$

Eq. (9.8) is in a form that shows the complete SCC function is a differential amplifier with a gain of 333.34. The selection and design of hardware to implement Eq. (9.8) are presented next.

9.4.5 Designing the SCC Hardware

To implement Eq. (9.6), see the *trial* SCC shown in Figure 9.10(a). A standard 2-op amp instrumentation amplifier is chosen with bootstrapping resistors R_4 and R_5 added to form a general purpose differential input to a bipolar current source output. The hardware equation for this circuit is given below in standard form as

$$I_L = \frac{A_v}{R_4} \, (V_1{-}V_2) \tag{9.9a}$$

This circuit responds to the difference voltage between V_1 and V_2. It sources a current into the load for $V_1 > V_2$ and sinks a current from the load when $V_1 < V_2$.

Differential gain (A_v) is controlled by adjustment of R_6 and is set according to the following expression:

$$A_v = 2 + \frac{2\,R_1}{R_6} \tag{9.9b}$$

Adjustment of gain (no units) with R_6 sets the conductance term of this circuit's hardware equation (Eq. 9.9a).

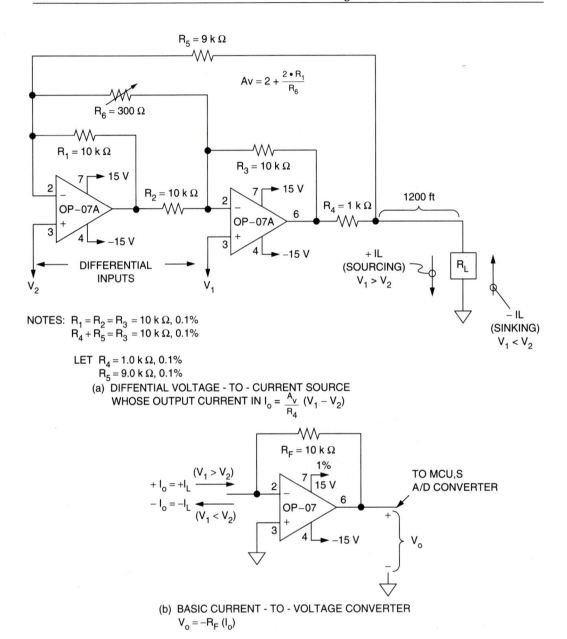

NOTES: $R_1 = R_2 = R_3 = 10$ k Ω, 0.1%
            $R_4 + R_5 = R_3 = 10$ k Ω, 0.1%

     LET $R_4 = 1.0$ k Ω, 0.1%
         $R_5 = 9.0$ k Ω, 0.1%

      (a) DIFFENTIAL VOLTAGE - TO - CURRENT SOURCE
            WHOSE OUTPUT CURRENT IN $I_o = \dfrac{A_v}{R_4} (V_1 - V_2)$

        (b) BASIC CURRENT - TO - VOLTAGE CONVERTER
               $V_o = -R_F (I_o)$

FIGURE 9.10 Signal conditioning circuit to interface, over long distances, the output of a pressure sensor to the input of a MCU

Some cautionary notes are in order before we design this SCC. First, Figure 9.10(a) is a current source, and as such, must maintain a large value of output resistance. To achieve a large R_o, make $R_1 = R_2$ and $R_4 + R_5 = R_3$ to a tolerance of at least 0.1%. Second, to obtain a high output voltage compliance, keep R_4 small. For this design we choose $R_1 = R_2 = R_3 = 10k\Omega$, 0.1%. Next select $R_4 = 1.0k\Omega$, 0.1%. Now $R_5 = 9.0k\Omega$, 0.1% to comply with the circuit restrictions.

Example 9.7:

Design Figure 9.10(a) to implement Eq. (9.6).

Solution:

First rewrite both design and hardware equations.

From Eq (9.6) $I_o = 66.67mv\ (V_3 - V_5)$

From Eq. (9.9a) $I_L = \dfrac{A_v}{1k\Omega}\ (V_1 - V_2)$

Comparing terms, let I_L of Figure 9.10(a) be I_o of our SCC. Notice the differential output of the pressure sensor $(V_3 - V_5)$ is applied to the input $(V_1 - V_2)$ of Figure 9.10(a).

To solve for the value of R_6 in order to set the circuit's conductance to $66.67m\mho$, first use Eq. (9.6) and then Eq. (9.9b).

Step #1 $66.67m\mho = A_v/1k\Omega$

$\therefore A_v = 66.67m\mho(1k\Omega) = 66.67$

Now substitute for A_v into Eq. (9.9b) to find R_G.

Step #2 $66.67 = 2 + \dfrac{2\ R_1}{R_6}$

$R_6 = \dfrac{2\ (10k\Omega)}{64.67} = 300\Omega$

Current-to-Voltage Converter Design

The output current of Figure 9.10(a) is next converted into a voltage by the current-to-voltage converter in Figure 9.10(b). Its hardware equation is given as

$$V_o = -R_F(I_o) \qquad\qquad (9.10)$$

Example 9.8:

Design hardware for Figure 9.10(b) to implement Eq. (9.6).

Solution:

Rewrite both design and hardware equations for comparison.

$$V_o = 5k\Omega(I_o)$$

$$V_o = -R_F(I_o)$$

Compare gain terms to find that for $5k\Omega(I_o)$ to equal $-R_F(I_o)$, (a) R_F must be set to $5k\Omega$, and (b) I_o must be made to be negative. Therefore, I_L from Figure 9.10(a) must be a *sinking* load current set by wiring $V_1 < V_2$ when a positive pressure is applied. A positive pressure occurs when $V_3 > V_5$; therefore wire the transducer's output to the current transmitter as follows:

Pin 3 of SCX01DNC to V_2
Pin 5 of SCX01DNC to V_1

9.4.6 Complete Pressure Sensor System

The complete pressure sensor system, interfaced to the MC68HC11 microcontroller is shown in Figure 9.11. The transducer, differential voltage-to-current converter, and current-to-voltage converter all work to sense differential pressure and transmit an analog signal over a long distance to the MCU.

To calibrate this system, apply 0 psid to the sensor and adjust R_1 until the voltage (V_o) at pin 45 (PE1 of the EVB) is 0V. Next apply 1 psid, and adjust R_6 until V_o at pin 45 (PE1 of the EVB) is 5.00V. Repeat until no further adjustment is required.

9.5

EVB PROGRAM FOR PRESSURE SENSOR DESIGN

The code provided in this section is a solution to the differential pressure problem defined in section 9.1. Figure 9.12 is a flow chart showing the logical steps of the program that checks the three pressure ranges and displays the system's condition on a monitor. Similar to the software design in Chapters 7 and 8, this program was written using the M68HC11 cross assembler on an IBM compartable computer and downloaded into the EVB's RAM.

The following code is one possible solution to the differential pressure problem defined in section 9.1. Figure 9.12 is a flow chart showing the logical steps of the program that checks the three pressure ranges and displays the appropriate message on the PC screen.

As shown in the flow chart of Figure 9.12 this is not in a continuous loop. Once the program is executed by using the Go command: (> G C900 <ENTER>), the program tests the pressure condition within the air duct, displays a message, and stops by returning control back to the EVB monitor. Hence the program is not in a continous loop constantly checking the pressure within the air duct at preset time intervals, this problem is left as a homework exercise (see Problem 9-11).

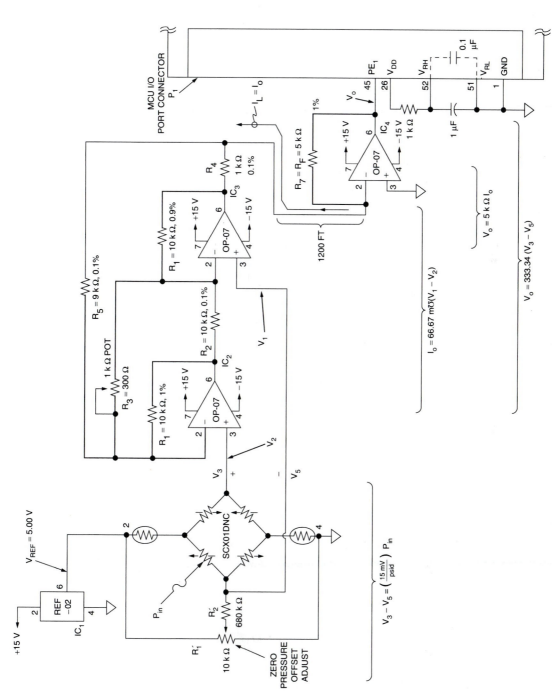

FIGURE 9.11 Complete pressure sensor system

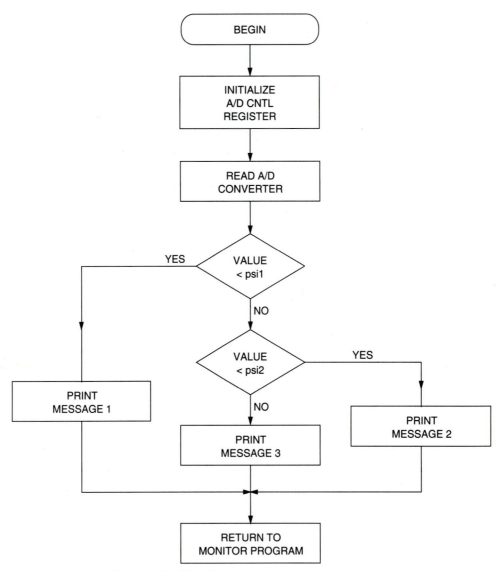

FIGURE 9.12 Flow chart for checking three pressure ranges

```
LINE  S PC   OPCO OPERANDS S LABEL   MNEMO OPERANDS COMMENT
00001                               NAM    Pressure Sensor Monitoring System
00002
00003                *****************************************************************
00004                *               EVB Utility Subroutine Address                  *
00005                *  Utility subroutines allow the user to perform a variety of input/  *
00006                *  output tasks and are described in Chapter 4.  They are stored in   *
00007                *  ROM and may be used by executing a JSR instruction to the applicable *
00008                *  address.  This application requires only one of the utility        *
00009                *  subroutines given in Chapter 4.                               *
00010                *****************************************************************
00011
00012  P 0000  ffc7      A OUTSTRG  EQU   $FFC7    Output message string until EOT ($04) include <CR> <LF>.
00013
00014                *****************************************************************
00015                *               Pounds per Square Inch Values                   *
00016                *  These psi equates are the limit values and are in hexadecimal so that *
00017                *  the input data after it is converted and stored in the A/D register  *
00018                *  can be compared immediately.                                 *
00019                *****************************************************************
00020
00021  P 0000  0032      A psi1     EQU   $32      An A/D value of 32hex = 1V.
00022  P 0000  00c8      A psi2     EQU   $C8      An A/D value of C8hex = 4V.
00023
00024
00025                *****************************************************************
00026                *                      Register Equates                         *
00027                *  These locations are fixed addresses in the memory map.        *
00028                *****************************************************************
00029
00030  P 0000  1030      A ADCTL    EQU   $1030    A/D control register.
00031  P 0000  1031      A ADR1     EQU   $1031    A/D register #1.
00032  P 0000  e0b2      A BUFFALO  EQU   $E0B2    Return to the EVB monitor program.
00033
00034
00035                *****************************************************************
00036                *                      Buffer Location                          *
00037                *  This buffer location is used to store in RAM the converted input data *
00038                *  for possible future use.  The starting address is $D900.      *
00039                *****************************************************************
00040
00041  A d900                          ORG   $D900    Assembler directive
00042
00043  A d900  01        A ADBUFF   RMB   1        Stores the A/D input.
00044
00045
00046                *****************************************************************
00047                *                      Display Messages                         *
00048                *  The following output messages are used to indicate the        *
00049                *  condition within the air duct.                               *
00050                *                       * * * * *                               *
00051                *  The messages are stored in memory beginning at location $D000. *
00052                *****************************************************************
00053
00054  A d000                          ORG   $D000    Assembler directive
00055
00056  A d000  57        A MSPRLO   FCC   'Warning air pressure is too low.  Install a filter immediately.'
00057  A d03f  04        A          FCB   $04      End-of-message mark.
00058
00059  A d040  46        A MSPROK   FCC   'Filter is installed and the system is working properly.'
00060  A d077  04        A          FCB   $04      End-of-message mark.
00061
00062  A d078  57        A MSPRHI   FCC   'Warning air pressure is too high.  Replace filter immediately.'
00063  A d0b6  04        A          FCB   $04      End-of-message mark.
00064
00065
00066                *****************************************************************
00067                *  This routine will be downloaded into the EVB RAM beginning at memory *
00068                *  location $C900.                                              *
00069                *****************************************************************
00070
00071  A c900                          ORG   $C900    Assembler directive
```

```
LINE   S PC   OPCO OPERANDS S LABEL   MNEMO OPERANDS COMMENT
00072
00073  A c900 86   21       A FILTER: LDAA  #$21     \ Initialize the
00074  A c902 b7   1030     A         STAA  ADCTL    / ADCTL register.
00075  A c905 c6   26       A         LDAB  #$26     Initialize counter for timing delay.
00076  A c907 5a            DELAY:    DECB           \ Timing delay for
00077  A c908 26   fd  c907           BNE   DELAY    / A/D conversion.
00078  A c90a b6   1031     A         LDAA  ADR1     Read A/D register.
00079  A c90d b7   d900     A         STAA  ADBUFF   Store A/D value for possible future use.
00080  A c910 81   32       A         CMPA  #psi1    Compare input value to psi1.
00081  A c912 25   0c  c920           BLO   PRINT1   If accumulator A < psi1, branch to PRINT1.
00082  A c914 81   c8       A         CMPA  #psi2    Compare input value to psi2.
00083  A c916 25   10  c928           BLO   PRINT2   If accumulator A < psi2, branch to PRINT2.
00084  A c918 ce   d078     A         LDX   #MSPRHI  Load message's starting address.
00085  A c91b bd   ffc7     A         JSR   OUTSTRG  Display MSPRHI message.
00086  A c91e 20   0e  c92e           BRA   PROMPT
00087
00088  A c920 ce   d000     A PRINT1: LDX   #MSPRLO  Load message's starting address.
00089  A c923 bd   ffc7     A         JSR   OUTSTRG  Display MSPRLO  message.
00090  A c926 20   06  c92e           BRA   PROMPT
00091
00092  A c928 ce   d040     A PRINT2: LDX   #MSPROK  Load message's starting address.
00093  A c92b bd   ffc7     A         JSR   OUTSTRG  Display MSPROK  message.
00094
00095  A c92e 7e   e0b2     A PROMPT: JMP   BUFFALO  Return to monitor program and output prompt.
00096
00097                                 END   $C900    Assembler directive.
00098
```

```
Total number of errors: 0
Total number of warnings: 0
Total number of lines: 98
Number of bytes in section ASCT: 233

Number of bytes in program: 233
```

```
              CROSS REFERENCE TABLE
NAME     ATTRB S VALUE P:LINE LINE1....N

ADBUFF         A d900 2:43        79
ADCTL    EQU   A 1030 2:30        74
ADR1     EQU   A 1031 2:31        78
BUFFALO  EQU   A e0b2 2:32        95
DELAY          A c907 3:76        77
FILTER         A c900 3:73
MSPRHI         A d078 3:62        84
MSPRLO         A d000 3:56        88
MSPROK         A d040 3:59        92
OUTSTRG  EQU   A ffc7 2:12        85  89  93
PRINT1         A c920 3:88        81
PRINT2         A c928 3:92        83
PROMPT         A c92e 3:95        86  90
psi1     EQU   A 0032 2:21        80
psi2     EQU   A 00c8 2:22        82
```

As discussed in previous chapters it is not necessary to build the entire signal conditioning circuit in order to test the program. Use Figure 5.9 and apply a known voltage such as 2.5V to port PE1 (pin 45). Now execute the program, the displayed message will be:

```
Filter is installed and the system is working properly.
```

The input voltage may be changed and the result for the three voltage ranges: $0 \leq Vin < 1.0V$, $1.0 \leq Vin < 4.0V$, and $4.0 < Vin \leq 5.0V$ may be checked.

As seen in the listing file the program only requires 20 lines of code. Since this is a short program, software troubleshooting is left as a homework exercise (see Problem (9.12).

This program is written for a single air duct however the program could easily be expanded for a larger system containing many air ducts and filters.

PROBLEMS

1. Convert the normal sea level pressure of 14.7psia into the following units:
   a) in of Hg
   b) in of H_2O
   c) mm of Hg
   d) cm of H_2O
2. Use the SCX01DNC data sheet given in Figure 9.6 to answer the following questions:
   a) Input impedance
   b) Find bridge current if V_s is set to 5.00V.
   c) Ratiometrically correct the sensitivity for a bridge bias of $V_s = 5.00V$.
   d) What is the full range of zero pressure offset?
3. Write the analog interface equation for a system that outputs 0 to 3V for an input that varies from 0 to 30psid. Show answer in the standard form ($y = mx + b$).
4. Use the equation derived in Problem 3 to determine V_o at (a) pin = 6psid, (b) 12psid, (c) 18psid and, (d) 24psid.
5. Refer to Figure 9.8(a). Determine I_{supply}, I_{ref} and $I_{10k\Omega(pot)}$ if V_s is changed to 5.00V [REF-02].
6. Refer to Figure 9.8(b). Write the ratiometrically corrected transducer equation for Figure 9.8(a) if V_s is set to 5.00V.
7. Write the SCC design equation for a block that accepts 0 to 10mV (differential) and outputs 0 to 20mA.
8. Write the SCC design equation for a block that accepts the 0 to 20mA current in Problem 8 above and converts it to 0 to 5V at the output.
9. Design Figure 9.10(a) to conform to the following SCC design equation. $I_O = 25mV (V_3 - V_5)$. Solve for RG, Av. Use Notes on Figure 9.10.
10. Rewrite the program in section 9.5 to display the following messages.
    a) High
    b) Low
    c) OK
11. Modify the program in section 9.5 so that the air duct pressure is measured at 30 second intervals for 10 minutes after which program control is returned to the EVB monitor.

12. For this software troubleshooting exercise, you do not have to apply a voltage at port PE1; just leave the terminal open. Insert a breakpoint at location $C90D Change the data in accumulator A to $04. What message will be displayed on the monitor when the program is continued? Use the proceed command and check your results. See Chapter 4 if you need a refresher on how to use the breakpoint, go, register modify, and proceed commands.

QUESTIONS

1. How is the seismic cavity formed on a silicon type pressure sensor?
2. What is the function of applying a SiO_2 layer over the piezo-resistive strain gage elements?
3. List the three types of pressure measurements and give at least one example of each.
4. Explain the difference between a manometer and a barometer.
5. When using an SCX15DNC pressure sensor, port B is applied with a pressure greater than that applied to port A. Which output pin (3 or 5) is more positive?

CHAPTER 10

Thermocouple High-Temperature Measurement with Software Linearization

10.0

INTRODUCTION

Some transducers have output-input characteristics that are partially or wholly nonlinear over their operating range. In this chapter we chose such a transducer to show how to convert its nonlinear output into a linear readout by appropriate hardware and software.

10.1

STATEMENT OF THE PROBLEM

Design a system to measure temperature of a soldering iron, in 5-second intervals, as it heats from ambient to final temperature. Measurements are to be stored in a microcontroller's memory and displayed. See Figure 10.1. From this data the soldering iron's time constant, thermal resistance, and thermal capacity can be calculated. As will be shown, the selected temperature transducer (thermocouple) has a nonlinear response. Therefore, the transducer's signal must be

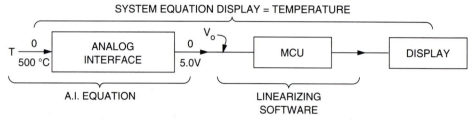

FIGURE 10.1 Soldering iron temperature is converted into a voltage by an analog interface, linearized by a MCU, and displayed on a printer

linearized. We will choose a software linearizing technique using a program loaded into the MCU.

Maximum soldering iron tip temperature ranges are approximately 290–400°C, 315–425°C and 340–450°C for 20, 25, and 30W irons respectively. The maximum temperature measuring capability of a semiconductor transducer is only about 150°C. Therefore, we must choose a thermocouple-type transducer whose measuring range can extend up to and beyond 500°C. Operating principles of thermocouples are reviewed as a prelude to design of the analog interface and writing a program for software linearization.

10.2

THERMOCOUPLE BASICS

10.2.1 Theory of Operation

A thermocouple is formed when two dissimilar metals make contact. They can be simply twisted together, soldered, or more often butt-welded. Iron (Fe) and constantan (C) metal wires form two thermocouple junctions as in Figure 10.2. Theoretically, each junction generates a thermoelectric voltage proportional to absolute temperature. A single junction voltage cannot be measured because other thermocouples are formed when a meter is connected to make the measurement. We can only measure the voltage *difference* between two junctions if they are at different temperatures.

10.2.2 Thermocouple Reference Tables

Thermocouples can be used to measure temperatures accurately over a very wide range (−270°C to 1800°C). Accurate data for each type of sensor is published in thermocouple N.I.S.T. (National Institute of Standards and Technology) reference tables. See also publications by Omega Engineering, Inc., P.O. Box 2284, Stamford, CT 06906.

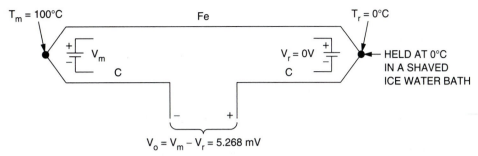

$$V_o = V_m - V_r = 5.268 \text{ mV}$$

FIGURE 10.2 Reference junction temperature $T_r = 0°C$ at the ice point and $V_r = 0V$. Measuring junction temperature V_m will increase as T_m increases.

Let us visualize how the table for a standard J-type, iron-constantan thermocouple might have been constructed. One junction in Figure 10.2 is placed in a shaved ice bath, stirred continually, and forced to be at a temperature of 0°C. This junction is *by definition* the *reference or cold junction* and its thermoelectric reference voltage is defined as $V_r = 0V$. Temperatures are measured with respect to T_r, by the remaining *measuring* junction, T_m. If T_m is placed in boiling water at $T_m = 100°C$, V_o will equal 5.268mV with the polarity shown in Figure 10.2.

This measurement allows us to (a) model measuring junction voltage V_m as a dc voltage in Figure 10.2, (b) show that the iron wire is positive with respect to constantan, and (c) write the thermocouple pair equation as:

$$V_o = V_m - V_r \tag{10.1}$$

Since $V_r = 0V$ in Eq. (10.1), $V_m = V_o = 5.268$mV. Look at the (partial) reference table given in Figure 10.3 to locate the entry $V_m = 5.268$mV at $T_m = 100°C$.

10.2.3 Thermocouple Temperature Measurement without an Ice-point Reference

Unknown temperature T_m can be measured without the inconvenient ice bath by reference to Figure 10.4. The technique is shown in the following example.

Example 10.1:

In Figure 10.4, reference junction T_r is at 25°C. If output voltage V_o is 3.991mV, find T_m.

Solution:

(a) Go to the type J thermocouple reference table in Figure 10.3. Enter the table at 25°C and read reference junction voltage $V_r = 1.277$mV.
(b) Substitute for V_r and V_o in Eq.(10.1):

DEG C	0	1	2	3	4	5	6	7	8	9	10	DEG C
0	0.000	0.050	0.101	0.151	0.202	0.253	0.303	0.354	0.405	0.456	0.507	0
10	0.507	0.558	0.609	0.660	0.711	0.762	0.813	0.865	0.916	0.967	1.019	10
20	1.019	1.070	1.122	1.174	1.225	1.277	1.329	1.381	1.432	1.484	1.536	20
30	1.536	1.588	1.640	1.693	1.745	1.797	1.849	1.901	1.954	2.006	2.058	30
40	2.058	2.111	2.163	2.216	2.268	2.321	2.374	2.426	2.479	2.532	2.585	40
50	2.585	2.638	2.691	2.743	2.796	2.849	2.902	2.956	3.009	3.062	3.115	50
60	3.115	3.168	3.221	3.275	3.328	3.381	3.435	3.488	3.542	3.595	3.649	60
70	3.649	3.702	3.756	3.809	3.863	3.917	3.971	4.024	4.078	4.132	4.186	70
80	4.186	4.239	4.293	4.347	4.401	4.455	4.509	4.563	4.617	4.671	4.725	80
90	4.725	4.780	4.834	4.888	4.942	4.996	5.050	5.105	5.159	5.213	5.268	90
100	5.268	5.322	5.376	5.431	5.485	5.540	5.594	5.649	5.703	5.758	5.812	100
110	5.812	5.867	5.921	5.976	6.031	6.085	6.140	6.195	6.249	6.304	6.359	110
120	6.359	6.414	6.468	6.523	6.578	6.633	6.688	6.742	6.797	6.852	6.907	120
130	6.907	6.962	7.017	7.072	7.127	7.182	7.237	7.292	7.347	7.402	7.457	130
140	7.457	7.512	7.567	7.622	7.677	7.732	7.787	7.843	7.898	7.953	8.008	140
150	8.008	8.063	8.118	8.174	8.229	8.284	8.339	8.394	8.450	8.505	8.560	150
160	8.560	8.616	8.671	8.726	8.781	8.837	8.892	8.947	9.003	9.058	9.113	160
170	9.113	9.169	9.224	9.279	9.335	9.390	9.446	9.501	9.556	9.612	9.667	170
180	9.667	9.723	9.778	9.834	9.899	9.944	10.000	10.055	10.111	10.166	10.222	180
190	10.222	10.277	10.333	10.388	10.444	10.499	10.555	10.610	10.666	10.721	10.777	190
200	10.777	10.832	10.888	10.943	10.999	11.054	11.110	11.165	11.221	11.276	11.332	200
210	11.332	11.387	11.443	11.498	11.554	11.609	11.665	11.720	11.776	11.831	11.887	210
220	11.887	11.943	11.998	12.054	12.109	12.165	12.220	12.276	12.331	12.387	12.442	220
230	12.442	12.498	12.553	12.609	12.664	12.720	12.776	12.831	12.887	12.942	12.998	230
240	12.998	13.053	13.109	13.164	13.220	13.275	13.331	13.386	13.442	13.497	13.553	240
250	13.553	13.608	13.664	13.719	13.775	13.830	13.886	13.941	13.997	14.052	14.108	250
260	14.108	14.163	14.219	14.274	14.330	14.385	14.441	14.496	14.552	14.607	14.663	260
270	14.663	14.718	14.774	14.829	14.885	14.940	14.995	15.051	15.106	15.162	15.217	270
280	15.217	15.273	15.328	15.383	15.439	15.494	15.550	15.605	15.661	15.716	15.771	280
290	15.771	15.827	15.882	15.938	15.993	16.048	16.104	16.159	16.214	16.270	16.325	290
300	16.325	16.380	16.436	16.491	16.547	16.602	16.657	16.713	16.768	16.823	16.879	300
310	16.879	16.934	16.989	17.044	17.100	17.155	17.210	17.266	17.321	17.376	17.432	310
320	17.432	17.487	17.542	17.597	17.653	17.708	17.763	17.818	17.874	17.929	17.984	320
330	17.984	18.039	18.095	18.150	18.205	18.260	18.316	18.371	18.426	18.481	18.537	330
340	18.537	18.592	18.647	18.702	18.757	18.813	18.868	18.923	18.978	19.033	19.089	340
350	19.089	19.144	19.199	19.254	19.309	19.364	19.420	19.475	19.530	19.585	19.640	350
360	19.640	19.695	19.751	19.806	19.861	19.916	19.971	20.026	20.081	20.137	20.192	360
370	20.192	20.247	20.302	20.357	20.412	20.467	20.523	20.578	20.633	20.688	20.743	370
380	20.743	20.798	20.853	20.909	20.964	21.019	21.074	21.129	21.184	21.239	21.295	380
390	21.295	21.350	21.405	21.460	21.515	21.570	21.625	21.680	21.736	21.791	21.846	390
400	21.846	21.901	21.956	22.011	22.066	22.122	22.177	22.232	22.287	22.342	22.397	400
410	22.397	22.453	22.508	22.563	22.618	22.673	22.728	22.784	22.839	22.894	22.949	410
420	22.949	23.004	23.060	23.115	23.170	23.225	23.280	23.336	23.391	23.446	23.501	420
430	23.501	23.556	23.612	23.667	23.722	23.777	23.833	23.888	23.943	23.999	24.054	430
440	24.054	24.109	24.164	24.220	24.275	24.330	24.386	24.441	24.496	24.552	24.607	440
450	24.607	24.662	24.718	24.773	24.829	24.884	24.939	24.995	25.050	25.106	25.161	450
460	25.161	25.217	25.272	25.327	25.383	25.438	25.494	25.549	25.605	25.661	25.716	460
470	25.716	25.772	25.827	25.883	25.938	25.994	26.050	26.105	26.161	26.216	26.272	470
480	26.272	26.328	26.383	26.439	26.495	26.551	26.606	26.662	26.718	26.774	26.829	480
490	26.829	26.885	26.941	26.997	27.053	27.109	27.165	27.220	27.276	27.332	27.388	490
500	27.388	27.444	27.500	27.556	27.612	27.668	27.724	27.780	27.836	27.893	27.949	500
510	27.949	28.005	28.061	28.117	28.173	28.230	28.286	28.342	28.398	28.455	28.511	510
520	28.511	28.567	28.624	28.680	28.736	28.793	28.849	28.906	28.962	29.019	29.075	520
530	29.075	29.132	29.188	29.245	29.301	29.358	29.415	29.471	29.528	29.585	29.642	530
540	29.642	29.698	29.755	29.812	29.869	29.929	29.983	30.039	30.096	30.153	30.210	540
550	30.210	30.267	30.324	30.381	30.439	30.496	30.553	30.610	30.667	30.724	30.782	550
560	30.782	30.839	30.896	30.954	31.011	31.068	31.126	31.183	31.241	31.298	31.356	560
570	31.356	31.413	31.471	31.528	31.586	31.644	31.702	31.759	31.817	31.875	31.933	570
580	31.933	31.991	32.048	32.106	32.164	32.222	32.280	32.338	32.396	32.455	32.513	580
590	32.513	32.571	32.629	32.687	32.746	32.804	32.862	32.921	32.979	33.038	33.096	590
600	33.096	33.155	33.213	33.272	33.330	33.389	33.448	33.506	33.565	33.624	33.683	600
610	33.683	33.742	33.800	33.859	33.918	33.977	34.036	34.095	34.155	34.214	34.273	610
620	34.273	34.332	34.391	34.451	34.510	34.569	34.629	34.688	34.748	34.807	34.867	620
630	34.867	34.926	34.986	35.046	35.105	35.165	35.225	35.285	35.344	35.404	35.464	630
640	35.464	35.524	35.584	35.644	35.704	35.764	35.825	35.885	35.945	36.005	36.066	640
650	36.066	36.126	36.186	36.247	36.307	36.368	36.428	36.489	36.549	36.610	36.671	650
660	36.671	36.732	36.792	36.853	36.914	36.975	37.036	37.097	37.158	37.219	37.280	660
670	37.280	37.341	37.402	37.463	37.525	37.586	37.647	37.709	37.770	37.831	37.893	670
680	37.893	37.954	38.016	38.078	38.139	38.201	38.262	38.324	38.386	38.448	38.510	680
690	38.510	38.572	38.633	38.695	38.757	38.819	38.882	38.944	39.006	39.068	39.130	690
700	39.130	39.192	39.255	39.317	39.379	39.442	39.504	39.567	39.629	39.692	39.754	700
710	39.754	39.817	39.880	39.942	40.005	40.068	40.131	40.193	40.256	40.319	40.382	710
720	40.382	40.445	40.508	40.571	40.634	40.697	40.760	40.823	40.886	40.950	41.013	720
730	41.013	41.076	41.139	41.203	41.266	41.329	41.393	41.456	41.520	41.583	41.647	730
740	41.647	41.710	41.744	41.837	41.901	41.965	42.028	42.092	42.156	42.219	42.283	740
750	42.283	42.347	42.411	42.475	42.538	42.602	42.666	42.730	42.794	42.858	42.922	750
760	42.922											760
DEG C	0	1	2	3	4	5	6	7	8	9	10	DEG C

Measuring Junction Temperature T_m – °C

Measuring Junction Voltage V_m ~ mV

FIGURE 10.3 Type J thermocouple reference table (N.I.S.T. National Institute of Standards and Technology Monograph 125). Values of V_m are given for a reference junction temperature $T_r = 0°C$ ($V_r = 0mV$).

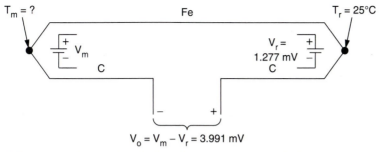

FIGURE 10.4 T_m can be calculated from reference table data if temperature of the reference junction is known.

$$V_o = V_m - V_r$$
$$3.991mV = V_m - 1.277mV$$

to find $V_m = (3.991 + 1.277)mV = 5.268mV$

(c) Enter Figure 10.3 at 5.268mV and read $T_m = 100°C$. Thus, T_m can always be measured if we know the temperature of the cold junction.

10.2.4 Identifying Thermocouples

Four of the most common types of standard thermocouple wire combinations are designated by their ANSI code letters, E, J, K, and T, as shown in Figure 10.5. The first named alloy is positive with respect to the second. For example, iron is positive with respect to constantan in a type J thermocouple. The iron wire is identified by its white insulation; the constantan's insulation is red. Each type of thermocouple has its own N.I.S.T. reference table.

ANSI CODE	ALLOY*	COLOR CODE	USEFUL RANGE	AVERAGE SENSITIVITY
E	CHROMEL-CONSTANTAN	PURPLE RED	−200°C TO 900°C	60.9 µV/°C
J	IRON-CONSTANTAN	WHITE RED	0°C TO 750°C	51.7 µV/°C
K	CHROMEL-ALUMEL	YELLOW RED	−200°C TO 1250°C	40.6 µV/°C
T	COPPER-CONSTANTAN	BLUE RED	−250°C TO 350°C	40.6 µV/°C

FIGURE 10.5 Thermocouple wire type is identified by the color of its insulation. The first named alloy* is positive with respect to the second. The average sensitivities are approximate and apply only at 25°C.

10.3

ELIMINATING ONE THERMOCOUPLE

10.3.1 Introduction

The basic thermocouple circuits in Figures 10.2 and 10.4 are tutorial in nature and are *not* encountered in real applications. In practice, you will see only a single thermocouple connected to a voltmeter via copper wires or connected to copper pads of a pc board containing signal conditioning circuitry. The transition from temperature measurement by two thermocouple junctions to a single thermocouple measurement is documented in Figure 10.6.

10.3.2 Intermediate Junctions

Two copper lead wires connect the two-junction thermocouple configuration of Figure 10.4 to a voltmeter. As shown in Figure 10.6(a), two additional (intermediate) copper-constantan junctions are created. If these junctions are held at the same temperature (isothermal), their thermoelectric voltages will cancel. Other intermediate junctions are encountered in practice: copper to solder on pc boards, as well as Kovar, gold, aluminum, and other metals within an integrated circuit. If each intermediate junction and its companion are at the same temperature their junction voltages cancel. If not, an error voltage is present. Careful attention to layout and thermal symmetry must be observed to ensure that each pair of intermediate junctions are isothermal.

In Figure 10.6(b), the iron-constantan reference junction and both intermediate copper-constantan junctions are shown at equal temperatures. The heavy-line constantan wire is an *intermediate metal* between the top iron wire and top copper wire. The empirical "law of intermediate metals" states that any third wire (C) between two dissimilar metals (Fe and Cu) has no effect on V_o as long as the two junctions (Fe-C and Cu-C) *are at the same temperature*. (If this law is not true, anyone could start their own electric company with a batch of dissimilar metals wired in series.) Since the constantan wire has no effect on V_o, it can be eliminated as shown in Figure 10.6(c).

10.3.3 Single Thermocouple Measurement

Suppose that Figure 10.6(c) represents a single Fe-C measuring thermocouple junction wired to the copper pads of a pc board. The reference junction is not immediately obvious. However, as long as the copper pads are isothermal, their temperature alone determines T_r of the reference junction. Both Fe-Cu and Cu-C junctions are treated as a single Fe-C reference junction as shown by the model in Figure 10.6(d). Any additional isothermal intermediate junction pairs have no effect on V_o.

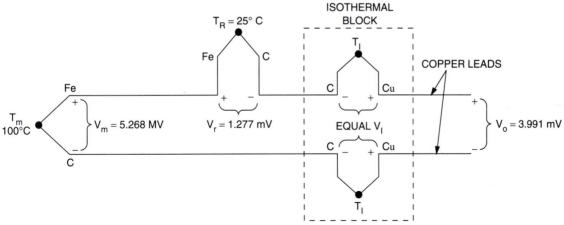

(a) COPPER LEADS FORM TWO IINTERMEDIATE JUNCTIONS LABELED T_I.
SINCE BOTH ADDED JUNCTIONS ARE AT EQUAL TEMPERATURES,
THEIR THERMOELECTRIC VOLTAGES CANCEL OUT.

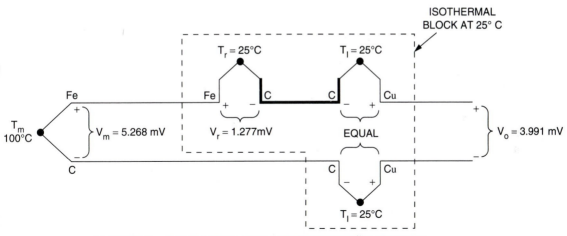

(b) SINCE $T_r = T_I$ THE (HEAVY LINE) CONSTANTAN WIRE BECOMES
AN INTERMEDIATE METAL. IT HAS NO EFFECT UPON THE
OUTPUT VOLTAGE, AND CAN BE ELIMINATED.

FIGURE 10.6 Eliminating one thermocouple

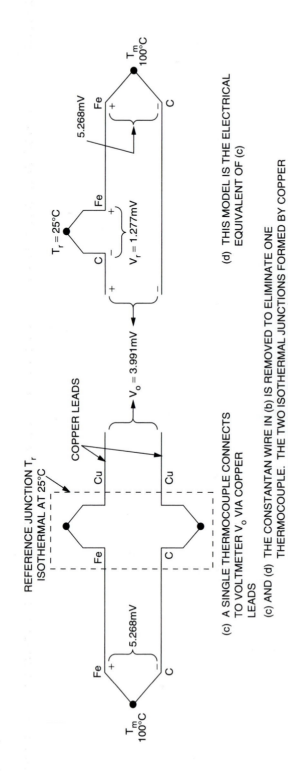

(c) A SINGLE THERMOCOUPLE CONNECTS TO VOLTMETER V_o VIA COPPER LEADS

(c) AND (d) THE CONSTANTAN WIRE IN (b) IS REMOVED TO ELIMINATE ONE THERMOCOUPLE. THE TWO ISOTHERMAL JUNCTIONS FORMED BY COPPER LEADS IN (c) BECOME THE NEW REFERENCE JUNCTION. TO CALCULATE T_m, V_r, AND V_o USE THE BASIC EQUIVALENT MODEL IN (d).

(d) THIS MODEL IS THE ELECTRICAL EQUIVALENT OF (c)

FIGURE 10.6 Eliminating one thermocouple (continued)

Type J tables are used to look up V_r, V_m, T_r, or T_m, and Eq. (10.1) is used to calculate V_o. The procedure to measure temperature with one thermocouple is illustrated by an example.

Example 10.2:

A single type J thermocouple is connected via copper leads to Kovar pads (within an IC) of a voltmeter as shown in Figure 10.7. If $V_o = 1.308\text{mV}$, find T_m.

Solution:

The iron and constantan wires first meet copper wires to identify the reference junction and its temperature $T_r = 25°C$. Model the Fe-Cu and Cu-C junctions as a single Fe-C reference junction. Look up $T_r = 25°C$ in Figure 10.3 and read $V_r = 1.277\text{mV}$. Use Eq. (10.1) to find V_m.

$V_o = 1.308\text{mV} = V_m - 1.277\text{mV}$
$V_m = 2.585\text{mV}$

Find $V_m = 2.585\text{mV}$ in Figure 10.3 and read $T_m = 50°C$. Note that the intermediate junctions at $35°C$ are isothermal and have *no* effect on V_o. They need not be drawn in the model.

10.4

COLD JUNCTION COMPENSATION

10.4.1 Need for Cold Junction Compensation

In a practical thermocouple measuring system, output V_o of the thermocouple pair (Figures 10.2, 10.4 and 10.6) should equal V_m. If we could insert a voltage in series opposition and equal to V_r, then there would be no need to (a) measure T_r, (b) look up V_r, and (3) use Eq. (10.1) to calculate V_m. Output V_o would equal V_m. Such a scheme is called ice-point or *cold junction* compensation (CJC).

10.4.2 Principle of Cold Junction Compensation

If an equal voltage can be connected in series opposition to reference voltage V_r, the thermocouple network's output voltage V_o would equal V_m. This principle is shown in Figure 10.8(a) where voltage V_c compensates for and cancels out the effect of V_r. In practice, reference temperature T_r will not be constant at a convenient value like $25°C$. For precise compensation, V_c must track V_r as T_r changes with its ambient. Thus the compensating voltage must be generated by a transducer circuit that (a) is isothermal with reference junction temperature T_r to (b) output a voltage that *tracks* V_r.

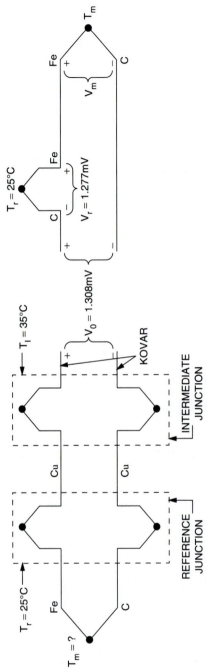

FIGURE 10.7 Circuit and equivalent model for Example 10.2

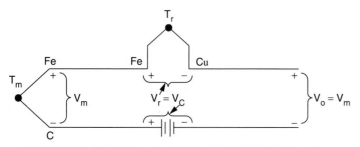

(a) REFERENCE VOLTAGE V_r IS CANCELLED BY INSERTING AN
     EQUAL AND OPPOSITE COMPENSATING VOLTAGE SO THAT $V_o = V_m$

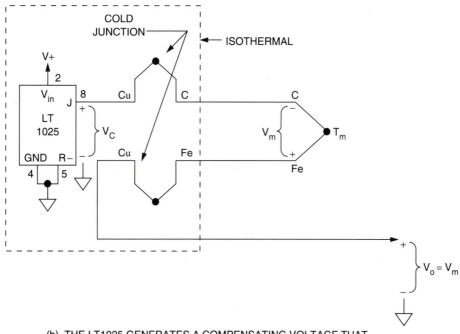

(b) THE LT1025 GENERATES A COMPENSATING VOLTAGE THAT
     CANCELS THE REFERENCE VOLTAGE SO THAT $V_o = V_m$

FIGURE 10.8 The principle of compensating for a reference voltage in (a) is accomplished by the practical circuit in (b).

One such circuit is shown in Figure 10.8(b). An integrated circuit, the LT1025 Cold Junction Compensator, must be maintained at exactly the same temperature as the reference junction formed by the Cu-C and Fe-Cu junctions (see Figures 10.6(c) and (d)). Its type J compensating voltage output V_c tracks and cancels V_r so that $V_o = V_m$. The LT1025 CJC accurately tracks V_r over a reference temperature range of 0 to 70°C. Its versatility is illustrated by a brief description.

10.4.3 LT1025 Micropower Thermocouple Cold Junction Compensator

Refer to the LT1025's functional block diagram in Figure 10.9(a) and (b). Reference temperature T_r is converted to 10mV/°C by a transducer circuit, corrected for the thermocouple characteristic's bow, and applied to a buffer op amp. The op amp's output equals 10mV/°C so that the LT1025 can be used to measure its own ambient temperature with a convenient 10 mV/°C sensitivity. V_o is then scaled by a precision resistance divider to give four compensating voltage outputs as shown. The output sensitivities are chosen to match each thermocouple's output voltage slope at 25°C. One application of the LT1025 is shown in Figure 10.13.

10.5

THERMOCOUPLE TRANSDUCER EQUATIONS

10.5.1 Thermocouple Nonlinearity

A Type J thermocouple's output–input characteristic seems to be reasonably linear as shown by the solid line graph of V_m vs. T_m in Figure 10.10(b). However, refer to the listings of corresponding V_m vs. T_m data point coordinates in Figure 10.10(a). The increase in V_m, or ΔV_m, is listed in column 3 for equal T_m increases of 10°C. If the thermocouple was linear, ΔV_m would be equal for each equal increase in ΔT_m. The sensitivity or slope $\alpha = \Delta V_m/10°C$ is calculated in column 4 and also shown for 10°C segments on the graph.

The slopes in column 4 increase as temperature increases to indicate the upward bow-shaped nonlinearity of V_m vs. T_m over even a limited range of 0 to 50°C. Note that the slope at approximately 25°C equals the LT1025's correction voltage for a type J thermocouple in Figure 10.10(a).

10.5.2 Linear Approximation Equations

A dashed line V_{m1} vs. T_m connects the end points in Figure 10.10(b) to construct a *trial* linear approximation of the actual solid V_m vs. T_m graph. The approximation has a rise of $\Delta V_{m1} = (2.585 - 0)$mV for a run of $\Delta T_m = (50 - 0)°C$, to yield an average slope of 51.7μV/°C. Since it passes through the origin, there is no offset term and the approximate transducer equation is

$$V_m = 51.7 \frac{mV}{°C} \times T_m \tag{10.2}$$

10.5.3 A Better Offset Linear Approximation

If a transducer has a slightly bow-shaped characteristic (bow up or down), a more accurate linear approximation transducer equation can be derived by constructing a straight line through the one-sixth and five-sixth operating points. The improvement is illustrated in the following example.

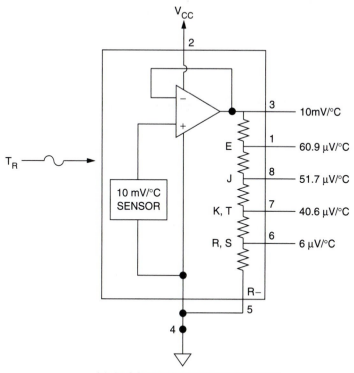

(a) BLOCK DIAGRAM OF THE LT1025

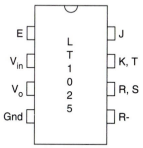

(b) PINOUT FOR HERMETIC
J OR MOLDED N DUAL-
IN-LINE PACKAGE

FIGURE 10.9 Block diagram and pinout for the LT1025 Micropower
Thermocouple Cold Junction Compensator

T_m	V_m	ΔV_m	SLOPE $\alpha = \Delta V_m/10°C$	V_{m1}	$V_{m1} - V_m$
0°C	0 mV	0.507 mV	50.7 µV/°C	0 mV	0 µV
10°C	0.507 mV	0.512 mV	51.2 µV/°C	0.517 mV	10 µV
20°C	1.019 mV	0.517 mV	51.7 µV/°C	1.034 mV	15 µV
30°C	1.536 mV	0.522 mV	52.2 µV/°C	1.551 mV	15 µV
40°C	2.058 mV	0.527 mV	52.7 µV/°C	2.068 mV	10 µV
50°C	2.585 mV			2.585 mV	0 µV

(a) TYPE J REFERENCE DATA

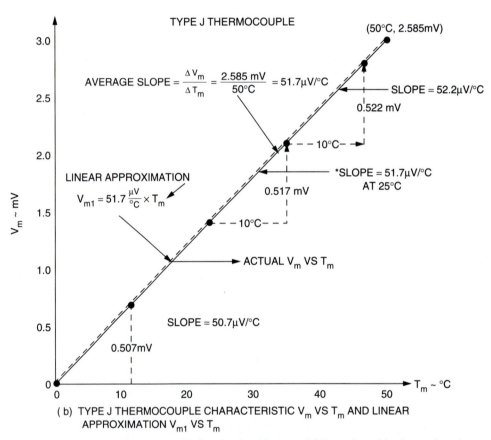

(b) TYPE J THERMOCOUPLE CHARACTERISTIC V_m VS T_m AND LINEAR APPROXIMATION V_{m1} VS T_m

FIGURE 10.10 Type J thermocouple data is plotted as a solid line. The table shows that slope $\propto$ increases with temperature. The approximate thermocouple equation between end points, $V_{m1} = 51.7\ \mu V/°C \times T_m$ is plotted as a dashed line.

Example 10.3:

Refer to the solid line V_{m2} vs. T_m approximation of a type J thermocouple characteristic in Figure 10.11(b). This graph is a straight line drawn between the one-sixth and five-sixths (temperature span) operating points. (a) Derive a transducer approximation equation from this graph. (b) Calculate the difference between V_{m2} and actual V_m at 10°C intervals to see if there is an improvement over the end point's approximation V_{m1} vs. T_m in Figure 10.10.

T_m	V_m	V_{m2}	$V_{m2} - V_m$
0°C	0mV	−0.008mV	−8μV
8°C	0.405mV	0.405mV	0μV
10°C	0.507mV	0.509mV	2μV
20°C	1.019mV	1.026mV	7μV
30°C	1.536mV	1.543mV	7μV
40°C	2.058mV	2.060mV	2μV
42°C	2.163mV	2.163mV	0μV
50°C	2.585mV	2.577mV	−8μV

(a) TABULATED DATA FOR (b)

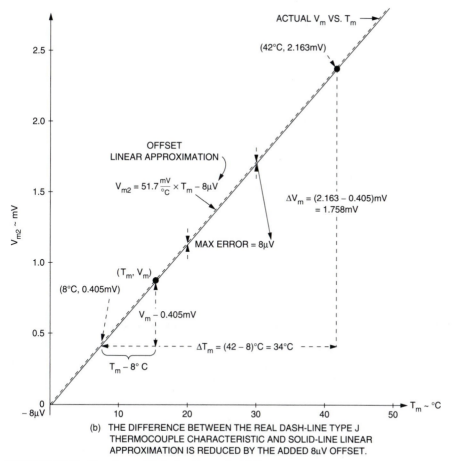

(b) THE DIFFERENCE BETWEEN THE REAL DASH-LINE TYPE J THERMOCOUPLE CHARACTERISTIC AND SOLID-LINE LINEAR APPROXIMATION IS REDUCED BY THE ADDED 8μV OFFSET.

FIGURE 10.11 Graphs and data for Example 10.3

335

Solution:

(a) Tabulate thermocouple operating point data points from Figure 10.3 in 10°C increments from 0 to 50°C. Add two more operating points at $T_m = 1/6 \times 50°C = 8°C$ and $T_m = 5/6 \times 50°C = 42°C$ as in columns 1 and 2 of Figure 10.11(a).

The solid V_{m2} vs. T_m graph does not pass through the origin but intercepts the vertical axis at $-8\mu V$. For this reason, V_{m2} vs. T_m is called an *offset linear approximation* of the transducer characteristic. Its equation is derived by first evaluating the slope:

$$\frac{\Delta V_{m2}}{\Delta T_m} = \frac{(2.163 - 0.405)mV}{(42 - 8)\,°C} = \frac{1.758mV}{34°C} = \frac{51.7\mu V}{°C}$$

The general slope at (T_m, V_m) is

$$\frac{\Delta V_{m2}}{\Delta T_m} = \frac{V_{m2} - 0.405\mu V}{T_m - 8°C}$$

Equate slopes:

$$\frac{V_{m2} - 0.405mV}{T_m - 8°C} = \frac{51.7\mu\,V}{°C}$$

solve for V_{m2} to get the *transducer's offset approximation equation*:

$$V_{m2} = 51.7\,\frac{\mu V}{°C} \times T_m - 8\mu V \tag{10.3}$$

(b) Calculate V_{m2} from Eq. (10.3) and list values in column 3 of Figure 10.11(a). List the difference between V_{m2} and actual V_m in column 4.

Note that the V_{m1} reads high by a maximum of $15\mu V$ in column 6 of Figure 10.10(a). Compare this with the maximum low reading of $-8\mu V$ in column 4 of Figure 10.11(a). Clearly the $-8\mu V$ offset in Eq. (10.3) causes an improvement over the end-point linear approximation by a factor of about 2 to 1. An error of $8\mu V$ in V_{m2} means a maximum worst case error of only 0.15°C.

10.5.4 Linearization Techniques

Nonlinear transducer characteristics can be linearized in real time by any one of four analog techniques. Offset linearization has been demonstrated in section 10.5.3 for a characteristic with only a slight nonlinearity. For characteristics with larger nonlinearities, the transducer's equation can be derived and implemented by IC hardware in one of three formats:

1. Piecewise linear approximation (op amps and diodes)
2. Polynomial approximations (multipliers and op amps)
3. Exponential, logarithmic, or power approximations (log or arthimetic computational ICs).

Hardware is available to construct circuits* whose output–input equations match one of these formats. Simply compare the transducer and hardware equations to accomplish the hardware design.

Linearization can also be accomplished by using software programmed into a microprocessor or microcontroller. This technique eliminates the need for trimming required by analog linearizing circuitry. Software solutions include look-up tables (requires much memory), power series expansions, or piecewise-linear approximations. In this chapter we select the piecewise-linear software approximation technique to show how it is accomplished within a microcontroller.

With the preceding background on thermocouple transducers and having chosen the type of linearization technique, we can now proceed with a design to solve the problem outlined in section 10.1.

10.6

TRANSDUCER APPROXIMATION FOR PIECEWISE SOFTWARE

10.6.1 Measuring System Overview

Figure 10.12 is a block diagram of a system to measure and record temperature of a soldering iron in 5-second intervals as it heats from room temperature to final temperature (see also Figure 10.1).

The thermocouple transducer circuit block represents a type J thermocouple and its associated LT1025 cold junction compensation IC. Input T_m ranges from 0 to 500°C and (from Figure 10.3) output $V_m = V_T$ ranges nonlinearly from 0 to

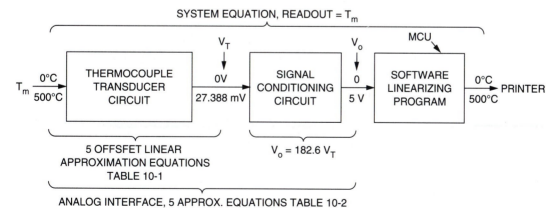

FIGURE 10.12 Block diagram of a system to measure and record soldering iron temperature

---

*See: D. H. Sheingold, "Nonlinear Circuits Handbook," Analog Devices; and J. Williams, "Application Note 28," Linear Technology Corp.

27.388mV. The transducer's characteristic will be divided (arbitrarily) into five equal temperature segments. An approximate equation will be derived for each segment in accordance with the offset linear technique presented in section 10.5.3. These equations will be amplified by a signal conditioning circuit to give five analog interface equations. The AI equations are required by the programmer to write the linearization program. Note: The equations have *nothing* to do with the design of the signal conditioning circuit.

10.6.2 Signal Conditioning Circuit Design

The signal conditioning must amplify V_T in Figure 10.12 to fill most of the 5.12V input span of the ADC in a MCU. For convenience, choose a range for V_o of 0 to 5V. The SCC must have a gain of:

$$\text{Slope} = \frac{\Delta V_o}{\Delta V_T} = \frac{(5-0)V}{(27.388-0)mV} = 182.6$$

and the SCC design equation is written by inspection:

$$V_o = 182.6 \times V_T \tag{10.4a}$$

Choose the noninverter amplifier in Figure 10.13 whose hardware equation is:

$$\frac{V_o}{V_T} = \left(1 + \frac{R_f}{R_i}\right) \tag{10.4b}$$

Arbitrarily choose $R_i = 1k\Omega$. Equate design and hardware equation gain terms to find $R_f = 181.6k\Omega$.

$$1 + \frac{R_f}{1k\Omega} = 182.6; R_f = 181.6k\Omega$$

The 100Ω pot in Figure 10.13 allows gain to be trimmed from about 170 to 190.

Five approximation equations must now be derived for the analog interface. This will complete the analog interface design and furnish data required by the MCU programmer to write the linearization program.

10.7

DERIVING THE PROGRAMMING LINEARIZATION EQUATIONS

10.7.1 Derivation Procedure

1. Construct a graph of the type J thermocouple's nonlinear V_T vs. T_m characteristic over the problem's range of 0 to 500°C. Divide the graph into equal piecewise-linear segments, for example, 100°C increments. Locate the one-sixth and five-sixth operating points on each segment. Derive an offset linear approximation

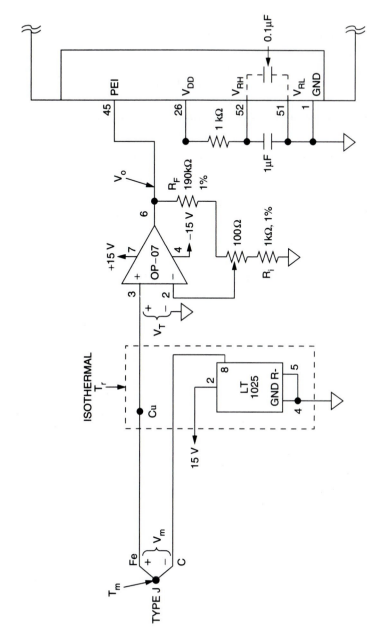

FIGURE 10.13 A cold-junction compensated type J thermocouple is connected to a noninverting amplifier SCC to complete the analog interface design.

339

equation of V_T vs. T_m for each segment. This procedure is shown in sections 10.7.2 and 10.7.3.

2. Multiply the V_T equations by the SCC's gain of 182.6 (Figure 10.12) to obtain an analog interface approximation equation, V_o vs. T_m, for *each* segment. These calculations are shown and tabulated in section 10.7.4.

3. Solve the V_o vs. T_m approximation equation of each segment for T_m and show the range of V_o for which the equation is valid. These are the equations required by the programmer to write the software linearization program. The T_m equations are listed in section 10.7.5.

10.7.2 Constructing the Piecewise-Linear Graph

Arbitrarily divide the input T_m span of 0 to 500°C into 5 equal increments of 100°C. Corresponding values of V_T are looked up from the type J thermocouple table in Figure 10.3 to obtain coordinates of five operating points plotted as circled points on Figure 10.14(a). For conceptual purposes only, these points are joined by alternated dashed and solid lines to form five segments. Identify the segments by their temperature range as shown in column 1 of Figure 10.14(b).

Choosing more segments would give a better approximation at the expense of increased complexity of the software linearization program, memory space, and program execution time.

10.7.3 Deriving the Type J Approximation Equations

We will derive an *offset* piecewise-linear approximation equation for each segment in Figure 10.14(a). List the one-sixth and five-sixth temperatures for each segment as in column 2 of Figure 10.14(b). Look up corresponding values for V_T from Figure 10.3, post them in column 3, and calculate ΔV_T for entry into column 4. Since each temperature increment is, for example $(83-17)°C = 66°C$, the slope of each *offset* linear segment is calculated from $\Delta V_T/66°C$ and listed in column 5.

Inspection of column 5 shows that the slopes of each segment are *not* equal. This evidence of nonlinearity is *not* readily apparent from the apparently linear type J thermocouple graph in Figure 10.14(a).

The approximation equations are next derived beginning with an example.

Example 10.4:

Derive an equation for the 200 to 300°C offset linear approximation segment in Figure 10.14(a).

Solution:

Coordinates for the one-sixth and five-sixth end points are 217°C, 11.720mV, and 283°C, 15.383mV. Refer to segment 3 in Figure 10.14(a). Evaluate the slope from coordinate data:

$$\text{Slope} = \frac{(15.383 - 11.720)\text{mV}}{(283 - 217)°\text{C}} = \frac{3.663\text{mV}}{66°\text{C}} = 55.5\frac{\mu\text{V}}{°\text{C}}$$

Express the general slope from point (T_m, V_T):

$$\text{Slope} = \frac{V_T - 11.720\text{mV}}{T_m - 217°\text{C}}$$

Equate slopes and force into standard form $y = mx + b$:

$$\frac{V_T - 11.720\text{mV}}{T_m - 217°\text{C}} = 55.5\frac{\mu\text{V}}{°\text{C}}$$

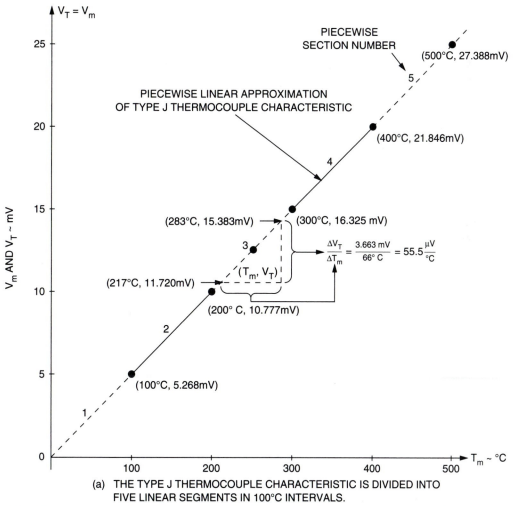

(a) THE TYPE J THERMOCOUPLE CHARACTERISTIC IS DIVIDED INTO
FIVE LINEAR SEGMENTS IN 100°C INTERVALS.

FIGURE 10.14 Data from (a) is used to plot a 5-segment linear approximation graph in (b). An offset linear approximation equation for each segment can then be derived as shown in Example 10.4.

SEGMENT	TEMP AT $\frac{1}{6}$ AND $\frac{5}{6}$	$V_T \sim$ mV	$\Delta V_T \sim$ mV	SLOPE IN μV/OC
0 TO 100°C	17° C $\Big\}$ 66°C 83° C	0.865 $\Big\}$ 4.347	3.482	52.7 $\frac{\mu V}{°C}$
100 TO 200°C	117 $\Big\}$ 66°C 183	6.195 $\Big\}$ 9.834	3.639	55.1 $\frac{\mu V}{°C}$
200 TO 300°C	217 $\Big\}$ 66°C 283	11.720 $\Big\}$ 15.383	3.663	55.5 $\frac{\mu V}{°C}$
300 TO 400°C	317 $\Big\}$ 66°C 383	17.266 $\Big\}$ 20.909	3.643	55.2 $\frac{\mu V}{°C}$
400 TO 500°C	417 $\Big\}$ 66°C 483	22.784 $\Big\}$ 26.439	3.655	55.4 $\frac{\mu V}{°C}$

(b)   THE INPUT SPAN OF T_m = 0 TO 500°C IS DIVIDED INTO 100°C SEGMENTS IN COLUMN 1. TEMPERATURES ARE LISTED AT THE 1/6 AND 5/6 POINT FOR EACH SEGMENT IN COLUMN 2 AND CORRESPONDING THERMOELECTRIC VOLTAGE IN COLUMN 3. ΔV_T IS LISTED IN COLUMN 4 FOR EQUAL ΔT_m OF 66°C. UNEQUAL SEGMENT SLOPES IN COLUMN 5 SHOW THE TYPE J THERMOCOUPLE NONLINEARITY.

FIGURE 10.14 Data from (a) is used to plot a 5-segment linear approximation graph in (b). An offset linear approximation equation for each segment can then be derived as shown in Example 10.4. (continued)

$$V_T - 11.720\text{mV} = \left(55.5\frac{\mu V}{°C}\right) \times T_m - 12.044\text{mV}$$

$$V_T = \left(55.5\frac{\mu V}{°C}\right) \times T_m - 0.324\text{mV} = \text{Offset approximation equation for } (200\text{–}300)°C$$

In similar fashion, equations are derived for each segment and the results are tabulated in Table 10.1.

TABLE 10.1   Offset Linear Approximation Equations in 100°C Increments for a Type J Thermocouple Characteristic. Measuring Temperature Range is 0–500°C. Thermoelectric Voltage Range is 0 to 27.388 mV.

Linear Approximation Equation	Valid in Range	
	T_m	V_T
$V_T = 52.75 \dfrac{\mu V}{°C} \times T_m - 0.0318 \text{mV}$	0 – 100°C	0 – 5.265mV
$V_T = 55.1 \dfrac{\mu V}{°C} \times T_m - 0.256 \text{mV}$	100 – 200°C	5.268 – 10.777mV
$V_T = 55.5 \dfrac{\mu V}{°C} \times T_m - 0.324 \text{mV}$	200 – 300°C	10.777 – 16.325mV
$V_T = 55.2 \dfrac{\mu V}{°C} \times T_m - 0.231 \text{mV}$	300 – 400°C	16.325 – 21.846mV
$V_T = 55.4 \dfrac{\mu V}{°C} \times T_m - 0.309 \text{mV}$	400 – 500°C	21.846 – 27.388mV

10.7.4 Analog Interface Equations

As shown in Figure 10.12, the SCC applies a gain of 182.6 to the transducer circuit's output V_T. The analog interface output V_o can also be represented by 5 approximation equations. From Eq. (10.4a), simply multiply the V_T approximation equations in Table 10.1 by 182.6. Results are tabulated in Table 10.2, and plotted in Fig. 10.15.

TABLE 10.2   Analog Interface Linear Approximation Equations

Analog Interface Approximation Equation	Valid Range	
	T_m	V_T
$V_o = 9.632 \dfrac{mV}{°C} \times T_m - 5.82 \text{mV}$	0 – 100°C	0 – 0.962V
$V_o = 10.061 \dfrac{mV}{°C} \times T_m - 46.74 \text{mV}$	100 – 200°C	0.962 – 1.967V
$V_o = 10.134 \dfrac{mV}{°C} \times T_m - 59.16 \text{mV}$	200 – 300°C	1.967 – 2.981V
$V_o = 10.079 \dfrac{mV}{°C} \times T_m - 42.181 \text{mV}$	300 – 400°C	2.981 – 3.989V
$V_o = 10.116 \dfrac{mV}{°C} \times T_m - 56.42 \text{mV}$	400 – 500°C	3.989 – 5.000V

10.7.5 The Programming Equations

The programming equation for each segment in Figure 10.15 is found by solving its analog interface equation for T_m. For example the AI equation for the third 200–300°C segment in Table 10.2 is:

$$V_o = 10.134 \ \frac{mV}{°C} \times T_m - 59.16mV$$

Solving for T_m:

$$T_m = \frac{V_o + 59.16mV}{10.134 \ \frac{mV}{°C}}, \quad \text{valid for } V_o = 1.967 \text{ to } 2.981V$$

The programming equations for all five segments are listed in Table 10.3 and shown graphically in Figure 10.15.

Example 10.5:

Check the accuracy of the programming equations at (a) $V_o = 472mV$, (b) $V_o = 1.462V$.

Solution:

(a) To see what the correct answer should be, find $V_T = V_o/182.6 = 472mV/182.6 = 2.585mV$. Find T_m from Figure 10.3; $T_m = 50°C$.

TABLE 10.3   Equations Required to Write a Software Linearization Program for the Analog Interface of Figure 10.13

If V_o is Between	Find T_m From	Equation	Segment
0–0.962V	$T_m = \dfrac{V_o + 5.82mV}{9.632mV/°C}$	(10.5a)	0–100°C
0.962–1.967V	$T_m = \dfrac{V_o + 46.74mV}{10.061mV/°C}$	(10.5b)	100–200°C
1.967–2.981V	$T_m = \dfrac{V_o + 59.16mV}{10.134mV/°C}$	(10.5c)	200–300°C
2.981–3.989V	$T_m = \dfrac{V_o + 42.181mV}{10.079mV/°C}$	(10.5d)	300–400°C
3.989–5.000V	$T_m = \dfrac{V_o + 56.42mV}{10.116mV/°C}$	(10.5e)	400–500°C

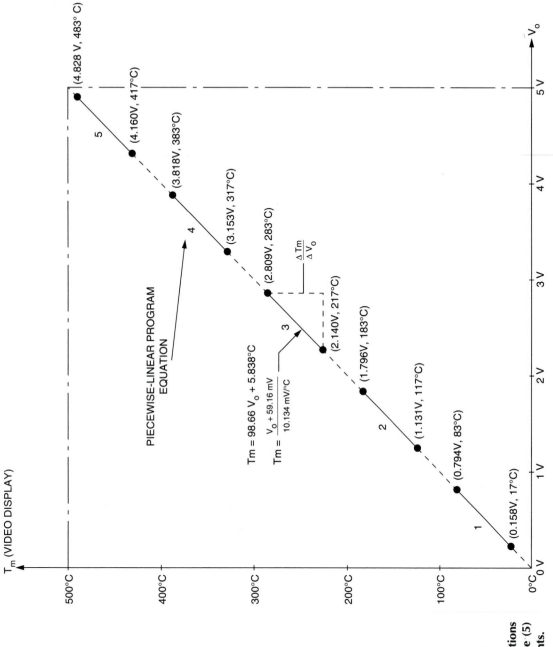

FIGURE 10.15 The piecewise-linear programming equations are divided into five (5) offset-linear segments.

Since V_o is between 0 and 0.962V, the program selects Eq.(10.5a) to solve for T_m:

$$T_m = \frac{472\text{mV} + 5.82\text{mV}}{9.632 \text{ mV}/°C} = 49.6°C$$

(b) Calculate $V_T = 1.462\text{V}/182.6 = 8.007\text{mV}$. T_m should equal 150°C from Figure 10.3. Since V_o lies between 0.962V and 1.967V, the program selects Eq. (10.5b) to find the readout for T_m:

$$T_m = \frac{1.462\text{V} + 46.74\text{mV}}{10.061 \text{ mV}/°C} = 149.96°C$$

The T_m readouts will be correct to within 0.25°C in the range 100 to 500°C and within 0.6°C from 0 to 100°C.

In similar fashion, equations are derived for each segment and the results are tabulated in Table 10.3. Now let's study how a microcontroller can be used to measure V_o, select the correct range, and calculate T_m.

10.8

SOFTWARE DESIGN

10.8.1 Introduction

Let's review the statement of the problem so we can define what the software must accomplish. A thermocouple is being used to measure a soldering iron's tip temperature at 5-second intervals (12 measurements per minute). What is not stated is how many measurements are necessary. A review of manufacturer's literature and our own measurements show that a soldering iron's tip usually reaches maximum temperature within 5 minutes. Therefore, the number of measurements must be

$$5 \text{ minutes} \times 12 \ \frac{\text{measurements}}{\text{minute}} = 60 \text{ measurements}$$

To ensure enough measurements and to account for variations in soldering irons, let's take 100 measurements. This value will be used as the interval count value in the program.

The temperature range is from 0°C to 500°C. Since a thermocouple's output is nonlinear, it has been divided into five subranges: 0°C–100°C, 100°C–200°C, 200°C–300°C, 300°C–400°C, and 400°C–500°C. Each of these subranges is approximated by a straight line with different offset (b values) and slope (m values) values. The task of the application program is to measure an input voltage from the signal conditioning circuit (V_o in Figure 10.13) and then determine which offset and slope values to use in the straight line equation to calculate the thermocouple's temperature. This process is known as piecewise linearization, and the application program as software linearization.

The general equation for the thermocouple temperature is

$$T_m = (V_o + b)\, 1/m \tag{10.5}$$

where V_o is the output voltage from the signal conditioning circuit and measured at port E (pin 45 on the MCU and on the EVB), b is the offset value, and $1/m$ is the reciprocal of the slope. The b and $1/m$ values are given in a table for each subrange at the beginning of the application program as shown in section 10.9. The program is also to display the temperature.

To help visualize the tasks to be accomplished, Figure 10.16 is an overall flow chart showing a logical sequence used to solve this problem. Many parts of this application have been studied in previous examples and used in other application programs. The following subsections follow the flow chart and refer to the labels used in the application program of section 10.9

10.8.2 CLEAR Routine

These few lines of code initialize the internal counter to 100 decimal and then clear 47 bytes of RAM that will be used to store data temporarily. The starting address of the RAM buffer is $DA00 set by the ORG directive. The first 7 bytes are used to store the b values and the buffer is labeled BBUFF. Refer to the buffer location heading in section 10.10 and Figure 10.18 to see how many locations are saved for each storage. Note that although 47 bytes are cleared, there are three areas labeled blank that are not used at this time but may be needed for future modifications to this program. Refer to section 10.9 for actual instructions and additional comments.

10.8.3 MEASTE Routine

This routine is similar to the MEASWE (measure weight) routine of Chapter 8. Like other routines used in this text with the A/D converter section, this routine accomplishes 5 tasks. They are: (1) initialize the A/D control register; (2) introduce a time delay so that the A/D converter has sufficient time to make the conversion; (3) read and temporarily store the contents of an A/D register; (4) convert the A/D reading to an equivalent voltage by multiplying the reading by 20mV/bit; (5) temporarily store the result of the multiplication.

The reason for storing the data in step 3 and step 5 is for convenience in later routines. The binary data saved in step 3 will be used to quickly determine the input voltage range in the RANGE routine. The BINBCD (binary-to-decimal) routine uses the result of step 5 to convert a 16-bit number to a 5-byte unpacked BCD value.

This application uses software to do the linearization and not the signal conditioning circuit. For each input voltage range, there is a different offset value and slope. Therefore, it is not possible to use the METEMP (measure temperature)

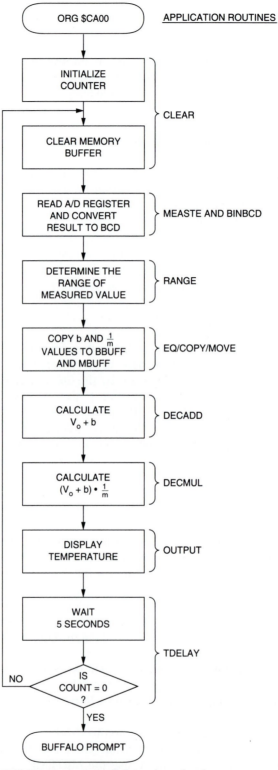

FIGURE 10.16 Overall flow chart for the software linearization program

routine of Chapter 7 in this application. The conversion from input binary data to temperature used in Chapter 7 is based on a constant slope and offset for the entire temperature range because of the characteristics of the temperature sensor that was used—the AD590. Also remember Chapter 7's temperature range was only from 0 to 100°C. The application in this chapter is from 0 to 500°C, which far exceeds the limits of the AD590 (–55 to 130°C), but there were several reasons for using the AD590 in the application of Chapter 7. Some of the reasons are the sensor's characteristics are linear in the desired temperature range and the sensor supplies a constant current. The MEASTE routine for this application only requires ten lines of code. Refer to this routine in section 10.9 for the lines of code and comments.

10.8.4 BINBCD Routine

This routine is the same routine used in Chapter 8 and originally written and studied in Chapter 3. Recall that this subroutine converts a 16-bit number stored in TREG1 to a 5-byte unpacked BCD value and stores it in a buffer labeled DBUFF. However, one difference between this routine and that used in Chapter 8 is the size of the buffer, DBUFF. In Chapter 8, the buffer size was set at 5 bytes; in this application 7 bytes have been saved (see assembler directive DBUFF RMB 7). The reason for reserving 7 bytes is that the converted value is expressed as a whole number times 10^{-4}. The decimal multiplication routine has been written to multiply the contents of two 7-byte buffers (DBUFF and MBUFF) and both numbers are expressed with a multiplier of 10^{-4}. The reader should now refer to the routine BINBCD in section 10.9 for the instructions and additional comments.

10.8.5 RANGE Routine

This section of the program selects one of the five ranges corresponding to the measured voltage. The range determines which equation values (b and 1/m) will be used in the calculation of temperature. Tables 10.2 and 10.3 show the range of V_o used in this application.

10.8.6 EQ/COPY/MOVE Routines

After the range has been found, it is necessary to copy the b and m values that correspond to the range into BBUFF and MBUFF respectively. The b and 1/m values are stored in a set of look-up tables beginning at $DA40. The assembler directive FCB (fixed constant byte) is used to set up the table. Refer to the application program of section 10.9.

The EQ (equation) instructions initialize the X register as a pointer. The COPY instructions initialize the Y register as a pointer and accumulator B as a counter for the number of bytes to be moved. The MOVE instructions copy the values from the look-up table to the BBUFF and MBUFF. Figure 10.17 shows a flow chart for these routines.

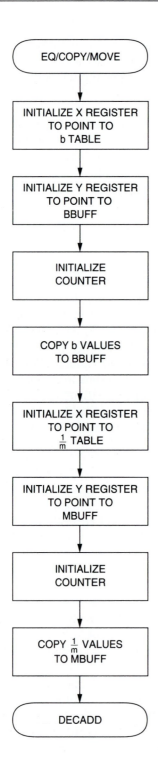

FIGURE 10.17 The flow chart for copying the b and 1/m values into the BBUFF and MBUFF, respectively

10.8.7 DECADD Routine

This subroutine adds the contents of two buffers, the DBUFF and BBUFF. Each buffer contains 7 bytes of unpacked BCD values. The result is stored back in DBUFF; therefore, the original values in DBUFF are lost. As given by Eq. (10.5) the general design equation is ,

$$T_m = \frac{V_o + b}{m}$$

The DECADD routine performs the operation of $V_o + b$. Refer to the routine labeled DECADD in section 10.9 for the program instructions and comments. If this program was to do just decimal addition, it would require fewer lines of code. However, the result is being stored as unpacked BCD. Therefore more programming steps are required.

10.8.8 DECMUL Routine

This decimal multiply (DECMUL) is very similar to the DECMUL routine used in Chapter 8. The differences are the number of bytes being multiplied, the names of the labels have been changed to reflect the names used in the different applications, and the location of the RAM buffers. Other than these differences, the routines are identical and thus perform the same functions; that is, to multiply the values in one buffer times the values in another buffer and store the product in a third buffer. In this application, the multiplicand values ($V_o + b$) have been stored in the DBUFF by the DECADD routine. The multiplier values ($1/m$) have been stored in the MBUFF by the COPYM and MOVE routines. The product will be stored in the buffer labeled TEBUFF (temperature buffer). Both the DBUFF and MBUFF store 7 unpacked BCD values. Thus, to hold the product, the TEBUFF is 14 bytes.

A flow chart for this application is similar to Figure 8.16 except for some name changes, that is total cost is now called temperature, price is now ($V_o + b$), and weight is $1/m$ values. Refer to the DECMUL routine in section 10.9 for the instructions and comments.

10.8.9 OUTPUT Routine

This routine displays the output temperature value. Examples of the format are:

Temperature: 509.7 degrees Celsius

and

Temperature: 0.6 degrees Celsius

These two examples are the highest and lowest readings possible with this system. All readings display one digit after the decimal point (resolution of one-tenth degree Celsius) and leading zero other than the units place are supressed. The decimal point is inserted by this routine. EVB utility subroutines are used to output the messages and values. Refer to section 10.9 for the line code of the OUTPUT routine.

10.8.10 TDELAY Routine

This routine is similar to the real time interrupt routine studied in Chapter 6 and used in Chapter 7. The routine introduces a 5-second time delay between temperature measurements before decrementing the interval count value. When the count equals zero, program execution returns to the EVB's monitor program and the BUFFALO prompt (>) is displayed. If the count value is set to 100 decimal, there will be 12 measurements per minute or a total time of 8 1/3 minutes for the software linearization program to process the 100 measurements. A soldering iron should reach its operating temperature within 5 minutes. Thus, ample time has been provided. For other applications, the interval count value can be changed for more or fewer measurements.

10.9

SOFTWARE LINEARIZATION APPLICATION PROGRAM

As with the other applications programs and many of the examples given in this text, the instructions were assembled on an IBM-compatible computer and downloaded into RAM on the EVB. This application begins with equate tables, reserve memory byte tables, tables for the b and 1/m values, and a listing of the display messages. The program begins at location $CA00 as given by the ORG directive. The directive ORG $DA00 shows the starting location of the memory buffer and ORG $D000 is the starting location that stores display messages.

After this application program is downloaded into the EVB RAM, it may be executed by using the G (Go) command.

> G CA00 <ENTER>

If the signal conditioning circuit is not connected and port PE1 is left open, the CPU reads all logic 1s (FF$_{hex}$) from A/D register 1. This reading is equivalent to the maximum possible temperature. The result displayed is 509.7°C. If you are unable to connect the signal conditioning circuit, and would like to simulate different input readings, refer to section 10.10.

```
LINE  S PC   OPCO OPERANDS  S LABEL   MNEMO OPERANDS COMMENT
00001                                 NAM   Software linearization
00002                       ***********************************************************************
00003                       *              EVB Utility Subroutine Addresses               *
00004                       *  Utility subroutines allow the user to perform a variety of  *
00005                       *  input/output tasks and are described in Chapter 4.  They are *
00006                       *  stored in ROM and may be used by executing a JSR instruction *
00007                       *  to the applicable address.                                  *
00008                       ***********************************************************************
```

```
LINE  S PC    OPCO OPERANDS  S LABEL    MNEMO OPERANDS COMMENT
00009
00010 P 0000  ffb5            A OUTRHLF   EQU   $FFB5      Convert right nibble to ASCII and output.
00011 P 0000  ffb8            A OUTA      EQU   $FFB8      Output character in accumulator A.
00012 P 0000  ffc7            A OUTSTRG   EQU   $FFC7      Output message string until $04 include leading <CR> <LF>.
00013 P 0000  ffca            A OUTSTRGO  EQU   $FFCA      Output message string until $04 no leading <CR> <LF>.
00014
00015                         ***************************************************************************
00016                         *                          Register Equates                              *
00017                         *  These locations are fixed addresses in the memory map.                *
00018                         ***************************************************************************
00019
00020 P 0000  00eb            A RTIVEC    EQU   $00EB      Pseudo vector location on the EVB.
00021 P 0000  1024            A TMSK2     EQU   $1024      Main timer interrupt mask register 2.
00022 P 0000  1025            A TFLG2     EQU   $1025      Timer interrupt flag register 2.
00023 P 0000  1026            A PACTL     EQU   $1026      Pulse accumulator control register.
00024 P 0000  1030            A ADCTL     EQU   $1030      A/D control register.
00025 P 0000  1031            A ADR1      EQU   $1031      A/D register #1.
00026 P 0000  e0b2            A BUFFALO   EQU   $E0B2      Starting location of the BUFFALO prompt.
00027
00028                         ***************************************************************************
00029                         *                          Buffer Locations                              *
00030                         *  These buffer locations are used to store temporary data in RAM.  The  *
00031                         *  starting address is $DA00.  Memory locations labeled BLANK1, BLANK2,   *
00032                         *  and BLANK3 are extra bytes of memory that have been included for        *
00033                         *  future expansion.                                                      *
00034                         ***************************************************************************
00035
00036 A da00                  ORG   $DA00      Assembler directive
00037 A da00  07              A BBUFF     RMB   7          Memory buffer for b values.
00038 A da07  02              A BLANK1    RMB   2          Memory locations not used at this time.
00039 A da09  07              A MBUFF     RMB   7          Memory buffer for 1/m values.
00040 A da10  07              A DBUFF     RMB   7          Memory buffer for the BCD values.
00041 A da17  02              A BLANK2    RMB   2          Memory locations not used at this time.
00042 A da19  01              A ADTEMP    RMB   1          Holds the input from the A/D converter.
00043 A da1a  02              A TREG1     RMB   2          Holds the product of A/D input x 20 mV/bit.
00044 A da1c  02              A DPNTR     RMB   2          Pointer to the DBUFF.
00045 A da1e  02              A MPNTR     RMB   2          Pointer to the MBUFF.
00046 A da20  02              A TEPNTR    RMB   2          Pointer to the TEBUFF.
00047 A da22  01              A DCNT      RMB   1          Holds the count value of the DBUFF.
00048 A da23  01              A MCNT      RMB   1          Holds the count value of the MBUFF.
00049 A da24  02              A TDREG     RMB   2          Holds the count value for the time delay loop.
00050 A da26  09              A BLANK3    RMB   9          Memory locations not used at this time.
00051 A da2f  01              A INTCNT    RMB   1          Holds the value for the interval counter.
00052 A da30  10              A TEBUFF    RMB   16         Memory buffer for the final temperature.
00053
00054                         ***************************************************************************
00055                         *         b value constants represented as whole numbers.                *
00056                         ***************************************************************************
00057 A da40  00050802        A B1VAL     FCB   0,5,8,2    b1 value.
00058 A da44  04060704        A B2VAL     FCB   4,6,7,4    b2 value.
00059 A da48  05090106        A B3VAL     FCB   5,9,1,6    b3 value.
00060 A da4c  04020108        A B4VAL     FCB   4,2,1,8    b4 value.
00061 A da50  05060402        A B5VAL     FCB   5,6,4,2    b5 value.
00062
00063                         ***************************************************************************
00064                         *         1/m value constants represented as whole numbers.              *
00065                         ***************************************************************************
00066 A da54  0100030802A M1VAL    FCB   1,0,3,8,2,1 1/m1 value.
00067 A da5a  0009090309A M2VAL    FCB   0,9,9,3,9,4 1/m2 value.
00068 A da60  0009080607A M3VAL    FCB   0,9,8,6,7,8 1/m3 value.
00069 A da66  0009090201A M4VAL    FCB   0,9,9,2,1,6 1/m4 value.
00070 A da6c  0009080805A M5VAL    FCB   0,9,8,8,5,3 1/m5 value.
00071
00072                         ***************************************************************************
00073                         *                          Display Messages                              *
00074                         *  The following messages are outputed with the temperature so the       *
00075                         *  data can be easily interpreted.  The messages are stored in memory     *
00076                         *  beginning at location $D000.                                           *
00077                         ***************************************************************************
00078 A d000                  ORG   $D000      Assembler directive
00079
00080 A d000  54              A MSTEMP    FCC   'Temperature: '
```

```
LINE   S PC    OPCO OPERANDS  S LABEL    MNEMO OPERANDS COMMENT
00081  A d00d  04             A          FCB   $04        End-of-message mark.
00082  A d00e  20             A MSDEG     FCC   ' degrees Celsius'
00083  A d01e  04             A          FCB   $04        End-of-message mark.
00084
00085                         *************************************************************************
00086                         *  This portion of the program initializes the interval counter to     *
00087                         *  100 decimal and clears 47 bytes of memory that will be used for       *
00088                         *  buffers and temporary registers.  Buffers labeled BBUFF,MBUFF,       *
00089                         *  and DBUFF each are seven bytes in length. TEBUFF is 14 bytes in      *
00090                         *  length but is cleared when the DECMUL routine is executed.            *
00091                         *************************************************************************
00092  A ca00                            ORG   $CA00      Assembler directive
00093
00094  A ca00 86  64          A          LDAA  #100       \ Initialize the interval counter.
00095  A ca02 b7  da2f        A          STAA  INTCNT     /
00096  A ca05 4f              CLEAR:     CLRA             Clear accumulator A.
00097  A ca06 ce  da00        A          LDX   #BBUFF     Initialize X register to the first location.
00098  A ca09 c6  2f          A          LDAB  #47        Initialize the count value.
00099  A ca0b a7  00          A C1:      STAA  00,X       Clear a location.
00100  A ca0d 08              INX              Increment X pointer.
00101  A ca0e 5a              DECB             Decrement count value.
00102  A ca0f 26  fa     ca0b BNE   C1         If count =/= 0, branch back to C1.
00103
00104
00105                         *************************************************************************
00106                         *  MEASTE:  This routine performs 5 functions: (1) initializes the A/D  *
00107                         *  control register, (2) introduces a time delay so that the A/D can make *
00108                         *  the conversion, (3) temporarily stores the binary input data in the   *
00109                         *  register labeled ADTEMP, (4) multiplies the binary value by 20mV/bit   *
00110                         *  and (5) stores the 16 bit result at the location called TREG1.         *
00111                         *************************************************************************
00112
00113  A ca11 86  21          A MEASTE:   LDAA  #$21       A/D control word.
00114  A ca13 b7  1030        A          STAA  ADCTL      Initialize ADCTL register.
00115  A ca16 c6  26          A          LDAB  #$26       Initialize time delay count.
00116  A ca18 5a              DELAY:     DECB             Decrement time delay count.
00117  A ca19 26  fd     ca18 BNE   DELAY      If count =/= 0, branch to DELAY.
00118  A ca1b b6  1031        A          LDAA  ADR1       Read A/D register.
00119  A ca1e b7  da19        A          STAA  ADTEMP     Temporarily store binary input data.
00120  A ca21 c6  14          A          LDAB  #20        Load multiplier 20 dec (14 hex).
00121  A ca23 3d              MUL              Multiply input data x 20 ---> D.
00122  A ca24 fd  da1a        A          STD   TREG1      Store product temporarily.
00123
00124                         *************************************************************************
00125                         *  BINBCD:  This part of the application program converts the 16 bit     *
00126                         *  value stored at TREG1 to a five digit BCD value. The converted         *
00127                         *  values are stored in a memory buffer labeled DBUFF as unpacked         *
00128                         *  BCD values.   Refer to buffer location table to see that 7 bytes       *
00129                         *  have been reserved for the DBUFF, the least significant bytes have      *
00130                         *  been cleared to logic 0s. This routine was studied in Example 3-24     *
00131                         *  and again in Chapter 8.                                                *
00132                         *************************************************************************
00133
00134  A ca27 fc  da1a        A BINBCD:   LDD   TREG1      Load 16 bit number to be converted.
00135  A ca2a ce  2710        A          LDX   #10000     Load divisor 10,000 (2710hex).
00136  A ca2d 02              IDIV             Integer divide.
00137  A ca2e 8f              XGDX             Save remainder in X register.
00138  A ca2f f7  da10        A          STAB  DBUFF      Store quotient in memory buffer.
00139  A ca32 8f              XGDX             Return remainder back to D.
00140  A ca33 ce  03e8        A          LDX   #1000      Load divisor 1,000 (3E8hex).
00141  A ca36 02              IDIV             Integer divide.
00142  A ca37 8f              XGDX             Save remainder in X register.
00143  A ca38 f7  da11        A          STAB  DBUFF+1    Store quotient in memory buffer.
00144  A ca3b 8f              XGDX             Return remainder back to D.
00145  A ca3c ce  0064        A          LDX   #100       Load divisor 100 (64hex).
00146  A ca3f 02              IDIV             Integer divide.
00147  A ca40 8f              XGDX             Save remainder in X register.
00148  A ca41 f7  da12        A          STAB  DBUFF+2    Store quotient in memory buffer.
00149  A ca44 8f              XGDX             Return remainder back to D.
00150  A ca45 ce  000a        A          LDX   #10        Load divisor 10 (Ahex).
00151  A ca48 02              IDIV             Integer divide.
00152  A ca49 8f              XGDX             Save remainder in X register.
```

```
LINE    S PC    OPCO OPERANDS  S LABEL    MNEMO OPERANDS COMMENT

00153   A ca4a f7   da13      A          STAB  DBUFF+3  Store quotient in memory buffer.
00154   A ca4d 8f             A          XGDX           Return remainder back to D.
00155   A ca4e f7   da14      A          STAB  DBUFF+4  Store quotient in memory buffer.
00156
00157                                    **********************************************************************
00158                         *  RANGE:  This portion of the program compares the input voltage to the  *
00159                         *  range limits. Thus the CPU determines which equation values to use for  *
00160                         *  the linearization.                                                      *
00161                                    **********************************************************************
00162
00163   A ca51 b6   da19      A RANGE:    LDAA  ADTEMP   Return the binary input data to accumulator A.
00164   A ca54 81   30        A          CMPA  #48      \ Is 0V < Vo < 0.962V
00165   A ca56 23   10    ca68           BLS   EQ1      / (0 to 100 degrees)
00166
00167   A ca58 81   62        A          CMPA  #98      \ Is 0.962V < Vo < 1.965V
00168   A ca5a 23   1b    ca77           BLS   EQ2      / (100 to 200 degrees)
00169
00170   A ca5c 81   95        A          CMPA  #149     \ Is 1.965V < Vo < 2.981V
00171   A ca5e 23   26    ca86           BLS   EQ3      / (200 to 300 degrees)
00172
00173   A ca60 81   c7        A          CMPA  #199     \ Is 2.981V < Vo < 3.989V
00174   A ca62 23   31    ca95           BLS   EQ4      / (300 to 400 degres)
00175
00176   A ca64 81   ff        A          CMPA  #255     \ Is 3.989V < Vo < 5.1V
00177   A ca66 23   3c    caa4           BLS   EQ5      / (400 to 510 degrees)
00178
00179                                    **********************************************************************
00180                         *  EQ:  This portion of the program initializes the X and Y registers to  *
00181                         *  be used as pointers for copying b and 1/m values into memory buffers.   *
00182                                    **********************************************************************
00183
00184   A ca68 ce   da43      A EQ1:      LDX   #B1VAL+3 Initialize X register to copy b values.
00185   A ca6b bd   cab3      A          JSR   COPYB
00186   A ca6e ce   da59      A          LDX   #M1VAL+5 Initialize X register to copy 1/m value.
00187   A ca71 bd   cabd      A          JSR   COPYM
00188   A ca74 7e   cad3      A          JMP   DECADD
00189
00190   A ca77 ce   da47      A EQ2:      LDX   #B2VAL+3 Initialize X register to copy b values.
00191   A ca7a bd   cab3      A          JSR   COPYB
00192   A ca7d ce   da5f      A          LDX   #M2VAL+5 Initialize X register to copy 1/m values.
00193   A ca80 bd   cabd      A          JSR   COPYM
00194   A ca83 7e   cad3      A          JMP   DECADD
00195
00196   A ca86 ce   da4b      A EQ3:      LDX   #B3VAL+3 Initialize X register to copy b values.
00197   A ca89 bd   cab3      A          JSR   COPYB
00198   A ca8c ce   da65      A          LDX   #M3VAL+5 Initialize X register to copy 1/m values.
00199   A ca8f bd   cabd      A          JSR   COPYM
00200   A ca92 7e   cad3      A          JMP   DECADD
00201
00202   A ca95 ce   da4f      A EQ4:      LDX   #B4VAL+3 Initialize X register to copy b values.
00203   A ca98 bd   cab3      A          JSR   COPYB
00204   A ca9b ce   da6b      A          LDX   #M4VAL+5 Initialize X register to copy 1/m values.
00205   A ca9e bd   cabd      A          JSR   COPYM
00206   A caa1 7e   cad3      A          JMP   DECADD
00207
00208
00209   A caa4 ce   da53      A EQ5:      LDX   #B5VAL+3 Initialize X register to copy b values.
00210   A caa7 bd   cab3      A          JSR   COPYB
00211   A caaa ce   da71      A          LDX   #M5VAL+5 Initialize X register to copy 1/m values.
00212   A caad bd   cabd      A          JSR   COPYM
00213   A cab0 7e   cad3      A          JMP   DECADD
00214
00215   A cab3 18ce da06      A COPYB:    LDY   #BBUFF+6 Initialize Y register to copy b values.
00216   A cab7 c6   04        A          LDAB  #4       Initialize acc B with a count value.
00217   A cab9 bd   cac7      A          JSR   MOVE
00218   A cabc 39             A          RTS
00219
00220   A cabd 18ce da0f      A COPYM:    LDY   #MBUFF+6 Initialize Y register to copy 1/m values.
00221   A cac1 c6   06        A          LDAB  #6       Initialize acc B with a count value.
00222   A cac3 bd   cac7      A          JSR   MOVE
00223   A cac6 39             A          RTS
```

```
LINE    S PC    OPCO OPERANDS  S LABEL      MNEMO OPERANDS COMMENT
00224                          ***********************************************************************
00225                          *  MOVE: This subroutine copies the table of constants to a memory buffer.*
00226                          *  On entry into this subroutine the X and Y registers have been loaded  *
00227                          *  with pointers.  The X register is used as the pointer to the table    *
00228                          *  of constants and the Y register is used as a pointer to the memory     *
00229                          *  buffer.  The contents of accumulator B are used as a count value and   *
00230                          *  is also preloaded.                                                     *
00231                          ***********************************************************************
00232
00233   A cac7 a6    00     A MOVE:    LDAA  00,X      Load acc A using the X index register.
00234   A cac9 18a7 00     A          STAA  00,Y      Store acc A using the Y index register.
00235   A cacc 09                     DEX             \ Change X and Y pointers.
00236   A cacd 1809                   DEY             /
00237   A cacf 5a                     DECB            Decrement count value.
00238   A cad0 26    f5   cac7        BNE   MOVE      If count =/= 0, branch back to MOVE.
00239   A cad2 39                     RTS             Return from subroutine.
00240
00241                          ***********************************************************************
00242                          *  DECADD: This routine is a decimal addition program.  The Vo values   *
00243                          *  stored in DBUFF are added to the b values stored in BBUFF and the     *
00244                          *  result is stored back in DBUFF.  If a carry from the most significant  *
00245                          *  bit occurs, it is also stored.                                         *
00246                          ***********************************************************************
00247
00248   A cad3 ce    da16   A DECADD:  LDX   #DBUFF+6  \ Initialize X and Y registers
00249   A cad6 18ce da06   A          LDY   #BBUFF+6  / as pointers.
00250   A cada c6    07     A          LDAB  #7        Set count value.
00251   A cadc 0c                      CLC             Clear carry flag.
00252   A cadd a6    00     A ADD:     LDAA  00,X      \
00253   A cadf 18a9 00     A          ADCA  00,Y      |
00254   A cae2 19                      DAA             |
00255   A cae3 81    10     A          CMPA  #$10      | Decimal addition and store
00256   A cae5 2d    07   caee        BLT   A1        | the result  back in DBUFF
00257   A cae7 84    0f     A          ANDA  #$0F      | as an unpacked BCD value.
00258   A cae9 0d                      SEC             |
00259   A caea a7    00     A          STAA  00,X      |
00260   A caec 20    03   caf1        BRA   A2        |
00261   A caee 0c               A1:    CLC             |
00262   A caef a7    00     A          STAA  00,X      /
00263   A caf1 09               A2:    DEX             \ Change pointer values.
00264   A caf2 1809                    DEY             /
00265   A caf4 5a                      DECB            Decrement count value.
00266   A caf5 26    e6   cadd        BNE   ADD       If count =/= 0, branch back to ADD.
00267
00268
00269                          ***********************************************************************
00270                          *  DECMUL:  This subroutine multiplies (Vo+b) times 1/m and then stores  *
00271                          *  the result in TEBUFF (temperature buffer).                            *
00272                          *  DPNTR, MPNTR, and TEPNTR hold the pointers to the memory buffers.      *
00273                          *  DCNT and MCNT hold the count values of the DBUFF and MBUFF.            *
00274                          ***********************************************************************
00275
00276   A caf7 18ce da30   A DECMUL:  LDY   #TEBUFF   Initialize Y register.
00277   A cafb c6    10     A          LDAB  #16       Initialize count value.
00278   A cafd 4f                      CLRA
00279   A cafe 18a7 00     A DM1:     STAA  00,Y      \  Clear partial product buffer
00280   A cb01 1808                    INY             |  (TEBUFF) which is 16 bytes
00281   A cb03 5a                      DECB            |  in length beginning at
00282   A cb04 26    f8   cafe        BNE   DM1       /  $DA30.
00283
00284   A cb06 cc    da16   A          LDD   #DBUFF+6  \
00285   A cb09 fd    da1c   A          STD   DPNTR     |
00286   A cb0c cc    da0f   A          LDD   #MBUFF+6  |
00287   A cb0f fd    da1e   A          STD   MPNTR     |
00288   A cb12 cc    da3d   A          LDD   #TEBUFF+13 | Initialize pointers and counters.
00289   A cb15 fd    da20   A          STD   TEPNTR    |
00290   A cb18 86    07     A          LDAA  #7        |
00291   A cb1a b7    da22   A          STAA  DCNT      |
00292   A cb1d 86    07     A          LDAA  #7        |
00293   A cb1f b7    da23   A          STAA  MCNT      /
00294
00295
```

```
LINE   S PC    OPCO OPERANDS  S LABEL    MNEMO OPERANDS COMMENT
00296  A cb22 18fe da20       A DM2:     LDY   TEPNTR   Initialize Y register.
00297  A cb26 fe   da1e       A DM3:     LDX   MPNTR    Initialize X register.
00298  A cb29 e6   00         A          LDAB  00,X     Load multiplier value.
00299  A cb2b c1   00         A          CMPB  #00      Check for multiplier equal to zero.
00300  A cb2d 27   23         cb52       BEQ   CONT     If multiplier = 0, branch to CONT (continue).
00301  A cb2f fe   da1c       A          LDX   DPNTR    Initialize X register.
00302  A cb32 a6   00         A          LDAA  00,X     Load multiplicand value.
00303  A cb34 3d                         MUL            Multiply A x B --> D.
00304  A cb35 ce   000a       A          LDX   #10      Load divisor 10dec = $0A.
00305  A cb38 02                         IDIV           Convert binary product to decimal
00306  A cb39 17                         TBA            Transfer B --> A.
00307  A cb3a bd   cb77       A          JSR   PARTPD   Jump to partial product subroutine.
00308
00309  A cb3d 8f                         XGDX           Move quotient to D register.
00310  A cb3e 17                         TBA            Transfer B --> A.
00311  A cb3f 1809                       DEY            Decrement Y register.
00312  A cb41 bd   cb77       A          JSR   PARTPD   Jump to partial product subroutine.
00313  A cb44 fc   da1c       A          LDD   DPNTR    \
00314  A cb47 83   0001       A          SUBD  #1       | Decrement multiplicand pointer.
00315  A cb4a fd   da1c       A          STD   DPNTR    /
00316  A cb4d 7a   da22       A          DEC   DCNT     Decrement multiplicand counter.
00317  A cb50 26   d4         cb26       BNE   DM3      If count =/= 0, branch to DM3.
00318  A cb52 86   07         A CONT:    LDAA  #7       \ Reset multiplicand counter.
00319  A cb54 b7   da22       A          STAA  DCNT     /
00320  A cb57 cc   da16       A          LDD   #DBUFF+6 \
00321  A cb5a fd   da1c       A          STD   DPNTR    |
00322  A cb5d fc   da1e       A          LDD   MPNTR    |
00323  A cb60 83   0001       A          SUBD  #1       |  Set buffer pointers for next
00324  A cb63 fd   da1e       A          STD   MPNTR    |  decimal multiplication.
00325  A cb66 fc   da20       A          LDD   TEPNTR   |
00326  A cb69 83   0001       A          SUBD  #1       |
00327  A cb6c fd   da20       A          STD   TEPNTR   /
00328  A cb6f 7a   da23       A          DEC   MCNT     Decrement multiplier count.
00329  A cb72 26   ae         cb22       BNE   DM2      If count =/= 0, branch to DM2.
00330  A cb74 7e   cb93       A          JMP   OUTPUT   Jump to OUTPUT routine.
00331
00332                                    ****************************************************************
00333                         *  PARTPD:  This subroutine adds the partial products thereby updating  *
00334                         *  the result in the TCBUFF.  At the end of the DECMUL program, the     *
00335                         *  total cost is stored in the buffer labeled TCBUFF.                   *
00336                         *            * * * * *                                                  *
00337                         *  Note: The contents of the Y register remain unchanged upon returning *
00338                         *  to the DECMUL program.                                               *
00339                                    ****************************************************************
00340
00341  A cb77 183c            PARTPD:    PSHY           Save Y register.
00342  A cb79 0c                         CLC            Clear C flag.
00343  A cb7a 18a9 00         A PP1:     ADCA  $00,Y    Add partial product + acc. A + C flag.
00344  A cb7d 19                         DAA            Decimal adjust.
00345  A cb7e 81   10         A          CMPA  #$10     Compare acc. A with 10hex.
00346  A cb80 2d   0b         cb8d       BLT   PP2      If A < 10hex, branch to PP2.
00347  A cb82 84   0f         A          ANDA  #$0F     Mask out upper nibble.
00348  A cb84 18a7 00         A          STAA  00,Y     Store result.
00349  A cb87 4f                         CLRA           Clear accumulator A.
00350  A cb88 0d                         SEC            Set C flag.
00351  A cb89 1809                       DEY            Decrement Y pointer.
00352  A cb8b 20   ed         cb7a       BRA   PP1      Branch to update partial product.
00353  A cb8d 18a7 00         A PP2:     STAA  00,Y     Store result.
00354  A cb90 1838                       PULY           Retrieve Y register.
00355  A cb92 39                         RTS            Return to DECMUL subroutine.
00356
00357                                    ****************************************************************
00358                         *  OUTPUT: The following routine outputs the temperature message and the *
00359                         *  temperature value stored in the TEBUFF.  Leading zeros are supressed. *
00360                                    ****************************************************************
00361
00362  A cb93 ce   d000       A OUTPUT:  LDX   #MSTEMP  Initialize X register.
00363  A cb96 bd   ffc7       A          JSR   OUTSTRG  Output the temperature message.
00364  A cb99 ce   da33       A          LDX   #TEBUFF+3 Initialize X register.
00365  A cb9c a6   00         A          LDAA  00,X     \
00366  A cb9e 81   00         A          CMPA  #0       |
00367  A cba0 27   0c         cbae       BEQ   OUT1     |
00368  A cba2 bd   ffb5       A          JSR   OUTRHLF  |
```

```
LINE   S PC   OPCO OPERANDS S LABEL    MNEMO OPERANDS  COMMENT
00369  A cba5 08                       INX              | Check for leading zeros
00370  A cba6 a6   00       A          LDAA  00,X       | and output hundredths,
00371  A cba8 bd   ffb5     A          JSR   OUTRHLF    | tenths, and units values.
00372  A cbab 7e   cbb8     A          JMP   OUT2       |
00373
00374  A cbae 08            OUT1:      INX              |
00375  A cbaf a6   00       A          LDAA  00,X       |
00376  A cbb1 81   00       A          CMPA  #0         |
00377  A cbb3 27   03       cbb8       BEQ   OUT2       |
00378  A cbb5 bd   ffb5     A          JSR   OUTRHLF    |
00379  A cbb8 08            OUT2:      INX              |
00380  A cbb9 a6   00       A          LDAA  00,X       |
00381  A cbbb bd   ffb5     A          JSR   OUTRHLF    /
00382  A cbbe 86   2e       A          LDAA  #$2E       \ Insert decimal point.
00383  A cbc0 bd   ffb8     A          JSR   OUTA       /
00384  A cbc3 08                       INX              \
00385  A cbc4 a6   00       A          LDAA  00,X       | Output the one-tenth value.
00386  A cbc6 bd   ffb5     A          JSR   OUTRHLF    /
00387  A cbc9 ce   d00e     A          LDX   #MSDEG     \ Initialize X register.
00388  A cbcc bd   ffca     A          JSR   OUTSTRGO   / Output MSDEG message.
00389
00390                  *****************************************************************
00391                  *                                                               *
00392                  * TDELAY:  This portion of the routine is a built in 5 second time  *
00393                  * delay.  It is similar to the procedure described in Chapter 6.    *
00394                  *                          * * * * *                             *
00395                  * The stack pointer is reset to location $004A so a user stack overflow *
00396                  * does not occur.  Remember from Chapter 4 that the user stack area  *
00397                  * begins at address $004A.                                       *
00398                  *****************************************************************
00399
00400  A cbcf 86   7e       A TDELAY:  LDAA  #$7E       \ Initialize the pseudo vector addresses
00401  A cbd1 97   eb       A          STAA  RTIVEC     | on the EVB for the real time interrupt
00402  A cbd3 cc   cbee     A          LDD   #CT        | function.
00403  A cbd6 dd   ec       A          STD   RTIVEC+1   /
00404
00405  A cbd8 86   03       A          LDAA  #$03       \ Set the RTRI and RTRO bits
00406  A cbda b7   1026     A          STAA  PACTL      / for a divide by 8 ratio.
00407
00408  A cbdd 86   40       A          LDAA  #$40       \ Set the RTII bit and
00409  A cbdf b7   1024     A          STAA  TMSK2      | clear the RTIF bit.
00410  A cbe2 b7   1025     A          STAA  TFLG2      /
00411
00412  A cbe5 cc   0099     A          LDD   #153       \ Store the count value at a location
00413  A cbe8 fd   da24     A          STD   TDREG      / called TDREG (time delay register).
00414
00415  A cbeb 0e                       CLI              Clear interrupt mask bit.
00416  A cbec 20   fe       cbec WAIT: BRA   WAIT       The CPU is waiting for an interrupt.
00417
00418  A cbee fc   da24     A CT:      LDD   TDREG      \
00419  A cbf1 83   0001     A          SUBD  #1         | Check to see if the routine has
00420  A cbf4 fd   da24     A          STD   TDREG      | looped 193 times to give a total
00421  A cbf7 1a83 0000     A          CPD   #0         | time delay of approximately 5 seconds.
00422  A cbfb 26   0e       cc0b       BNE   CLRFLG     /
00423
00424  A cbfd 8e   004a     A          LDS   #$004A     Reset the user stack pointer in the EVB.
00425  A cc00 7a   da2f     A          DEC   INTCNT     Decrement the interval count value.
00426  A cc03 27   03       cc08       BEQ   T1         If count = 0, branch to T1.
00427  A cc05 7e   ca05     A          JMP   CLEAR      Jump back to CLEAR for the next measurement.
00428
00429  A cc08 7e   e0b2     A T1:      JMP   BUFFALO    Jump to the EVB monitor program.
00430
00431  A cc0b 86   40       A CLRFLG:  LDAA  #$40       \ Clear the RTIF bit in
00432  A cc0d b7   1025     A          STAA  TFLG2      /  the TFLG2 register.
00433  A cc10 3b                       RTI              Return from interrupt.
00434
00435                                  END   $CA00      Assembler directive.


Total number of errors: 0
Total number of warnings: 0
Total number of lines: 435
```

Number of bytes in section ASCT: 674

Number of bytes in program: 674

CROSS REFERENCE TABLE

NAME	ATTRB	S	VALUE	P:LINE	LINE1....N
A1		A	caee	7:261	256
A2		A	caf1	7:263	260
ADCTL	EQU	A	1030	2:24	114
ADD		A	cadd	6:252	266
ADR1	EQU	A	1031	2:25	118
ADTEMP		A	da19	2:42	119 163
B1VAL		A	da40	3:57	184
B2VAL		A	da44	3:58	190
B3VAL		A	da48	3:59	196
B4VAL		A	da4c	3:60	202
B5VAL		A	da50	3:61	209
BBUFF		A	da00	2:37	97 215 249
BINBCD		A	ca27	4:134	
BLANK1		A	da07	2:38	
BLANK2		A	da17	2:41	
BLANK3		A	da26	2:50	
BUFFALO	EQU	A	e0b2	2:26	429
C1		A	ca0b	3:99	102
CLEAR		A	ca05	3:96	427
CLRFLG		A	cc0b	10:431	422
CONT		A	cb52	8:318	300
COPYB		A	cab3	6:215	185 191 197 203 210
COPYM		A	cabd	6:220	187 193 199 205 212
CT		A	cbee	10:418	402
DBUFF		A	da10	2:40	138 143 148 153 155 248 284 320
DCNT		A	da22	2:47	291 316 319
DECADD		A	cad3	6:248	188 194 200 206 213
DECMUL		A	caf7	7:276	
DELAY		A	ca18	4:116	117
DM1		A	cafe	7:279	282
DM2		A	cb22	7:296	329
DM3		A	cb26	7:297	317
DPNTR		A	da1c	2:44	285 301 313 315 321
EQ1		A	ca68	5:184	165
EQ2		A	ca77	5:190	168
EQ3		A	ca86	5:196	171
EQ4		A	ca95	5:202	174
EQ5		A	caa4	6:209	177
INTCNT		A	da2f	2:51	95 425
M1VAL		A	da54	3:66	186
M2VAL		A	da5a	3:67	192
M3VAL		A	da60	3:68	198
M4VAL		A	da66	3:69	204
M5VAL		A	da6c	3:70	211
MBUFF		A	da09	2:39	220 286
MCNT		A	da23	2:48	293 328
MEASTE		A	ca11	4:113	
MOVE		A	cac7	6:233	217 222 238
MPNTR		A	da1e	2:45	287 297 322 324
MSDEG		A	d00e	3:82	387
MSTEMP		A	d000	3:80	362
OUT1		A	cbae	9:374	367
OUT2		A	cbb8	9:379	372 377
OUTA	EQU	A	ffb8	2:11	383
OUTPUT		A	cb93	8:362	330
OUTRHLF	EQU	A	ffb5	2:10	368 371 378 381 386
OUTSTRG	EQU	A	ffc7	2:12	363
OUTSTRGO	EQU	A	ffca	2:13	388
PACTL	EQU	A	1026	2:23	406
PARTPD		A	cb77	8:341	307 312
PP1		A	cb7a	8:343	352
PP2		A	cb8d	8:353	346
RANGE		A	ca51	5:163	
RTIVEC	EQU	A	00eb	2:20	401 403
T1		A	cc08	10:429	426
TDELAY		A	cbcf	9:400	
TDREG		A	da24	2:49	413 418 420

```
                    CROSS REFERENCE TABLE
        NAME    ATTRB S VALUE P:LINE LINE1....N
        TEBUFF        A da30  2:52        276  288  364
        TEPNTR        A da20  2:46        289  296  325  327
        TFLG2   EQU   A 1025  2:22        410  432
        TMSK2   EQU   A 1024  2:21        409
        TREG1         A da1a  2:43        122  134
        WAIT          A cbec  9:416       416
```

10.10

TESTING AND DEBUGGING THE APPLICATION PROGRAM

Most of the testing and debugging of this application program can be done using the following BUFFALO commands:

- BR—Breakpoint set
- G—Execute program
- MD—Memory display
- P—Proceed/continue from breakpoint
- RM—Register modify

By inserting a breakpoint at the end of a routine, the program may be executed up to the breakpoint. Then using the MD command, the contents of the memory buffers may be checked. Since the buffer locations are from $DA00 to $DA3F, the command format is

> MD DA00 DA3F <ENTER>

This command will display 4 lines with 16 bytes per line. Figure 10.18 shows the location of each buffer with its corresponding label. The designation XX refers to a byte of data. The location of the b and 1/m values are stored starting at location $DA40. The reader should check this by using the MD command. If you wish to see both the contents of the buffers and the stored table values, use

> MD DA00 <ENTER>

Now 9 lines with 16 bytes per line will be displayed.

10.10.1 Simulating a SCC Voltage Input

As previously mentioned, if the signal conditioning circuit is not connected to port PE1, the A/D register stores FF_{hex} and the displayed temperature is 509.7° Celsius. If you would like to simulate different input readings, it can be done in two ways. The first method is to apply a known voltage to port PE1 (pin 45). To do this, refer to Figure 5.9 for a typical circuit diagram. By setting the voltage at PE1 and using the correct range equation of Table 10.3, the temperature can be

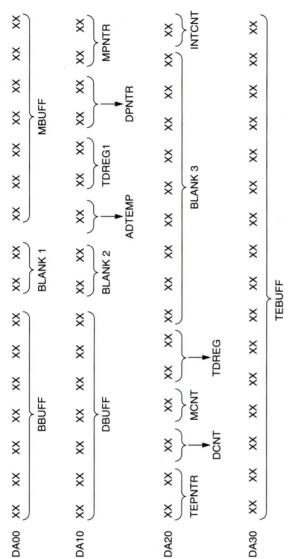

FIGURE 10.18 A memory map guide for the locations of the buffers when using the MD command

calculated. Now execute the software linearization program and record the displayed result and compare it to the calculated value.

The second method uses only software and there is no connection to PE1. Insert a breakpoint at address $CA1E. Now when the program is executed, it stops after the A/D register is read into accumulator A but before the data is stored. Change the data in accumulator A by using the RM A command and then use the P command to continue. The format is

```
> RM A <ENTER>
P CA1E  X ----  Y ----  A FF  B --   C --  S ----    (-- indicates
                                                      typical data)

A-FF 00 <ENTER>          Simulates 0 °C.
>P <ENTER>
```

The result now displayed is

Temperature: 0.6 degrees Celsius

This is the same result given by the general equation. The nonlinearity of a thermocouple causes an inherent offset. Since the breakpoint is still inserted and the program is in a loop (count value is not equal to zero), program execution will again stop at the same point. Remember the program has a 5-second time delay routine so wait for the delay. By using this procedure, new values may be loaded into accumulator A to test other input ranges.

PROBLEMS

1. Compute V_o for Figure 10.2 if T_m - 75°C. Note: Use the type J thermocouple table given in Figure 10.3 for your data.
2. Calculate T_m in Figure 10.4 if V_o is changed to (a) 2.585mV and (b) 1.277mV.
3. Refer to Figure 10.7. Determine the value of T_m if T_r is held at 0°C and the intermediate junctions are at 25°C. V_o equals 5.268mV.
4. Solve for the correction voltage developed at pin 8 of an LT1025 CJC IC if the device temperature T_r is (a) 20°C, (b) 25°C, and (c) 30°C.
5. A type J thermocouple is to measure temperatures ranging from 0 to 255°C. Design an analog interface, using Figure 10.13 as a guide, to fill the 0 to 2.55V input span of an 8-bit analog-to-digital converter.
6. Repeat Problem 5 above when T_m is changed to 0 to 100°C and the ADC's input span is 0 to 10V.
7. Use the data plotted in Figure 10.14(a) to write five (5) *end-point* linear equations ($V_T = mT_m + b$) for the five segments shown.
8. Create five (5) analog interface approximation equations ($V_o = mT_m + b$) from Problem 7 by multiplying each by the 182.6 gain term (Eq. 10.4a).

9. Use the analog interface approximation equations developed in Problems 7 and 8 to determine T_m if (a) $V_o = 472mV$ and (b) $V_o = 1.467V$.
10. Compare the end-point results in Problem 9 with the offset linear results in Example 10.5. Which method produces the best approximation to actual data?

QUESTIONS

1. Why isn't it possible to measure the measurement junction voltage (V_m) of a single thermocouple directly?
2. Define the term isothermal.
3. Define, in your own words, the "law of intermediate metals" as it applies to thermocouples.
4. How do you determine which wire is the chromel wire of a type E thermocouple?
5. Which thermocouple type, supported by the LT1025 CJC IC has (a) the greatest sensitivity to changes in temperature, (b) the least sensitivity to changes in temperature?
6. Would thermocouple linearization be necessary if $\Delta V_m/\Delta T_m$ equaled a constant 52mV/°C?
7. Which linearization technique (offset linear or end-point linear) contributes to the least amount of error?
8. List the five tasks accomplished by the MEASTE subroutine when the MCU is asked to measure temperature at one of its ADC inputs.
9. If the CLEAR routine was changed to also clear TEBUFF, would the INTCNT register have to be relocated? Explain your answer.
10. If the CLEAR routine also cleared TEBUFF, what instructions in the DECMUL routine could be eliminated?
11. In the range from 0 to 100°C, what is the temperature change per bit ?
12. If the MCU did not have a Y index register, what programming steps would you need to copy the b table into the BBUFF?
13. Could the OUTPUT routine be used in another application to display numbers up to 999.9?
14. Which instruction(s) in the TDELAY routine must be changed to create a 10-second time delay?

M68HC11 Instruction Set

INSTRUCTIONS, ADDRESSING MODES, AND EXECUTION TIMES

Source Form(s)	Operation	Boolean Expression	Addressing Mode for Operand	Machine Coding (Hexadecimal)		Bytes	Cycle	Condition Codes							
				Opcode	Operand(s)			S	X	H	I	N	Z	V	C
ABA	Add Accumulators	A + B → A	INH	1B		1	2	-	-	↕	-	↕	↕	↕	↕
ABX	Add B to X	IX + 00:B → IX	INH	3A		1	3	-	-	-	-	-	-	-	-
ABY	Add B to Y	IY + 00:B → IY	INH	18 3A		2	4	-	-	-	-	-	-	-	-
ADCA (opr)	Add with Carry to A	A + M + C → A	A IMM	89	ii	2	2	-	-	↕	-	↕	↕	↕	↕
			A DIR	99	dd	2	3								
			A EXT	B9	hh ll	3	4								
			A IND,X	A9	ff	2	4								
			A IND,Y	18 A9	ff	3	5								
ADCB (opr)	Add with Carry to B	B + M + C → B	B IMM	C9	ii	2	2	-	-	↕	-	↕	↕	↕	↕
			B DIR	D9	dd	2	3								
			B EXT	F9	hh ll	3	4								
			B IND,X	E9	ff	2	4								
			B IND,Y	18 E9	ff	3	5								

Source Form(s)	Operation	Boolean Expression	Addressing Mode for Operand	Machine Coding (Hexadecimal) Opcode	Operand(s)	Bytes	Cycle	Condition Codes S	X	H	I	N	Z	V	C
ADDA (opr)	Add Memory to A	A + M → A	A IMM	8B	ii	2	2	-	-	↕	-	↕	↕	↕	↕
			A DIR	9B	dd	2	3								
			A EXT	BB	hh ll	3	4								
			A IND,X	AB	ff	2	4								
			A IND,Y	18 AB	ff	3	5								
ADDB (opr)	Add Memory to B	B + M → B	B IMM	CB	ii	2	2	-	-	↕	-	↕	↕	↕	↕
			B DIR	DB	dd	2	3								
			B EXT	FB	hh ll	3	4								
			B IND,X	EB	ff	2	4								
			B IND,Y	18 EB	ff	3	5								
ADDD (opr)	Add 16-Bit to D	D + M:M + 1 → D	IMM	C3	jj kk	3	4	-	-	-	-	↕	↕	↕	↕
			DIR	D3	dd	2	5								
			EXT	F3	hh ll	3	6								
			IND,X	E3	ff	2	6								
			IND,Y	18 E3	ff	3	7								
ANDA (opr)	AND A with Memory	A•M → A	A IMM	84	ii	2	2	-	-	-	-	↕	↕	0	-
			A DIR	94	dd	2	3								
			A EXT	B4	hh ll	3	4								
			A IND,X	A4	ff	2	4								
			A IND,Y	18 A4	ff	3	5								

Source Form	Operation	Boolean Expression	Addressing Mode	Opcode	Operand	~	#	S	X	H	I	N	Z	V	C
ANDB (opr)	AND B with Memory	B•M → B	B IMM	C4	ii	2	2	–	–	–	–	↕	↕	0	–
			B DIR	D4	dd	3	2								
			B EXT	F4	hh ll	4	3								
			B IND,X	E4	ff	4	2								
			B IND,Y	18 E4	ff	5	3								
ASL (opr)	Arithmetic Shift Left	C ← [b7 … b0] ← 0	EXT	78	hh ll	6	3	–	–	–	–	↕	↕	↕	↕
			IND,X	68	ff	6	2								
			IND,Y	18 68	ff	7	3								
ASLA			A INH	48		2	1								
ASLB			B INH	58		2	1								
ASLD	Arithmetic Shift Left Double	C ← [b15 … b0] ← 0	INH	05		3	1	–	–	–	–	↕	↕	↕	↕
ASR (opr)	Arithmetic Shift Right	[b7 … b0] → C	EXT	77	hh ll	6	3	–	–	–	–	↕	↕	↕	↕
			IND,X	67	ff	6	2								
			IND,Y	18 67	ff	7	3								
ASRA			A INH	47		2	1								
ASRB			B INH	57		2	1								
BCC (rel)	Branch if Carry Clear	? C = 0	REL	24	rr	3	2	–	–	–	–	–	–	–	–
BCLR (opr) (msk)	Clear Bit(s)	M•($\overline{\text{mm}}$) → M	DIR	15	dd mm	6	3	–	–	–	–	↕	↕	0	–
			IND,X	1D	ff mm	7	3								
			IND,Y	18 1D	ff mm	8	4								
BCS (rel)	Branch if Carry Set	? C = 1	REL	25	rr	3	2	–	–	–	–	–	–	–	–
BEQ (rel)	Branch if = Zero	? Z = 1	REL	27	rr	3	2	–	–	–	–	–	–	–	–

Source Form(s)	Operation	Boolean Expression	Addressing Mode for Operand	Machine Coding (Hexadecimal) Opcode	Operand(s)	Bytes	Cycle	S	X	H	I	N	Z	V	C
BGE (rel)	Branch if ≥ Zero	?N⊕V=0	REL	2C	rr	2	3	-	-	-	-	-	-	-	-
BGT (rel)	Branch if >Zero	?Z+(N⊕V)=0	REL	2E	rr	2	3	-	-	-	-	-	-	-	-
BHI (rel)	Branch if Higher	?C+Z=0	REL	22	rr	2	3	-	-	-	-	-	-	-	-
BHS (rel)	Branch if Higher or Same	?C=0	REL	24	rr	2	3	-	-	-	-	-	-	-	-
BITA (opr)	Bit(s) Test A with Memory	A•M	A IMM	85	ii	2	2	-	-	-	-	↕	↕	0	-
			A DIR	95	dd	2	3								
			A EXT	B5	hh ll	3	4								
			A IND,X	A5	ff	2	4								
			A IND,Y	18 A5	ff	3	5								
BITB (opr)	Bit(s) Test B with Memory	B•M	B IMM	C5	ii	2	2	-	-	-	-	↕	↕	0	-
			B DIR	D5	dd	2	3								
			B EXT	F5	hh ll	3	4								
			B IND,X	E5	ff	2	4								
			B IND,Y	18 E5	ff	3	5								
BLE (rel)	Branch if ≤Zero	?Z+(N⊕V)=1	REL	2F	rr	2	3	-	-	-	-	-	-	-	-
BLO (rel)	Branch if Lower	?C=1	REL	25	rr	2	3	-	-	-	-	-	-	-	-
BLS (rel)	Branch if Lower or Same	?C+Z=1	REL	23	rr	2	3	-	-	-	-	-	-	-	-

Mnemonic	Description	Boolean / Operation	Mode	Opcode	Operand	~	#	S	X	H	I	N	Z	V	C
BLT (rel)	Branch If < Zero	? N ⊕ V = 1	REL	2D	rr	2	3	-	-	-	-	-	-	-	-
BMI (rel)	Branch if Minus	? N = 1	REL	2B	rr	2	3	-	-	-	-	-	-	-	-
BNE (rel)	Branch if Not = Zero	? Z = 0	REL	26	rr	2	3	-	-	-	-	-	-	-	-
BPL (rel)	Branch if Plus	? N = 0	REL	2A	rr	2	3	-	-	-	-	-	-	-	-
BRA (rel)	Branch Always	? 1 = 1	REL	20	rr	2	3	-	-	-	-	-	-	-	-
BRCLR(opr)	Branch if Bit(s) Clear	? M• mm = 0	DIR	13	dd mm rr	4	6	-	-	-	-	-	-	-	-
(msk)			IND,X	1F	ff mm rr	4	7								
(rel)			IND,Y	18 1F	ff mm rr	5	8								
BRN (rel)	Branch Never	? 1 = 0	REL	21	rr	2	3	-	-	-	-	-	-	-	-
BRSET(opr)	Branch if Bit(s) Set	? ($\overline{M}$)•mm = 0	DIR	12	dd mm rr	4	6	-	-	-	-	-	-	-	-
(msk)			IND,X	1E	ff mm rr	4	7								
(rel)			IND,Y	18 1E	ff mm rr	5	8								
BSET(opr)	Set Bit(s)	M + mm → M	DIR	14	dd mm	3	6	-	-	-	-	↕	↕	0	-
(msk)			IND,X	1C	ff mm	3	7								
			IND,Y	18 1C	ff mm	4	8								
BSR (rel)	Branch to Subroutine	See Special Ops	REL	8D	rr	2	6	-	-	-	-	-	-	-	-
BVC (rel)	Branch if Overflow Clear	? V = 0	REL	28	rr	2	3	-	-	-	-	-	-	-	-
BVS (rel)	Branch if Overflow Set	? V = 1	REL	29	rr	2	3	-	-	-	-	-	-	-	-
CBA	Compare A to B	A – B	INH	11		1	2	-	-	-	-	↕	↕	↕	↕
CLC	Clear Carry Bit	0 → C	INH	0C		1	2	-	-	-	-	-	-	-	0
CLI	Clear Interrupt Mask	0 → I	INH	0E		1	2	-	-	-	0	-	-	-	-

Source Form(s)	Operation	Boolean Expression	Addressing Mode for Operand	Machine Coding (Hexadecimal) Opcode	Operand(s)	Bytes	Cycle	S	X	H	I	N	Z	V	C
CLR (opr)	Clear Memory Byte	0 → M	EXT	7F	hh ll	3	6	-	-	-	-	0	1	0	0
			IND,X	6F	ff	2	6								
			IND,Y	18 6F	ff	3	7								
CLRA	Clear Accumulator A	0 → A	A INH	4F		1	2	-	-	-	-	0	1	0	0
CLRB	Clear Accumulator B	0 → B	B INH	5F		1	2	-	-	-	-	0	1	0	0
CLV	Clear Overflow Flag	0 → V	INH	0A		1	2	-	-	-	-	-	-	0	-
CMPA (opr)	Compare A to Memory	A − M	A IMM	81	ii	2	2	-	-	-	-	↕	↕	↕	↕
			A DIR	91	dd	2	3								
			A EXT	B1	hh ll	3	4								
			A IND,X	A1	ff	2	4								
			A IND,Y	18 A1	ff	3	5								
CMPB (opr)	Compare B to Memory	B − M	B IMM	C1	ii	2	2	-	-	-	-	↕	↕	↕	↕
			B DIR	D1	dd	2	3								
			B EXT	F1	hh ll	3	4								
			B IND,X	E1	ff	2	4								
			B IND,Y	18 E1	ff	3	5								
COM (opr)	1's Complement Memory Byte	$FF − M → M	EXT	73	hh ll	3	6	-	-	-	-	↕	↕	0	1
			IND,X	63	ff	2	6								
			IND,Y	18 63	ff	3	7								

Mnemonic	Operation	Boolean/Arithmetic	Addressing Mode	Opcode	Operand	#	~	S	X	H	I	N	Z	V	C
COMA	1's Complement A	$FF − A → A	A INH	43		1	2	–	–	–	–	↕	↕	0	1
COMB	1's Complement B	$FF − B → B	B INH	53		1	2	–	–	–	–	↕	↕	0	1
CPD (opr)	Compare D to Memory 16-Bit	D − M:M+1	IMM	1A 83	jj kk	4	5	–	–	–	–	↕	↕	↕	↕
			DIR	1A 93	dd	3	6								
			EXT	1A B3	hh ll	4	7								
			IND,X	1A A3	ff	3	7								
			IND,Y	CD A3	ff	3	7								
CPX (opr)	Compare X to Memory 16-Bit	IX − M:M+1	IMM	8C	jj kk	3	4	–	–	–	–	↕	↕	↕	↕
			DIR	9C	dd	2	5								
			EXT	BC	hh ll	3	6								
			IND,X	AC	ff	2	6								
			IND,Y	CD AC	ff	3	7								
CPY (opr)	Compare Y to Memory 16-Bit	IY − M:M+1	IMM	18 8C	jj kk	4	5	–	–	–	–	↕	↕	↕	↕
			DIR	18 9C	dd	3	6								
			EXT	18 BC	hh ll	4	7								
			IND,X	1A AC	ff	3	7								
			IND,Y	18 AC	ff	3	7								
DAA	Decimal Adjust A	Adjust Sum to BCD	INH	19		1	2	–	–	–	–	↕	↕	↕	↕
DEC (opr)	Decrement Memory Byte	M − 1 → M	EXT	7A	hh ll	3	6	–	–	–	–	↕	↕	↕	–
			IND,X	6A	ff	2	6								
			IND,Y	18 6A	ff	3	7								
DECA	Decrement Accumulator A	A − 1 → A	A INH	4A		1	2	–	–	–	–	↕	↕	↕	–
DECB	Decrement Accumulator B	B − 1 → B	B INH	5A		1	2	–	–	–	–	↕	↕	↕	–
DES	Decrement Stack Pointer	SP − 1 → SP	INH	34		1	3	–	–	–	–	–	–	–	–

Source Form(s)	Operation	Boolean Expression	Addressing Mode for Operand	Machine Coding (Hexadecimal) Opcode	Machine Coding (Hexadecimal) Operand(s)	Bytes	Cycle	Condition Codes S	X	H	I	N	Z	V	C
DEX	Decrement Index Register X	IX − 1 → IX	INH	09		1	3	-	-	-	-	↕	↕	↕	-
DEY	Decrement Index Register Y	IY − 1 → IY	INH	18 09		2	4	-	-	-	-	↕	↕	↕	-
EORA (opr)	Exclusive OR A with Memory	A ⊕ M → A	A IMM	88	ii	2	2	-	-	-	-	↕	↕	0	-
			A DIR	98	dd	2	3								
			A EXT	B8	hh ll	3	4								
			A IND,X	A8	ff	2	4								
			A IND,Y	18 A8	ff	3	5								
EORB (opr)	Exclusive OR B with Memory	B ⊕ M → B	B IMM	C8	ii	2	2	-	-	-	-	↕	↕	0	-
			B DIR	D8	dd	2	3								
			B EXT	F8	hh ll	3	4								
			B IND,X	E8	ff	2	4								
			B IND,Y	18 E8	ff	3	5								
FDIV	Fractional Divide 16 by 16	D/IX → IX; r → D	INH	03		1	41	-	-	-	-	-	↕	↕	↕
IDIV	Integer Divide 16 by 16	D/IX → IX; r → D	INH	02		1	41	-	-	-	-	-	↕	0	↕
INC (opr)	Increment Memory Byte	M + 1 → M	EXT	7C	hh ll	3	6	-	-	-	-	↕	↕	↕	-
			IND,X	6C	ff	2	6								
			IND,Y	18 6C	ff	3	7								
INCA	Increment Accumulator A	A + 1 → A	A INH	4C		1	2	-	-	-	-	↕	↕	↕	-
INCB	Increment Accumulator B	B + 1 → B	B INH	5C		1	2	-	-	-	-	↕	↕	↕	-

Mnemonic	Description	Operation	Mode	Opcode	~	#	S	X	H	I	N	Z	V	C
INS	Increment Stack Pointer	SP + 1 → SP	INH	31	1	3	–	–	–	–	–	–	–	–
INX	Increment Index Register X	IX + 1 → IX	INH	08	1	3	–	–	–	–	–	↕	–	–
INY	Increment Index Register Y	IY + 1 → IY	INH	18 08	2	4	–	–	–	–	–	↕	–	–
JMP (opr)	Jump	See Special Ops	EXT	7E hh ll	3	3	–	–	–	–	–	–	–	–
			IND,X	6E ff	2	3								
			IND,Y	18 6E ff	3	4								
JSR (opr)	Jump to Subroutine	See Special Ops	DIR	9D dd	2	5	–	–	–	–	–	–	–	–
			EXT	BD hh ll	3	6								
			IND,X	AD ff	2	6								
			IND,Y	18 AD ff	3	7								
LDAA (opr)	Load Accumulator A	M → A	A IMM	86 ii	2	2	–	–	–	–	↕	↕	0	–
			A DIR	96 dd	2	3								
			A EXT	B6 hh ll	3	4								
			A IND,X	A6 ff	2	4								
			A IND,Y	18 A6 ff	3	5								
LDAB (opr)	Load Accumulator B	M → B	B IMM	C6 ii	2	2	–	–	–	–	↕	↕	0	–
			B DIR	D6 dd	2	3								
			B EXT	F6 hh ll	3	4								
			B IND,X	E6 ff	2	4								
			B IND,Y	18 E6 ff	3	5								

Source Form(s)	Operation	Boolean Expression	Addressing Mode for Operand	Machine Coding (Hexadecimal) Opcode Operand(s)		Bytes	Cycle	Condition Codes S X H I N Z V C
LDD (opr)	Load Double Accumulator D	M → A, M + 1 → B	IMM	CC	jj kk	3	3	- - - - ↕ ↕ 0 -
			DIR	DC	dd	2	4	
			EXT	FC	hh ll	3	5	
			IND,X	EC	ff	2	5	
			IND,Y	18 EC	ff	3	6	
LDS (opr)	Load Stack Pointer	M:M + 1 → SP	IMM	8E	jj kk	3	3	- - - - ↕ ↕ 0 -
			DIR	9E	dd	2	4	
			EXT	BE	hh ll	3	5	
			IND,X	AE	ff	2	5	
			IND,Y	18 AE	ff	3	6	
LDX (opr)	Load Index Register X	M:M + 1 → IX	IMM	CE	jj kk	3	3	- - - - ↕ ↕ 0 -
			DIR	DE	dd	2	4	
			EXT	FE	hh ll	3	5	
			IND,X	EE	ff	2	5	
			IND,Y	CD EE	ff	3	6	
LDY (opr)	Load Index Register Y	M:M + 1 → IY	IMM	18 CE	jj kk	4	4	- - - - ↕ ↕ 0 -
			DIR	18 DE	dd	3	5	
			EXT	18 FE	hh ll	4	6	
			IND,X	1A EE	ff	3	6	
			IND,Y	18 EE	ff	3	6	

Mnemonic	Operation	Boolean/Arithmetic Operation	Addressing Mode	Opcode	Operand	~	#	S	X	H	I	N	Z	V	C
LSL (opr)	Logical Shift Left	C ← [b7...b0] ← 0	EXT	78	hh ll	3	6	–	–	–	–	↕	↕	↕	↕
			IND,X	68	ff	2	6								
			IND,Y	18 68	ff	3	7								
LSLA			A INH	48		1	2								
LSLB			B INH	58		1	2								
LSLD	Logical Shift Left Double	C ← [b15...b0] ← 0	INH	05		1	3	–	–	–	–	↕	↕	↕	↕
LSR (opr)	Logical Shift Right	0 → [b7...b0] → C	EXT	74	hh ll	3	6	–	–	–	–	0	↕	↕	↕
			IND,X	64	ff	2	6								
			IND,Y	18 64	ff	3	7								
LSRA			A INH	44		1	2								
LSRB			B INH	54		1	2								
LSRD	Logical Shift Right Double	0 → [b15...b0] → C	INH	04		1	3	–	–	–	–	0	↕	↕	↕
MUL	Multiply 8 by 8	A×B → D	INH	3D		1	10	–	–	–	–	–	–	–	↕
NEG (opr)	2's Complement Memory Byte	0 – M → M	EXT	70	hh ll	3	6	–	–	–	–	↕	↕	↕	↕
			IND,X	60	ff	2	6								
			IND,Y	18 60	ff	3	7								
NEGA	2's Complement A	0 – A → A	A INH	40		1	2	–	–	–	–	↕	↕	↕	↕
NEGB	2's Complement B	0 – B → B	B INH	50		1	2	–	–	–	–	↕	↕	↕	↕
NOP	No Operation	No Operation	INH	01		1	2	–	–	–	–	–	–	–	–

Source Form(s)	Operation	Boolean Expression	Addressing Mode for Operand	Machine Coding (Hexadecimal) Opcode	Operand(s)	Bytes	Cycle	S	X	H	I	N	Z	V	C
ORAA (opr)	OR Accumulator A (Inclusive)	A + M → A	A IMM	8A	ii	2	2	-	-	-	-	↕	↕	0	-
			A DIR	9A	dd	2	3								
			A EXT	BA	hh ll	3	4								
			A IND,X	AA	ff	2	4								
			A IND,Y	18 AA	ff	3	5								
ORAB (opr)	OR Accumulator B (Inclusive)	B + M → B	B IMM	CA	ii	2	2	-	-	-	-	↕	↕	0	-
			B DIR	DA	dd	2	3								
			B EXT	FA	hh ll	3	4								
			B IND,X	EA	ff	2	4								
			B IND,Y	18 EA	ff	3	5								
PSHA	Push A onto Stack	A→Stk, SP=SP−1	A INH	36		1	3	-	-	-	-	-	-	-	-
PSHB	Push B onto Stack	B→Stk, SP=SP−1	B INH	37		1	3	-	-	-	-	-	-	-	-
PSHX	Push X onto Stack (Lo First)	IX→Stk, SP=SP−2	INH	3C		1	4	-	-	-	-	-	-	-	-
PSHY	Push Y onto Stack (Lo First)	IY→Stk, SP=SP−2	INH	18 3C		2	5	-	-	-	-	-	-	-	-
PULA	Pull A from Stack	SP=SP+1, A→Stk	A INH	32		1	4	-	-	-	-	-	-	-	-
PULB	Pull B from Stack	SP=SP+1, B→Stk	B INH	33		1	4	-	-	-	-	-	-	-	-
PULX	Pull X from Stack (Hi First)	SP=SP+2, IX→Stk	INH	38		1	5	-	-	-	-	-	-	-	-
PULY	Pull Y from Stack (Hi First)	SP=SP+2, IY→Stk	INH	18 38		2	6	-	-	-	-	-	-	-	-

Mnemonic	Operation	Boolean Expression	Addressing Mode	Opcode	Operand	~	#	H	I	N	Z	V	C
ROL (opr)	Rotate Left	C ← [b7 ← b0] ← C	EXT	79	hh ll	3	6	-	-	↕	↕	↕	↕
			IND,X	69	ff	2	6	-	-	↕	↕	↕	↕
			IND,Y	18 69	ff	3	7	-	-	↕	↕	↕	↕
ROLA			A INH	49		1	2	-	-	↕	↕	↕	↕
ROLB			B INH	59		1	2	-	-	↕	↕	↕	↕
ROR (opr)	Rotate Right	C → [b7 → b0] → C	EXT	76	hh ll	3	6	-	-	↕	↕	↕	↕
			IND,X	66	ff	2	6	-	-	↕	↕	↕	↕
			IND,Y	18 66	ff	3	7	-	-	↕	↕	↕	↕
RORA			A INH	46		1	2	-	-	↕	↕	↕	↕
RORB			B INH	56		1	2	-	-	↕	↕	↕	↕
RTI	Return from Interrupt	See Special Ops	INH	3B		1	12	↕	↕	↕	↕	↕	↕
RTS	Return from Subroutine	See Special Ops	INH	39		1	5	-	-	-	-	-	-
SBA	Subtract B from A	A − B → A	INH	10		1	2	-	-	↕	↕	↕	↕
SBCA (opr)	Subtract with Carry from A	A − M − C → A	A IMM	82	ii	2	2	-	-	↕	↕	↕	↕
			A DIR	92	dd	2	3	-	-	↕	↕	↕	↕
			A EXT	B2	hh ll	3	4	-	-	↕	↕	↕	↕
			A IND,X	A2	ff	2	4	-	-	↕	↕	↕	↕
			A IND,Y	18 A2	ff	3	5	-	-	↕	↕	↕	↕
SBCB (opr)	Subtract with Carry from B	B − M − C → B	B IMM	C2	ii	2	2	-	-	↕	↕	↕	↕
			B DIR	D2	dd	2	3	-	-	↕	↕	↕	↕
			B EXT	F2	hh ll	3	4	-	-	↕	↕	↕	↕
			B IND,X	E2	ff	2	4	-	-	↕	↕	↕	↕
			B IND,Y	18 E2	ff	3	5	-	-	↕	↕	↕	↕

Source Form(s)	Operation	Boolean Expression	Addressing Mode for Operand	Machine Coding (Hexadecimal) Opcode	Operand(s)	Bytes	Cycle	Condition Codes S	X	H	I	N	Z	V	C
SEC	Set Carry	1→C	INH	0D		1	2	-	-	-	-	-	-	-	1
SEI	Set Interrupt Mask	1→I	INH	0F		1	2	-	-	-	1	-	-	-	-
SEV	Set Overflow Flag	1→V	INH	0B		1	2	-	-	-	-	-	-	1	-
STAA (opr)	Store Accumulator A	A→M	A DIR	97	dd	2	3	-	-	-	-	↕	↕	0	-
			A EXT	B7	hh ll	3	4								
			A IND,X	A7	ff	2	4								
			A IND,Y	18 A7	ff	3	5								
STAB (opr)	Store Accumulator B	B→M	B DIR	D7	dd	2	3	-	-	-	-	↕	↕	0	-
			B EXT	F7	hh ll	3	4								
			B IND,X	E7	ff	2	4								
			B IND,Y	18 E7	ff	3	5								
STD (opr)	Store Accumulator D	A→M, B→M+1	DIR	DD	dd	2	4	-	-	-	-	↕	↕	0	-
			EXT	FD	hh ll	3	5								
			IND,X	ED	ff	2	5								
			IND,Y	18 ED	ff	3	6								
STOP	Stop Internal Clocks		INH	CF		1	2	-	-	-	-	-	-	-	-
STS (opr)	Store Stack Pointer	SP→M:M+1	DIR	9F	dd	2	4	-	-	-	-	↕	↕	0	-
			EXT	BF	hh ll	3	5								
			IND,X	AF	ff	2	5								
			IND,Y	18 AF	ff	3	6								

Mnemonic	Operation	Addressing Mode	Opcode	Operand	Bytes	Cycles	S	X	H	I	N	Z	V	C
STX (opr)	Store Index Register X	IX → M:M+1					–	–	–	–	↕	↕	0	–
		DIR	DF	dd	2	4								
		EXT	FF	hh ll	3	5								
		IND,X	EF	ff	2	5								
		IND,Y	CD EF	ff	3	6								
STY (opr)	Store Index Register Y	IY → M:M+1					–	–	–	–	↕	↕	0	–
		DIR	18 DF	dd	3	5								
		EXT	18 FF	hh ll	4	6								
		IND,X	1A EF	ff	3	6								
		IND,Y	18 EF	ff	3	6								
SUBA (opr)	Subtract Memory from A	A – M → A					–	–	–	–	↕	↕	↕	↕
		A IMM	80	ii	2	2								
		A DIR	90	dd	2	3								
		A EXT	B0	hh ll	3	4								
		A IND,X	A0	ff	2	4								
		A IND,Y	18 A0	ff	3	5								
SUBB (opr)	Subtract Memory from B	B – M → B					–	–	–	–	↕	↕	↕	↕
		B IMM	C0	ii	2	2								
		B DIR	D0	dd	2	3								
		B EXT	F0	hh ll	3	4								
		B IND,X	E0	ff	2	4								
		B IND,Y	18 E0	ff	3	5								
SUBD (opr)	Subtract Memory from D	D – M:M+1 → D					–	–	–	–	↕	↕	↕	↕
		IMM	83	jj kk	3	4								
		DIR	93	dd	2	5								
		EXT	B3	hh ll	3	6								
		IND,X	A3	ff	2	6								
		IND,Y	18 A3	ff	3	7								
SWI	Software Interrupt	See Special Ops					–	–	–	1	–	–	–	–
		INH	3F		1	14								

Source Form(s)	Operation	Boolean Expression	Addressing Mode for Operand	Machine Coding (Hexadecimal) Opcode	Operand(s)	Bytes	Cycle	S	X	H	I	N	Z	V	C
TAB	Transfer A to B	A → B	INH	16		1	2	-	-	-	-	↕	↕	0	-
TAP	Transfer A to CC Register	A → CCR	INH	06		1	2	↕	↕	↕	↕	↕	↕	↕	↕
TBA	Transfer B to A	B → A	INH	17		1	2	-	-	-	-	↕	↕	0	-
TEST	TEST (Only in Test Modes)	Address Bus Counts	INH	00		1	*	-	-	-	-	-	-	-	-
TPA	Transfer CC Register to A	CCR → A	INH	07		1	2	-	-	-	-	-	-	-	-
TST (opr)	Test for Zero or Minus	M − 0	EXT	7D	hh ll	3	6	-	-	-	-	↕	↕	0	0
			IND, X	6D	ff	2	6								
			IND, Y	18 6D	ff	3	7								
TSTA		A − 0	A INH	4D		1	2	-	-	-	-	↕	↕	0	0
TSTB		B − 0	B INH	5D		1	2	-	-	-	-	↕	↕	0	0
TSX	Transfer Stack Pointer to X	SP + 1 → IX	INH	30		1	3	-	-	-	-	-	-	-	-
TSY	Transfer Stack Pointer to Y	SP + 1 → IY	INH	18 30		2	4	-	-	-	-	-	-	-	-
TXS	Transfer X to Stack Pointer	IX − 1 → SP	INH	35		1	3	-	-	-	-	-	-	-	-
TYS	Transfer Y to Stack Pointer	IY − 1 → SP	INH	18 35		2	4	-	-	-	-	-	-	-	-
WAI	Wait for Interrupt	Stack Regs & WAIT	INH	3E		1	**	-	-	-	-	-	-	-	-
XGDX	Exchange D with X	IX → D, D → IX	INH	8F		1	3	-	-	-	-	-	-	-	-
XGDY	Exchange D with Y	IY → D, D → IY	INH	18 8F		2	4	-	-	-	-	-	-	-	-

NOTES:

Cycle:

    *   = Infinity or until reset occurs

  ** = 12 cycles are used beginning with the opcode fetch. A wait state is entered which remains in effect for an integer number of MPU E-clock cycle (n) until an interrupt is recognized. Finally, two additional cycles are used to fetch the appropriate interrupt vector (total = 14 + n).

Operands:

dd = 8-bit direct address $0000-$00FF. (High byte assumed to be $00.)
ff   = 8-bit positive offset $00 (0) to $FF (255) added to index.
hh = High order byte of 16-bit extended address.
ii   = One byte of immediate data.
jj   = High order byte of 16-bit immediate data.
kk = Low order byte of 16-bit immediate data.
ll   = Low order byte of 16-bit extended address.
mm = 8-bit mask (set bits to be affected).
rr   = Signed relative offset $80 (−128) to $7F (+127). Offset relative to the address following the machine code offset byte.

Condition Codes:

  —   Bit not changed
  0   Always cleared (logic 0).
  1   Always set (logic 1).
 ↕   Bit cleared or set depending on operation.
 ↓   Bit may be cleared, cannot become set.

381

M68HC24 Port Replacement Unit (PRU)

MOTOROLA SEMICONDUCTORS

3501 ED BLUESTEIN BLVD., AUSTIN, TEXAS 78721

Advance Information

PORT REPLACEMENT UNIT (PRU)

The MC68HC24 is a peripheral device which replaces Ports B and C of the MC68HC11 microcomputer (MCU). These ports are lost when the MCU is placed in the expanded or special test modes of operation. Port B is a general purpose output port. Port C is a general purpose input/output port complemented by full handshake capability. This device can also be used in an emulator as a replacement for Port B, Port C, STRA, and STRB. Applications requiring external memory in early production or top of the line models can also use the MC68HC24 for parallel I/O. When used in these expanded systems, a later switch to a single chip solution will be transparent to software.

The MC68HC24 is not restricted to simply replacing MC68HC11 ports. The MC68HC24 should be considered as a cost-effective solution for any CMOS microcomputer system requiring I/O expansion, parallel printer interface, or interprocessor communications in multiple MCU systems.

HARDWARE FEATURES
- Supports All Handshake and I/O Modes of the MC68HC11 Ports
- Automatic Conformance to the MC68HC11's Variable Memory Map
- Multiplexed Address/Data Bus
- 3.0-5.5 Volt Operation
- Can Be Used with the MC68HC11, MC68HC01, MC146805E2, MC146805E3, and other CMOS Microcomputers
- 0 to 2.1 MHz Operation

SOFTWARE FEATURES
- Software Compatible to MC68HC11 in Single-Chip Mode
- Minimizes Software Overhead for Parallel I/O Handshake Protocols

---

MC68HC24

HCMOS
(HIGH-DENSITY, HIGH-PERFORMANCE SILICON GATE)

PORT REPLACEMENT UNIT (PRU)

P SUFFIX
PLASTIC PACKAGE
CASE 711

L SUFFIX
CERAMIC PACKAGE
CASE 715

FN SUFFIX
PCC QUAD PACKAGE

PIN ASSIGNMENT
(DUAL-IN-LINE)

```
IO TEST  1      40  CS
   A15   2      39  MODE
   A14   3      38  RS
   A13   4      37  E
   A12   5      36  R/W
  STRA   6      35  RESET
   PC0   7      34  AD0
   PC1   8      33  AD1
   PC2   9      32  AD2
   PC3  10      31  AD3
   PC4  11      30  AD4
   PC5  12      29  AD5
   PC6  13      28  AD6
   PC7  14      27  AD7
   VDD  15      26  VSS
  STRB  16      25  IRQ
   PB7  17      24  PB0
   PB6  18      23  PB1
   PB5  19      22  PB2
   PB4  20      21  PB3
```

PIN ASSIGNMENT
(QUAD)

```
        A12  A13  A14  A15 IO TEST N/C  CS  MODE  RS   E  R/W
         6    5    4    3    2    1   44   43   42  41  40

STRA  7                                                    39  RESET
PC0   8                                                    38  AD0
PC1   9                                                    37  AD1
PC2  10                                                    36  AD2
PC3  11                                                    35  AD3
N/C  12                                                    34  N/C
PC4  13                                                    33  AD4
PC5  14                                                    32  AD5
PC6  15                                                    31  AD6
PC7  16                                                    30  AD7
VDD  17                                                    29  VSS
      18   19   20   21   22   23   24   25   26   27   28
     STRB  PB7  PB6  PB5  PB4  N/C  PB3  PB2  PB1  PB0  IRQ
```

©MOTOROLA INC., 1985   ADI1046

FIGURE 1 MC68HC24 Port Replacement Unit Block Diagram

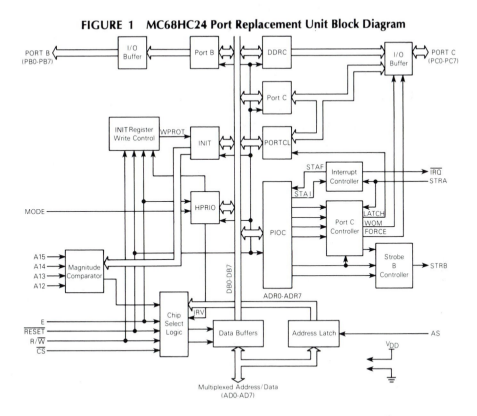

MAXIMUM RATINGS

Rating	Symbol	Value	Unit
Supply Voltage	V_{DD}	-0.5 to $+7.0$	V
Input Voltage	V_{in}	$V_{SS} -0.5$ to $V_{DD} +0.5$	V
Current Drain per Pin	I_{IK}	25	mA
Operating Temperature Range	T_A	-40 to $+85$	°C
Storage Temperature Range	T_{stg}	-55 to $+150$	°C

THERMAL CHARACTERISTICS

Characteristic	Symbol	Value	Unit
Thermal Resistance Ceramic 40 Pin DIP Plastic 40 Pin DIP Plastic 44 Pin Quad Pack	θ_{JA}	50 100 TBD	°C/W

 MOTOROLA *Semiconductor Products Inc.*

THERMAL CHARACTERISTICS

This device contains circuitry which protects the inputs against damage due to high static voltages or electric fields; however, it is advised that normal precautions be taken to avoid applications of any voltage higher than maximum rated voltages to this high-impedance circuit. For proper operation, it is recommended that V_{in} and V_{out} be constrained to the range $V_{SS} \leq (V_{in}$ or $V_{out}) \leq V_{DD}$. Unused inputs must always be tied to an appropriate logic voltage level (e.g., either V_{SS} or V_{DD}).

POWER CONSIDERATIONS

The average chip-junction temperature, T_J, in °C can be obtained from:

$$T_J = T_A + (P_D \bullet \theta_{JA}) \tag{1}$$

Where:

$T_A \equiv$ Ambient Temperature, °C

$\theta_{JA} \equiv$ Package Thermal Resistance, Junction-to-Ambient, °C/W

$P_D \equiv P_{INT} + P_{PORT}$

$P_{INT} \equiv I_{CC} \times V_{CC}$, Watts — Chip Internal Power

$P_{PORT} \equiv$ Port Power Dissipation, Watts — User Determined

For most applications $P_{PORT} \ll P_{INT}$ and can be neglected. P_{PORT} may become significant if the device is configured to drive Darlington bases or sink LED loads.

An approximate relationship between P_D and T_J (if P_{PORT} is neglected) is:

$$P_D = K \div (T_J + 273°C) \tag{2}$$

Solving equations 1 and 2 for K gives:

$$K = P_D \bullet (T_A + 273°C) + \theta_{JA} \bullet P_D{}^2 \tag{3}$$

Where K is a constant pertaining to the particular part. K can be determined from equation (3) by measuring P_D (at equilibrium) for a known T_A. Using this value of K, the values of P_D and T_J can be obtained by solving equations (1) and (2) iteratively for any value of T_A.

MODE SELECTION ELECTRICAL CHARACTERISTICS ($V_{DD} = 5.0$ V $\pm$ 10%, $V_{SS} = 0$ Vdc, $T_A = 25$°C unless otherwise noted; see Figure 2 for timing diagram)

Characteristic	Symbol	Min	Typ	Max	Unit
Mode Programming Voltage Low	V_{MPL}	0	–	$0.2 \times V_{DD}$	V
Mode Programming Voltage High	V_{MPH}	$0.7 \times V_{DD}$	–	V_{DD}	V
$\overline{RESET}$ Low Input Pulse Width	PW_{RSTL}	2	–	–	E_{cyc}
Mode Programming Setup Time	t_{MPS}	2	–	–	E_{cyc}
Mode Programming Hold Time	t_{MPH}	0	–	–	E_{cyc}

FIGURE 2   Mode Selection Timing

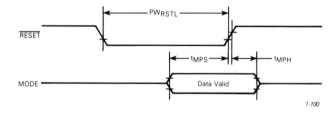

1-100

DC ELECTRICAL CHARACTERISTICS (V_{DD} = 5.0 V ± 10%, V_{SS} = 0 Vdc, T_A = −40°C to +85°C unless otherwise noted)

Characteristic		Symbol	Min	Max	Unit
Output Voltage (I_{Load} = ± 10 μA)	All Outputs	V_{OL}	—	0.1	V
	All Outputs Except $\overline{IRQ}$ (see Note 1)	V_{OH}	V_{DD}−0.1	—	
Output Low Voltage (I_{Load} = 1.6 mA)		V_{OL}	—	0.4	V
Output High Voltage (I_{Load} = −0.8 mA, V_{DD} = 4.5 V)		V_{OH}	V_{DD}−0.8	—	V
	All Outputs Except $\overline{IRQ}$ (see Note 1)				
Input Low Voltage	All Inputs	V_{IL}	V_{SS}	0.2 × V_{DD}	V
Input High Voltage	All Inputs	V_{IH}	0.7 × V_{DD}	V_{DD}	V
I/O Ports, 3-State Leakage (V_{in} = V_{DD} or V_{SS}) PB0-PB7, PC0-PC7, AD0-AD7		I_{OZ}	—	± 10	μA
Input Current (V_{in} = V_{DD} or V_{SS})		I_{IN}	—	± 1	μA
E, AS, R/$\overline{W}$, $\overline{CS}$, MODE, A12-A15, IOTEST, STRA					
Total Supply Current (see Note 2)		I_{DD}	—	5	mA
Input Capacitance E, AS, R/$\overline{W}$, $\overline{CS}$, MODE, A12-15, IOTEST, STRA		C_{in}	—	8.0	pF
PB0-PB7, PC0-PC7, AD0-AD7			—	12.0	
Power Dissipation		P_D	—	25	mW

NOTES:
1. V_{OH} specification for $\overline{IRQ}$ is not applicable because it is an open drain output pin.
2. Test conditions for total supply current are as follows:
    a. C_L = 90 pF on Port B and AD0 through AD7, no dc loads, t_{cyc} = 500 ns.
    b. Port C programmed as inputs.
    c. V_{IL} = V_{SS} + 0.2 V for PC0-PC7, AD7-AD2 and AD0 (during E = V_{IL}), $\overline{CS}$
       V_{IH} = V_{DD} − 0.2 V for $\overline{RESET}$, R/$\overline{W}$, AD1 (during E = V_{IL}), MODE.
    d. The E input is a squarewave from V_{SS} + 0.2 V to V_{DD} − 0.2 V.
    e. AS input is 25% duty cycle from V_{SS} + 0.2 V to V_{DD} − 0.2 V.

PERIPHERAL PORT TIMING (V_{DD} = 5.0 V ± 10%, all timing is shown with respect to 20% V_{DD} and 70% V_{DD} unless otherwise noted)

Characteristics	Symbol	Min	Max	Unit	Fig. No.
Peripheral Data Setup Time (Port C)	t_{PDSU}	200	—	ns	4
Peripheral Data Hold Time (Port C)	t_{PDH}	10	—	ns	4
Delay Time, E Negative Transition to Peripheral Data Valid (Ports B and C, see Note 1)	t_{PWD}	—	100	ns	3
Input Data Setup Time (Port C)	t_{IS}	50	—	ns	6, 7
Input Data Hold Time (Port C)	t_{IH}	10	—	ns	6, 7
Delay Time, E Positive Transition to STRB Asserted (see Note 2)	t_{DEB}	—	80	ns	5, 8, 9
Delay Time, E Positive Transition to STRB Negated Hand-shake Mode (see Note 2)	t_{DEBN}	—	80	ns	7, 9
Setup Time, STRA Asserted to E Negative Transition (see Note 3)	t_{AES}	0	—	ns	7, 8, 9
Delay Time, STRA Asserted to Port C Data Out Valid	t_{PCD}	—	100	ns	9
Hold Time, STRA Negated to Port C Data	t_{PCH}	10	—	ns	9
Three-State Hold Time	t_{PCZ}	—	150	ns	9
STRA Cycle Time	t_{Scyc}	2	—	E_{cyc}	6, 7

NOTES:
1. The method of calculating the timing for this characteristic differs from the MC68HC11.
2. If this setup time is met, STRB will be acknowledged in the next cycle. If it is not met, the response will be delayed one more cycle.
3. Port C timing is only valid for active drive (CWOM bit not set in PIOC).

(M) MOTOROLA *Semiconductor Products Inc.*

FIGURE 3   Port Write Timing

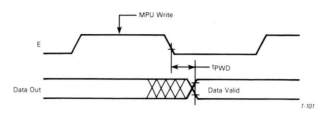

1-101

FIGURE 4   Port C Static Read Timing

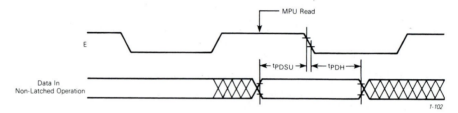

1-102

FIGURE 5   Simple Output Strobe Timing

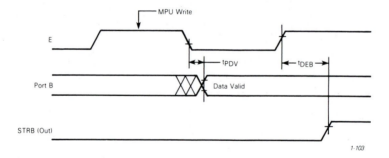

1-103

FIGURE 6   Simple Input Strobe Timing

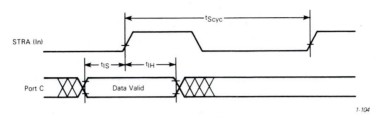

1-104

FIGURE 7   Port C Input Handshake Timing

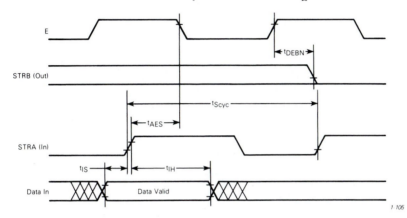

1-105

FIGURE 8   Port C Output Handshake Timing

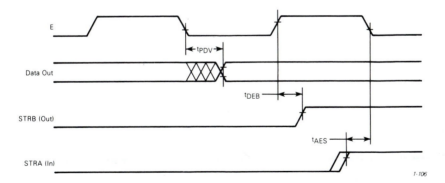

1-106

 MOTOROLA *Semiconductor Products Inc.*

FIGURE 9 Port C Three-State Output Handshake Timing

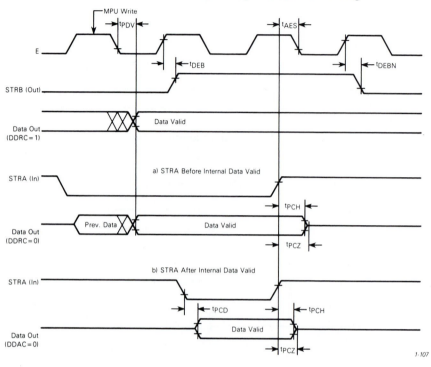

1-107

MOTOROLA *Semiconductor Products Inc.*

BUS TIMING CHARACTERISTICS (V_{DD} = 5.0 V ± 10%, V_{SS} = 0 Vdc, T_A = – 40° to + 85°C unless otherwise noted; see Figure 10 for detailed timing diagrams)

Ident. Number	Characteristic	Symbol	1 MHz		2.1 MHz		Unit
			Min	Max	Min	Max	
1	Cycle Time	t_{cyc}	1000	–	476	–	ns
2	Pulse Width, E Low	PW_{EL}	430	–	200	–	ns
3	Pulse Width, E High	PW_{EH}	450	–	210	–	ns
4	Input and Clock Rise and Fall Time	t_r, t_f	–	25	–	20	ns
8	R/$\overline{W}$ Hold Time	t_{RWH}	20	–	10	–	ns
13	Setup Time before Rising Edge of E (R/$\overline{W}$, $\overline{CS}$)	t_{RWS}	100	–	50	–	ns
15	Chip Select Hold Time ($\overline{CS}$)	t_{CSH}	20	–	20	–	ns
18	Read Data Hold Time	t_{DHR}	10	50	10	50	ns
21	Write Data Hold Time	t_{DHW}	10	–	10	–	ns
24	Muxed Address Valid Time to AS Fall	t_{ASL}	60	–	30	–	ns
25	Muxed Address Hold Time	t_{AHL}	40	–	20	–	ns
26	Delay Time, E Fall to AS Rise	t_{ASD}	60	–	30	–	ns
27	AS Pulse Width High	t_{WASH}	150	–	75	–	ns
28	AS Fall to E Rise	t_{ASED}	60	–	30	–	ns
30	Peripheral Output Data Delay Time from E Rise (Read)	T_{DDR}	20	240	10	120	ns
31	Peripheral Data Setup Time (Write)	t_{DSW}	150	–	75	–	ns

FIGURE 10   Bus Timing Diagram

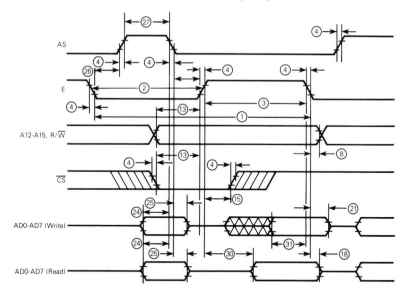

1-108

 MOTOROLA *Semiconductor Products Inc.*

PIN DESCRIPTION

The input and output pins (or signals) for the port replacement unit are described in the following paragraphs.

V_DD AND V_SS

Power is supplied to the peripheral using these two pins. Power is V_{DD} and ground is V_{SS}.

RESET (RESET)

This active-low control input pin is used to initialize the MC68HC24 to a known start-up state. The system state after a reset is detailed in the **STATE AFTER RESET** section. This pin must remain at a low level for a minimum of two E-clock cycles to be recognized.

ENABLE (E)

The E-clock input is the basic MPU/MCU clock. This clock provides most timing reference information to the MC68HC24. In general, when E is low, an internal process is taking place. When E is high, data is being accessed.

The E-clock runs at the external bus rate of the MPU/MCU and may range in frequency from dc to the maximum operating frequency of the device (i.e., this peripheral part is static). More information on the timing relationships between the various signals may be found in the **PERIPHERAL PORT TIMING** and **BUS TIMING CHARACTERISTICS** sections.

ADDRESS STROBE (AS)

The AS input pulse serves to demultiplex the address/data bus. The falling edge of AS causes the addresses AD0 through AD7 to be latched within the MC68HC24.

READ/WRITE (R/W)

The read/write pin is a high-impedance input signal which is used to control the direction of data flow along the multiplexed address/data bus. When the device is selected and the R/W input is high, the data output buffers are enabled and a selected register is read.

Data is written into the selected register when the chip is selected with R/W low. The R/W signal is not latched by the MC68HC24. In order to guarantee that register contents are not corrupted, R/W must be stable prior to the rising edge of the E-clock and must remain stable throughout the E-clock high time.

CHIP SELECT (CS)

This input pin serves as the device chip select. The MC68HC24 is selected when (1) CS is low, (2) the contents of the INIT register match address lines A12 through A15, and (3) the lower order address lines (AD0 through AD7) select an internal register address. All three of these conditions must be met to access the internal registers. The CS signal is latched on the rising edge of the E-clock and must be stable prior to that edge.

No action will take place within the MC68HC24 during bus cycles in which (1) CS is not asserted, (2) the A12 through A15 address lines do not match the contents of the INIT register, or (3) an internal register is not addressed.

ADDRESS AND DATA (AD0 through AD7)

Multiplexed bus microprocessors save pins by presenting the address during the first portion of the bus cycle and using those same pins during the second portion of the bus cycle for data. Address and data multiplexing does not slow the access time of the MC68HC24 since the bus reversal from address to data occurs during the internal register access time.

The low-order address must be stable (valid) prior to the fall of AS at which time the MC68HC24 latches the address present on AD0 through AD7. If the latched address is decoded, if CS is asserted, and if A12 through A15 match the contents of the INIT register, a selected register will be accessed.

Although a 64-byte register block is reserved for the registers, only seven of the locations are currently implemented. See the **INTERNAL REGISTER DESCRIPTION** section for details about specific addresses.

Valid write data must be presented by the MPU/MCU during the E high period of the write cycle. In a read cycle, the MC68HC24 outputs eight bits of data during the second half of the read bus cycle and then ceases driving the bus (returns to a high impedance state) after the falling edge of E.

HIGH ORDER ADDRESS (A12 through A15)

The address lines, A12 through A15, are the non-multiplexed high-order address lines of the MPU/MCU. These signals are used internally to establish a partial decoding for the chip select. They are latched by the rising edge of the E-clock and must be stable prior to this edge. A magnitude comparator checks the value of these lines against a value stored in the INIT register. If they match, CS is asserted, and an internal register is addressed, the device will be accessed during the current bus cycle.

PORT B (PB0 through PB7)

Port B (PB0 through PB7) is an 8-bit general purpose output port. In the simple strobed mode of operation, STRB is pulsed for each write to Port B. See the **I/O PORTS** section for more information.

PORT C (PC0 through PC7)

Each line of Port C is individually programmable as either an input or an output via its data direction register (DDRC). An I/O pin is an input when its corresponding DDR bit is a logic zero and an output when the DDR bit is a logic one. Several handshake modes are available on this port (see **I/O PORTS** section).

STROBE A (STRA)

Strobe A is an edge detecting input used by Port C. In the simple strobed and input handshake modes of operation, the programmed edge on STRA will latch the data on the Port C inputs into PORTCL. In the output handshake mode, STRA is an edge-sensitive acknowledge input signal indicating that Port C output data has been accepted by the external device.

Ⓜ MOTOROLA *Semiconductor Products Inc.*

STROBE B (STRB)

While operating in the simple strobed I/O mode, Strobe B is a strobe output which pulses for each write to Port B. In the full handshake mode of parallel I/O, STRB acts as a handshake output line. The STRB pin is a READY output in the input handshake mode, inhibiting the external device from strobing new data into Port C. In the output handshake mode, STRB is again a READY output; however, in this case it indicates that new data has been written to Port C by the microprocessor.

INTERRUPT REQUEST (IRQ)

The IRQ output pin is an open drain, active low signal that may be used to interrupt the microprocessor with a service request. The open drain output allows multiple devices to be wire-ORed together. This configuration requires an external resistor to V_{DD} as no internal pullup is provided.

The MC68HC11 I/O port interrupts share the same vector address as IRQ. As a result, an expanded MC68HC11 system incorporating an MC68HC24 (to replace the displaced I/O features) will appear to the software as a single chip solution. Refer to the **INTERNAL REGISTER DESCRIPTION—PIOC** and the **I/O PORTS—FULL HANDSHAKE I/O** sections for additional information.

I/O TEST (IOTEST)

This is a factory test feature and the IOTEST pin must be tied directly to V_{SS} for normal operation.

I/O PORTS

There are two 8-bit parallel I/O ports on the MC68HC24. Port B is a general purpose output-only port, whereas Port C may be used as general purpose input and/or output pins as specified by DDRC. In conjunction with STRA and STRB, Ports B and C may be used for special strobed and handshake modes of parallel I/O as well as general purpose I/O.

GENERAL PURPOSE I/O (PORT C)

When used as general purpose I/O signals, each bit has associated with it one bit in the PORTC data register and one bit in the corresponding position in the data direction register (DDRC). The DDRC is used to specify the primary direction of data on the I/O pin; however, specification of a line as an output does not disable the ability to read the line as a latched input.

When a bit which is configured as an output is read, the value returned will be the value at the input to the pin driver. When a pin is configured as an input (by clearing the DDRC bit) the pin becomes a high impedance input. When writing to a bit that is configured as an input, the value will not affect the I/O pin; however, the bit will be stored to an internal latch so that if the line is later reconfigured as an output this value will appear at the I/O pin.

This operation can be used to preset a value for an output port prior to configuring it as an output, so that glitches of an output state which are not defined for the external system may be avoided. Reset configures the port for input by clearing both the DDR and the data register.

FIXED DIRECTION I/O (PORT B)

Port B is a general purpose output-only port. The data direction is fixed in order to properly emulate the operation of the MC68HC11 Port B. Reads of Port B return the levels sensed at the input of the pin drivers. Write data is stored in an internal latch which directly drives the output pin driver. Reset clears the data register forcing the outputs low.

SIMPLE STROBED I/O

The simple strobed mode of parallel I/O is controlled by the parallel I/O control (PIOC) register. This mode is selected when the HNDS bit in the PIOC register is clear. This mode forces PORTCL to be a strobed input port with the STRA pin used as the edge detecting latch command input. Also, Port B becomes a strobed output port with the STRB pin acting as the output strobe.

Strobed Input Port C

In this mode, there are two addresses where Port C may be read—PORTC data register and PORTCL latch register. Even when the strobed input mode is selected, one or all of the bits in Port C may be used as general purpose I/O lines. In other words, the DDRC register still controls the data direction of all Port C pins.

The STRA pin is used as an edge-detecting input. Either falling or rising edges may be specified as the significant edge by use of the EGA bit in PIOC. Whenever the selected active edge is detected at the STRA pin, the current logic levels at Port C are latched into the PORTCL register and the Strobe A flag (STAF) bit in PIOC is set.

If the STAI bit in PIOC is also set, then an interrupt sequence is requested on the IRQ pin. The STAF flag is automatically cleared by reading the PIOC register (with STAF set) followed by a read of the PORTCL register. Additional active edges of STRA continue to latch new data into PORTCL regardless of the state of the STAF flag. Consecutive active edges on STRA must be a minimum of two E-clock cycles apart.

Reads of the PORTCL register return the last value latched, while reads of PORTC return the static level of the Port C pins (inputs) or the level at the input to the pin driver (outputs).

Strobed Output Port B

In this mode, the STRB pin is a strobe output which is pulsed each time there is a write to Port B. Data written to PORTB is stored in a latch which drives the Port B pin drivers. Reads of Port B return the levels at the inputs of those pin drivers.

The INVB bit in the PIOC register controls the polarity of the pulse out of the STRB pin. If the INVB bit is set, the strobe pulse will be a high going pulse (two E-clock periods long) on a normally low line. If the INVB bit is clear, the strobe pulse will be low-going pulse (two E-clock periods long) on a normally high line.

FULL HANDSHAKE I/O

The full handshake modes of parallel I/O involve Port C, STRA, and STRB. There are two basic modes (input and output) and an additional variation on the output handshake mode that allows for three-state operation of Port C. In all

M MOTOROLA *Semiconductor Products Inc.*

handshake modes, STRA is an edge detecting input and STRB is a handshake output line. The effect of DDRC is discussed in the detailed description of the input and output protocols found in this section.

Input Handshake Protocol

In the input handshake scheme, Port C is a latching input port, STRA is an edge-sensitive latch command from the external system that is driving Port C and STRB is a READY output line controlled by logic in the MC68HC24.

In a typical system, an external device wishing to pass data to Port C would test the READY line (STRB). When a ready condition was recognized, the external device would place data on the Port C inputs followed by a pulse on the STRA input to the MC68HC24. The active edge on the STRA line would latch the Port C data into the PORTCL register, set the STAF flag (optionally causing an interrupt), and deassert the READY line (STRB). Deassertion of the READY line would automatically inhibit the external device from strobing new data into Port C. Reading the PORTCL latch register, after reading PIOC with STAF set, clears the STAF flag. Whenever PORTCL is read, the READY (STRB) line is asserted indicating that new data may now be strobed into Port C.

The STRB line can be configured (with the PLS control bit) to be a pulse output (pulse mode) or a static output (interlocked mode). The only difference between the pulse and interlock modes is that in pulse mode, the READY line pulses (asserts) for only two E-clock periods after the latched data becomes available. While in interlock mode, the asserted state of the READY line lasts until new data is strobed into Port C via the STRA input line.

The Port C DDR bits should be cleared (input) for each bit that is to be used as a latched input bit. It is, however, possible to use some Port C bits as latched inputs with the input handshake protocol and at the same time use other Port C bits as static inputs and still other Port C bits as static output bits.

The input handshake protocol has no effect on the use of Port C bits as static inputs or static outputs. Reads of the PORTC register always return the static logic level at the Port C pins (for lines configured as input by DDRC bit equals zero) or at the inputs to the pin drivers (for lines configured as outputs by DDRC bit equals one). Data latched into PORTCL always reflects the level at the Port C pins. Writes to either the PORTC address or the PORTCL address will write information to the Port C output register without affecting the input handshake strobes.

NOTE

After programming PIOC to enter the input handshake mode, STRB will remain in the inactive state. This precaution has been taken to ensure that the external system will not strobe data into PORTCL before all initialization is complete. When ready to accept data, the MPU/MCU should perform a dummy read of the PORTCL address. This operation will assert STRB initiating the input handshake protocol.

Output Handshake Protocol

In the output handshake scheme, Port C is an output port, STRB is a READY output, and STRA is an edge-sensitive acknowledge input signal indicating that Port C output data has been accepted by the external device. In a variation of this output handshake operation, STRA is used as an output enable input as well as an edge-sensitive acknowledge input.

In a typical system, the controlling processor writes to the MC68HC24, placing data in the Port C output latch. Stable data on the Port C pins is indicated by the automatic assertion of the MC68HC24 READY (STRB) line. The external device then processes the available data and pulses the STRA input to indicate that new data may be placed on the Port C output lines. The active edge on STRA causes the READY (STRB) line to be automatically deasserted and the STAF status flag to be set (optionally causing an interrupt). In response to STAF being set, the program puts out new data on Port C as required.

There are two addresses associated with the Port C data register, the normal PORTC data address and a second address (PORTCL) that accesses the input latch on reads and the normal port on writes. On writes to the second address (PORTCL), the data goes to the same port output register as it would on a write to the PORTC address but the STAF flag bit is cleared (provided PIOC was first read with the STAF bit set). This allows an automatic clearing mechanism in output handshake modes to co-exist with normal Port C outputs.

All eight bits in Port C must be used as outputs while the output handshake protocol is selected. That is, part of Port C may not be used for static or latched inputs while the remaining bits are being used for output handshake. The following section covers this limitation in more detail.

Output Handshake Protocol, Three-State Variation

There is a variation to the output handshake protocol that allows three-state operation of Port C. It is possible to directly interconnect this 8-bit parallel port to other 8-bit three-state devices with no additional external parts.

The STRA signal is used as an acknowledge/enable input whose sense is controlled by the EGA bit in the PIOC register. The EGA bit specifies the transition from the asserted to the deasserted state of the STRA input signal. If EGA is zero, the asserted state is high and falling edges are interpreted as acknowledge signals. If EGA is one, the asserted state is low and rising edges are interpreted as acknowledge signals.

As long as the STRA input pin is negated, all Port C bits obey the data direction specified by DDRC. Bits which are configured as inputs (DDR bit equals zero) will be high impedance. When the STRA input is asserted, all Port C lines are forced to be outputs regardless of the data in DDRC.

This operation limits the ability to use some Port C bits as static inputs while using others as handshake outputs. However, it does not interfere with the use of some Port C bits as static outputs while others are being used as three-state handshake outputs. Port C bits which are to be used as static outputs or normal handshake outputs should have their corresponding DDRC bits set. Bits which are to be used as three-state handshake outputs should have their corresponding DDRC bits clear.

Interaction of Handshake and General Purpose I/O

There are two addresses associated with the Port C data register: the normal PORTC address and a second address

MOTOROLA *Semiconductor Products Inc.*

(PORTCL) that accesses the input latch on reads and the normal port on writes. On writes to the second address (PORTCL), the data goes to the same port output register as it would on a write to the port output address. When operating in the output handshake mode, writing to PORTC will not clear the STAF bit whereas writing to PORTCL will clear it. This allows an automatic clearing mechanism to co-exist with normal Port C outputs.

When full input handshake protocol is specified, both general purpose input and/or general purpose output can co-exist at Port C. When full output handshake protocol is specified, general purpose outputs can co-exist with the handshake outputs at Port C. However, the three-state feature of the output handshake mode interferes with general purpose inputs in two ways.

First, in full output handshake, the Port C pins are forced to be driven outputs during any period in which STRA is in its active state regardless of the state of the DDRC bits. This potentially conflicts with any device trying to drive Port C unless the external device has an open-drain type output driver.

Secondly, the value returned on reads of Port C is the state at the inputs to the pin drivers regardless of the state of the DDRC bits. This allows data written for output handshake to be read even if the pins are in a three-state condition.

The following is an example of Port C being used for full input handshake, general purpose input, and general purpose output all at the same time. Assume that the PIOC and DDRC control registers are set up as follows:

```
PIOC = 0111 0000   /STAF/STAI/CWOM/HNDS/.../OIN/PLS/EGA/INVB/
DDRC = 0000 1100   /MSB...        ...LSB/
```

In this example, Port C bits b7 through b4 will be used for input handshake, bits b3 and b2 will be used as open-drain type general purpose outputs, and bits b0 and b1 will be used as general purpose inputs. The DDRC register is configured such that bits b2 and b3 are outputs and the rest of the Port C bits are inputs. The PIOC register is configured such that full-input handshake is specified (HNDS equals one and OIN equals zero). CWOM equals one so any pins in Port C which are configured as outputs will behave as open-drain type outputs. The other bits in the PIOC are not important for the discussion of this example.

When data is latched into PORTCL according to the input handshake protocol, all eight bits are captured although only the four MSBs are of interest to the input handshake software. The data latched into all eight bits of PORTCL will be the levels present at Port C pins.

Software driving the bits b2 and b3 general-purpose outputs would perform writes to PORTC which would not affect the handshake protocol or the latching of data into PORTCL. Data written to Port C bits b0, b1, and b4 through b7 would also be latched into the internal Port C output latch but since the corresponding DDRC bits are zeros, the corresponding Port C pins would remain unaffected.

Bit manipulation and read-modify-write instructions could be used on PORTC because reads of PORTC do not affect the input handshake functions. Although writes to PORTCL would also cause data to be written to Port C, this address should not be used for general purpose output. This is because bit manipulation and read-modify-write instructions

read the location before writing to it and this read would interfere with the input handshake protocol.

Finally, to use bits 0 and 1 for general purpose inputs, simply read PORTC which will return the desired information and will not interfere with the input handshake protocol. Note that the current state of the Port C bits b4 through b7 are also read which means that even the pins which are being used for input handshake can be read at any time without disturbing the input handshake function.

INTERNAL REGISTER DESCRIPTION

A 64-byte address space is reserved for internal register access, although not all 64 addresses are used. The ABSOLUTE locations where these addresses will appear are specified by the reset initialization software and chip select logic provided by the end user (see INIT register). The following list summarizes the register mnemonics and their associated addresses.

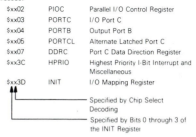

$xx02	PIOC	Parallel I/O Control Register
$xx03	PORTC	I/O Port C
$xx04	PORTB	Output Port B
$xx05	PORTCL	Alternate Latched Port C
$xx07	DDRC	Port C Data Direction Register
$xx3C	HPRIO	Highest Priority I-Bit Interrupt and Miscellaneous
$xx3D	INIT	I/O Mapping Register

— Specified by Chip Select Decoding
— Specified by Bits 0 through 3 of the INIT Register

PARALLEL I/O CONTROL REGISTER (PIOC)

The PIOC register is an 8-bit read/write register except for bit 7 which is a read-only flag bit.

b7	b6	b5	b4	b3	b2	b1	b0	
STAF	STAI	CWOM	HNDS	OIN	PLS	EGA	INVB	$xx02
0	0	0	0	0	0	1	1	RESET

b7, STAF   The STAF (Strobe A Interrupt Status Flag) bit is set when a selected active edge is detected by the STRA input pin. If b6 (STAI) is set, then an interrupt sequence using the IRQ output pin will also be requested whenever the STAF flag is set. This bit is cleared by reset to indicate no interrupt request is pending.

There is an automatic clearing mechanism on this flag bit (STAF) which depends on the operating mode selected. There are three basic strobed modes (see b4, HNDS and b3, OIN).

When HNDS is zero, the simple strobed mode is specified and the OIN bit has no meaning or effect. In this mode, the STAF flag is automatically set by detection of the selected edge on the STRA input pin indicating that new data is available in the

Port C latch. The STAF flag is automatically cleared by a read of the PIOC register (with STAF set) followed by a read of the PORTCL latch register.

When HNDS is one and OIN is zero, the input handshake mode is specified. In this mode, the STAF flag is automatically set by detection of the selected edge on the STRA input pin indicating that new data is available in the Port C latch. The STAF bit is automatically cleared by a read of the PIOC register (with STAF set) followed by a read of the PORTCL latch register.

When HNDS is one and OIN is one, the output handshake mode is specified. In this mode, the STAF flag is automatically set by detection of the selected edge on the STRA input pin indicating that data from Port C has been accepted by the external system. The STAF flag is automatically cleared by a read of the PIOC register (with STAF set) followed by a write to the PORTCL latch register.

b6, STAI
The STAI (Strobe A Interrupt Enable Mask) bit is used to specify whether or not a hardware interrupt sequence is to be requested whenever STAF is set. To request a hardware interrupt, both the STAI interrupt enable bit and the STAF flag bit must be set. This bit is cleared by $\overline{\text{RESET}}$ so that parallel I/O interrupts are inhibited. The user must write this bit to a one in order to use the strobed and handshake I/O functions in an interrupt-driven rather than a polled environment.

b5, CWOM
When the CWOM (Port C Wire-OR Mode) bit is zero, the Port C output pins operate normally. When this bit is set to one, the Port C outputs behave as open-drain type drivers allowing wired-OR type external connections. When CWOM equals one, the top driver device is disabled so that pins may be driven low by writing zeros or become three-state by writing ones. With an external pull-up resistor, the non-driven lines are pulled to logic ones.

This permits Port C output pins to be safely wired in parallel with other similar CMOS output drivers without fear of contentions which could otherwise cause destructive latch-up. This bit is cleared by $\overline{\text{RESET}}$ so Port C pins which are configured as outputs will operate normally.

b4, HNDS
When HNDS (Handshake Mode) bit is clear, the STRA pin acts as a simple input strobe to latch incoming data into the PORTCL latch register and the STRB pin acts as a simple output strobe that pulses after any write to Port B. When HNDS is set, it specifies that a handshake protocol involving Port C, STRA, and STRB is in effect. In all modes, STRA is an edge-sensitive input and $\overline{\text{STRB}}$ is an output. This bit is cleared by $\overline{\text{RESET}}$. The strobe and handshake modes are described in greater detail in the I/O PORTS section.

b3, OIN
The OIN (Output or Input Handshake) bit has no meaning or effect unless HNDS is set to one. When this bit is zero, input handshake protocol is specified. When this bit is a one, output handshake protocol is specified. See the I/O PORTS section for a more detailed description of the handshake protocols.

b2, PLS
The PLS (Pulse/Interlocked Handshake) bit has no meaning or effect unless HNDS is set to one. When this bit is zero, interlocked handshake operation is specified. When this bit is one, pulse mode handshake operation is specified.

In interlocked modes, the STRB output line, once activated, remains active indefinitely until the selected edge is detected on the STRA input line. In pulse modes, the STRB output line, once activated, remains active for only two MCU E-clock cycles and then automatically reverts to the inactive state. This bit is cleared by $\overline{\text{RESET}}$. For more details on the handshake protocols, see the I/O PORTS section.

b1, EGA
The EGA (Active Edge for STRA) bit is used to specify which edge (rising or falling) on the STRA input pin is to be considered the active edge. When this bit is zero, the active edge is the falling edge and when this bit is one, the active edge is the rising edge. This bit is set to one by $\overline{\text{RESET}}$.

When output handshake mode is specified, this bit is used to control the PORT C three-state variation as well as select the active acknowledge edge. In the three-state variation, the EGA bit specifies the trailing edge polarity for the STRA input pin which is interpreted as the enable/acknowledge signal. Assertion of STRA overrides the DDRC specification to force Port C to be outputs and the edge of negation is the active edge acknowledge command.

If EGA is zero, the falling edge at STRA is the active edge which causes STAF to be set and STRB to be negated. Additionally, if EGA is zero, Port C bits obey the DDRC specification while STRA is low but Port C is forced to be an output when STRA is high.

If EGA is one, the rising edge at STRA is the active edge. This causes STAF to be set and STRB to be negated. In addition, Port C bits obey the DDRC specification while

MOTOROLA *Semiconductor Products Inc.*

STRA is high, but Port C is forced to be an output when STRA is low.

b0, INVB   The INVB (Invert Strobe B) bit is used to specify whether or not to invert the normal Strobe B (STRB) logic output levels. When this bit is one, no inversion is specified and the active level on the strobe B output line is logic one. When this bit is zero, inversion is specified and the active level on the strobe B output line is logic zero. This bit is set to one by RESET so that the STRB output will initially be in the low state out of reset. For a more detailed description of the handshake protocols, see the I/O PORTS section.

PORT C DATA REGISTER (PORTC)

	b7	b6	b5	b4	b3	b2	b1	b0	
	PC7	PC6	PC5	PC4	PC3	PC2	PC1	PC0	$xx03
	0	0	0	0	0	0	0	0	RESET

Port C (PORTC) is a general purpose input/output port complemented by full handshake capability. For bits that are configured as inputs, reads of this address return the level sensed at the pin. For bits configured as outputs, reads return the level sensed at the input to the pin driver. When a Port C pin is being used for the three-state variation of parallel output handshake, reads return the level sensed at the input to the pin driver even if the DDR bits suggest that the pin is configured as an input.

Writes to Port C cause the value to be latched in the 8-bit Port C data register. (Note that this is not the same register as the PORTCL latch register described later.) When the corresponding DDRC bit is set, the value in the Port C data register is driven out of the Port C pin. This data latch allows the programmer to initialize the data prior to turning on the output drivers by setting bits in the DDRC. The PORTC register is cleared by RESET.

PORTB (PORT B DATA REGISTER)

	b7	b6	b5	b4	b3	b2	b1	b0	
	PB7	PB6	PB5	PB4	PB3	PB2	PB1	PB0	$xx04
	0	0	0	0	0	0	0	0	RESET

Port B (PORTB) is a general purpose output-only port. Reads of this address return the level sensed at the input to the pin driver. Writes to Port B cause the value to be latched in the 8-bit Port B data register. The PORTB register is set to zero by RESET.

PORT C LATCHED DATA REGISTER (PORTCL)

	b7	b6	b5	b4	b3	b2	b1	b0	
	PCL7	PCL6	PCL5	PCL4	PCL3	PCL2	PCL1	PCL0	$xx05
	U	U	U	U	U	U	U	U	RESET

The Port C latch register (PORTCL) allows alternate access to Port C information. This register is used in conjunction with the strobed parallel I/O modes. Input data is latched into the PORTCL register on each selected edge on the STRA pin. The latched data is the level at the pins regardless of the operating mode selected. Reads of PORTCL return the contents of the Port C input latch. Reads also act as part of an automatic flag clearing sequence in the input handshake modes of Port C.

Writes to the PORTCL register are equivalent to writes to the PORTC register except that PORTCL writes are used as part of an automatic flag clearing sequence in the output handshake modes of Port C. For more information on the Port C strobed and handshake modes, see the I/O PORTS section. The contents of PORTCL are not affected by RESET.

DATA DIRECTION REGISTER C (DDRC)

	b7	b6	b5	b4	b3	b2	b1	b0	
	DDRC7	DDRC6	CCRC5	DDRC4	DDRC3	DDRC2	DDRC1	DDRC0	$xx07
	0	0	0	0	0	0	0	0	RESET

The data direction register C (DDRC) is a read/write register used in conjunction with Port C to specify the direction of data flow at each of the Port C pins. A Port C pin is an input if the corresponding bit in DDRC is zero. The pin is an output if the corresponding bit in DDRC is set to one. During reset, all bits in the DDRC are cleared to zero. The effects of DDRC are overridden in the three-state variation of the output handshake mode. For additional information, see the I/O PORTS, Output Handshake Protocol, Three-State Variation section.

HIGHEST PRIORITY INTERRUPT REGISTER (HPRIO)

	b7	b6	b5	b4	b3	b2	b1	b0	
	—	SMOD	—	IRV	—	—	—	—	$xx3C
	0	—	0	—	0	0	0	0	RESET

NOTE
Reset condition of SMOD and IRV depend on initialization mode.

b7, b5, b3, b2, b1, b0—Not Implemented

These bits are not implemented. Writes have no meaning or effect on them. Reads of these bits will always return a logic zero value.

b6, SMOD   The SMOD (Special Test Mode) bit is a read only bit which reflects the operating mode of the peripheral as selected by the MODE input. The inverted state of MODE is latched into SMOD by the rising edge of RESET. When SMOD equals zero (MODE equals one), the peripheral is operating in the normal mode. When SMOD equals one (MODE equals zero), the special test mode is selected.

The special test mode may be exited under software control by writing SMOD from a

MOTOROLA *Semiconductor Products Inc.*

one to a zero. However, the special test mode may not be reentered by writing the bit back to one. This SMOD bit becomes write-protected once written to zero. This implies that the normal operating mode can be entered either through a hardware reset or through software while the special test mode may only be entered through a hardware reset.

b4, IRV   The IRV (Internal Read Visibility) control bit eliminates potential bus conflict problems when this device is used in conjunction with the MC68HC11. To allow a logic analyzer to monitor the internal bus activity of the MC68HC11, provisions have been made for the MPU to selectively drive the external data bus during internal reads as well as writes. The selection of this feature is controlled by the IRV bit.

The state following reset and the programming characteristics of the MC68HC24 IRV bit are the same as the MC68HC11 IRV bit. However, the functional characteristics are the opposite. The MC68HC24 IRV functions as follows:

Logic 0 — Reads of the INIT and HPRIO registers will enable the multiplexed address/data buffers, placing the contents of the selected register on the bus.

Logic 1 — Reads of the INIT and HPRIO registers do *not* enable the multiplexed address/data bus drivers.

This bit may be read at any time, although the multiplexed address/data bus will remain high-impedance during reads when IRV equals one. Only one write will be acknowledged and then only if SMOD equals one. The IRV bit is forced to zero (reads of HPRIO and INIT enabled) when SMOD is written from a one to a zero (entering normal mode). Reset clears this bit in the normal mode and sets this bit in the special test mode.

INIT (I/O MAPPING REGISTER)

b7	b6	b5	b4	b3	b2	b1	b0	
—	—	—	—	REG3	REG2	REG1	REG0	$xx3D
0	0	0	0	0	0	0	1	RESET

The INIT (I/O Mapping) register is a special purpose 8-bit register that is used (optionally) during initialization to change the default locations of the MC68HC24 internal registers in the MPU/MCU memory map. The lower four bits of the MC68HC24 INIT register are duplicates of the MC68HC11 INIT register. These four bits are used to specify the active state of the four high order address bits to the register address decoding logic. This register functions identically to the MC68HC11 INIT register with the following exceptions: (1) only the lower four bits are implemented, and (2) the protection mechanism is not time dependent.

The default starting address of the 64-byte internal register space is $1x00 (i.e., INIT is initialized to $01). Initialization software can move the registers to any 4K boundary within the memory map. External decoding of A8 through A11 specifies where in the 4K block (on a 256-byte boundaries) the 64-byte register space is located. As an example, assume that the initialization software wrote the value $09 to the INIT register and that $\overline{CS}$ was true when A8 through A11 were low. This would place the registers from $9000 through $903F in the memory map. Decoding A8 through A11 so that the chip is selected when all four address lines are low maps the MC68HC24 registers to the same address as the MC68HC11 registers.

The INIT register is special in that there is a write-protect mechanism associated with it. In the normal mode, the register may be written once at any time after reset. This *differs* from the operation of the MC68HC11 INIT register which becomes write protected after the first 64 E-clock cycles, whether or not a write to the register has occurred. After the first write, the MC68HC24 INIT register becomes write-protected and thereafter is a read-only register.

While in the special test mode (SMOD equals one), the protection mechanism is overridden and the INIT register may be written repeatedly as long as SMOD remains a one. When SMOD is written to a zero (to enter the normal operating mode), the write-protect mechanism is enabled. One additional write, regardless of the number of writes performed while in the special test mode, is allowed after entering normal operating mode. Writes to the upper four bits of the INIT register have no effect on the register contents and reads will always return zeroes in the most significant bit positions.

SYSTEM CONFIGURATION

The MC68HC24 allows an end user to configure the peripheral to his specific MCU system through the use of hard wired options such as the mode select pin (MODE) and by the use of internal registers under software control. The following section describes those options which are fixed through hardware. Other configuration options, which can be changed dynamically, are discussed in the sections entitled **I/O PORTS** and **MODES OF OPERATION**.

MODE SELECTION

A dedicated mode select pin (MODE) determines which of two operating modes the MC68HC24 enters out of $\overline{RESET}$. Both modes properly emulate the action of Ports B and C of the MC68HC11. The modes are the normal and special test modes. Another dedicated pin (IOTEST) is used to test the output buffers.

The state of the mode select pin (MODE) is latched into the peripheral by the rising edge of $\overline{RESET}$ with the inverse of the latched value reflected in the SMOD bit of the HPRIO register. Normal mode is indicated by SMOD equals zero (MODE equals one). Special Test mode is indicated by SMOD equals one (MODE equals zero). The difference between these two modes is limited to the operation of the INIT and HPRIO registers.

The MODE input corresponds (in function, but not voltage levels) to the MODB/VPGM input of the MC68HC11. The MC68HC11 requires either V_{DD} or a level $1.4 \times V_{DD}$ on the

 MOTOROLA *Semiconductor Products Inc.*

MODB pin to select the operating mode; whereas, the MC68HC24 requires only logic level signals. The $1.4 \times V_{DD}$ level required by the MC68HC11 coresonds to a logic low on the MC68HC24. The V_{DD} level required by the MC68HC11 corresponds to a logic high on the MC68HC24. In normal operation, the special test mode is not used and the mode pin on both the MC68HC11 and the MC68HC24 can be tied to V_{DD}.

STATE AFTER RESET

When a low level is sensed on the $\overline{RESET}$ pin, the MC68HC24 enters the reset state. Most of the registers and control bits are forced to a specific state during reset and, if a user requires a different configuration, he must write the desired values into these registers in his initialization software. For detailed information about the options available, see the **INTERNAL REGISTER DESCRIPTION** section.

Note that $\overline{RESET}$ is synchronized to the system clock (E) before being used internally. For this reason, $\overline{RESET}$ must be held low for a minimum of two E-clock cycles to be recognized. Once recognized, the peripheral is initialized as described below.

Most of the configuration state after reset is indepedent of the selected operating mode. The STAF, STAI, and HNDS bits in the PIOC register are initialized to zeros so that no interrupt is pending or enabled and the simple strobed mode (rather than full handshake modes) of parallel I/O is selected. The CWOM bit is initialized to zero (Port C not operating in wired-OR mode). Port C is initialized as a general purpose, high-impedance input port (DDRC equals $00), STRA as an edge-sensitive strobe input, and the active edge is initially configured to detect rising edges (EGA bit set to one by $\overline{RESET}$). The STRB strobe output is initially a zero (INVB bit is initialized to one), while Port B is initialized with all outputs forced low.

The SMOD and IRV bits in the HPRIO register reflect the status of the MODE input at the rising edge of $\overline{RESET}$. Reset also deselects the chip and forces the multiplexed address/data bus to high impedance inputs.

MODES OF OPERATION

SPECIAL TEST MODE

The special test mode is selected with MODE equal to zero at the rising of edge of RESET. Initialization into this mode loads HPRIO with $50 (SMOD and IRV equal one) and disables the INIT register write-protect mechanism.

While in special test mode (SMOD bit equals one), the INIT register write-protect mechanism is overridden and INIT remains writable as long as SMOD remains one. When SMOD is written to a zero (to enter the normal operating mode), the write-protect mechanism is enabled. One additional write is allowed after entering normal operating mode regardless of the number of writes performed while in the special test mode.

The reset state of IRV is one in the special test mode. An attempted read of either the INIT or HPRIO register with IRV equal to one will leave the data bus in a high impedance state with the output buffers disabled. If IRV equals zero, the data buffers are enabled and the contents of the selected register are placed on the data bus. The IRV bit is writable only one

time while in the special test mode. Entering the normal mode forces the IRV bit to zero, enabling the data bus output buffers on reads of these two addresses. Table 1 summarizes the chip select options.

TABLE 1 — MC68HC24 CHIP SELECT
ACTION SUMMARY

$\overline{CS}$	IRV	Action Taken
0	0	Chip selected. HPRIO & INIT reads enabled.
0	1	Chip selected. HPRIO & INIT reads disabled.
1	X	Chip not selected.

NORMAL MODE

Normal mode is selected when the MODE input is at a logic high level at the rising edge of $\overline{RESET}$. The HPRIO register is initialized to $00 (SMOD and IRV equal zero). The INIT register write-protect mechanism is enabled, allowing only a single write to INIT. Reads of both the INIT and HPRIO register enable the output buffers, thus providing visibility into the contents of these registers. The HPRIO register is write-protected while in the normal mode. A reset sequence must be initiated to change the contents of this register.

NOTE

A write to the INIT register must be included in the initialization software whether or not the registers are to be relocated. This write will ensure that an accidental write to the register at a later time will not cause the registers to be remapped. THIS IS ONE OF THE FUNCTIONAL DIFFERENCES BETWEEN THE MC68HC11 PORTS AND THE MC68HC24 IMPLEMENTATION.

MC68HC11 AND MC68HC24 OPERATIONAL DIFFERENCES

INIT REGISTER WRITE-PROTECT MECHANISM

The MC68HC11 INIT register write-protect mechanism automatically disables writes to the INIT register 64 E-clock cycles after the rising edge of $\overline{RESET}$. The MC68HC24 write-protect circuitry IS NOT TIME DEPENDENT. Only a write to the INIT register will disable further writes. Both the MC68HC11 and MC68HC24 INIT registers can be written repeatedly in the special test mode of operation (see the **SPECIAL TEST MODE** section) or once in the normal mode.

This difference dictates that the user should not rely on the timeout feature of the MC68HC11 to write-protect the INIT register if he plans to utilize the same software with the MC68HC24. Instead, a write to the INIT register should be done during initialization, even if the remapping feature is not going to be used.

STRA PULSE WIDTH

Due to differences in implementation technology, the MC68HC24 incorporates an additional level of synchronization (over the MC68HC11) on the STRA input. Under normal

operating conditions, the end user will be unaware of this anomaly. Only systems which continually strobe new data into PORTCL are affected.

In order to allow the STRA signal to propagate through the internal feedback mechanism, a minimum delay of two E-clock cycles between active edges has been specified. This delay should not concern most users, since the time required to acknowledge the receipt of data and to read the data is much greater than two cycles.

STRB SYNCHRONIZATION

The MC68HC11 synchronizes changes of Port B, Port C, and STRB data to an internal quadrature clock. This method of implementation makes internal buffer delays transparent to the end user. This internal clock is generated from the 4X clock, and as a result, cannot be duplicated by the MC68HC24. Port B and Port C data are synchronized to the E-clock and become valid t_{PWD} *after* the falling edge of E instead of during the setup time before E.

The most noticeable change involves STRB. The STRB signal is synchronized to the rising edge of E instead of the quadrature clock as in the MC68HC11. At slow clock rates (much less than 1 MHz), the delay between valid data on the port pins and the assertion of STRB could be considerable.

PACKAGE DIMENSIONS

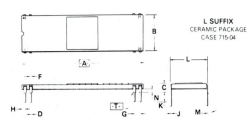

L SUFFIX
CERAMIC PACKAGE
CASE 715-04

DIM	MILLIMETERS		INCHES	
---	MIN	MAX	MIN	MAX
A	50.29	51.31	1.980	2.020
B	14.63	15.49	0.576	0.610
C	2.79	4.32	0.110	0.170
D	0.38	0.53	0.015	0.021
F	0.76	1.52	0.030	0.060
G	2.54 BSC		0.100 BSC	
J	0.20	0.33	0.008	0.013
K	2.54	4.57	0.100	0.180
L	14.99	15.65	0.590	0.616
M	–	10°	–	10°
N	1.02	1.52	0.040	0.060

NOTES:
1. DIMENSION -A- IS DATUM.
2. POSITIONAL TOLERANCE FOR LEADS:

⊕ | 0.25 (0.010) Ⓜ | T | A Ⓜ |

3. -T- IS SEATING PLANE.
4. DIMENSION "L" TO CENTER OF LEADS WHEN FORMED PARALLEL.
5. DIMENSIONING AND TOLERANCING PER ANSI Y14.5, 1973.

MOTOROLA *Semiconductor Products Inc.*

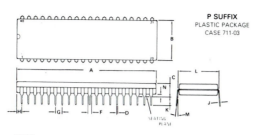

P SUFFIX
PLASTIC PACKAGE
CASE 711-03

DIM	MILLIMETERS		INCHES	
	MIN	MAX	MIN	MAX
A	51.69	52.45	2.035	2.065
B	13.72	14.22	0.540	0.560
C	3.94	5.08	0.155	0.200
D	0.36	0.56	0.014	0.022
F	1.02	1.52	0.040	0.060
G	2.54 BSC		0.100 BSC	
H	1.65	2.16	0.065	0.085
J	0.20	0.38	0.008	0.015
K	2.92	3.43	0.115	0.135
L	15.24 BSC		0.600 BSC	
M	0°	15°	0°	15°
N	0.51	1.02	0.020	0.040

NOTES:
1. POSITIONAL TOLERANCE OF LEADS (D),
   SHALL BE WITHIN 0.25 mm (0.010) AT
   MAXIMUM MATERIAL CONDITION, IN
   RELATION TO SEATING PLANE AND
   EACH OTHER.
2. DIMENSION L TO CENTER OF LEADS
   WHEN FORMED PARALLEL.
3. DIMENSION B DOES NOT INCLUDE
   MOLD FLASH.

FN SUFFIX
PCC QUAD PACKAGE
PRELIMINARY MECHANICAL DETAIL

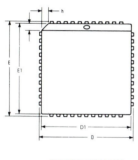

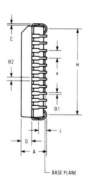

DIM	MILLIMETERS		INCHES	
	MIN	MAX	MIN	MAX
A	4.24	4.50	1.67	1.77
B1	0.33	0.53	0.013	0.021
B2	0.66	0.81	0.026	0.032
C	0.13	0.38	0.005	0.015
D	17.45	17.60	0.687	0.693
D1	16.51	16.66	0.650	0.656
E	17.45	17.60	0.687	0.693
E1	16.51	16.66	0.650	0.656
e	1.27 BSC		0.050 BSC	
H	15.75 BSC		0.620 BSC	
h	1.07	1.22	0.042	0.048
J	1.07	1.22	0.42	0.48
L	0.64	1.02	0.025	0.040
Q	1.78	2.03	0.070	0.080

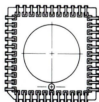

Ⓜ **MOTOROLA** *Semiconductor Products Inc.*

3501 ED BLUESTEIN BLVD., AUSTIN, TEXAS 78721 ● A SUBSIDIARY OF MOTOROLA INC.

A18615 PRINTED IN USA 2-85 IMPERIAL LITHO C28659 18,000   AD11046

Interrupt Vector Flowcharts

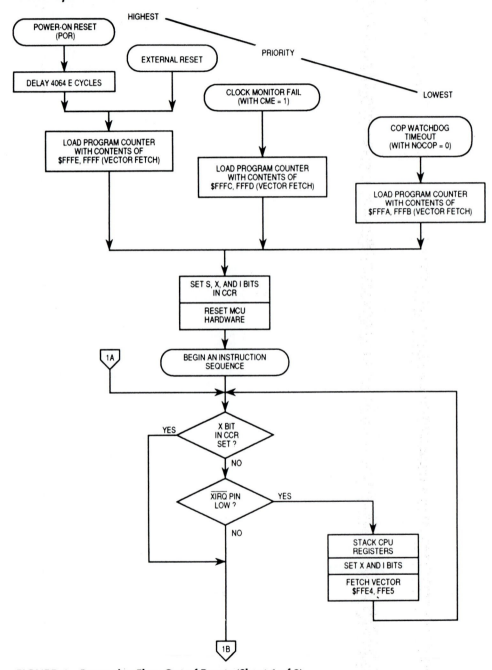

FIGURE 1   Processing Flow Out of Resets (Sheet 1 of 2)

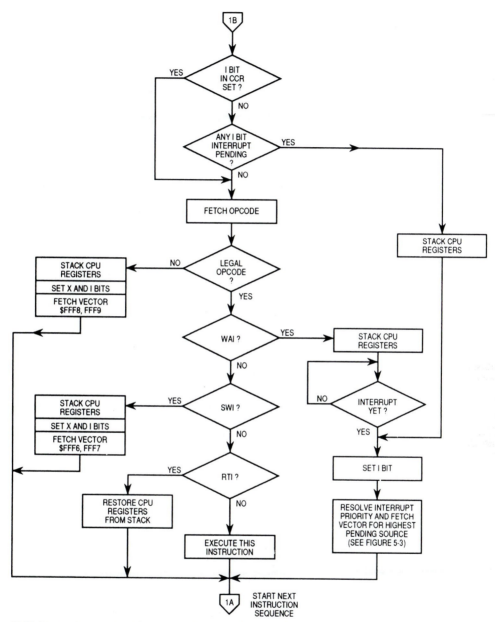

FIGURE 1 Processing Flow Out of Resets (Sheet 2 of 2)

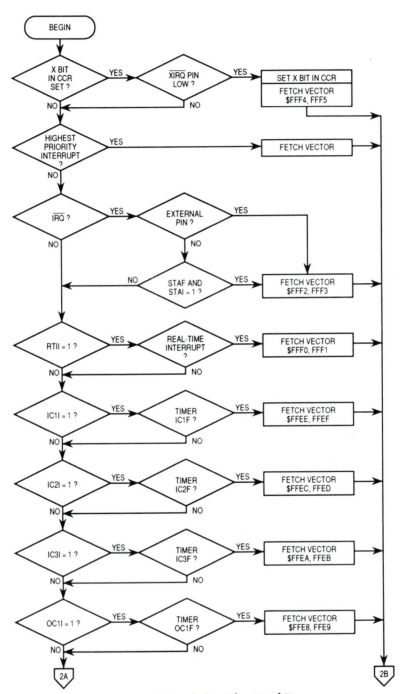

FIGURE 2   Interrupt Priority Resolution (Sheet 1 of 2)

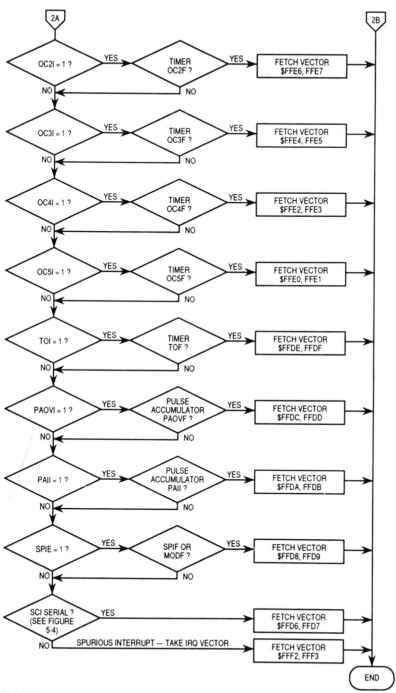

FIGURE 2   Interrupt Priority Resolution (Sheet 2 of 2)

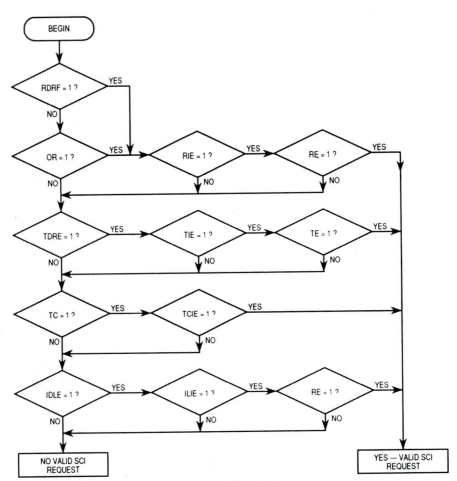

FIGURE 3   Interrupt Source Resolution within SCI

ASCII Character Set

Most Significant Bits
$b_7\ b_6\ b_5$

	Hex Codes →	**0** 000	**1** 001	**2** 010	**3** 011	**4** 100	**5** 101	**6** 110	**7** 111
0000	0	NUL	DLE	SP	0	@	P	`	p
0001	1	SOH	DC1	!	1	A	Q	a	q
0010	2	STX	DC2	"	2	B	R	b	r
0011	3	ETX	DC3	#	3	C	S	c	s
0100	4	EOT	DC4	$	4	D	T	d	t
0101	5	ENQ	NAK	%	5	E	U	e	u
0110	6	ACK	SYN	&	6	F	V	f	v
0111	7	BEL	ETB	'	7	G	W	g	w
1000	8	BS	CAN	(	8	H	X	h	x
1001	9	HT	EM	)	9	I	Y	i	y
1010	A	LF	SUB	*	:	J	Z	j	z
1011	B	VT	ESC	+	;	K	[	k	{
1100	C	FF	FS	,	<	L	\	l	|
1101	D	CR	GS	–	=	M	]	m	}
1110	E	SO	RS	.	>	N	^	n	~
1111	F	SI	US	/	?	O	—	o	DEL

Least Significant Bits $b_4\ b_3\ b_2\ b_1$

OP-07 Operational Amplifier

FEATURES

- **Low V_{OS}** .... 25μV Max
- **Low V_{OS} Drift** .... 0.6μV/°C Max
- **Ultra-Stable vs Time** .... 1.0μV/Month Max
- **Low Noise** .... 0.6V_{p-p} Max
- **Wide Input Voltage Range** .... ±14V
- **Wide Supply Voltage Range** .... ±3V to ±18V
- **Fits 725, 108A/308A, 741, AD510 Sockets**
- **125°C Temperature-Tested Dice**

ORDERING INFORMATION †

$T_A = +25°C$ V_{OS} MAX (μV)	PACKAGE				OPERATING TEMPERATURE RANGE
	TO-99	CERDIP 8-PIN	PLASTIC 8-PIN	LCC 20-CONTACT	
25	OP07AJ*	OP07AZ*	—	—	MIL
75	OP07EJ	OP07EZ	OP07EP	—	COM
75	OP07J*	OP07Z*	—	OP07RC/883	MIL
150	OP07CJ	OP07CZ	OP07CP	—	XIND
150	—	—	OP07CS††	—	XIND
150	OP07DJ	—	OP07DP	—	XIND

* For devices processed in total compliance to MIL-STD-883, add /883 after part number. Consult factory for 883 data sheet.

† Burn-in is available on commercial and industrial temperature range parts in CerDIP, plastic DIP, and TO-can packages.

†† For availability and burn-in information on SO and PLCC packages, contact your local sales office.

GENERAL DESCRIPTION

The OP-07 has very low input offset voltage (25μV max for OP-07A) which is obtained by trimming at the wafer stage. These low offset voltages generally eliminate any need for external nulling. The OP-07 also features low input bias current (±2nA for OP-07A) and high open-loop gain (300V/mV for OP-07A). The low offsets and high open-loop gain make the OP-07 particularly useful for high-gain instrumentation applications.

The wide input voltage range of ±13V minimum combined with high CMRR of 110dB (OP-07A) and high input impedace provides high accuracy in the noninverting circuit configuration. Excellent linearity and gain accuracy can be maintained even at high closed-loop gains.

Stability of offsets and gain with time or variations in temperture is excellent. The accuracy and stability of the OP-07, even at high gain, combined with the freedom from external nulling have made the OP-07 a new industry standard for instrumentation and military applications.

The OP-07 is available in five standard performance grades. The OP-07A and the OP-07 are specified for operation over the full military range of −55°C to +125°C; the OP-07E is specified for operation over the 0°C to +70°C range, and OP-07C and D over the −40°C to +85°C temperature range.

The OP-07 is available in hermetically-sealed TO-99 metal can or ceramic 8-pin Mini-DIP, and in epoxy 8-pin Mini-DIP. It is a direct replacement for 725, 108A, and OP-05 amplifiers; 741-types may be directly replaced by removing the 741's nulling potentiometer. The OP-207, a dual OP-07, is available for applications requiring close matching of two OP-07 amplifiers. For improved specifications, see the OP-77/OP-177.

PIN CONNECTIONS

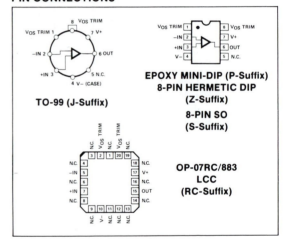

SIMPLIFIED SCHEMATIC

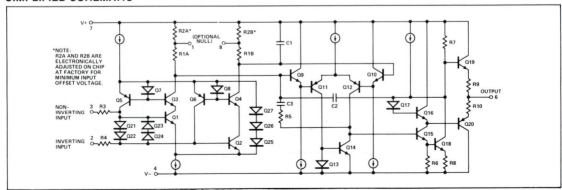

ABSOLUTE MAXIMUM RATINGS (Note 1)

Supply Voltage .... ±22V
Differential Input Voltage .... ±30V
Input Voltage (Note 2) .... ±22V
Output Short-Circuit Duration .... Indefinite
Storage Temperature Range
  J, RC and Z Packages .... −65°C to +150°C
  P Package .... −65°C to +125°C
Operating Temperature Range
  OP-07A, OP-07, OP-07RC .... −55°C to +125°C
  OP-07E .... 0°C to +70°C
  OP-07C, OP-07D .... −40°C to +85°C
Lead Temperature (Soldering, 60 sec) .... +300°C
Junction Temperature (T_j) .... +150°C

PACKAGE TYPE	Θ_{JA} (Note 3)	Θ_{JC}	UNITS
TO-99 (J)	150	18	°C/W
8-Pin Hermetic DIP (Z)	148	16	°C/W
8-Pin Plastic DIP (P)	103	43	°C/W
20-Contact LCC	98	38	°C/W
8-Pin SO (S)	158	43	°C/W

NOTES:
1. Absolute maximum ratings apply to both DICE and packaged parts, unless otherwise noted.
2. For supply voltages less than ±22V, the absolute maximum input voltage is equal to the supply voltage.
3. Θ_{JA} is specified for worst case mounting conditions, i.e., Θ_{JA} is specified for device in socket for TO, CerDIP, P-DIP, and LCC packages; Θ_{JA} is specified for device soldered to printed circuit board for SO package.

ELECTRICAL CHARACTERISTICS at $V_S = \pm 15V$, $T_A = 25°$ C, unless otherwise noted.

PARAMETER	SYMBOL	CONDITIONS	OP-07A MIN	OP-07A TYP	OP-07A MAX	OP-07 MIN	OP-07 TYP	OP-07 MAX	UNITS
Input Offset Voltage	V_{OS}	(Note 1)	—	10	25	—	30	75	µV
Long-Term Input Offset Voltage Stability	ΔV_{OS}/Time	(Note 2)	—	0.2	1.0	—	0.2	1.0	µV/Mo
Input Offset Current	I_{OS}		—	0.3	2.0	—	0.4	2.8	nA
Input Bias Current	I_B		—	±0.7	±2.0	—	±1.0	±3.0	nA
Input Noise Voltage	e_{np-p}	0.1Hz to 10Hz (Note 3)	—	0.35	0.6	—	0.35	0.6	µV$_{p-p}$
Input Noise Voltage Density	e_n	f_O = 10Hz (Note 3)	—	10.3	18.0	—	10.3	18.0	nV/$\sqrt{Hz}$
		f_O = 100Hz (Note 3)	—	10.0	13.0	—	10.0	13.0	
		f_O = 1000Hz (Note 3)	—	9.6	11.0	—	9.6	11.0	
Input Noise Current	i_{np-p}	0.1Hz to 10Hz (Note 3)	—	14	30	—	14	30	pA$_{p-p}$
Input Noise Current Density	i_n	f_O = 10Hz (Note 3)	—	0.32	0.80	—	0.32	0.80	pA/$\sqrt{Hz}$
		f_O = 100Hz (Note 3)	—	0.14	0.23	—	0.14	0.23	
		f_O = 1000Hz (Note 3)	—	0.12	0.17	—	0.12	0.17	
Input Resistance — Differential-Mode	R_{IN}	(Note 4)	30	80	—	20	60	—	MΩ
Input Resistance — Common-Mode	R_{INCM}		—	200	—	—	200	—	GΩ
Input Voltage Range	IVR		±13	±14	—	±13	±14	—	V
Common-Mode Rejection Ratio	CMRR	$V_{CM} = \pm 13V$	110	126	—	110	126	—	dB
Power Supply Rejection Ratio	PSRR	$V_S = \pm 3V$ to ±18V	—	4	10	—	4	10	µV/V
Large-Signal Voltage Gain	A_{VO}	$R_L \geq 2k\Omega$, $V_O = \pm 10V$	300	500	—	200	500	—	V/mV
		$R_L \geq 500\Omega$, $V_O = \pm 0.5V$, $V_S = \pm 3V$ (Note 4)	150	400	—	150	400	—	
Output Voltage Swing	V_O	$R_L \geq 10k\Omega$	±12.5	±13.0	—	±12.5	±13.0	—	V
		$R_L \geq 2k\Omega$	±12.0	±12.8	—	±12.0	±12.8	—	
		$R_L \geq 1k\Omega$	±10.5	±12.0	—	±10.5	±12.0	—	
Slew Rate	SR	$R_L \geq 2k\Omega$ (Note 3)	0.1	0.3	—	0.1	0.3	—	V/µs
Closed-Loop Bandwidth	BW	$A_{VCL} = +1$ (Note 3)	0.4	0.6	—	0.4	0.6	—	MHz
Open-Loop Output Resistance	R_O	$V_O = 0$, $I_O = 0$	—	60	—	—	60	—	Ω
Power Consumption	P_d	$V_S = \pm 15V$, No Load	—	75	120	—	75	120	mW
		$V_S = \pm 3V$, No Load	—	4	6	—	4	6	
Offset Adjustment Range		$R_P = 20k\Omega$	—	±4	—	—	±4	—	mV

NOTES:
1. OP-07A grade V_{OS} is measured approximately one minute after application of power. For all other grades V_{OS} is measured approximately 0.5 seconds after application of power.
2. Long-Term Input Offset Voltage Stability refers to the averaged trend line of V_{OS} vs. Time over extended periods after the first 30 days of operation.

Excluding the initial hour of operation, changes in V_{OS} during the first 30 operating days are typically 2.5µV — refer to typical performance curves. Parameter is sample tested.
3. Sample tested.
4. Guaranteed by design.

ELECTRICAL CHARACTERISTICS at $V_S = \pm 15V$, $-55°C \leq T_A \leq +125°C$, unless otherwise noted.

PARAMETER	SYMBOL	CONDITIONS	OP-07A MIN	OP-07A TYP	OP-07A MAX	OP-07 MIN	OP-07 TYP	OP-07 MAX	UNITS
Input Offset Voltage	V_{OS}	(Note 1)	—	25	60	—	60	200	µV
Average Input Offset Voltage Drift Without External Trim	TCV_{OS}	(Note 2)	—	0.2	0.6	—	0.3	1.3	µV/°C
With External Trim	TCV_{OSn}	$R_P = 20k\Omega$ (Note 3)	—	0.2	0.6	—	0.3	1.3	µV/°C
Input Offset Current	I_{OS}		—	0.8	4	—	1.2	5.6	nA
Average Input Offset Current Drift	TCI_{OS}	(Note 2)	—	5	25	—	8	50	pA/°C
Input Bias Current	I_B		—	±1	±4	—	±2	±6	nA
Average Input Bias Current Drift	TCI_B	(Note 2)	—	8	25	—	13	50	pA/°C
Input Voltage Range	IVR		±13	±13.5	—	±13	±13.5	—	V
Common-Mode Rejection Ratio	CMRR	$V_{CM} = \pm 13V$	106	123	—	106	123	—	dB
Power Supply Rejection Ratio	PSRR	$V_S = \pm 3V$ to $\pm 18V$	—	5	20	—	5	20	µV/V
Large-Signal Voltage Gain	A_{VO}	$R_L \geq 2k\Omega$, $V_O = \pm 10V$	200	400	—	150	400	—	V/mV
Output Voltage Swing	V_O	$R_L \geq 2k\Omega$	±12	±12.6	—	±12	±12.6	—	V

NOTES:
1. OP-07A grade V_{OS} is measured approximately one minute after application of power. For all other grades V_{OS} is measured approximately 0.5 seconds after application of power.
2. Sample tested.
3. Guaranteed by design.

TYPICAL OFFSET VOLTAGE TEST CIRCUIT

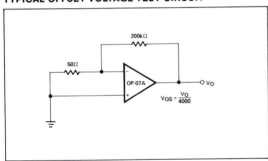

TYPICAL LOW-FREQUENCY NOISE TEST CIRCUIT

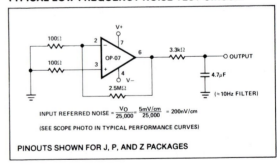

OPTIONAL OFFSET NULLING CIRCUIT

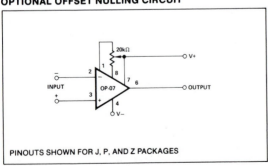

BURN-IN CIRCUIT

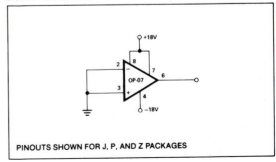

ELECTRICAL CHARACTERISTICS at $V_S = \pm 15V$, $T_A = 25°C$, unless otherwise noted.

PARAMETER	SYMBOL	CONDITIONS	OP-07E			OP-07C			OP-07D			UNITS
			MIN	TYP	MAX	MIN	TYP	MAX	MIN	TYP	MAX	
Input Offset Voltage	V_{OS}	(Note 1)	—	30	75	—	60	150	—	60	150	μV
Long-Term V_{OS} Stability	V_{OS}/Time	(Note 2)	—	0.3	1.5	—	0.4	2.0	—	0.5	3.0	μV/Mo
Input Offset Current	I_{OS}		—	0.5	3.8	—	0.8	6.0	—	0.8	6.0	nA
Input Bias Current	I_B		—	± 1.2	± 4.0	—	± 1.8	± 7.0	—	± 2.0	± 12	nA
Input Noise Voltage	e_{np-p}	0.1Hz to 10Hz (Note 3)	—	0.35	0.6	—	0.38	0.65	—	0.38	0.65	μV_{p-p}
Input Noise Voltage Density	e_n	$f_O = 10$Hz $f_O = 100$Hz (Note 3) $f_O = 1000$Hz	— — —	10.3 10.0 9.6	18.0 13.0 11.0	— — —	10.5 10.2 9.8	20.0 13.5 11.5	— — —	10.5 10.3 9.8	20.0 13.5 11.5	nV/$\sqrt{\text{Hz}}$
Input Noise Current	i_{np-p}	0.1Hz to 10Hz (Note 3)	—	14	30	—	15	35	—	15	35	pA$_{p-p}$
Input Noise Current Density	i_n	$f_O = 10$Hz $f_O = 100$Hz (Note 3) $f_O = 1000$Hz	— — —	0.32 0.14 0.12	0.80 0.23 0.17	— — —	0.35 0.15 0.13	0.90 0.27 0.18	— — —	0.35 0.15 0.13	0.90 0.27 0.18	pA/$\sqrt{\text{Hz}}$
Input Resistance — Differential-Mode	R_{IN}	(Note 4)	15	50	—	8	33	—	7	31	—	MΩ
Input Resistance — Common-Mode	R_{INCM}		—	160	—	—	120	—	—	120	—	GΩ
Input Voltage Range	IVR		± 13	± 14	—	± 13	± 14	—	± 13	± 14	—	V
Common-Mode Rejection Ratio	CMRR	$V_{CM} = \pm 13$V	106	123	—	100	120	—	94	110	—	dB
Power Supply Rejection Ratio	PSRR	$V_S = \pm 3$V to ± 18V	—	5	20	—	7	32	—	7	32	μV/V
Large-Signal Voltage Gain	A_{VO}	$R_L \geq 2k\Omega$, $V_O = \pm 10$V $R_L \geq 500\Omega$ $V_O = \pm 0.5$V $V_S = \pm 3$V (Note 4)	200 150	500 400	— —	120 100	400 400	— —	120 —	400 400	— —	V/mV
Output Voltage Swing	V_O	$R_L \geq 10k\Omega$ $R_L \geq 2k\Omega$ $R_L \geq 1k\Omega$	± 12.5 ± 12.0 ± 10.5	± 13.0 ± 12.8 ± 12.0	— — —	± 12.0 ± 11.5 —	± 13.0 ± 12.8 ± 12.0	— — —	± 12.0 ± 11.5 —	± 13.0 ± 12.8 ± 12.0	— — —	V
Slew Rate	SR	$R_L \geq 2k\Omega$ (Note 3)	0.1	0.3	—	0.1	0.3	—	0.1	0.3	—	V/μs
Closed-Loop Bandwidth	BW	$A_{VCL} = +1$ (Note 5)	0.4	0.6	—	0.4	0.6	—	0.4	0.6	—	MHz
Open-Loop Output Resistance	R_O	$V_O = 0$, $I_O = 0$	—	60	—	—	60	—	—	60	—	Ω
Power Consumption	P_d	$V_S = \pm 15$V, No Load $V_S = \pm 3$V, No Load	— —	75 4	120 6	— —	80 4	150 8	— —	80 4	150 8	mW
Offset Adjustment Range		$R_P = 20k\Omega$	—	± 4	—	—	± 4	—	—	± 4	—	mV

NOTES:
1. Input Offset Voltage measurements are performed by automated test equipment approximately 0.5 seconds after application of power.
2. Long-Term Input Offset Voltage Stability refers to the averaged trend line of V_{OS} vs. Time over extended periods after the first 30 days of operation. Excluding the initial hour of operation, changes in V_{OS} during the first 30 operating days are typically 2.5μV — refer to typical performance curves. Parameter is sample tested.
3. Sample tested.
4. Guaranteed by design.
5. Guaranteed but not tested.

ELECTRICAL CHARACTERISTICS at $V_S = \pm15V$, $0°C \le T_A \le +70°C$ for OP-07E, and $-40°C \le T_A \le +85°C$ for OP-07C/D, unless otherwise noted.

PARAMETER	SYMBOL	CONDITIONS	OP-07E			OP-07C			OP-07D			UNITS
			MIN	TYP	MAX	MIN	TYP	MAX	MIN	TYP	MAX	
Input Offset Voltage	V_{OS}	(Note 1)	—	45	130	—	85	250	—	85	250	μV
Average Input Offset Voltage Drift Without External Trim	TCV_{OS}	(Note 3)	—	0.3	1.3	—	0.5	1.8	—	0.7	2.5	$\mu V/°C$
With External Trim	TCV_{OSn}	$R_P = 20k\Omega$ (Note 3)	—	0.3	1.3	—	0.4	1.6	—	0.7	2.5	$\mu V/°C$
Input Offset Current	I_{OS}		—	0.9	5.3	—	1.6	8.0	—	1.6	8.0	nA
Average Input Offset Current Drift	TCI_{OS}	(Note 2)	—	8	35	—	12	50	—	12	50	pA/°C
Input Bias Current	I_B		—	±1.5	±5.5	—	±2.2	±9.0	—	±3.0	±14	nA
Average Input Bias Current Drift	TCI_B	(Note 2)	—	13	35	—	18	50	—	18	50	pA/°C
Input Voltage Range	IVR		±13.0	±13.5	—	±13.0	±13.5	—	±13.0	±13.5	—	V
Common-Mode Rejection Ratio	CMRR	$V_{CM} = \pm13V$	103	123	—	97	120	—	94	106	—	dB
Power Supply Rejection Ratio	PSRR	$V_S = \pm3V$ to $\pm18V$	—	7	32	—	10	51	—	10	51	$\mu V/V$
Large-Signal Voltage Gain	A_{VO}	$R_L \ge 2k\Omega$ $V_O = \pm10V$	180	450	—	100	400	—	100	400	—	V/mV
Output Voltage Swing	V_O	$R_L \ge 2k\Omega$	±12	±12.6	—	±11	±12.6	—	±11	±12.6	—	V

NOTES:
1. Input offset voltage measurements are performed by automated test equipment approximately 0.5 seconds after application of power.
2. Sample tested.
3. Guaranteed by design.

DICE CHARACTERISTICS (125°C TESTED DICE AVAILABLE)

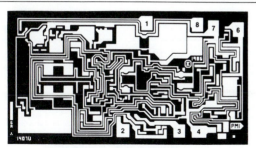

DIE SIZE 0.100 × 0.055 inch, 5500 sq. mils
(2.54 × 1.40 mm, 3.56 sq. mm)

1. BALANCE
2. INVERTING INPUT
3. NONINVERTING INPUT
4. V−
6. OUTPUT
7. V+
8. BALANCE

WAFER TEST LIMITS at $V_S = \pm 15V$, $T_A = 25°C$ for OP-07N, OP-07G and OP-07GR devices; $T_A = 125°C$ for OP-07NT and OP-07GT devices, unless otherwise noted.

PARAMETER	SYMBOL	CONDITIONS	OP-07NT LIMIT	OP-07N LIMIT	OP-07GT LIMIT	OP-07G LIMIT	OP-07GR LIMIT	UNITS
Input Offset Voltage	V_{OS}		140	40	210	80	150	µV MAX
Input Offset Current	I_{OS}		4.0	2.0	5.6	2.8	6.0	nA MAX
Input Bias Current	I_B		±4	±2	±6	±3	±7	nA MAX
Input Resistance Differential-Mode	R_{IN}	(Note 2)	—	20	—	20	8	MΩ MIN
Input Voltage Range	IVR		±13	±13	±13	±13	±13	V MIN
Common-Mode Rejection Ratio	CMRR	$V_{CM} = \pm 13V$	100	110	100	110	100	dB MIN
Power Supply Rejection Ratio	PSRR	$V_S = \pm 3V$ to $\pm 18V$	20	10	20	10	30	µV/V MAX
Output Voltage Swing	V_O	$R_L = 10k\Omega$ $R_L = 2k\Omega$ $R_L = 1k\Omega$	— ±12.0 —	±12.5 ±12.0 ±10.5	— ±12.0 —	±12.0 ±11.5 ±10.5	±12.0 ±11.5 —	V MIN
Large-Signal Voltage Gain	A_{VO}	$R_L = 2k\Omega$ $V_O = \pm 10V$	200	200	150	120	120	V/mV MIN
Differential Input Voltage			±30	±30	±30	±30	±30	V MAX
Power Consumption	P_d	$V_{OUT} = 0V$	—	120	—	120	150	mW MAX

NOTES:
1. For 25°C characteristics of OP-07NT and OP-07GT, see OP-07N and OP-07G characteristics, respectively.

2. Guaranteed by design.

Electrical tests are performed at wafer probe to the limits shown. Due to variations in assembly methods and normal yield loss, yield after packaging is not guaranteed for standard product dice. Consult factory to negotiate specifications based on dice lot qualification through sample lot assembly and testing.

TYPICAL ELECTRICAL CHARACTERISTICS at $V_S = \pm 15V$, $T_A = +25°C$, unless otherwise noted.

PARAMETER	SYMBOL	CONDITIONS	OP-07NT TYPICAL	OP-07N TYPICAL	OP-07GT TYPICAL	OP-07G TYPICAL	OP-07GR TYPICAL	UNITS
Average Input Offset Voltage Drift	TCV_{OS}	$R_S = 50\Omega$	0.2	0.2	0.3	0.3	0.7	µV/°C
Nulled Input Offset Voltage Drift	TCV_{OSn}	$R_S = 50\Omega$, $R_P = 20k\Omega$	0.2	0.2	0.3	0.3	0.7	µV/°C
Average Input Offset Current Drift	TCI_{OS}		5	5	8	8	12	pA/°C
Slew Rate	SR	$R_L \geq 2k\Omega$	0.3	0.3	0.3	0.3	0.3	V/µs
Closed-Loop Bandwidth	BW	$A_{VCL} = +1$	0.6	0.6	0.6	0.6	0.6	MHz

TYPICAL PERFORMANCE CHARACTERISTICS

OPEN-LOOP GAIN vs TEMPERATURE

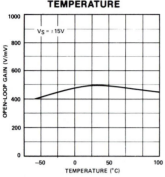

OFFSET VOLTAGE CHANGE DUE TO THERMAL SHOCK

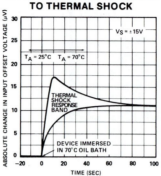

WARM-UP DRIFT

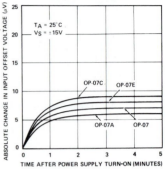

MAXIMUM ERROR vs SOURCE RESISTANCE

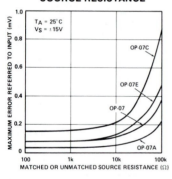

MAXIMUM ERROR vs SOURCE RESISTANCE

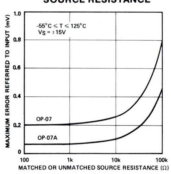

MAXIMUM ERROR vs SOURCE RESISTANCE

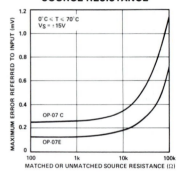

INPUT BIAS CURRENT vs DIFFERENTIAL INPUT VOLTAGE

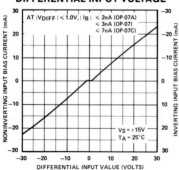

INPUT BIAS CURRENT vs TEMPERATURE

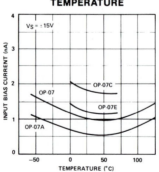

INPUT OFFSET CURRENT vs TEMPERATURE

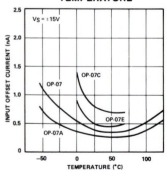

TYPICAL PERFORMANCE CHARACTERISTICS

OP-07 LOW FREQUENCY NOISE

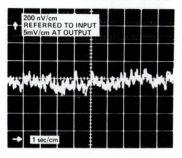

**TOTAL INPUT NOISE VOLTAGE
vs FREQUENCY**

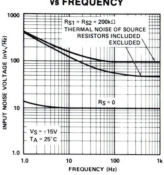

**INPUT WIDEBAND NOISE vs
BANDWIDTH (0.1Hz TO
FREQUENCY INDICATED)**

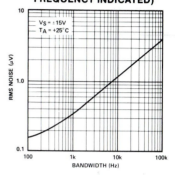

CMRR vs FREQUENCY

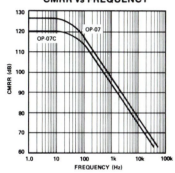

PSRR vs FREQUENCY

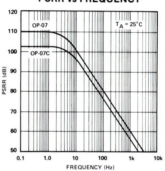

**OPEN-LOOP GAIN vs
POWER SUPPLY VOLTAGE**

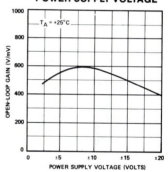

**OPEN-LOOP
FREQUENCY RESPONSE**

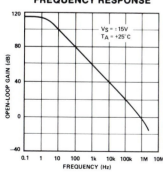

**CLOSED-LOOP RESPONSE
FOR VARIOUS
GAIN CONFIGURATIONS**

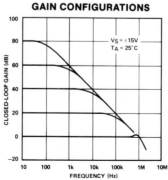

**MAXIMUM OUTPUT SWING
vs FREQUENCY**

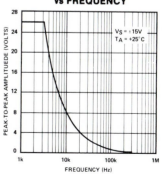

TYPICAL PERFORMANCE CHARACTERISTICS

MAXIMUM OUTPUT VOLTAGE vs LOAD RESISTANCE

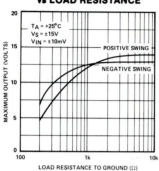

POWER CONSUMPTION vs POWER SUPPLY

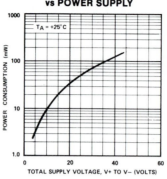

OUTPUT SHORT-CIRCUIT CURRENT vs TIME

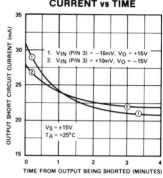

UNTRIMMED OFFSET VOLTAGE vs TEMPERATURE

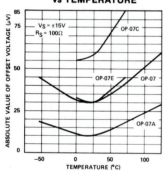

TRIMMED OFFSET VOLTAGE vs TEMPERATURE

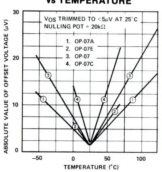

OFFSET VOLTAGE STABILITY vs TIME

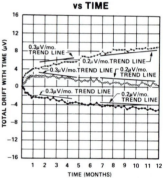

TYPICAL APPLICATIONS

HIGH SPEED, LOW V$_{OS}$, COMPOSITE AMPLIFIER

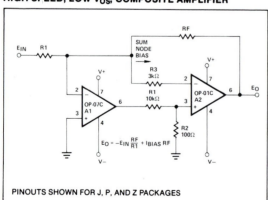

PINOUTS SHOWN FOR J, P, AND Z PACKAGES

ADJUSTMENT-FREE PRECISION SUMMING AMPLIFIER

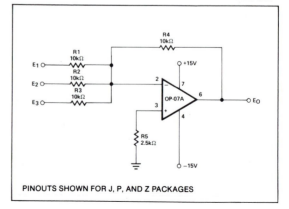

PINOUTS SHOWN FOR J, P, AND Z PACKAGES

AD590 Two-Terminal IC Temperature Transducer

FEATURES
Linear Current Output: 1μA/K
Wide Range: –55°C to +150°C
Probe Compatible Ceramic Sensor Package
Two-Terminal Device: Voltage In/Current Out
Laser Trimmed to ±0.5°C Calibration Accuracy (AD590M)
Excellent Linearity: ±0.3°C Over Full Range (AD590M)
Wide Power Supply Range: +4V to +30V
Sensor Isolation from Case
Low Cost

PIN DESIGNATIONS

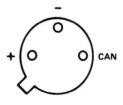

BOTTOM VIEW

PRODUCT DESCRIPTION

The AD590 is a two-terminal integrated circuit temperature transducer which produces an output current proportional to absolute temperature. For supply voltages between +4V and +30V the device acts as a high impedance, constant current regulator passing 1μA/K. Laser trimming of the chip's thin film resistors is used to calibrate the device to 298.2μA output at 298.2K (+25°C).

The AD590 should be used in any temperature sensing application below +150°C in which conventional electrical temperature sensors are currently employed. The inherent low cost of a monolithic integrated circuit combined with the elimination of support circuitry makes the AD590 an attractive alternative for many temperature measurement situations. Linearization circuitry, precision voltage amplifiers, resistance measuring circuitry and cold junction compensation are not needed in applying the AD590.

In addition to temperature measurement, applications include temperature compensation or correction of discrete components, biasing proportional to absolute temperature, flow rate measurement, level detection of fluids and anemometry. The AD590 is available in chip form making it suitable for hybrid circuits and fast temperature measurements in protected environments.

The AD590 is particularly useful in remote sensing applications. The device is insensitive to voltage drops over long lines due to its high impedance current output. Any well-insulated twisted pair is sufficient for operation hundreds of feet from the receiving circuitry. The output characteristics also make the AD590 easy to multiplex: the current can be switched by a CMOS multiplexer or the supply voltage can be switched by a logic gate output.

*Covered by Patent No. 4,123,698.

PRODUCT HIGHLIGHTS

1. The AD590 is a calibrated two terminal temperature sensor requiring only a dc voltage supply (+4V to +30V). Costly transmitters, filters, lead wire compensation and linearization circuits are all unnecessary in applying the device.

2. State-of-the-art laser trimming at the wafer level in conjunction with extensive final testing insures that AD590 units are easily interchangeable.

3. Superior interference rejection results from the output being a current rather than a voltage. In addition, power requirements are low (1.5mW's @ 5V @ +25°C). These features make the AD590 easy to apply as a remote sensor.

4. The high output impedance ($>10M\Omega$) provides excellent rejection of supply voltage drift and ripple. For instance, changing the power supply from 5V to 10V results in only a 1μA maximum current change, or 1°C equivalent error.

5. The AD590 is electrically durable: it will withstand a forward voltage up to 44V and a reverse voltage of 20V. Hence, supply irregularities or pin reversal will not damage the device.

One Technology Way; P. O. Box 9106; Norwood, MA 02062-9106 U.S.A.
Tel: 617/329-4700   Twx: 710/394-6577
Telex: 924491   Cables: ANALOG NORWOODMASS

■■■■ **Specifications** (@ +25°C and V_S = 5V Unless Otherwise Noted)

Model	AD590J			AD590K			Units
	Min	Typ	Max	Min	Typ	Max	
ABSOLUTE MAXIMUM RATINGS							
Forward Voltage (E+ to E−)			+44			+44	Volts
Reverse Voltage (E+ to E−)			−20			−20	Volts
Breakdown Voltage (Case to E+ or E−)			±200			±200	Volts
Rated Performance Temperature Range[1]	−55		+150	−55		+150	°C
Storage Temperature Range[1]	−65		+155	−65		+155	°C
Lead Temperature (Soldering, 10 sec)			+300			+300	°C
POWER SUPPLY							
Operating Voltage Range	+4		+30	+4		+30	Volts
OUTPUT							
Nominal Current Output @ +25°C (298.2K)		298.2			298.2		µA
Nominal Temperature Coefficient		1			1		µA/K
Calibration Error @ +25°C			±5.0			±2.5	°C
Absolute Error (over rated performance temperature range)							
Without External Calibration Adjustment			**±10**			**±5.5**	°C
With +25°C Calibration Error Set to Zero			**±3.0**			**±2.0**	°C
Nonlinearity			**±1.5**			**±0.8**	°C
Repeatability[2]			±0.1			±0.1	°C
Long Term Drift[3]			±0.1			±0.1	°C
Current Noise		40			40		pA/√Hz
Power Supply Rejection							
+4V≤V_S≤+5V		0.5			0.5		µA/V
+5V≤V_S≤+15V		0.2			0.2		µA/V
+15V≤V_S≤+30V		0.1			0.1		µA/V
Case Isolation to Either Lead		10^{10}			10^{10}		Ω
Effective Shunt Capacitance		100			100		pF
Electrical Turn-On Time		20			20		µs
Reverse Bias Leakage Current[4]							
(Reverse Voltage = 10V)		10			10		pA
PACKAGE OPTIONS							
TO-52 (H-03A)		AD590JH			AD590KH		
Flat Pack (F-2A)		AD590JF			AD590KF		

NOTES

[1]The AD590 has been used at −100°C and +200°C for short periods of measurement with no physical damage to the device. However, the absolute errors specified apply to only the rated performance temperature range.

[2]Maximum deviation between +25°C readings after temperature cycling between −55°C and +150°C; guaranteed not tested.

[3]Conditions: constant +5V, constant +125°C; guaranteed, not tested.

[4]Leakage current doubles every 10°C.

[5]See Section 20 for package outline information.

Specifications subject to change without notice.

Specifications shown in boldface are tested on all production units at final electrical test. Results from those tests are used to calculate outgoing quality levels. All min and max specifications are guaranteed, although only those shown in **boldface** are tested on all production units.

Model	AD590L			AD590M			
	Min	Typ	Max	Min	Typ	Max	Units
ABSOLUTE MAXIMUM RATINGS							
Forward Voltage (E + to E −)			+ 44			+ 44	Volts
Reverse Voltage (E + to E −)			− 20			− 20	Volts
Breakdown Voltage (Case to E + or E −)			± 200			± 200	Volts
Rated Performance Temperature Range[1]	− 55		+ 150	− 55		+ 150	°C
Storage Temperature Range[1]	− 65		+ 155	− 65		+ 155	°C
Lead Temperature (Soldering, 10 sec)			+ 300			+ 300	°C
POWER SUPPLY							
Operating Voltage Range	+ 4		+ 30	+ 4		+ 30	Volts
OUTPUT							
Nominal Current Output @ + 25°C (298.2K)		298.2			298.2		μA
Nominal Temperature Coefficient		1			1		μA/K
Calibration Error @ + 25°C			± 1.0			± 0.5	°C
Absolute Error (over rated performance temperature range)							
Without External Calibration Adjustment			± 3.0			± 1.7	°C
With + 25°C Calibration Error Set to Zero			± 1.6			± 1.0	°C
Nonlinearity			± 0.4			± 0.3	°C
Repeatability[2]			± 0.1			± 0.1	°C
Long Term Drift[3]			± 0.1			± 0.1	°C
Current Noise		40			40		pA√Hz
Power Supply Rejection							
+ 4V ≤ V_S ≤ + 5V		0.5			0.5		μA/V
+ 5V ≤ V_S ≤ + 15V		0.2			0.2		μA/V
+ 15V ≤ V_S ≤ + 30V		0.1			0.1		μA/V
Case Isolation to Either Lead		10^{10}			10^{10}		Ω
Effective Shunt Capacitance		100			100		pF
Electrical Turn-On Time		20			20		μs
Reverse Bias Leakage Current[4]							
(Reverse Voltage = 10V)		10			10		pA
PACKAGE OPTION							
TO-52 (H-03A)		AD590LH			AD590MH		
Flat Pack (F-2A)		AD590LF			AD590MF		

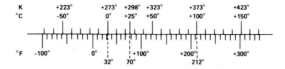

TEMPERATURE SCALE CONVERSION EQUATIONS

$$°C = \frac{5}{9} (°F - 32) \qquad K = °C + 273.15$$

$$°F = \frac{9}{5} °C + 32 \qquad °R = °F + 459.7$$

The 590H has 60µ inches of gold plating on its Kovar leads and Kovar header. A resistance welder is used to seal the nickel cap to the header. The AD590 chip is eutectically mounted to the header and ultrasonically bonded to with 1 MIL aluminum wire. Kovar composition: 53% iron nominal; 29% ±1% nickel; 17% ±1% cobalt; 0.65% manganese max; 0.20% silicon max; 0.10% aluminum max; 0.10% magnesium max; 0.10% zirconium max; 0.10% titanium max; 0.06% carbon max.

The 590F is a ceramic package with gold plating on its Kovar leads, Kovar lid, and chip cavity. Solder of 80/20 Au/Sn composition is used for the 1.5 mil thick solder ring under the lid. The chip cavity has a nickel underlay between the metalization and the gold plating. The AD590 chip is eutectically mounted in the chip cavity at 410°C and ultrasonically bonded to with 1 mil aluminum wire. Note that the chip is in direct contact with the ceramic base, not the metal lid. When using the AD590 in die form, the chip substrate must be kept electrically isolated, (floating), for correct circuit operation.

In the AD590, this PTAT voltage is converted to a PTAT current by low temperature coefficient thin film resistors. The total current of the device is then forced to be a multiple of this PTAT current. Referring to Figure 1, the schematic diagram of the AD590, Q8 and Q11 are the transistors that produce the PTAT voltage. R5 and R6 convert the voltage to current. Q10, whose collector current tracks the collector currents in Q9 and Q11, supplies all the bias and substrate leakage current for the rest of the circuit, forcing the total current to be PTAT. R5 and R6 are laser trimmed on the wafer to calibrate the device at +25°C.

Figure 2 shows the typical V−I characteristic of the circuit at +25°C and the temperature extremes.

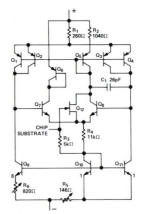

FIGURE 1   Schematic Diagram

METALIZATION DIAGRAM

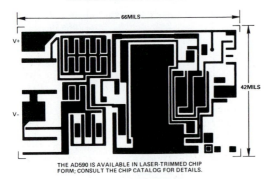

THE AD590 IS AVAILABLE IN LASER-TRIMMED CHIP FORM; CONSULT THE CHIP CATALOG FOR DETAILS.

CIRCUIT DESCRIPTION[1]

The AD590 uses a fundamental property of the silicon transistors from which it is made to realize its temperature proportional characteristic: if two identical transistors are operated at a constant ratio of collector current densities, r, then the difference in their base-emitter voltages will be $(kT/q)(\ln r)$. Since both k, Boltzman's constant and q, the charge of an electron, are constant, the resulting voltage is directly porportional to absolute temperature (PTAT).

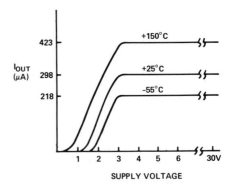

FIGURE 2   V−I Plot

[1] For a more detailed circuit description see M.P. Timko, "A Two-Terminal IC Temperature Transducer," IEEE J. Solid State Circuits, Vol. SC-11, p. 784-788, Dec. 1976.

EXPLANATION OF TEMPERATURE SENSOR SPECIFICATIONS

The way in which the AD590 is specified makes it easy to apply in a wide variety of different applications. It is important to understand the meaning of the various specifications and the effects of supply voltage and thermal environment on accuracy.

The AD590 is basically a PTAT (proportional to absolute temperature)[1] current regulator. That is, the output current is equal to a scale factor times the temperature of the sensor in degrees Kelvin. This scale factor is trimmed to $1\mu A/K$ at the factory, by adjusting the indicated temperature (i.e. the output current) to agree with the actual temperature. This is done with 5V across the device at a temperature within a few degrees of $25°C$ (298.2K). The device is then packaged and tested for accuracy over temperature.

CALIBRATION ERROR

At final factory test the difference between the indicated temperature and the actual temperature is called the calibration error. Since this is a scale factor error, its contribution to the total error of the device is PTAT. For example, the effect of the $1°C$ specified maximum error of the AD590L varies from $0.73°C$ at $-55°C$ to $1.42°C$ at $150°C$. Figure 3 shows how an exaggerated calibration error would vary from the ideal over temperature.

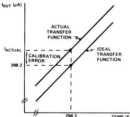

FIGURE 3 Calibration Error vs. Temperature

The calibration error is a primary contributor to maximum total error in all AD590 grades. However, since it is a scale factor error, it is particularly easy to trim. Figure 4 shows the most elementary way of accomplishing this. To trim this circuit the temperature of the AD590 is measured by a reference temperature sensor and R is trimmed so that $V_T = 1mV/K$ at that temperature. Note that when this error is trimmed out at one temperature, its effect is zero over the entire temperature range. In most applications there is a current to voltage conversion resistor (or, as with a current input ADC, a reference) that can be trimmed for scale factor adjustment.

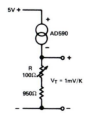

FIGURE 4 One Temperature Trim

[1] $T(°C) = T(K) -273.2$; Zero on the Kelvin scale is "absolute zero"; there is no lower temperature.

ERROR VERSUS TEMPERATURE: WITH CALIBRATION ERROR TRIMMED OUT

Each AD590 is also tested for error over the temperature range with the calibration error trimmed out. This specification could also be called the "variance from PTAT" since it is the maximum difference between the actual current over temperature and a PTAT multiplication of the actual current at $25°C$. This error consists of a slope error and some curvature, mostly at the temperature extremes. Figure 5 shows a typical AD590K temperature curve before and after calibration error trimming.

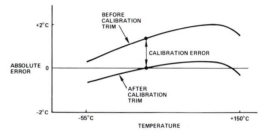

FIGURE 5 Effect of Scale Factor Trim on Accuracy

ERROR VERSUS TEMPERATURE: NO USER TRIMS

Using the AD590 by simply measuring the current, the total error is the "variance from PTAT" described above plus the effect of the calibration error over temperature. For example the AD590L maximum total error varies from $2.33°C$ at $-55°C$ to $3.02°C$ at $150°C$. For simplicity, only the larger figure is shown on the specification page.

NONLINEARITY

Nonlinearity as it applies to the AD590 is the maximum deviation of current over temperature from a best-fit straight line. The nonlinearity of the AD590 over the $-55°C$ to $+150°C$ range is superior to all conventional electrical temperature sensors such as thermocouples, RTD's and thermistors. Figure 6 shows the nonlinearity of the typical AD590K from Figure 5.

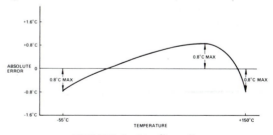

FIGURE 6 Nonlinearity

Figure 7A shows a circuit in which the nonlinearity is the major contributor to error over temperature. The circuit is trimmed by adjusting R_1 for a 0V output with the AD590 at $0°C$. R_2 is then adjusted for 10V out with the sensor at $100°C$. Other pairs of temperatures may be used with this procedure as long as they are measured accurately by a reference sensor. Note that for +15V output ($150°C$) the V+ of the op amp must be greater than 17V. Also note that V− should be at least −4V: if V− is ground there is no voltage applied across the device.

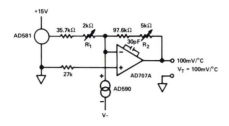

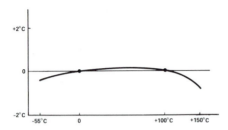

FIGURE 7A   Two Temperature Trim

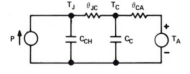

FIGURE 7B   Typical Two-Trim Accuracy

VOLTAGE AND THERMAL ENVIRONMENT EFFECTS

The power supply rejection specifications show the maximum expected change in output current versus input voltage changes. The insensitivity of the output to input voltage allows the use of unregulated supplies. It also means that hundreds of ohms of resistance (such as a CMOS multiplexer) can be tolerated in series with the device.

It is important to note that using a supply voltage other than 5V does not change the PTAT nature of the AD590. In other words, this change is equivalent to a calibration error and can be removed by the scale factor trim (see previous page).

The AD590 specifications are guaranteed for use in a low thermal resistance environment with 5V across the sensor. Large changes in the thermal resistance of the sensor's environment will change the amount of self-heating and result in changes in the output which are predictable but not necessarily desirable.

The thermal environment in which the AD590 is used determines two important characteristics: the effect of self heating and the response of the sensor with time.

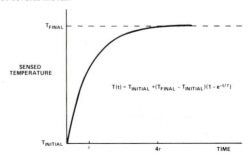

FIGURE 8   Thermal Circuit Model

Figure 8 is a model of the AD590 which demonstrates these characteristics. As an example, for the TO-52 package, θ_{JC} is the thermal resistance between the chip and the case, about

$26°C/watt$. θ_{CA} is the thermal resistance between the case and its surroundings and is determined by the characteristics of the thermal connection. Power source P represents the power dissipated on the chip. The rise of the junction temperature, T_J, above the ambient temperature T_A is:

$$T_J - T_A = P\,(\theta_{JC} + \theta_{CA}).\qquad\text{Eq. 1}$$

Table I gives the sum of θ_{JC} and θ_{CA} for several common thermal media for both the "H" and "F" packages. The heat-sink used was a common clip-on. Using Equation 1, the temperature rise of an AD590 "H" package in a stirred bath at +25°C, when driven with a 5V supply, will be 0.06°C. However, for the same conditions in still air the temperature rise is 0.72°C. For a given supply voltage, the temperature rise varies with the current and is PTAT. Therefore, if an application circuit is trimmed with the sensor in the same thermal environment in which it will be used, the scale factor trim compensates for this effect over the entire temperature range.

MEDIUM	$\theta_{JC} + \theta_{CA}$ (°C/watt)		τ (sec)(Note 3)	
	H	F	H	F
Aluminum Block	30	10	0.6	0.1
Stirred Oil[1]	42	60	1.4	0.6
Moving Air[2]				
With Heat Sink	45	–	5.0	–
Without Heat Sink	115	190	13.5	10.0
Still Air				
With Heat Sink	191	–	108	–
Without Heat Sink	480	650	60	30

[1] Note: τ is dependent upon velocity of oil; average of several velocities listed above.
[2] Air velocity $\cong$ 9ft/sec.
[3] The time constant is defined as the time required to reach 63.2% of an instantaneous temperature change.

Table I. Thermal Resistances

The time response of the AD590 to a step change in temperature is determined by the thermal resistances and the thermal capacities of the chip, C_{CH}, and the case, C_C. C_{CH} is about 0.04 watt-sec/°C for the AD590. C_C varies with the measured medium since it includes anything that is in direct thermal contact with the case. In most cases, the single time constant exponential curve of Figure 9 is sufficient to describe the time response, T(t). Table I shows the effective time constant, τ, for several media.

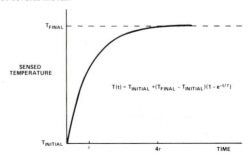

FIGURE 9   Time Response Curve

GENERAL APPLICATIONS

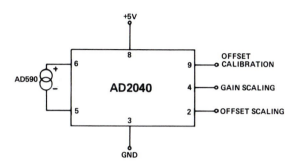

FIGURE 10   Variable Scale Display

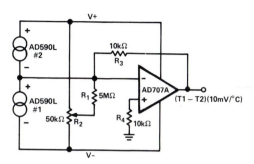

FIGURE 12   Differential Measurements

Figure 10 demonstrates the use of a low-cost Digital Panel Meter for the display of temperature on either the Kelvin, Celsius or Fahrenheit scales. For Kelvin temperature Pins 9, 4 and 2 are grounded; and for Fahrenheit temperature Pins 4 and 2 are left open.

The above configuration yields a 3 digit display with $1°C$ or $1°F$ resolution, in addition to an absolute accuracy of $±2.0°C$ over the $-55°C$ to $+125°C$ temperature range if a one-temperature calibration is performed on an AD590K, L, or M.

a desired temperature difference. For example, the inherent offset between the two devices can be trimmed in. If V+ and V− are radically different, then the difference in internal dissipation will cause a differential internal temperature rise. This effect can be used to measure the ambient thermal resistance seen by the sensors in applications such as fluid level detectors or anemometry.

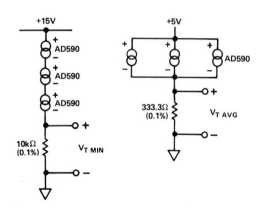

FIGURE 11   Series & Parallel Connection

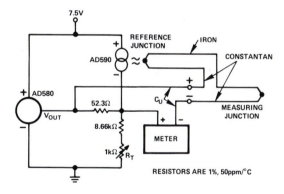

FIGURE 13   Cold Junction Compensation Circuit for Type J Thermocouple

Connecting several AD590 units in series as shown in Figure 11 allows the minimum of all the sensed temperatures to be indicated. In contrast, using the sensors in parallel yields the average of the sensed temperatures.

The circuit of Figure 12 demonstrates one method by which differential temperature measurements can be made. R_1 and R_2 can be used to trim the output of the op amp to indicate

Figure 13 is an example of a cold junction compensation circuit for a Type J Thermocouple using the AD590 to monitor the reference junction temperature. This circuit replaces an ice-bath as the thermocouple reference for ambient temperatures between $+15°C$ and $+35°C$. The circuit is calibrated by adjusting R_T for a proper meter reading with the measuring junction at a known reference temperature and the circuit near $+25°C$. Using components with the T.C.'s as specified in Figure 13, compensation accuracy will be within $±0.5°C$ for circuit temperatures between $+15°C$ and $+35°C$. Other thermocouple types can be accommodated with different resistor values. Note that the T.C.'s of the voltage reference and the resistors are the primary contributors to error.

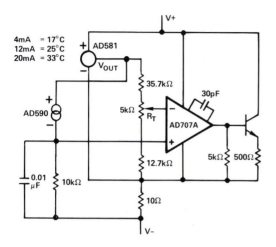

FIGURE 14   4 to 20mA Current Transmitter

Figure 14 is an example of a current transmitter designed to be used with 40V, 1kΩ systems; it uses its full current range of 4mA to 20mA for a narrow span of measured temperatures. In this example the 1μA/K output of the AD590 is amplified to 1mA/°C and offset so that 4mA is equivalent to 17°C and 20mA is equivalent to 33°C. R_T is trimmed for proper reading at an intermediate reference temperature. With a suitable choice of resistors, any temperature range within the operating limits of the AD590 may be chosen.

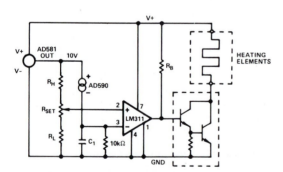

FIGURE 15   Simple Temperature Control Circuit

Figure 15 is an example of a variable temperature control circuit (thermostat) using the AD590. R_H and R_L are selected to set the high and low limits for R_{SET}. R_{SET} could be a simple pot, a calibrated multi-turn pot or a switched resistive divider. Powering the AD590 from the 10V reference isolates the AD590 from supply variations while maintaining a reasonable voltage (~7V) across it. Capacitor C_1 is often needed to filter extraneous noise from remote sensors. R_B is determined by the β of the power transistor and the current requirements of the load.

Figure 16 shows how the AD590 can be configured with an 8-bit DAC to produce a digitally controlled set point. This

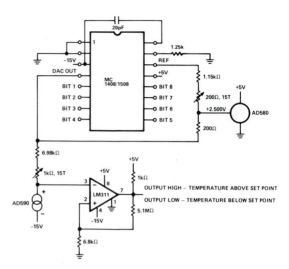

FIGURE 16   DAC Set Point

particular circuit operates from 0 (all inputs high) to +51°C (all inputs low) in 0.2°C steps. The comparator is shown with 1°C hysteresis which is usually necessary to guard-band for extraneous noise; omitting the 5.1MΩ resistor results in no hysteresis.

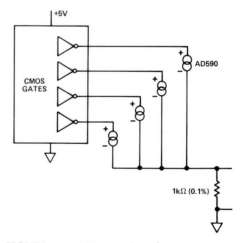

FIGURE 17   AD590 Driven from CMOS Logic

The voltage compliance and the reverse blocking characteristic of the AD590 allows it to be powered directly from +5V CMOS logic. This permits easy multiplexing, switching or pulsing for minimum internal heat dissipation. In Figure 17 any AD590 connected to a logic high will pass a signal current through the current measuring circuitry while those connected to a logic zero will pass insignificant current. The outputs used to drive the AD590's may be employed for other purposes, but the additional capacitance due to the AD590 should be taken into account.

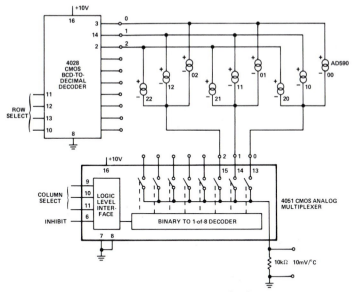

FIGURE 18   Matrix Multiplexer

CMOS Analog Multiplexers can also be used to switch AD590
current. Due to the AD590's current mode, the resistance of
such switches is unimportant as long as 4V is maintained
across the transducer. Figure 18 shows a circuit which combines
the principal demonstrated in Figure 17 with an 8 channel
CMOS Multiplexer. The resulting circuit can select one of
eighty sensors over only 18 wires with a 7 bit binary word. The
inhibit input on the multiplexer turns all sensors off for minimum dissipation while idling.

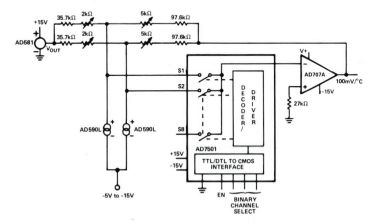

FIGURE 19   8-Channel Multiplexer

Figure 19 demonstrates a method of multiplexing the AD590
in the two-trim mode (Figure 7). Additional AD590's and their
associated resistors can be added to multiplex up to 8 channels
of $\pm0.5°$C absolute accuracy over the temperature range of
$-55°$C to $+125°$C. The high temperature restriction of $+125°$C
is due to the output range of the op amps; output to $+150°$C
can be achieved by using a $+20$V supply for the op amp.

OUTLINE DIMENSIONS
AND PIN DESIGNATIONS

Dimensions shown in inches and (mm).

TO-52 PACKAGE: DESIGNATION "H"

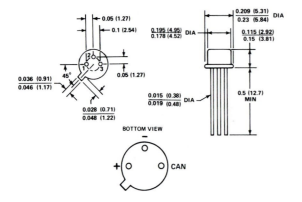

BOTTOM VIEW

Platform Load Cell

Platform Load Cell 0-2 to 0-200 lbs

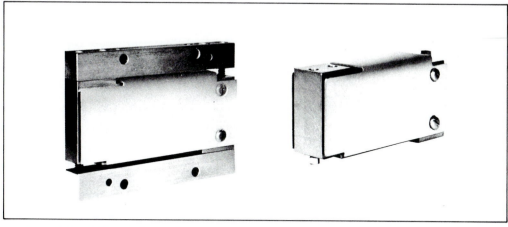

- EXCELLENT LINEARITY, HYSTERESIS, CREEP
- HIGH SHOCK LOAD CAPABILITY
- DUAL INTEGRAL OVERLOAD STOPS
- LOW PROFILE
- INTEGRAL MOUNTING BOSSES
- LOW ECCENTRIC LOAD SENSITIVITY
- MEETS REQUIREMENTS OF NEW H-44 CODE

The PLC triple beam platform load cell is ideal for precision weight and force measurement in commercial, postal, counting and check weighing applications. Unique, integral dual overload stops provide high tolerance to shock loads, off-center loading and repeated overloads. The PLC attaches directly to the upper and lower scale structures, simplifying assembly and lowering manufacturing costs. Optional foldback arms allow the user to take full advantage of the dual overload stops without having to make modifications to their scale structure.

■■■■ TECHNICAL DATA

Rated Capacity (lbs)	2	5	10	20	50	100	200
Rated Output (mV/V)	2.0 ± 0.4			2.2 ± 0.2			
Nonlinearity (%)				0.02			
Hysteresis (%)				0.02			
Nonrepeatability (%)				0.01			
Creep in 20 min. (%)				0.03			
Zero Balance (%)				5.0			
Compensated Temp. Range (°F/°C)				+15 to +115/−10 to +45			
Temp. Effect: Output (% of load/100F)				0.08			
Zero Balance (%/100F)				0.15			
Terminal Resistance: Input (ohms min.)				400			
Output (ohms)				350 ± 3			
Excitation Voltage: Maximum VDC or VAC rms				15			
Insulation Resistance (megohms min.)				5000 at 50 VDC			
Max. Load*, Safe (%) (overload stops adjusted)				150			
Max. Load*, Ultimate without overload stops engaged (%)				300			
Max Load*, Ultimate with overload stops engaged (%)				1000			
Eccentric Load Sensitivity,** 50% Cap. (%/in.)	0.008	0.008	0.008	0.007	0.006	0.005	0.010
Max. Moment, Operating (lb. in.)	6	15	30	60	150	375	750
Max. Moment, Safe (lb. in.)	12	30	60	120	300	750	1500
Deflection at Rated Load (inches)	0.016	0.021	0.018	0.012	0.008	0.009	0.005
Weight (lbs)				0.9			1.2

Percentages relative to rated output, except as noted.   *With load centered.
**Percent of reading.
REQUEST CERTIFIED DRAWINGS BEFORE DESIGNING MOUNTINGS OR FIXTURES—DIMENSIONS AND SPECIFICATIONS ARE SUBJECT TO CHANGE WITHOUT NOTICE.

PLC
Platform Load Cell
0-2 to 0-200 lbs

DIMENSIONS

2-100 lbs

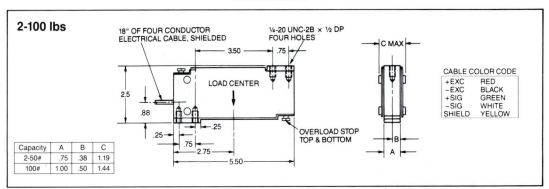

Capacity	A	B	C
2-50#	.75	.38	1.19
100#	1.00	.50	1.44

CABLE COLOR CODE
+EXC	RED
−EXC	BLACK
+SIG	GREEN
−SIG	WHITE
SHIELD	YELLOW

200 lbs

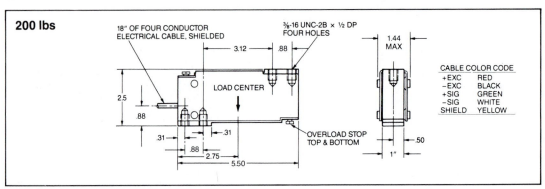

CABLE COLOR CODE
+EXC	RED
−EXC	BLACK
+SIG	GREEN
−SIG	WHITE
SHIELD	YELLOW

With Foldback Arms

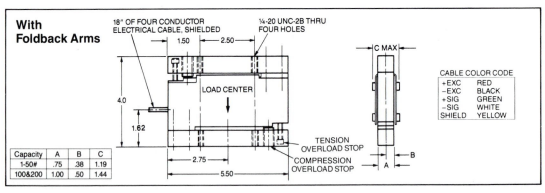

Capacity	A	B	C
1-50#	.75	.38	1.19
100&200	1.00	.50	1.44

CABLE COLOR CODE
+EXC	RED
−EXC	BLACK
+SIG	GREEN
−SIG	WHITE
SHIELD	YELLOW

HOTTINGER BALDWIN MEASUREMENTS, INC.
P.O. Box 1500
Framingham, MA 01701
Phone: (617) 875-8282 Telex: 681-7140

REQUEST CERTIFIED DRAWINGS BEFORE DESIGNING MOUNTINGS OR FIXTURES—
DIMENSIONS AND SPECIFICATIONS ARE SUBJECT TO CHANGE WITHOUT NOTICE

PWS

SINGLE POINT LOAD CELL

7 TO 150 KG

- STAINLESS STEEL
- LOW PROFILE
- RESISTANT TO SHOCK LOADING
- AVAILABLE NTEP CERTIFIED

The PWS is a single point cell, constructed of stainless steel and designed to perform in harsh, high shock load environments. These features have made the PWS ideal for platform scales and packaging and process weighing equipment.

TECHNICAL DATA

	7	10	15	30	60	100	150
Rated Capacity (KG)	7	10	15	30	60	100	150
Rated Output (mV/V)			2.0 ± 0.2				
Combined Error Due to Non-Linearity and Hysteresis (%)			0.03				
Nonrepeatability (%)			0.01				
Creep in 20 min. (%)			0.03				
Zero Balance (%)			5.0				
Compensated Temp. Range (°F/°C)			+15 to +104/-10 to +40				
Temp. Effect: Output (% of load/100°F)			0.25				
Zero Balance (%/100°F)			0.25				
Terminal Resistance: Input (ohms min.)			350				
Output (ohms)			350 ± 3				
Excitation Voltage: Maximum VDC or VAC rms			15				
Insulation Resistance (megohms min.)			5000 at 50 VDC				
Max. Load*, Safe (%)			150				
Max. Load* Ultimate (%)			300				
Eccentric Load Sensitivity,** 50% Cap. (%/100 mm)			0.05				
Deflection at Rated Load (mm)	.30	.30	.35	.35	.35	.45	.45
Weight (KG)			2.5		3.5		4.5

Percentages relative to rated output, except as noted.

REQUEST CERTIFIED DRAWINGS BEFORE DESIGNING MOUNTINGS OR FIXTURES. DIMENSIONS AND SPECIFICATIONS ARE SUBJECT TO CHANGE WITHOUT NOTICE.

PWS
Single Point Load Cell
7 to 150 KG

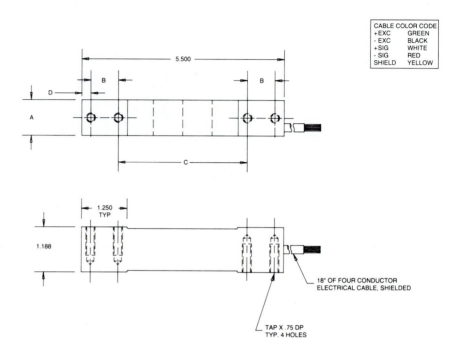

CABLE COLOR CODE

+EXC	GREEN
- EXC	BLACK
+SIG	WHITE
- SIG	RED
SHIELD	YELLOW

5.500

B   B

D

A

C

1.250
TYP

1.188

18" OF FOUR CONDUCTOR
ELECTRICAL CABLE, SHIELDED

TAP X .75 DP
TYP. 4 HOLES

CAPACITY	A	B	C	D	TAP
7, 10, 15 KG	.75	.75	3.50	.25	1/4-20 UNF-2B
30, 60 KG	.94	.75	3.50	.25	1/4-20 UNF-2B
100, 150 KG	1.20	.88	3.12	.31	3/8-16 UNF-2B

HBM, INC.
19 Bartlett Street
Marlboro, MA 01752
Tel. (508) 624-4500
Fax (508) 485-7480

SCX C Series Pressure Sensors

FEATURES

■ **Low Cost**

■ **Temperature Compensation**

■ **Calibrated Zero and Span**

■ **Small Size**

■ **Low Noise**

■ **High Impedance for Low Power Applications**

APPLICATIONS

■ **Medical Equipment**

■ **Computer Peripherals**

■ **Pneumatic Controls**

■ **HVAC**

EQUIVALENT CIRCUIT

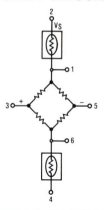

ELECTRICAL CONNECTION

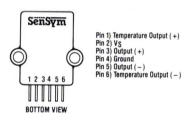

Pin 1) Temperature Output (+)
Pin 2) Vs
Pin 3) Output (+)
Pin 4) Ground
Pin 5) Output (−)
Pin 6) Temperature Output (−)

1 2 3 4 5 6

BOTTOM VIEW

Note: The polarity indicated is for pressure applied to port B. (For Absolute devices, pressure is applied to port A and the output polarity is reversed.)

GENERAL DESCRIPTION

The SCX C series sensors will provide a very cost effective solution for pressure applications that require operation over a wide temperature range. These internally calibrated and temperature compensated sensors give an accurate and stable output over a 0°C to 70°C temperature range. This series is intended for use with non-corrosive, non-ionic working fluids such as air, dry gases, and the like.

Devices are available to measure absolute, differential, and gage pressures from 1psi (SCX01) up to 100psi (SCX100). The Absolute (A) devices have an internal vacuum reference and an output voltage proportional to absolute pressure. The Differential (D) devices allow application of pressure to either side of the pressure sensing diaphragm and can be used for gage or differential pressure measurements.

The SCX devices feature an integrated circuit sensor element and laser trimmed thick film ceramic housed in a compact nylon case. This package provides excellent corrosion resistance and provides isolation to external package stresses. The package has convenient mounting holes and pressure ports for ease of use with standard plastic tubing for pressure connection.

All SCX devices are calibrated for span to within ±5% and provide an offset (zero pressure output) of ±1 millivolt maximum. These parts were designed for low cost applications where the user can typically provide fine adjustment of zero and span in external circuitry. For higher accuracies, refer to the standard SCX series datasheet. If the application requires extended temperature range operation, beyond 0 to 70°C, two pins which provide an output voltage proportional to temperature are available for use with external circuitry.

The output of the bridge is ratiometric to the supply voltage and operation from any D.C. supply voltage up to +30V is acceptable.

Because these devices have very low noise and 100 microsecond response time they are an excellent choice for medical equipment, computer peripherals, and pneumatic control applications.

For further technical information on the SCX series, please contact your local Sensym office or the factory.

Pressure Sensor Characteristics   *SCX C Series*

▬▬▬ STANDARD PRESSURE RANGES

PART NUMBER	OPERATING PRESSURE	PROOF PRESSURE*	FULL-SCALE SPAN
SCX01DNC	0–1 psid	20 psid	18 mV
SCX05DNC	0–5 psid	20 psid	60 mV
SCX15ANC	0–15 pisa	30 psia	90 mV
SCX15DNC	0–15 psid	30 psid	90 mV
SCX30ANC	0–30 pisa	60 psia	90 mV
SCX30DNC	0–30 psid	60 psid	90 mV
SCX100ANC	0–100 pisa	150 psia	100 mV
SCX100DNC	0–100 psid	150 psid	100 mV

*Maximum pressure above which causes permanent sensor failure.

Maximum Ratings (For All Devices)

Supply Voltage, V_S	$+30\,V_{DC}$
Common-mode Pressure	50 psig
Lead Temperature	
(Soldering, 10 seconds)	300 °C

Environmental Specifications (For All Devices)

Temperature Range

Compensated	0 to 70 °C
Operating	-40 °C to $+85$ °C
Storage	-55 °C to $+125$ °C
Humidity Limits	0 to 100% RH

▬▬▬ SCX01DNC PERFORMANCE CHARACTERISTICS (NOTE 1)

CHARACTERISTIC	MIN	TYP	MAX	UNIT
Operating Pressure Range		—	1	psid
Sensitivity	—	18	—	mV/psi
Full-scale Span (Note 2)	17.00	18.00	19.00	mV
Zero Pressure Offset	-1.0	0	$+1.0$	mV
Combined Linearity and Hysteresis (Note 3)	—	±0.2	±1.0	%FSO
Temperature Effect on Span (0–70 °C) (Note 4)	—	±0.4	±2.0	%FSO
Temperature Effect on Offset (0–70 °C) (Note 4)	—	±0.20	±1.0	mV
Repeatability (Note 5)	—	±0.2	±0.5	%FSO
Input Impedance (Note 6)	—	4.0	—	kΩ
Output Impedance (Note 7)	—	4.0	—	kΩ
Common-mode Voltage (Note 8)	5.7	6.0	6.3	V_{DC}
Response Time (Note 9)	—	100	—	μsec
Long Term Stability of Offset and Span (Note 10)	—	±0.1	—	%FSO

Pressure Sensor Characteristics (Cont.)   *SCX C Series*

■■■■ SCX05DNC PERFORMANCE CHARACTERISTICS (NOTE 1)

CHARACTERISTIC	MIN	TYP	MAX	UNIT
Operating Pressure Range		—	5	psid
Sensitivity	—	12.0	—	mV/psi
Full-scale Span (Note 2)	57.5	60.0	62.5	mV
Zero Pressure Offset	−1.0	0	+1.0	mV
Combined Linearity and Hysteresis (Note 3)	—	±0.1	±1.0	%FSO
Temperature Effect on Span (0–70°C) (Note 4)	—	±0.4	±2.0	%FSO
Temperature Effect on Offset (0–70°C) (Note 4)	—	±0.20	±1.0	mV
Repeatability (Note 5)	—	±0.2	±0.5	%FSO
Input Impedance (Note 6)	—	4.0	—	kΩ
Output Impedance (Note 7)	—	4.0	—	kΩ
Common-mode Voltage (Note 8)	5.7	6.0	6.3	V_{DC}
Response Time (Note 9)	—	100	—	μsec
Long Term Stability of Offset and Span (Note 10)	—	±0.1	—	%FSO

■■■■ SCX15C PERFORMANCE CHARACTERISTICS (NOTE 1)

CHARACTERISTIC	MIN	TYP	MAX	UNIT
Operating Pressure Range		—	15	psi
Sensitivity	—	6.0	—	mV/psi
Full-scale Span (Note 2)	85.0	90.0	95.0	mV
Zero Pressure Offset	−1.0	0	+1.0	mV
Combined Linearity and Hysteresis (Note 3)	—	±0.1	±1.0	%FSO
Temperature Effect on Span (0–70°C) (Note 4)	—	±0.4	±2.0	%FSO
Temperature Effect on Offset (0–70°C) (Note 4)	—	±0.20	±1.0	mV
Repeatability (Note 5)	—	±0.2	±0.5	%FSO
Input Impedance (Note 6)	—	4.0	—	kΩ
Output Impedance (Note 7)	—	4.0	—	kΩ
Common-mode Voltage (Note 8)	5.7	6.0	6.3	V_{DC}
Response Time (Note 9)	—	100	—	μsec
Long Term Stability of Offset and Span (Note 10)	—	±0.1	—	%FSO

Pressure Sensor Characteristics (Cont.)   *SCX C Series*

■■■■■ SCX30C PERFORMANCE CHARACTERISTICS (NOTE 1)

CHARACTERISTIC	MIN	TYP	MAX	UNIT
Operating Pressure Range		—	30	psi
Sensitivity	—	3.0	—	mV/psi
Full-scale Span (Note 2)	85.0	90.0	95.0	mV
Zero Pressure Offset	− 1.0	0	+ 1.0	mV
Combined Linearity and Hysteresis (Note 3)	—	± 0.2	± 1.0	% FSO
Temperature Effect on Span (0–70°C) (Note 4)	—	± 0.4	± 2.0	% FSO
Temperature Effect on Offset (0–70°C) (Note 4)	—	± 0.2	± 1.0	mV
Repeatability (Note 5)	—	± 0.2	± 0.5	% FSO
Input Impedance (Note 6)	—	4.0	—	kΩ
Output Impedance (Note 7)	—	4.0	—	kΩ
Common-mode Voltage (Note 8)	5.7	6.0	6.3	V_{DC}
Response Time (Note 9)	—	100	—	μsec
Long Term Stability of Offset and Span (Note 10)	—	± 0.1	—	% FSO

■■■■■ SCX100C PERFORMANCE CHARACTERISTICS (NOTE 1)

CHARACTERISTIC	MIN	TYP	MAX	UNIT
Operating Pressure Range		—	100	psi
Sensitivity	—	1.0	—	mV/psi
Full-scale Span (Note 2)	95.0	100.0	105.0	mV
Zero Pressure Offset	− 1.0	0	+ 1.0	mV
Combined Linearity and Hysteresis (Note 3)	—	± 0.2	± 1.0	% FSO
Temperature Effect on Span (0–70°C) (Note 4)	—	± 0.4	± 2.0	% FSO
Temperature Effect on Offset (0–70°C) (Note 4)	—	± 0.20	± 1.0	mV
Repeatability (Note 5)	—	± 0.2	± 0.5	% FSO
Input Impedance (Note 6)	—	4.0	—	kΩ
Output Impedance (Note 7)	—	4.0	—	kΩ
Common-mode Voltage (Note 8)	5.7	6.0	6.3	V_{DC}
Response Time (Note 9)	—	100	—	μsec
Long Term Stability of Offset and Span (Note 10)	—	± 0.1	—	% FSO

Typical Performance Characteristics   *SCX C Series*

Voltage at Pin 1 vs. Temperature

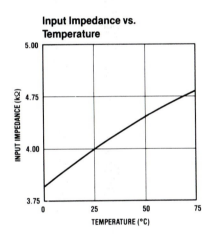

Voltage at Pin 6 vs. Temperature

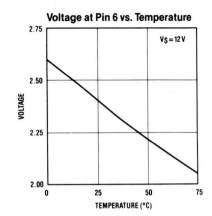

Input Impedance vs. Temperature

0.1 Hz to 10 Hz Noise

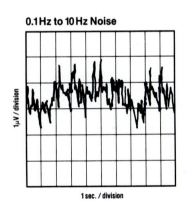

Specification Notes: (For All Devices)

Note 1: Reference Conditions: Unless otherwise noted: Supply Voltage, $V_S = 12\,V_{DC}$, $T_A = 25\,°C$, Common-mode Line Pressure = 0 psig, Pressure Applied to Port B. For absolute devices only, pressure is applied to Port A and the output polarity is reversed.

Note 2: Span is the algebraic difference between the output voltage at full-scale pressure and the output at zero pressure. Span is ratiometric to the supply voltage.

Note 3: See Definition of Terms.
Hysteresis — the maximum output difference at any point within the operating pressure range for increasing and decreasing pressure.

Note 4: Maximum error band of the offset voltage and the error band of the span, relative to the 25°C reading.

Note 5: Maximum difference in output at any pressure with the operating pressure range and temperature within 0°C to +70°C after:
a) 1,000 temperature cycles, 0°C to +70°C
b) 1.5 million pressure cycles, 0 psi to full-scale span.

Note 6: Input impedance is the impedance between pins 2 and 4.

Note 7: Output impedance is the impedance between pins 3 and 5.

Note 8: This is the common-mode voltage of the output arms (Pins 3 and 5) for $V_S = 12\,V_{DC}$.

Note 9: Response time for a 0 psi to full-scale span pressure step change, 10% to 90% rise time.

Note 10: Long term stability over a one year period.

GENERAL DISCUSSION

The SCX series devices give a voltage output which is directly proportional to applied pressure. The devices will give an increasing positive going output when increasing pressure is applied to pressure port P_B of the device. If the input pressure connections are reversed, the output will increase with decreases in pressure. The devices are ratiometric to the supply voltage and changes in the supply voltage will cause proportional changes in the offset voltage and full-scale span. Since for absolute device pressure is applied to port P_A, output polarity will be reversed.

User Calibration

The SCX devices are fully calibrated for offset and span and should therefore require little user adjustment in most applications. For precise span and offset adjustments, refer to the applications section herein or contact the Sensym factory.

Vacuum Reference (Absolute Devices)

Absolute sensors have a hermetically sealed vacuum reference chamber. The offset voltage on these units is therefore measured at vacuum, 0 psia. Since all pressure is measured relative to a vacuum reference, all changes in barometric pressure or changes in altitude will cause changes in the device output.

Media Compatibility

SCX devices are compatible with most non-corrosive gases. Because the circuitry is coated with a protective silicon gel, many otherwise corrosive environments can be compatible with the sensors. As shown in the physical construction diagram below, fluids must generally be compatible with silicon gel, plastic, aluminum, RTV, silicon, and glass for use with Port B. For questions concerning media compatibility, contact the factory.

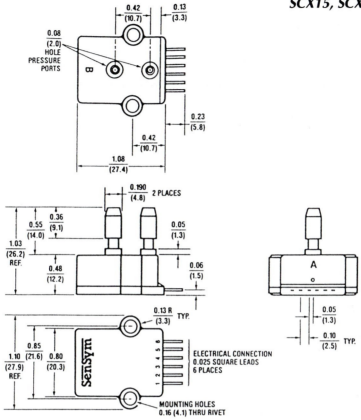

DIMENSIONS IN INCHES (MILLIMETERS)
WEIGHT: 5 GRAMS
CASE MATERIAL: GLASS FILLED NYLON

WETTED MATERIAL
PORT A: GLASS FILLED NYLON, RTV, SILGEL
PORT B: GLASS FILLED NYLON, SILICON, RTV
SEE PHYSICAL CONSTRUCTION DRAWING

ORDERING INFORMATION

To order, use the following part numbers:

DESCRIPTION	PART NUMBER
0 to 1 psi Differential/Gage	SCX01DNC
0 to 5 psi Differential/Gage	SCX05DNC
0 to 15 psi Absolute	SCX15ANC
0 to 15 psi Differential/Gage	SCX15DNC
0 to 30 psi Absolute	SCX30ANC
0 to 30 psi Differential/Gage	SCX30DNC
0 to 100 psi Absolute	SCX100ANC
0 to 100 psi Differential/Gage	SCX100DNC

1255 Reamwood Avenue
Sunnyvale, California 94089
Telephone: (408) 744-1500
TELEX: 176376
TWX: 910 339 9625

SenSym

Index